# DECISION MODELS FOR MANAGEMENT

# McGraw-Hill Series in Quantitative Methods for Management

**Consulting Editor**

**Martin K. Starr,** *Columbia University*

# DECISION MODELS
# FOR MANAGEMENT

**Jack Byrd, Jr.**
**L. Ted Moore**
*Professors of Industrial Engineering*
*West Virginia University*

**McGraw-Hill Book Company**

New York  St. Louis  San Francisco  Auckland  Bogotá  Hamburg
Johannesburg  London  Madrid  Mexico  Montreal  New Delhi
Panama  Paris  São Paulo  Singapore  Sydney  Tokyo  Toronto

This book was set in Times Roman by Automated Composition Service, Inc.
The editors were Donald G. Mason and Edwin Hanson;
the production supervisor was John Mancia.
The drawings were done by ECL Art Associates, Inc.
Fairfield Graphics was printer and binder.

**DECISION MODELS FOR MANAGEMENT**

1234567890 FGFG 898765432

ISBN 0-07-009511-6

**Library of Congress Cataloging in Publication Data**

Byrd, Jack.
   Decision models for management.

   Includes index.
   1. Decision-making—Mathematical models.
2. Operations research.   I. Moore, L. Ted.
II. Title.
HD30.23.B9        658.4′03        81-11747
ISBN 0-07-009511-6                  AACR2

To Jay Stern
and Curtis Tompkins
*Jack Byrd, Jr.*


To Charlene
*L. Ted Moore*

# CONTENTS

# Part 2   Planning and Policy Decisions

## 4   Developing Plans     90

## 5   Evaluating Risks     133

## 8   Service Decisions

## 9   Scheduling Decisions

## 10   Distribution Decisions     323

## 11   Facility Decisions     348

# Part 4   Summary

# PREFACE

This book attempts to reconcile management's decision making needs with the tools available for providing quantitative assistance with those needs. As a result, the book is organized according to decision categories instead of according to quantitative techniques. In this way, this book differs from most texts used in operations research, production/operations management, and quantitative methods courses. The authors believe that the book's unique organization reflects the developing level of maturity of the art of managerial application of quantitative models and methods to the everyday world.

Chapters of this text are intended to represent separate functional areas of managerial decision making. This division of topics is more difficult to determine than is the division of topics according to techniques, but the authors feel that the needs of modern management require greater emphasis upon management aspects of problems than upon rather abstract mathematical formalisms.

Each chapter begins with a brief description of what is to follow and what the chapter is intended to convey. The role of each chapter in the overall scheme of the text is also explained.

After the introductory comments, each chapter begins with a case study of an organization. This case is referred to as a continuing theme throughout the chapter. Techniques for addressing some of the problems of the organization are introduced as necessary to facilitate their applications to the case studied. Each main case in a chapter is intended to demonstrate the managerial decision environment and the possible role of quantitative models in making the required decisions.

Each chapter ends with two problem sets. The first problem set reviews the specific information in that chapter. The second problem set consists of exercises which encourage the student to enlarge upon his or her understanding of the chapter's conceptual basis.

The exercises are followed by caselets, which are minicases exhibiting the same category of decision problems as did the main case of the chapter.

After all the problems, exercises, and caselets, short cases complete each chapter. These cases present short but fairly detailed examples of decision situations and the implementation of the modeling techniques discussed in the chapter.

As a guide for the instructor, a teaching manual accompanies the text. This manual suggests day-by-day topics and procedures for the course, relates the course materials to those in standard courses on quantitative methods, operations research, and production/operations management, and suggests supplementary readings and topics with which the instructor may wish to augment the text.

*Jack Byrd, Jr.*
*L. Ted Moore*

# DECISION MODELS FOR MANAGEMENT

## DECISION MAKING CONCEPTS

# INTRODUCTION TO PART ONE
# DECISION MAKING CONCEPTS

This book is divided into four parts. The first part presents general considerations pertaining to the decision making process. The second part discusses broad organizational decisions. The third part focuses on operational decisions, and the last part summarizes the prior three parts and attempts to generalize their lessons.

The entire book aims at presenting a comprehensive view of decision making that looks at the personality of the decision maker as well as the character of the decision itself. Although the nominal emphasis of this text is upon models and their applications, the authors believe that a broader understanding of decision making is required to make the use of models effective.

In Part 1 the general decision making environment is described, as are the characteristics of the decision maker. The decision maker is usually described in each case in enough detail as to provide an insight into the personal side of the decision.

The role of models in decision making is discussed in general terms, and the interaction between model, modeler, and decision maker is presented as a natural part of the decision process.

A range of responsibilities which can be given models is reviewed, but it is stressed that the educated experience and judgment of the decision maker should be enhanced by a model.

The preliminary and general outline of some of the realities of the use of models in decision making should prepare the reader for the specific cases in the rest of the text. In order to focus the chapters properly, each chapter of Parts 2 and 3 deals with very limited topics. Only in Part 4 is a deliberate attempt made to present a complex decision situation. Part 1 should be read with the view in mind that it will provide the background against which the other parts are painted.

# ONE

## DECISION MAKING CONCEPTS

## SYNOPSIS OF THE CHAPTER

Decision making is not a precise activity. It is often not clear why a decision is necessary or whether a decision made was effective. Yet there are some organizing principles which can be brought to the decision making process. These principles are illustrated by this chapter.

The introductory case—the Citron Company—shows a company faced with a variety of problems. As a means of reducing the complexity of the decision making situation, a single problem definition is proposed along with a single, quantitative measure of the effectiveness of any decision.

Conflicting philosophies within the Citron management complicate the implementation of decisions. Thus, two problems must be addressed at once: disarming philosophic opposition to analytical procedures and determining what analytical procedures should be followed.

The modeling and quantitative analysis activities are not emphasized because the major points being made deal with the realities of obtaining effective management action.

After the Citron case has introduced some of the characteristics of real-life management decision making, the chapter explains the varieties of influences which must be considered in deriving, implementing, and understanding management decisions.

Decision making is presented as an activity which must be viewed holistically and which cannot be made into or represented as a purely quantitative impersonal process. The integration of the skills possessed by quantitative modelers and analysts with those of experienced managers is suggested as a procedure for making effective decisions.

## MAJOR CONCEPTS PRESENTED IN THIS CHAPTER

1. Decisions involve the complex interrelationships of people and organizations and are influenced by societal forces.
2. The standard assumption that models often make is that decisions made by individuals and organizations are rational. This assumption is often invalid when the real-life nature of decisions is considered.
3. Decision makers have their own style that is often different from the scientific method.
4. Influencing factors on individual decision making include such forces as perceptual processes, subconscious processes, intuitive processes, uncertainty, stress conditions, and personal habits.
5. Organizational decision making is influenced by the collective behavior of the individual decision makers. Additional influences include the behavior of individuals in groups, the influences of power and authority, and the consequences of organizational equilibrium and inertia.
6. Societal forces influence decision making by both individuals and organizations. Ethics, legal restrictions, societal norms, and cultural forces are important factors that shape and constrain individuals and organizations as decision makers.


## EXPECTATIONS OF THE STUDENTS

The student, after studying this chapter, should be able to do the following:

1. Analyze the factors that influence decision making by both individuals and organizations
2. Analyze the decision making styles of individuals with respect to the following:
   *a.* Tolerance of ambiguity
   *b.* Risk taking
   *c.* Reliance on intuition
   *d.* Willingness to accept outside input
   *e.* Use of the scientific method
3. Describe, both generally and for specific situations, how each of the following factors influence decision making:
   *a.* Decision models
   *b.* Perceptions of situations
   *c.* Subconscious forces
   *d.* Uncertainty
   *e.* Stress
   *f.* Personal habits
4. Discuss how the development of a decision model influences power and authority relationships within an organization
5. Describe the factors within an organization that influence decision making
6. Discuss the external forces that influence decision making in an organization

# A DECISION MAKING CASE STUDY— THE CITRON COMPANY

Harvey Kincaid of Citron Company had a problem. As the manager of market planning and development for Citron, he had been appointed by the new company president as chairman of a task force, the members of which are outlined in the organizational chart of Fig. 1.1. This task force was charged with deter-

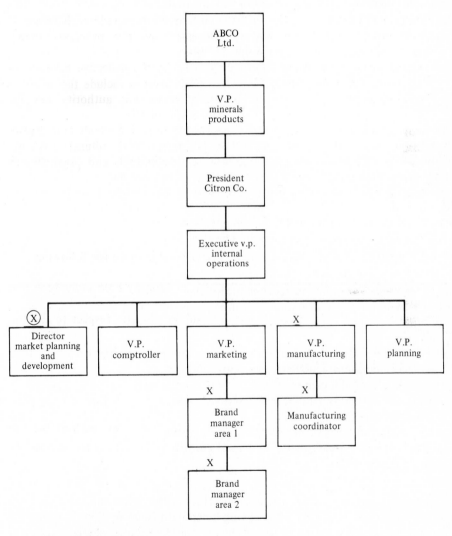

X   = Member of Task Force
(X) = Chairman of the Task Force

**Figure 1.1** Placement of task force members in the organizational chart for Citron Company (Division of ABCO Ltd.).

mining how to improve Citron's profits on its fastest-growing product line. The background of Harvey's problem included instances of sales being lost because of long product lead times and confused marketing policies.

Over the past few years, Citron had been losing profit and market share. Even though tonnage had declined, order lead times had lengthened from four weeks to fifteen weeks. As a result, Citron's market position had weakened and the price of its stock had dropped.

ABCO had bought Citron when its stock was low and had installed a dynamic president, Vince Todd, to restore its profitability. According to the purchase agreement, the former Citron president, James Harder, was retained as general manager of operations, and vice presidents for marketing and manufacturing continued to report to Harder. However, the comptroller (a vice president) and the vice president for planning were to report directly to Vince Todd.

After being with the company for only a short time, Todd lost patience with the marketing department's lack of direction. Politics prevented his removing the vice president for marketing, Peter Duvalier, because of his relationship with James Harder and some major stockholders of ABCO, so Todd created the position of director of market planning and development and gave this individual (Harvey Kincaid, who was organizationally equal to the vice presidents) authority to "take on any sacred cows" he thought appropriate.

The problem of declining profits led Todd to ask Harvey Kincaid to chair the specialties product task force. The charge of this group was to determine what could be done to improve the company's market share in a vital segment of its business, the specialities market. The task force met and outlined an ambitious program:

Define maximum manufacturing capabilities and capacity.
Define maximum physical volume and profit contribution.
Determine ways and costs to round out production capacity in optimum product mix.
Perform design and cost studies of the low-cost specialty production facility that achieves maximum machine-rate contribution.
Perform plant location cost studies.
Perform analysis of overall return on investment and cash flow on capacity expansion designs.
Establish standard costs of products.
Examine margins, capacity cost, and total contribution by product of possible product mixes.

How to proceed in this program was Harvey's problem, and it perplexed him for some time. One day, while having lunch with Gene Watkins, a computer consultant, Harvey mentioned his problem, and Gene offered his assistance. While Gene's company did not normally engage in business of this type, Gene suggested to Harvey that a former professor of his might be of help. Harvey asked Gene to arrange a meeting with his professor, Jack Vogel.

## Initial Meeting

At the meeting, Harvey Kincaid introduced Professor Vogel to the various members of the task force and presented the problem statement. Although the problem seemed vague, Professor Vogel decided to enter into a consulting arrangement with the company. A colleague of Professor Vogel's, Professor Ted Mehr, was also asked to join the project, because it appeared that the effort involved would be extensive.

The two consultants began by attempting to simplify the problem definition. After several visits to the company, the problem became clearer: the company was concerned about the product mix it was marketing, the manufacturing facilities were thought to be operating at full capacity, and long lead times seemed to be causing lost sales. Harvey himself told the consultants that he believed greater profits could be obtained from the existing plants by choosing a better product mix. Too much time seemed to be devoted to making time-consuming low-profit items.

Jack Vogel and Ted Mehr also learned something about the company's politics in these early meetings. Harvey Kincaid and the vice president for marketing were bitter enemies. Organizationally, they were equals, but their marketing philosophies differed significantly. Harvey was outspoken and flamboyant but a very shrewd marketing expert. He wanted to consolidate the existing product line and initiate innovative marketing programs. The vice president, Peter Duvalier, was a conservative administrator whose ruling doctrine was the maintenance of the status quo. Over the years, he had fought for and obtained many company policies favored by salesmen. Some of these policies included allowing small-volume special products to be made for high-volume customers and allowing special orders to interfere with existing manufacturing schedules. Jack Vogel and Ted Mehr sensed that they were involved in a corporate power struggle between two opposing factions. At the same time, a third faction, the manufacturing side of the organization, had to be considered. Cognizant of the internal politics of the organization, the consultants decided to develop a prototype model to illustrate the basic principles they proposed to apply. In effect, the prototype effort was to be an opening salvo in the product mix battle.

## A Prototype Model

The prototype model was developed for a single hypothetical plant producing five products. The results of the model both created interest and led to improved communications between the consultants and company personnel. Harvey Kincaid and Dick Rush, the manufacturing coordinator, each began to acquire a "feel" for the model and made many useful suggestions for the full model yet to be developed. The consultants were asked to visit the plant which was to be modeled and to talk with plant personnel about the model. The plant visit accomplished several ends, the most important of which was that it acquainted the consultants with the true plant conditions and established a communication link between the consultants and plant personnel.

## Data Collection

In attempting to develop the full-scale model, the consultants discovered that much of the data they needed was not available. Considerable effort was spent attempting to convince the company that new data needed to be collected on the manufacturing processes, but little progress was made toward that end. (The consultants suspected that the operating managers did not want data collected which reflected true plant operating conditions.) The plant model was eventually fashioned from the available data.

## Initial Model Results

The model showed that packaging of finished material was the major constraint. This result was counter to what the manufacturing personnel knew to be true. By reviewing the model they discovered that the consultants had considered only one of three packaging lines in their model. The consultants had been unaware of the distinctions between the three lines. The model was revised to reflect the correct plant operation, and the model results were presented again.

During this second presentation, the consultants were alerted to a material-handling limitation which the manufacturing personnel felt should be included in the model. The new revisions were made, and an acceptable model was eventually developed.

## Final Model Results

Model results indicated that the past year's profits could have been increased by over 90 percent simply by making a different product mix. Further results showed that a $2.5 million plant expansion already approved would have a minimal impact on profit compared to that obtainable by a shift to an improved product mix. The consultants were asked to develop a list of products which should be emphasized in order to increase profits. They were also asked to develop procedures for stocking high-volume items as a means of reducing lead times and thereby improving market share. Finally, they were asked to report their recommendations formally.

Vince Todd delayed action on the recommendations until he was sure the figures presented were realistic. The president's inaction prompted Harvey Kincaid to write a memorandum pointing out the company's declining market share in the last quarter as strong justification for convening a management meeting to discuss the consultants' studies. The president agreed to a meeting.

In an effort to gain the desired action from the meeting. Harvey Kincaid developed a strategy advocating that a new warehouse be built to store inventories of high-volume products. He decided to deemphasize the reduction of product lines in order to strengthen his warehouse position. Harvey felt that brand reduction was too big a step to push for its acceptance first, largely because of the opposition he knew would come from the vice president of marketing.

## Implementation Meeting

The meeting was heated, and both sides presented well-prepared arguments for their views. The president heard both sides of the issues and decided, contrary to Harvey Kincaid's expectation, that the company should proceed with brand reduction. The construction of a warehouse was delayed, however, until the impact of reducing product lines could be studied. At the end of the meeting the president asked Harvey Kincaid to prepare a strategy for consolidating the product line. It was suggested that he pursue options such as selling high-volume products as substitutes for low-volume products, raising the prices of low-volume products, and promsing short lead times only for high-volume products as ways to reduce the number of items in the product line.

## DECISION MODELS AND DECISION MAKING— STATE OF THE ART

The above vignette is based upon a real instance of a decision model being used to assist a company in determining corporate policy. It is an example of the act of decision making, which is one of the most common of human activities, but one of the least understood. The behavioral makeup of the decision maker, the organizational framework and environment for decision making, the contributions of other individuals, the amount of information available, the nature of legal restrictions, and even the cultural setting for the decision affect the way that decisions are made.

If a model is to be successfully integrated into the decision process, then the role of the model in that process must be understood by both the modeler and the decision maker. The position promoted in this text is that quantitative models *must* be integrated into modern managerial decision making.

To effect the blend of approaches to decision making that this text advocates, managerial decision styles and quantitative modeling procedures must be reconciled. Since this text attempts to relate modeling techniques to the decision environments to which they would likely apply, the chapters refer to categories of decisions instead of categories of mathematical methods.

The quantitative techniques presented throughout the text are predominantly those associated with the disciplines called operations research (OR), management science (MS), and production/operations management (P/OM). These fields of study each deal with the application of quantitative modeling concepts to problems of operating systems. The implicit philosophy of these quantitative disciplines is that models can sufficiently well represent the important characteristics of operational systems to contribute helpful information about these systems.

Although modeling techniques may be interesting as isolated objects of study, they are of little use unless they are incorporated by managers into their decision making processes. It is, therefore, a surprising fact that most quantitative texts touch only superficially on the manner in which decisions are made.

Few empirical studies have traced the incorporation of mathematical formalisms such as operations research into the decision making process.

A strange situation exists; decision models are being presented in textbooks as though they were independent of the decision process. At the same time, theories of decision making have often ignored the impact of models on the decision process. One of the major themes of this text will be a study of the interface between decision maker, modeler, and model. The decision making procedures advocated in this text require that there be a quantitative model which can provide information which bears upon the decisions to be made. The model should be built by a quantitative analyst, or modeler, in close cooperation with the appropriate managerial decision makers. To be of any practical value, the model must include the realties of the decision making environment and the constraints imposed upon decision makers by this environment.

The limitations upon possible decisions which result from the attitudes of the individual, the organization, and society will now be considered. First, the psychology of the individual decision maker will be examined. Then a discussion of the organizational viewpoint will analyze the actions of individual decision makers as they work together in an organization. Finally, the effect that society itself has on organizational decision makers will be investigated. This chapter contains only a limited treatment of these subjects; however, subsequent chapters on decision models will further develop the concepts presented.

## THE INDIVIDUAL ASPECT OF DECISION MAKING

Quantitative modeling theory, if it considers the psychology of the decision maker at all, assumes that the decision maker's behavior will be rational. The best available evidence suggests that this assumption is not valid. Simon (1976, p. 76) theorizes: "It is impossible for the behavior of a single, isolated individual to reach any high degree of rationality. The number of alternatives he must explore is so great, the information he would need to evaluate them so vast, that even an approximation to objective rationality is hard to conceive. Individual choice takes place in an environment of 'givens'—premises that are accepted by the subject as bases for his choice; and behavior is adaptive only within the limits set by these 'givens.'" Even a formal definition of rational behavior is a point of dispute among authors in the fields of administrative science and behavioral psychology.

Decision making strategies have been described by numerous theorists. Simon (1976, p. 25) uses the term "satisficing" to describe the behavior of an individual who seeks a solution good enough to satisfy a minimum set of conditions. Miller and Starr (1967) speak of "incremental improvements" as a satisficing strategy which moves the decision maker gradually toward an improved solution. Lindbloom (1959) describes this process as "muddling through"; Etzioni (1967) proposes a process he calls "mixed scanning" to describe decision making behavior. He sees a process of suboptimizing being used to make the fundamental decision combined with incremental modifications of this process as minor decisions are required. While none of these procedures is universally accepted, they are important in that they describe the "nonrational" character of decision making. It is interesting to contrast these theories with the decision theory so often described in quantitative literature.

The quantitative disciplines view decision making as a rational process approximating the scientific method. In general, this method consists of a series of steps such as the following:

1. Identify the problem.
2. Determine goals and objectives for solving the problem.
3. Gather the necessary data.
4. Formulate an analytic model of the problem.
5. Select alternatives to be evaluated.
6. Evaluate alternatives.
7. Select the preferred alternative.
8. Implement the preferred alternative.

No matter how logical and appealing the above approach may be, it is unlikely that an individual's decision process conforms to it. As Morris (1972, pp. 192–193) concludes:

> These recipes are the subject of numerous articles and books on how to make decisions. They are appealing in that they sound very reasonable and appear to be obviously "the right way to do it." There appears to be very little evidence, however, that they have any interesting effect on the actual decision-making behavior of experienced persons. Although the evidence is admittedly experimental, the best hypothesis appears to be that if one really wanted to alter the behavior of an intuitive decider, these pseudo-logical schemes are not going to be very effective.

While the process that an individual or organization goes through in making a decision is not well understood, there is some evidence revealing the psychological influences on an individual during decision making. Some of these influences are clearly important and need to be recognized if models and their analyses are to be effective aids to decision makers.

## Perceptual Processes

The traditional view in the quantitative literature has been that a clear, unbiased problem statement is available from which a decision model can be formulated. Perceptions of the decision maker(s) and subordinates about the problem are often ignored. Litterer (1965, pp. 62–63) describes the perceptual process as consisting of three elements: selectivity, closure, and interpretation. The decision maker selectively accepts information and tends to classify it for further use. This information is then compiled (the closure operation) into a meaningful whole. Finally, the decision maker uses experience and intuitive processes to interpret the information then collected and filed away.

This perceptual process may lead to difficulties in developing a decision model. The problem as seen by management may not be the true problem, and the original problem definition may need to be revised as the study proceeds.

In the example of the Citron Company, the task force's definition of the problem was extremely broad and encompassed almost every phase of the company's operation. After considerable effort, the consultants and the task force agreed that the problem was to determine the optimal product mix for one of the company's plants. Understanding and working with management perceptions are important parts of the quantitative analyst's job, since these perceptions often influence the eventual model structure.

Perceptions also influence data collection efforts. Individuals exaggerate the importance of their immediate concerns. Therefore, the modeler who obtains data based upon these perceptions may miss significant information relevant to the problem. To Citron's management, materials handling was not perceived to be a problem. However, during the project, model results contradicted this view. Fortunately, the model was easily corrected.

Perceptions influence the evaluations and selection of alternatives. Managers may not endorse recommendations they see as hard to implement, controversial, or threatening to their power base. In the Citron Company example, Harvey Kincaid went into the planning committee meeting with a strategy of advocating the construction of a warehouse. Kincaid perceived the recommendation that brand proliferation be reversed as overly controversial, and so he was not prepared to promote it. As the meeting progressed, brand reduction became the focus of discussion, and a decision was made to implement this recommendation. Kincaid's perception had been wrong, but the decision he wanted was made.

Perceptual processes can influence every phase of model design, construction, and implementation. Analysts must evaluate these perceptions and develop models from as correct a perceptual base as possible. At the same time, analysts must be prepared to work with decision makers to alter their perceptual biases, and decision makers must be prepared to guide analysts in the appropriate direction.

## Subconscious Processes

The role of the subconscious mind in decision making is not well understood. The Freudian view, for example, pictures the individual as self-centered and as subconsciously distorting realities to reflect inner needs. Rationalizations are created as "good" reasons for subconscious desires. No matter whether this is an accurate view, subconscious processes are difficult to identify and confront. Ferber (1967) examines subconscious processes in several case studies which show subconscious processes as significant obstacles for an objective manager to overcome. In the Citron Company the reluctance of some managers to allow the collection of realistic cost data seemed to stem from a subconscious fear that such data would reveal embarrassments. (The fear may well have been conscious.)

## Intuitive Processes

One function of a model is the replacement of intuition. Opposition to intuitive decision making is based on the contention that the human mind cannot cope with problem complexity. Forrester (1971, p. 1) states: "It is my basic theme that the human mind is not adapted to interpreting how social systems behave. Our social systems belong to a class of multi-loop, non-linear feedback systems. . . . Evolutionary processes have not given us the mental skill needed to properly interpret the dynamic behavior of the systems of which we have now become a part."

In contrast with Forrester's viewpoint, Drucker (1973, p. 513) theorizes: "Insight, understanding, ranking of priorities, and a 'feel' for the complexity of an area are as important as precise, beautifully elegant mathematical models— and in fact usually infinitely more useful and indeed even more 'scientific.' They reflect the reality of the manager's universe and of his tasks."

In the same light, Little concludes that a decision calculus is needed which has as its goal the updating of a manager's intuition. As he sees it (1970, p. B470), such a decision calculus would have as its goal developing a "set of procedures for processing data and judgments to assist a manager in his decision making."

There exists little experimental evidence to support one viewpoint over the other. Pegels (1970, p. 70) performed a study on college students in which he asked them to make production-related decisions, and then he compared their decisions to those of a model. He concluded in this case that the model was better than student judgment. His experiment, however, had a flawed design biased in favor of the model. Tversky and Kahneman (1974, pp. 1124–1131) discuss biases that result when intuitive judgments are made in situations of uncertainty. While their study dealt primarily with probability estimates, Tversky and Kahneman provide convincing arguments that faulty judgments result from an overreliance on intuition.

On the other side of the issue, there is evidence supporting the proposition that models aimed at augmenting intuition are the most successful. Studies such as those of Angel et al. (1972), Caruso and Kokat (1973), Easingwood (1973), and Frankfurter et al. (1974) are examples of models developed to make more efficient use of intuition. Each of these studies has been more successful than comparable purely analytical studies. Morris (1972, p. 97) concludes that "The techniques likely to succeed are those that do not require a great amount of special training or 'selling' and that the decision maker finds naturally assimilable into his own personal style."

In an attempt to enlist intuition as an ally, the analysts for Citron studied the language and viewpoints common to the company and its industry. Subsequent oral and written reports were expressed as far as possible in this language. Similarly, only "cases" which were clearly implied by day-to-day operations were investigated. Technical data and presentations which would have seemed foreign were avoided.

The enhancement of intuition is a desirable and important goal, although requiring a different structure of quantitative modeling. Subsequent chapters in this text will delve more fully into this point.

## Attitudes about Uncertainty

A manager's attitude toward uncertainty affects the success of a decision model. From his reivew of research studies, Harrison (1975, p. 157) concludes:

The propensity to accept risk is obviously influenced by at least the following variables:

(1) the intelligence and other personality traits of the decision maker
(2) the expectations of the decision maker
(3) the amount of information available to the decision maker
(4) the amount of time within which the choice must be made
(5) the complexity (however defined) of the choice itself

Intelligence, the first factor in the list, has been found to be inversely related to risk taking. The more intelligent the decision makers, the more likely they are to develop consistent low-risk alternatives which promise modest levels of success versus a minimal chance of failure. The less intelligent decision makers appear more willing to take risks if there is some chance of large reward.

Morlock (1967) has shown that decision makers who have low expectations of success will require more information to decide upon a course of action than those who have a high expectation of success. Decision makers who display high degrees of apprehension are also prone to search for more information in decision making.

Time pressure also affects decision making. A common pattern is as follows. As the difficulty of decision making increases, the time required to make a decision can be expected to increase. However, once the decision difficulty has reached a sufficiently high level, the required decision time decreases, since the decision maker has declining hopes of finding a good solution and makes a snap decision.

To the modeler, management attitudes about uncertainty are central to the success of a modeling effort. A decision maker with a low tolerance for uncertainty may not be willing to accept the standard mathematical approaches to risk. The level of expectation, the complexity, and the pressure of time may also affect a manager's willingness to initiate a modeling effort.

Some managers prefer an uncertain situation, since it allows them to demonstrate their decision making skill. Other managers avoid uncertainty. In either case, the manager's attitudes toward uncertainty affect the successful application of quantitative aids.

At Citron, Harvey Kincaid understood the role of uncertainty. "Well, even if the data you used is 30 percent off, the results are *still* startling," he told the consultants. Peter Duvalier, on the other hand, felt that making any change in marketing policy would insert so much uncertainty into the operations that literally *nothing* would remain predictable.

## Stress Conditions and Decision Making

Stress is the final psychological aspect of decision making. Janis and Mann (1976, p. 657) describe stress as resulting from fear of two consequences: material and social losses from a decision and loss in esteem as a decision maker. Of all the psychological aspects of decision making, perhaps more is known about stress than any other aspect. The work of Testlinger (1964) is another example of work on this subject.

Janis and Mann (1977) outline five coping patterns that a decision maker may employ in making decisions:

1. Unconflicted adherence—the decision maker continues as before and ignores evidence indicating that a change is necessary.
2. Unconflicted change—the decision maker uncritically goes along with a new course of action.
3. Defensive avoidance—the decision maker avoids the decision by shifting the responsibility to others or by using rationalizations to procrastinate.
4. Hypervigilance—the decision maker frantically searches in all directions for a solution and adopts the first solution that promises some immediate relief.
5. Vigilance—the decision maker follows a well-organized search for a solution.

The vigilance pattern appears to be the best for a decision maker to follow, but in many cases the first four patterns dominate. Most Citron personnel opted for the first and third patterns.

To the modeler, these concepts are important. If a vigilant pattern of decision making is not characteristic of a manager, a decision model may be of little help. The modeler must be conscious of stress patterns and the limitations they impose.

A complete understanding of the individual decision maker does not yet exist, but research to date has offered important insights, such as the fact that the decision maker may not act as rationally as is often assumed. A quantitative analyst trying to provide assistance to a decision maker should be aware that the decision maker's perceptions, subconscious, intuitive process, and attitude toward uncertainty all contribute to a decision making process which is much different and more complex than that of a mathematical model.

## Personal Habits

Decision makers must be studied in order to predict their decision-making style. Over the years individual decision makers tend to develop habits of thinking which produce predictable decisions. Harry S Truman saw the President's job as that of a high-level decision maker. He was fully capable of deciding in favor of an atomic bomb attack and then relaxing, satisfied that the decision was finished and relatively unconcerned with its consequences.

Adolph Hitler felt himself bound by his own decisions. Once he had determined to attack Poland, France, or Russia, his mind was permanently made up. He was unable to let go of his decisions even when logic might show that they were wrong decisions. He could not rest until he had carried out the decisions.

Truman's approach to the Presidency contrasted markedly with that of Eisenhower, who was a delegator of authority and decisions. However, in each case the pattern was habitual.

Habit played a role in all of the Nazi chieftain's decisions and was an integral part of his style. Although Hitler's decisional monomania likely won successes in the seizure of Czechoslovakia and Austria, his attack on Russia was undertaken in the same spirit and was a serious error.

At Citron, Harvey Kincaid was careful, but persistent. His habit was to proceed cautiously but without cowardice. Peter Duvalier was a backbiter who characteristically made reactionary, snap judgments. President Todd was almost in the Truman mold.

There is little chance of deterring a decision maker from adhering to form, but an analyst working with one must be conscious of the limitations that habit imposes and try to avoid impossible situations. Peter Duvalier at Citron never did accept the idea of eliminating some brands from his market list.

## THE ORGANIZATIONAL VIEW OF DECISION MAKING

To the individual trained in management, the organizational aspect of decision making is paramount. Extensive discussions exist on the subject of organization theory and how it relates to decision making. It is ironic that quantitative texts give little if any exposure to the organizational influence on decision models. The organization is virtually ignored in the development of many quantitative decision models. While a complete discussion of organizational influences is beyond the scope of this text, certain concepts must be described in sufficient detail that the reader will be aware of the importance of those influences on decision making.

### Group Decision Making

More and more organizations have adopted consensus styles of management in which a group is established to study a particular decision. In most cases, the group is made up of individuals with opposing viewpoints and conflicting objectives. Therefore, any model employed must be able to accommodate multiple and conflicting objectives. Technical methods for resolving multiple objectives are not well developed for practical use. Although many "scientific" ranking schemes have been developed, administrators do not view these procedures as being very useful.

An analyst working with a group must be able to deal with the conflicting desires of the group members. To each member of the group, the analyst must be perceived as an unbiased observer and recorder of information. In reality, the analyst must decide what information is important and build a data base around this information. To accomplish this task without antagonizing the members of the group is often difficult. In fact, the analyst may spend more time on diplomatic efforts than on model development.

Little empirical evidence contrasting the acceptance of modeling efforts done for groups with those done for individuals exists. Models done for group decision making efforts should be substantially more difficult, since the analyst must play the two roles of technical expert and group mediator. In the Citron Company, the task force composed of both marketing and production representatives had to agree on the form of the product mix model before it could be accepted as a tool for use in the planning process.

On the other hand, models accepted by an entire group have a much greater chance of implementation than do models prepared for an individual in the group. Models developed from a single individual's perspective may not be implemented, especially if other viewpoints have not been included.

## Power and Authority

The interaction of models with organizational power and authority may occur in different ways. Administrators may view decision models as devices for usurping their decision making responsibilities. While models are unlikely to displace decision makers from a major portion of their administrative responsibilities, the fear of such an event dominates the thinking of some administrators. Thus, an administrator may view the modeling process as a threat.

For example, a warehouse manager has operated the facility over the years as a personal fiefdom. The manager dispenses poor-quality service to those parts of the organization that fail to "buckle under." Supplies are delayed, and orders may be sent to the wrong place, or they may contain the wrong materials. An inventory model, no matter how well developed, is certain to incur the wrath of this warehouse manager. The warehouse manager correctly believes that such a model would potentially infringe on his or her power and authority.

In another example, a city council has funded a study of several fire station locations. The study estimates the capital costs, expected loss in lives, and expected property damage resulting from each of five different locations. The study shows that two of the possible sites are better in all cases than are the other three. The city council president, however, is a strong advocate of one of the three less desirable sites. The political power and authority of the council president is being challenged by the model.

In the Citron Company, the planning model implied marketing strategies which were perceived by the vice president for marketing as a challenge to his authority. He had frequently used low-volume brands as his tool to penetrate special markets. Since the model indicated that production disruptions resulting from these small-volume products were not worth the hypothesized marketing advantages, the vice president saw the model as a threat to his activities.

Decision models can also be used to *acquire* power and authority. In a sense, managers who have quantitative experts "on their side" can wield an assortment of analytical tools to support their positions in an organizational dispute. Depending upon the quality and the organizational acceptance of a modeling project, its long-range effect may be the enhancement of the prestige of the administrator who initiated the project.

Harvey Kincaid, director of market planning and development at Citron, had seen the product mix study as a step in his assumption of the major marketing responsibilities at Citron. As the study progressed, it was evident that the results would support his position. When the recommendations from the consultants were accepted, his power did increase, and he was even given the responsibility of reducing the brand list.

The potential for the use of a decision model as a tool for power acquisition by a manager can present significant problems to the modeler. A successful modeling effort initiated by one branch of an organization may be seen in its other parts as an attempt by that group to seize power. In many cases, this fear is unfounded, but if the perception is there, the modeler may find avoiding this organizational conflict difficult.

## Organizational Equilibrium and Inertia

Organizations, whether public or private, are complex entities. While the stated goals of such organizations may be expressed as maximizing profits or as maximizing the level of service for the tax dollar, the true goal is often the maintenance of the status quo of the organization. Thus, the decision analyst must confront not only the conflicting "stated" objectives as discussed earlier but also the "hidden" objectives that really direct the organization. Procedures which maximize profit but disturb organizational equilibrium may not be acceptable.

Consider the case of a model designed to distribute cigarette production among a group of five manufacturing facilities. The results of the model indicate that profit would be maximized if one of the plants were closed or if it were shifted to making different cigarettes than it had been making. Such a solution may be difficult to implement. The harmful impact on the community which houses the endangered manufacturing facility is an important consideration in implementing the original solution; however, organizational problems may also limit what can be done.

The elimination of one facility in five will have implications for the administrative framework of the organization. What will happen to the supervisory staff at the facility to be shut down? Some of them will be absorbed into the central administrative staff, thus setting off a chain of events destined to disturb the equilibrium of the entire organization. The ability of the organization to undergo such a transformation may have a significant impact on acceptance of the strategy dictated by the model.

Organizational inertia is another impediment to the success of a decision modeling effort. The problem of getting things done in an organization is a much-discussed concern of management, but the difficulty in overcoming organizational inertia limits many modeling efforts.

Three major sources of inertia are the three governing P's of an organization: policies, precedents, and procedures. To cynics, frustrated by their inability to move their organizations in a new direction, the three P's seem to be merely organizational ploys to allow administrators to avoid making difficult decisions in unfamiliar situations. It is easier, it seems, to fall back on established policies as an excuse not to venture into an area of risk. At the same time, innovative ideas requiring thought are easily rejected when some prohibitive precedent can be cited.

Consider, for example, the application of a model developed for a regional office of a union retail store. The results of the model analyses dictated that a 20 percent improvement in customer service (delivery time) would be achieved by reallocating personnel within the office. The new pattern would have violated existing procedures which established the work loads for various employees in the office. Management, upon reviewing the suggested allocation, rejected it because it would have established a precedent for local control displacing central control, and it violated the principle of standardization of administration.

Group decisions in general are complex organizational phenomena. A successful modeling effort must deal with such group relationships as power and authority, organizational inertia and equilibrium, organizational conflicts, and the desire to preserve the status quo. A modeling effort may disturb any or all of these relationships. Subsequent chapters will emphasize the roles of specific types of models in organizational decision making.

## THE SOCIETAL ASPECT OF DECISION MAKING

Individual and organizational attitudes toward decision making are tempered by societal considerations. Such factors as social norms, standards of ethical behavior, legal restrictions, and even the cultural setting of the organization affect how decisions are made.

### Social Norms

Social norms are influences which affect decisions made by individuals and organizations. Ebert and Mitchell (1975, p. 211) define a social norm to be "an evaluative scale (i.e., a yardstick) designating an acceptable latitude and an objectionable latitude for behavior, activity, events, beliefs, or any object of concern to members of a social unit. In other words, the social norm is the standard and accepted way of making judgments." To the extent that modeling is a pioneering activity within an organization, it may be considered outside the social norm. Ebert and Mitchell (1975, p. 222) describe seven general principles which explain the role of social norms in decision making:

1. The more ambiguous or uncertain the situation, the greater is the role played by norms and influence.
2. The more anonymous the information exchanged, the less influence is exerted.
3. The more confident and competent the decision maker, the less he is likely to be influenced.
4. Increasing pressure by increasing the number of people exerting the pressure does not seem very effective past groups of five.
5. The more unanimous the pressure, the greater the influence.
6. The more cohesive and interdependent the group members, the greater the likelihood of conformity.
7. Certain persons can be identified who conform less than others (e.g., flexible, bright, independent individuals).

It is interesting to apply these seven principles to the decision making situation at the Citron Company. The strongest advocate of the modeling effort was

Harvey Kincaid, the director of market planning and development. He was a nonconformist but was also a confident and competent individual. He was able to withstand pressure from the marketing side of Citron, and, as the study results became known, he was an outspoken advocate of the implied plan of action. The task force itself was not cohesive. Each member was rather independent. As the results of the model were presented, various members of the task force began to exert pressure on the marketing vice president to adopt some of the recommendations of the study. Finally, when the president supported part of the recommendations, overt resistance to them disappeared.

Social norms, as seen in this one example, can be influential in any decision making effort. At Citron, the norm was "the way we do things around here." Changing such a pattern of behavior requires the support of innovative, dynamic individuals. The success of any modeling activity may depend heavily upon such support.

## Ethical Behavior

The social attitudes of the 60s and 70s often cast the large organization in the role of the villain of society. Corporations were accused of lacking social responsibility. The view of managers as being only concerned with profits became commonplace. However, the attitudes of managers were and are often determined by ethical considerations.

Maximum profit is *not* the sole operating goal of management, and ethical behavior *is* considered to be important in decision making. Peter Drucker (1973) explains the mistrust by the public as a result of the business executive's rhetoric stressing profit. He chides business executives for not doing their job in explaining economic realities.

Models may also be influenced by the rhetoric of profit so that modeled objectives stress monetary considerations to the exclusion of social responsibilities. For example, a pollution control model may seek the method for exactly meeting pollution control standards, but its major objective is to hold down control costs. So strong is the economic orientation of modelers and managers that such models rarely pursue the best way to minimize pollution.

Models are not intrinsically incapable of including ethical and social considerations. The skill of the modeler and the will of management can bring the power of quantitative methods to the analysis of problems with these aspects included. The realization that problems are multidimensional and that diverse objectives must be included in all problems that affect larger issues is the basic requirement for developing models with the necessary flexibility.

## Legal Restrictions

Perhaps the most powerful issue of the 80s and 90s will be the role of government in regulating private industry. Regulations can result in a range of effects, good and bad. Most regulations represent limits on the flexibility of industry operations and must be dealt with as best the industry can. Models can be used to show companies the best way to comply with regulations, but they can also be used to study the regulations themselves. As a means of resolving conflicting claims as to the costs and benefits of regulations, models can be developed to study different regulations.

Regulations represent constraints, but they also offer opportunities to accomplish objectives that may not have been economically feasible otherwise. The Occupational Safety and Health Administration (OSHA) regulations limiting the weight loaded on trucks may prompt a study of the truck routing and loading regulations of a company. Environmental Protection Agency (EPA) regulations on pollutant discharges may prompt a study of product scheduling. In each of these cases, the modeling effort may have been a low-priority project before the advent of the regulation, but a regulation can be turned into at least a partial advantage in such cases.

Regulations may, however, offer decision makers an excuse to neglect their responsibilities. Low productivity can be conveniently blamed on federal rules, when, in fact, low productivity may have been due to poor management. The constant barrage of regulations may also leave decision makers with a feeling of lost authority; they may view any decision as one of strict adherence to regulations rather than one of thoughtful decision making.

To the quantitative analyst, regulations present both opportunities and impediments. The skillful analyst can use a regulation as an opportunity for improved decision making. The extent to which this can be accomplished is largely a function of the organization's acceptance of government controls.

## Cultural Dimensions

In recent years there has been increased interest in comparing management and decision styles in different countries, particularly Japan and the United States.

In an article in the *Harvard Business Review*, Peter Drucker (1971) contrasts decision making in America and Japan. He describes the Japanese style as one of decision by consensus in which a decision is debated throughout the organization until an agreement is reached. To the Japanese, the crucial element in decision making is defining the question. Debate centers on whether a problem exists. Once the essence of the problem is defined, the answer to the problem closely parallels its definition.

What the Japanese system produces is a decision which needs little selling to implement. Since consensus must be reached on every decision, the implementation phase tends to be nearly instantaneous.

What does this particular cultural dimension mean to the modeler? In America, a frequent complaint about quantitative decision models is their lack of success in being implemented. If a model is an accepted contributor to attaining consensus, it would seem that its implementation would be less difficult in the Japanese culture. In America, models are used to generate solutions which must then be sold. In Japan, models are used to investigate the problem. While such models are probably more difficult to develop, their eventual success should be enhanced. Little study has been done to evaluate the cultural aspect of decision making or decision models.

Other factors peculiar to individual countries affect decision making style. The economic system of a country is another dimension which undoubtedly affects the success of modeling efforts. What effect the nature of an economic system has on the acceptance of decision models is little understood. Also, while the cultural heritage of a country is believed to have an effect on decision making, little is known about the relative acceptance of models in different cultures.

# REFERENCES

Angel, R. D., W. L. Caudle, R. Noonan, and A. Whinston: "Computer-Assisted School Bus Scheduling," *Management Science*, vol. 18, no. 6, 1972, pp. B279–B282.

Caruso, F. A., and J. J. Kokat: "Coil-Slitting—A Shop Floor Solution," *Industrial Engineering*, November 1973, pp. 18–23.

Drucker, Peter F.: *Management, Tasks, Responsibilities, Practices*, Harper and Row, New York, 1973.

_____: "What We Can Learn from Japanese Management," *Harvard Business Review*, March–April 1971, pp. 110–122.

Easingwood, C.: "A Heuristic Approach to Selecting Sales Regions and Territories," *Operational Research Quarterly*, vol. 24, no. 4, 1973, pp. 527–534.

Ebert, Ronald J., and Terence R. Mitchell: *Organizational Decision Processes*, Crane, Russak and Co., New York, 1975.

Etzioni, A.: "Mixed Scanning: A Third Approach to Decision Making," *Public Administration Review*, vol. 27, 1967, pp. 385–392.

Ferber, Robert C.: "The Role of the Subconscious in Executive Decision Making," *Management Science*, vol. 13, no. 8, 1967, B519–B526.

Forrester, Jay W.: "Counterintuitive Behavior of Social Systems," *Technological Forecasting and Social Change*, vol. 3, no. 1, 1971.

Frankfurter, G. M., K. E., Kendall, and C. E. Pegels: "Management Control of Blood through a Short-Term Supply—Demand Forecast System," *Management Science*, vol. 21, no. 4, 1974, pp. 444–452.

Harrison, E. Frank: *The Managerial Decision-Making Process*, Houghton Mifflin, Boston, 1975.

Janis, Irving L., and Leon Mann: "Coping with Decision Conflict," *American Scientist*, vol. 64, 1976, pp. 657–667.

_____ and _____: *Decision Making*, Free Press, New York, 1977.

Lindbloom, C. E.: "The Science of Muddling Through," *Public Administration Review*, vol. 10, 1959, pp. 79–99.

Litterer, Joseph A.: *The Analysis of Organizations*, Wiley, New York, 1965.

Little, John D. C.: "Models and Managers: The Concept of a Decision Calculus," *Management Science*, vol. 16, no. 8, 1970, pp. B466–B485.

Miller, David W., and Martin K. Starr: *The Structure of Human Decisions*, Prentice-Hall, Englewood Cliffs, N.J., 1967.

Morlock, Henry: "The Effect of Outcome Desirability on Information Required for Decision," *Behavioral Science*, July 1967, pp. 296–300.

Morris, William T.: "Matching Decision Aids with Intuitive Styles," in Henry S. Brinkers (ed.), *Decision Making*, Ohio State University Press, Columbus, 1972.

Pegels, Carl: "Human Decision vs. Math Model: An Experiment," *Industrial Engineering*, December 1970, pp. 41–44.

Simon, Herbert: *Administrative Behavior*, 3d ed., Free Press, New York, 1976.
Testlinger, Leon: *Conflict, Decision and Dissonance*, Stanford University Press, Stanford, Calif., 1964.
Tversky, Amos and Daniel Kahneman: "Judgment under Uncertainty: Heuristics and Biases," *Science*, vol. 185, 1974, pp. 1124–1131.

# QUESTIONS

1 What was the decision that Citron needed to make?

2 How did the description of the decision situation change as the technical study proceeded?

3 Why was the task force appointed to look at the decision? What was the influence of the task force on the action taken as a result of the study?

4 How did the decision model influence the decision process of the task force?

5 What is the scientific method of decision making? Is this approach applied universally in decision making?

6 How are perceptions formed? How do perceptions influence decision making?

7 How do subconscious forces influence rational decision making?

8 Does the use of intuitive processes in decision making limit the use of decision models?

9 What factors influence the attitudes that a person may have with regard to uncertainty?

10 What is the likely behavior of a football quarterback faced with a changing defensive pattern? How does this behavior relate to the coping pattern for dealing with stress?

11 How does group behavior influence decision making in organizations?

12 How can the development of a decision model influence the power and authority relationships within an organization?

13 What changing social norms have influenced business decision making in the past ten years?

14 What are some of the major areas of decision making that the federal government influences through the use of regulatory bodies or other legislative powers?

# EXERCISES

1 Analyze your personal decision making style with regard to the following:
   (*a*) Tolerance of ambiguity
   (*b*) Comfort with risk taking
   (*c*) Effect of high stress levels
   (*d*) Role of intuition
Illustrate your analysis with two specific cases: one involving the selection of a college and the second involving the selection of a major.

2 Analyze the decision making style of someone you have worked for or know well according to the following:
   (*a*) Tolerance of ambiguity
   (*b*) Comfort with risk taking
   (*c*) Effect of high stress levels
   (*d*) Role of intuition
   (*e*) Willingness to accept outside input

3 Select five decisions that you have made and evaluate your initial perceptions about the decision in contrast to the reality of the decision situation.

4 Discuss a company's decision to resist union organization efforts with respect to the power and authority relationships within the organization.

5 From an article you have read in *Fortune, Business Week*, or some other business magazine, analyze the individual and organizational aspects of the decision discussed.

6 You are faced with a vital decision that must be made within a week. Describe as carefully as possible your personal habits in making such a decision.

7 What social forces of the 60s and 70s have influenced business decision making? Discuss this influence in terms of the following decision areas:
  (*a*) Capital investments
  (*b*) Personnel policies
  (*c*) Quality control
  (*d*) Facility location

8 For the most recent Super Bowl, analyze the attitudes of both teams with regard to risk taking. Identify key plays in the game and analyze how influential risk taking behavior was to the outcome of the play.

9 Analyze a crucial play of a World Series game as outlined in Exercise 8.

10 For a group that you belong to, analyze the respective role of each member of the group in a group decision making effort. If a decision model were to be developed for such a group, which member would be the most influential in the acceptance of the model.

11 What are your existing perceptions about the role of mathematical models in decision making situations?

12 What decision that you have made have you personally learned the most from? Why do you think this decision was so instructive?

# CASELETS*

1. Gloria Wexler is an industrial engineering junior. She has a 3.5 grade point average and seems to enjoy her courses very much. She has been active in the American Institute of Industrial Engineers and a sorority. During the past year, she has been disturbed by a problem concerning her future. Although she is happy in engineering, the thought of a forty-year career is not appealing to her. She would like to have a family with three children. The men she meets at sorority parties are generally turned off by the fact that she is in engineering and that she made more money on a summer job than they might make on a full-time job. Although she has met a lot of men in her engineering classes, none of them appeal to her. She has begun to think that an engineering husband is not for her. In addition, the thought of graduating and going to work in a new area is frightening. As a result of her dilemma, Gloria is thinking of changing her major to a more "acceptable" field for women.

   (*a*) Describe Gloria Wexler's view of her career decision in terms of the following:
     (1) Her perception of factors affecting the decision
     (2) The subconscious influences affecting her decision
     (3) The role of intuition in the decision

*The stereotypes encountered occasionally in the caselets are, unfortunately, encountered in real life. They do not reflect the views of the authors or the publisher.

(4) The role of social norms in the decision
(5) Her attitudes about uncertainty

2. Hal Johnson, plant manager of a large equipment manufacturer, was expressing his feelings to John Walker, the chief industrial engineer. John had been called to Hal Johnson's office to discuss misrouting of their warehouse shipments. Orders were increasingly being sent to the wrong place. For example, an order the previous week had been sent incorrectly to San Diego instead of Jacksonville. Hal Johnson was incensed.

"Those employees we have are worthless. We just spent 2 million dollars last year on a completely automated warehouse where all the workers need to do is ride around the plant and go to a location we tell them. They hardly have to lift a finger. They used to have to remember where everything was. Now all they have to do is read a card, go to the right place, and pick up the item. John, what's wrong?"

Before responding to Hal Johnson, John thought back to the work situation in the warehouse prior to the change. Most of the laborers were long-time employees of the company who up to a year ago had been thought of as some of the most productive workers in the plant. They had decorated their forklift trucks with sayings and names. They had given special names to different areas of the warehouse such as Cathy's Corner and Beulah's Bay. They had frequently staged races against the clock to see how fast they could find and deliver orders to the loading dock. All of a sudden their productivity had declined and incorrect shipments had become common.

(a) Describe Hal Johnson's view of the warehouse problem in terms of the following:
   (1) His perception of the problem
   (2) Subconscious influences
(b) What social forces are influencing Johnson's attitudes?
(c) What factors were not taken into account in the decision to automate the warehouse?

## CASE 1.1: ALUMNI STADIUM

Alumni Stadium was the home of Mountaineer University's football program. The 38,000-seat stadium was considered one of the best fields in the country for watching football. The stands were practically on top of the field. Although the viewing was great for Mountaineer fans, opposing teams were often intimidated by the stadium. In an effort to alleviate the conditions at Alumni Stadium, the opposing teams demanded that the stadium be expanded or that the traditional home-and-away schedules would be abandoned. Although their arguments were based upon economic criteria, it was clear that many of Mountaineer's rivals were tired of bringing highly rated teams into the stadium only to be upset.

## The University's Recommendation

The decision on whether to build a new stadium was an emotional one. Members of the university debated the issue and decided that some action had to be taken to either improve the existing stadium or build a new one. The office of intercollegiate athletics and the athletic council weighed a number of factors in making their decision. Foremost among their considerations were the following:

1. The cost of the alternatives
2. The impact of the decision on the community
3. The desires of the alumni association
4. The desires of state citizens
5. The desires of the student body
6. The impact of the decision on the football program
7. Available land for each alternative
8. Necessary support services (e.g., parking, sewers, highways)
9. Other uses for the stadium
10. Tradition and competitive advantages
11. Potential legislative support

A cost estimate was developed for expanding the existing stadium. Taking into consideration land purchases and all necessary construction, an estimate of $14 million was developed. This alternative would have added 15,000 seats to the stadium.

Although a specific cost estimate for a new stadium was not prepared, experience with similar facilities indicated that $20 million would be needed for a new field. This estimate did not include the cost of any infrastructure for a new stadium.

In comparing the alternatives, the university considered the cost to be the deterrent to the new facility. The state legislature had been very cool to the university in recent years, particularly as demonstrated by faculty salaries, equipment and travel support, and current expenses. Thinking that it would be lucky to receive any support, the university requested support for the expanded stadium instead of a new facility.

## Legislative Action

The recommendation from the university was forwarded without comment to the state legislature from the board of regents. Several of the delegates from the university district were upset with the university proposal. They seemed particularly disturbed at not being consulted on the decision. They seemed more than willing to do battle with their legislative colleagues for a new stadium. For some time they had felt that other districts had received more than their fair share of public works funds.

As the delegates prepared a strategy to gain the approval for a new building, the governor shocked the state legislature as well as the university. In his budget message to the legislature, he proposed the building of a new stadium. When asked about the $20 million cost estimate which was not based on any engineering or architectural study, the governor seemed unworried. "If the stadium needs more money, so be it."

The legislature went along with the governor's proposal with a minimum of its usual bickering. An engineering firm was hired to make detailed plans for the facility, prepared a detailed budget, and select a site. The stadium was set to open in three years from the signing of the bill.

## The Site Selection Decision

Until the stadium received final approval, the university and the surrounding community seemed hesitant to express any views on the new facility. Suddenly the reality of the situation began to concern the community. Where would the new facility be built?

The engineering firm narrowed down its choices for the new stadium to three possible sites:

A—University property on a golf course located between the university hospital and the law school

B—University property on one of the farms outside of the main campus area

C—Private property 5 miles from campus, but close to the interstate highway

Each of the sites had major weaknesses. Alternative A would remove the university's golf course and would be disruptive to the hospital. It would also adversely affect local property values. Local roads, sewer lines, and parking were also insufficient to handle the increased loads.

Alternative B suffered from inadequate highway access, which made the site less accessible to university students. Research programs in the college of agriculture might also be affected by this alternative.

Alternative C had sufficient access, but its distance from campus made the stadium unusable for anything other than football and special events, and the cost of the property was high.

As the disadvantages of each site became clear, local community support for the new stadium deteriorated. A movement to reconsider the renovation of the old stadium was proposed. The stadium became an issue in the legislative races. After a six-month study of the sites was completed, consultants recommended alternative A. The option of renovating the old stadium was dismissed because it would violate the conditions of the bonds that were to be issued to fund the stadium.

Protests continued for some time, but eventually the decision became final. The local community continued to complain about its lack of input into the decision process. Town-gown relationships, which had been strained for years, continued to grow worse.

## Discussion Guide

1 What factors influenced the university's original decision to expand the seating of its football facility?

2 What perceptions influenced the university's recommendation to expand the old stadium?

3 What were some likely influences underlying the governor's recommendation to build a new stadium?

4 What were the likely influences which caused the choice of the site for the new stadium?

5 What were the aspects of the decision process used in this case that led to the town-gown problems?

6 Could a decision model have been used in this case to circumvent some of the problems caused by the decision?

7 If you were hired by the consultant to make a similar study at another university, what would you have done differently?

# TWO

## MODELS IN DECISION MAKING

## SYNOPSIS OF THE CHAPTER

This chapter stresses the requirements imposed upon models by the decision situation itself. If the combination of the skills of the modeler, the attributes of the model, and the judgment of the decision maker is to produce useful results, the model must be adapted toward this end. This chapter demonstrates some of the personality traits and realities which can affect the modeling and decision making environment.

Specific methods are suggested for the development of models that are flexible enough to fill the proper role. Among topics discussed are how models can do what they should and when modeling may be inappropriate or inadvisable.

During the discussion of the role of models, it is suggested that the main goal of models should be to clarify the insights of the decision maker. In order to satisfy the goal, models must adapt closely to the needs of the decision making environment. Specific methods are suggested for adapting models effectively.

The need for fitting the model to the requirements of the decision maker is emphasized along with the need for open communication between modeler and decision maker during the modeling process.

Chapters 1 and 2 together form the philosophic basis for the following chapters, each of which deals with a particular type of decision or a special way of viewing a decision. The philosophy espoused holds that managerial decision making should avail itself of the insights available from quantitative models. This philosophy further holds that neither models nor modelers can displace the decision making function of the manager but that the role of the modeler in the modern management environment should be the adaptation of modeling tools to the real needs of the decision situation. The ideal situation, in the view of this philosophy, is the smooth blending of model, modeler, and decision maker into an effective unit.

## MAJOR CONCEPTS PRESENTED IN THIS CHAPTER

1. The role of decision models should be the enhancement of the decision maker's insight.

2. The decision model should be compatible with the individual decision style of the decision maker(s).
3. For the communications process between model and manager to be effective, there must be a level of mutual understanding between the model builder and the manager.
4. Success of a model should be measured whenever possible by tangible results achieved. The insights provided by the model to the decision making effort are also a valuable indicator of the success of the model.
5. There are attitudes within an organization and problems affecting the decision to be made which may limit chances for successful application of a decision model.

## EXPECTATIONS OF THE STUDENT

The student, after studying this chapter, should be able to do the following:

1. Identify and explain the proper role of models in decision making
2. Identify a decision maker's personal style and adapt the model to this style
3. Analyze the interaction between the model builder and the decision maker
4. Describe a model building process that will enhance the implementation success of the model
5. Identify a successful model
6. Identify the decision conditions where models are unlikely to be successful

Students, after reading and and studying this chapter, should be aware of the model development process. The ability to apply many of the concepts presented here requires considerable experience, but additional insights should evolve as the ensuing chapters are covered.

## MORGAN COUNTY EMERGENCY MEDICAL SERVICES

The Morgan County Emergency Medical Services (MCEMS) faced the problem of where to locate. Since its inception two years earlier, it had been housed in the second floor and the garage of a building owned by a beer distributor. The station, although conveniently located, was physically inadequate.

The garage supports would not safely accommodate the weight of the vehicles, and the garage owner was unwilling to have the facility repaired. As the MCEMS expanded, space became cramped, and several vehicles had to be parked along the highway. The MCEMS decided to ask the county commissioners for funds to lease or purchase adequate facilities.

The administrative assistant to the county commission, John Eishart, was approached separately and asked to give his support to the request for a new facility. John, a former military officer, was in favor of the request but did not believe the commissioner could be convinced of its validity. He gave vent to his feelings in the presence of Sue Mullen, the head of the MCEMS, telling of his continuing frustration with the county commission.

"I swear, I think only one of those three guys can read. You're not going to get any support for any project that costs money unless it involves a matter of life or death or unless it has potential for high levels of political gain. They love to get their pictures taken coming to the rescue of some distressed family. You'd also think they owned stock in pipe the way they build sewers and water lines. You know as well as I do that the rural parts of the county swing the elections and that the commissioners never forget who put them in office. I don't think you can get their ear unless you approach them just right.

"You know, a thought just came to me. I once took a short course in college that discussed a model for locating a fire station. I bet the same thing could be done for the MCEMS garage. If you could show that the present garage location is costing lives, I think those guys would have to listen."

Sue Mullen was amazed at John Eishart's candor in describing the county commission. She was fully convinced that his perception of the commissioners' thinking was correct and agreed to devise a model to test alternative locations for the MCEMS facility. She was actually reluctant to pursue this line of undertaking, since she felt that she already knew where the MCEMS facility should be located, but the possibilities that this effort might please Eishart and might help sell the commissioners were factors that moved her to initiate the model.

Eishart called William Marshall, the director of short courses at Morgan College, and asked him if he could help. As it turned out, one of Marshall's students, Wesley Baker, had just had his third thesis topic "fall through." A meeting between Eishart, Mullen, Marshall, and Baker was arranged, and it led to general agreement that a model could help in the location decision. Throughout the meeting, Baker was uncharacteristically subdued, so after the meeting, Marshall asked him to come into his office.

Baker was dubious of the value of the study. He had been involved in other quantitative studies that had failed, and he wanted to be sure that this project would be worth his efforts. He wasn't sure what the study could tell the county commission.

"It seems to me that you should simply locate the facility where you have the greatest number of accidents," said Baker.

"I agree, Wes, but you also need to know the effect of each location on the rest of the county. You know as well as I do that the big shots that live out along the lake are going to complain if any suggestion is made to locate the MCEMS facility further from them."

"I know, but it just seems to me that I'm going to prepare a model for some politician to use in protecting his rear end."

"I'd consider that a valid application, Wes. Don't worry, I think Eishart really wants your input to this decision."

As a result of Marshall's encouragement, Baker reluctantly began his study. His first step was to meet with Mullen and develop a documented flowchart of the steps in emergency medical care. At the same time he began outlining the data he thought he would need.

While data describing all calls for assistance were kept, the emergency work performed was of such urgency that most of the data was only recorded after the accident. Because of this retrospective aspect of the data, Baker felt that much of it was inaccurate. He delayed fully committing himself to what he viewed as a questionable project for some time.

Baker did obtain some data on the locations of calls for emergency services in Morgan County. As he had suspected, 48 percent of the calls came from the city of Morgan, the county seat. An additional 14 percent of the calls originated in the suburbs. Since 62 percent of the calls came from such a limited portion of the county, Baker became steadily more convinced that his model would only confirm the obvious.

Extensive discussions were held between Marshall and Baker on the nature of the model, the data needed, and the simplifying assumptions required. The discussions seemed to Marshall to be a stalling maneuver, but Baker appeared convinced that he was using this time profitably in further refining the model. Marshall kept insisting that Baker keep Mullen aware of his progress, but for some reason Baker was hesitant to keep in touch with the MCEMS people.

Finally, Baker became ready to make a full-time commitment to the study. He reluctantly returned to the MCEMS facility, and, as was predictable, Mullen was upset.

"Where have you been? We thought you gave up on us."

Baker, in his typical, honest fashion, explained that he had had a heavy teaching load, Mullen seemed to understand but still was not mollified. The MCEMS facility had become even more inadequate, and it was now clear that some decision about a new facility had to be made soon. She communicated this sense of urgency to Baker. Baker, throughout his academic days, had been a student who would work well only if sufficient pressure were applied to him. Mullen's sense of urgency presented a challenge to him that put him into high gear. His crash effort began.

During marathon research sessions, Baker collected the data he needed from past emergencies. He chose three potential locations for the new facility and collected data on the travel times implied for each location. A simulation model was written, and, after a week of debugging, the three alternatives were tested. One of the alternatives investigated (A) was an abandoned vocational studies building in downtown Morgan, owned by the board of education. Another location (B) was distant from the city but close to the major highways that provided access to all parts of the county. He also included the existing location (C) to provide a base case for validation of the simulation model.

His model gave predictable results as shown in Table 2.1.

Baker prepared an executive summary of his work and presented it to Sue Mullen. She seemed pleased with the results and asked Baker a great number of questions about the assumptions he had made. Convinced that the model would demonstrate the need for a new facility, Mullen asked Baker to present his results to a regular meeting of the MCEMS Authority.

Elated at a chance to present his results to a group of public decision makers, Baker prepared carefully for the meeting. When he arrived, he was somewhat dis-

**Table 2.1 Simulated response times to various parts of Morgan County, in minutes**

| | Facility location alternatives | | | |
| --- | --- | --- | --- | --- |
| | Downtown location (A) | Interstate location (B) | Present location (C) | Percent of calls |
| Morgan | 3.4 | 5.1 | 6.1 | 48 |
| Suburbs | 5.5 | 8.4 | 9.4 | 14 |
| Rural areas | 10.3 | 13.3 | 14.3 | 36 |
| Lakeside areas | 9.9 | 7.9 | 7.9 | 2 |

appointed to find that other topics seemed to take precedence over the facility location problem. One of these topics, a complaint by a local, privately operated ambulance service, seemed to be of prime interest to the newspaper reporters in attendance (Exhibit 2.1).

Finally, Baker got a chance to present his results. The MCEMS Authority seemed impressed by his thoroughness and clearly supported the relocation of the MCEMS facility at the downtown location. They asked Baker to share his model with Sue Mullen so that other locations could be tested.

A complete copy of the study was submitted to John Eishart so he could prepare a thorough proposal to the county commission. Unfortunately, the county commission was simultaneously being harassed by local landlords, developers, and businesspeople over a proposed county subdivision. John Eishart, the author of the proposal, was being reviled as a communist sympathizer.

For weeks Eishart was involved in a series of public meetings over the proposed subdivision. His reputation as an effective aide to the county commission was in question and he was almost fully occupied in defending himself.

While the subdivision debate raged, Baker completed his graduate degree and left town to further his education. By the time Eishart's attention was again focused on the MCEMS facility location problem, he had become very sensitive to the political nuances of the location decision. The decision to relocate the MCEMS building downtown was sure to aggravate the same segment of the population that had attacked him over the subdivision proposal. A location in the Sevenmile part of town was politically more acceptable to this vociferous minority, and the travel times approximated those from the present location. Eishart supported this location, since it would avoid the dense traffic of the downtown location. He decided to formally recommend to the county commission that a new facility be built in Sevenmile.

Sue Mullen went along with Eishart's decision, since it meant that the MCEMS would get a new building instead of a renovated one. She reasoned that this location would give response times no worse than the present location, and the original goal of responding to 90 percent of the calls within fifteen minutes could still be met.

As Eishart had expected, the Sevenmile location was approved with little dissent.

## EXHIBIT 2.1: Press coverage of the EMS meeting

### EMS SQUAD DENIES ACCUSATION IT MAKES NONEMERGENCY RUNS

Morgan County Emergency Medical Services Authority members last night denied accusations that the group is making nonemergency calls and defended the actions of its employees.

Herschel Mullins, owner of the private Morgan Ambulance Service, complained to the county comission Monday that EMS is infringing upon his business by answering nonemergency calls.

EMS coordinator Sue Mullen told the authority the complaint apparently stemmed from the transporting of a body to a local funeral home.

She said the EMS vehicle was called to the scene and found a man wearing a beekeeper's outfit, who had apparently died of cardiac arrest. She said the EMS unit administered resuscitation efforts which proved unsuccessful and then was told to transport the man's body to the funeral home.

The members agreed to write to the county commission and inform it that the EMS is not seeking nonemergency business and refers this business to the private ambulance service. But the members agreed there will continue to be areas in which it is not clear if it is an emergency situation and agreed to sit down with Mullins to discuss any problem areas.

Authority president Tom Vanlandingham told the members that there have been instances in which the private ambulance service personnel "have acted in a nonprofessional manner, used foul language, and showed no professional courtesy."

In other action, the authority decided to purchase a $7000 piece of equipment that would be used to cut and pry wreck victims from mangled vehicles. The instrument has been in the planning stages for several years but hasn't been funded. The members agreed to spend about a week looking for matching state or federal funds to help pay for the instrument but in their absence to go ahead and buy the equipment. It would take four to six weeks to order the equipment and train the paramedics to use it.

In an unrelated matter, the authority approved salary increases for the EMS employees for the coming fiscal year. The seven paramedics will get $11,000 each, an increase of $1000. The coordinator of the program will get $15,720 compared to $14,300 this year. The bookkeeper will get $9000 compared to $7200 this year.

In another matter, Morgan College student, Wes Baker, told the authority he has just completed his master's degree and has studied possible sites for locating the EMS facilities as his thesis topic. He said he concluded that locating the facilities in the old county Vo-Tech Building or in another facility in Morgan would be preferable to location outside the city.

Baker said he studied the present Route 7 location, another location on Route 7, and the Vo-Tech location. He said that by locating the facilities at the Vo-Tech location, two to three minutes could be shaved from the response time to some areas, that some would remain the same, and that some areas would see a three-minute or less increase in response time. Baker said that one-half the calls received are inside the city while only one-twelfth of the calls are from Route 7 eastward.

So far the county commission has made no decision about making the Vo-Tech Building available to the EMS. The authority members decided to send a copy of Baker's master's thesis to the county commission with a letter stressing the importance of a quick decision on the request for using the building.

The current facility on Route 7 is too small and some of the vehicles must be parked outside the building. There are also problems with the flooring, the authority members said.

# THE PROPER ROLE OF THE MODEL

One misconception about decision models is that their purpose is to present an optimal decision, already made, to the decision maker about some course of action. Although most quantitative texts refute this view in their introductory remarks, their ensuing approach to models implies that models are the salvation of the great mass of managers. Managers are often pictured in examples and problems as tied to inadequate seat-of-the-pants approaches to problems. Little credence is given to the usefulness of judgment and experience.

The facts of the matter are quite different. The role of the decision model should be navigating rather than piloting. A model can point to the general consequences of certain decisions, but it cannot make the decision.

As Geoffrion (1976) has aptly stated, "The role of models should be the provision of insights not numbers." He supports his view by stating that "few if any applications lead to a single perfect numerical model whose solution is directly translatable into practical action . . . purely numerical results must be supplemented by intuitively reasonable explanations as to why the results are as they are."

Little (1970) makes the same point when he states that the role of a model should be updating a manager's intuition. "If we want a manager to use a model, we should make it his, an extension of his ability to think about and analyze his operation." He calls the integrated process "decision calculus." "A decision calculus will be defined as a model-based set of procedures for processing data and judgments to assist a manager in his decision making."

Combining these ideas, *the role of the decision model should be to provide decision makers with insights regarding the decision effort in such a way as to enhance their overall intuitive decision making ability.* The decision model should not be viewed as a device to isolate "optimal" solutions from lists of alternatives nor should managerial judgment be ignored in the modeling process. The decision model should be viewed as one of many possible inputs into the eventual decision.

The model employed in the MCEMS location decision was not designed to identify an optimal location. In fact, John Eishart felt that the political consequences outweighed relative response time, the criterion studied by the model. Was the model used in this case? John Eishart most likely understood the implications of the model and intuitively considered the response time consequences of his decision. Without a model, he would not have had this insight as a foundation for his decision. Even though Eishart did not accept one of the locations Baker had analyzed with the model, the decision model still played a useful role in the eventual decision.

# ADAPTING THE MODEL TO THE DECISION MAKER

At any gathering of quantitative professionals, a frequent complaint heard is that management does not understand what the modeler is trying to do. Extensive discussions are devoted to how to develop training programs for management. Conceptual models of the implementation process are presented, and occasionally working managers are invited to provide "witness" on their experiences with successful modeling projects.

Morris (1972) argues very persuasively that the modeling effort ought to explicitly consider managerial style in the development of the model. For a highly intuitive decision maker, the model should be structured in an interactive format so that the decision maker can pursue an entire series of possibilities. For an analytic decision maker, the model can be more structured. This type of manager is likely to have greater confidence in analytic complexity.

Conservative managers may want a complete analysis of every phase of the decision. For these managers' style, their belief in model validity is extremely important, since they probably will not take any action without strong assurances that all their facts are in order.

In the view of decision makers who like to "wing it," the model should be a quick simplification of the situation. These decision makers thrive on the psychic reward they receive from making decisions bereft of unnecessary detail.

Skinner (1978) presents sixteen attributes of executive style (see Table 2.2) which must be considered in adapting model to decision maker.

In each of these sixteen areas, the model may have to be adapted to the style of the executive. This adaptation process requires an extensive knowledge of the executive which may not always be available. In some cases, the decision maker may actually be a group of individuals with differing styles, thus complicating the model development task. The adaptation of the model to the decision maker is often difficult to achieve, but, if realized, it can mean a substantial improvement in the usefulness of the model.

In the MCEMS case, the decision making style of neither John Eishart nor the county commission was readily known and no extensive effort was made to

**Table 2.2 Attributes of executive style**

| Attributes | Range or continuum |
|---|---|
| Analytical patterns | Intuitive——Analytical |
| Cognitive style | Inductive——Deductive, use of generalization |
| Decision making | Authoritative——Consultative |
| Decision making speed | Fast, quick——Studied, worried |
| Delegation | Little——Much |
| Explicit "rules of thumb" | Few——Many |
| Type of follow-up | Loose, little——Much, rigorous |
| Communication | Informal, verbal——Formal, written |
| Personal relationships | Supportive——Demanding, challenging |
| Pressure, pace | Relaxed——Rigorous, energetic |
| Availability | Easily available——Remote |
| Boldness, audacity | Bold, risk taking——Cautious, risk aversive |
| Focus on time dimension | Seldom——Continuous |
| Openness to persuasion | Flexible——Dogged, persistent, single-minded |
| Work with subordinates | One-on-one——In a group |
| Work with superior | Wants support——Works alone |

identify decision styles. Even if the effort to do so had been made, the styles might have been difficult to identify. The boldness exhibited by John Eishart at the beginning of the study later turned to caution. The county commission seemed to have a "rule-of-thumb" style that was primarily political.

The executive style of a decision maker is often ignored in the development of models, as was the case in the MCEMS study. The usual picture of managers presented in quantitative texts, that of seat-of-the-pants decision makers who are desperately seeking a more rational approach to problem solving, is a simplistic view and rarely accurate. The decision style of the manager does need to be understood by the modeler, and communications between the two should be properly developed to achieve the best results.

## THE COMMUNICATION PROCESS IN DECISION MODELS

Communication between the decision maker, model developers, and the model itself is not well understood. A communication format that works well in one decision environment fails in seemingly similar circumstances. Churchman and Schainblatt (1965) have postulated a matrix describing the interaction between the model developer and manager, as shown in Table 2.3.

The ideal state of mutual understanding requires that the model designer be aware of the decision maker's type as discussed in the previous section. The decision maker also has an obligation to understand the creative process that goes into the construction of a decision model if it is to be a useful tool.

In the MCEMS case, Wesley Baker had continuing doubts as to the need for a model. John Eishart perhaps contributed to these doubts because of his belief that the model would confirm the obvious and protect the county commission politically. Eishart's initial position and Baker's involvement in other activities contributed to a lack of mutual understanding.

The work of Churchman and Schainblatt is perhaps the best known of the numerous studies of the communications process between model builder and manager. However, Schultz and Slevin (1975) are the editors of a series of important papers on the subject of model implementation, and Martin and Pendse (1977) provide a transactional analysis approach to the work of Churchman and Schainblatt.

**Table 2.3 The Churchman-Schainblatt communications matrix**

|  | Model builder understands manager | Model builder does not understand manager |
|---|---|---|
| Manager understands model builder | *Mutual understanding* | *Communication* of what's right |
| Manager does not understand model builder | Model builder *persuades* manager because model builder understands manager's personality. | Statement of what is right— take it or leave it. Separate function |

The communication process between the model itself and the decision maker has been studied to a lesser degree. The interaction between model and decision maker can be described as either active or passive. In the active case, the model is designed with interactive features which permit the manager to converse directly with the model. The model asks questions of the decision maker and responds by indicating the results implied by the decision maker's answers. In a passive role, the model is used to investigate options devised by the model builder, which are then reported to the decision maker for selection. However, the decision maker may propose that additional options be investigated. Both active and passive roles can be effective, but the personal style of the decision maker and the nature of the decision must be considered in either case.

There is empirical evidence to support the contention that an integrated modeling and decision making process is an effective one. Fromm et al. (1975), in a study of decision models constructed with federal funds, have identified the "closeness" between model building, the model itself, and the decision maker as a key determinant of the eventual success of a model. When a model was prepared for a research organization but intended for use by another client group, the model generally was not successful in being applied.

There are undoubtedly many procedures which can be suggested for gaining the interest of a decision maker in the development and use of a decision model. Some such procedures offered below are largely a reflection of the authors' experience in modeling.

Doing a pilot study is a quick way to involve the decision maker in the analysis. A pilot study produces a small, simplified model used to demonstrate the type of input and output to be expected from the eventual model. It may be only approximate. It may contain completely fictitious data, but it must clearly illustrate what assistance a model can offer.

The advantages of a pilot model are numerous. First, it gives the decision maker an early look at what can be expected from the full model. It can be used to maintain the enthusiasm which usually wanes soon after a project's initiation. A pilot model, as a simplification of the eventual model, can be completed quickly enough to maintain the level of enthusiasm at a rather high level since the decision maker can soon see some tangible results.

A pilot study is also advantageous in that it is a vehicle for discussing such issues as data requirements, output formats, and computational assumptions. While discussions of these matters could take place without a pilot study, the existence of examples adds meaning and interest to the discussion. It is not uncommon for significant data modifications and output changes to result from such discussions, a further advantage in that they are made prior to the primary modeling effort.

A recent study by Byrd and Moore (1977) examined a decision model devised to suggest an improved product mix. The analysts prepared a small, pilot model to illustrate the basic principles of the planned full model. The small model facilitated the achievement of several important objectives. First, it gave the task force which sponsored the model a chance to see what the model would be able to do. The task force chairperson became so excited about the model that the chair requested several additional computer runs, even though the small model was hypothetical. The modelers also presented the pilot study to other company members to obtain their advice on improving its design. Refinements included correcting the model's assumptions and redefining data requirements. The enthusiasm that developed from the pilot model carried through the entire study and greatly aided in its eventual implementation.

A pilot study was not prepared for the MCEMS case, and as a result Wesley Baker failed to inspire the decision maker's enthusiasm early into the project. Subsequent implementation problems can often be attributed to the failure on the part of quantitative specialists to respond quickly with an early analysis and then to maintain the momentum once achieved.

In general, once the pilot study has been demonstrated and future directions agreed upon, the next step is the development of the full model. A *user-directed, step-by-step approach* to this development can facilitate the eventual implementation of the model. This approach asks decision makers to take part in a directing capacity. Modelers should begin with a simple model which is demonstrated to the decision makers; changes to the model should then be suggested by the decision makers and facilitated by the modelers.

This approach simultaneously accomplishes several objectives. It builds the decision makers' trust in the model, since they have provided the major direction for it. Even though the initial model may be an oversimplification, it gives the decision makers a chance to use the model at its most elementary level and gain confidence in its use. As the model's complexity grows, the decision makers can adjust to the added detail.

This step-by-step modeling approach also allows decision makers to eliminate unnecessary detail from the model. Since they have been involved with the model on a continuing basis, they are good judges of when the modeling effort has reached a point of diminishing returns.

In the product mix example described earlier, the quantitative analysts developed the model in incremental stages. As each new feature was added to the model, the results were presented to the decision makers. At each step in the process, the analysts solicited advice on future directions to take. The task force requested that several new features be added to the model, including an increase in the number of modeled products and an additional processing step.

Collecting data for a modeling effort can often be a difficult process. Decision makers may not see the need to provide all the data requested. In this regard, the approach to take is to first *develop the model with the data available*. If the step-by-step approach works as planned, the decision maker will be increasingly interested in the modeling effort. As successive stages of the model are developed, the decision maker will be more receptive to seeing that necessary additional data are provided.

In the study mentioned, the task force chairperson had the staff prepare the data for twenty-nine products. Since these products characteristically contributed 75 percent of the company's profits, data for these products were considered to be representative of the entire operation. However, once the results of this study were developed, the task force was anxious to have the full ninety-eight-item product line modeled, and readily provided the necessary data. The step-by-step approach in this case had the effect of making additional data collection much easier.

A final approach to the process of gaining and keeping interest in the modeling effort is to adopt a policy that revisions are to be expected, *a no-fault revision policy*. Revisions are inevitable in a decision modeling effort. Sometimes they will result from misunderstandings between decision maker and analyst; in other cases they may result from requests for additional detail. Analysts may become defensive about any necessary revisions, while the policy maker may view the necessity for revisions as evidence of a lack of insight on the part of the analyst. Since the assignment of blame for revisions does not contribute to the success of any project, a policy of no-fault revisions can make a substantial contribution to the eventual implementation of recommendations derived from the model. The acceptance of revisions as a natural fact of life helps the entire project and avoids rancor.

In the study mentioned earlier, several revisions were necessary in the model. Some of the original data were incorrect and the processing configuration originally used was in error. In each case, the analysts and decision makers accepted the model changes without recriminations. This spirit of cooperation was a major contributing factor to the model's success.

There are many other approaches that could be suggested as means of gaining the interest of the decision maker in the modeling process. The suggestions discussed above have been tried and found effective in the course of several modeling projects. They serve as prime ingredients in the development of effective decision models.

## APPLICATION OF DECISION MODELS

What types of decisions lend themselves to analysis via decision models? Po-Kempner (1977) suggests several dimensions to consider in addressing this question. One dimension is the degree of structure. Another dimension might relate to the contrast between decisions made to support daily operation versus more encompassing planning decisions. A third dimension might be the relation of the decision to the major functional areas of business: finance, general management, logistics, production, and sales and marketing. In this text, decisions will largely be distinguished according to the planning versus operational dimensions.

Resource allocation, strategy development, business forecasting, and risk-venture analysis are categories of planning decisions to which decision models have been applied. In each of these areas, a decision tends to be unstructured and unique. Planning decisions also tend to involve more qualitative input than do operational decisions because these decisions are more complicated. There is generally more than one objective, and the decisions may involve conflicts between various parts of the organization.

Operational decisions involve such organizational responsibilities as providing for material supplies, analyzing capacity, scheduling operations, distributing products, and developing facilities. Each of these decisions is made frequently and is fairly well structured. Each tends to be more quantitative in nature than do planning decisions and not nearly as controversial in the organization.

In this text both planning and operational decisions are discussed. The Citron decision of Chap. 1 is illustrative of a planning type of decision in that it delved into the future product mix policies of Citron. The facility decision of the Morgan County Emergency Medical Services, on the other hand, was primarily operational. Chapters 3 through 6 concern themselves with analyses of planning decisions, while Chaps. 7 through 11 concentrate on the operational variety.

## WHEN MODELS ARE NOT USED

Decision models are not panaceas. Making decisions is one of the most common daily undertakings of every manager; yet very few of these ordinary decisions are modeled. Why?

In the first place, models require *managerial support* to be successful. In organizations that have a limited history of analytical performance measurement, there may be a limited conceptual base for the use of a decision model. Models are most successful in those organizations that measure performance and are comfortable with the evaluation of alternatives on at least some analytical basis. In other situations, *there is not enough time.* Decision models take time to formulate and many decisions require rapid, even split-second, reactions. Even in those cases where the time to make a decision is longer, there may not be enough lead time to use decision models effectively.

Many decisions offer *little incentive* for the use of a formal decision model. Decision models cost money. The decision alternatives may be similar enough that the expected benefit of using a model may not be sufficient to warrant the development of a model. A lack of belief that a decision model could provide more information than experienced judgment may be another reason for not using one. Ignorance and fear of models may also prevent their use.

A decision may be dominated by *qualitative considerations* which seem to preclude the use of a model. Decision models employ a comparison of alternatives according to some measure of effectiveness. Although qualitative considerations can be incorporated into decision models, many decision makers feel more comfortable making qualitative decisions intuitively.

Other decisions may involve quantitative considerations, but there *may not be sufficient data* to use a decision model effectively. Lack of data often combines with other factors to prevent the use of a decision model.

*Organizational factors* may impede the use of a decision model. Such problems as the size of the available staff and availability of experienced personnel and computational facilities may limit or prohibit the use of decision models.

## WHEN CAN MODELS BE CALLED SUCCESSFUL?

There are few instances when a model can unequivocally be called successful. In such cases, there is usually a "before" situation which can readily be contrasted with an "after" situation, showing conditions to be better after the advent of the model. For instance, a company that uses a model to increase production can clearly call the model application a success. Rarely is the judgment of models so simple.

A more realistic assessment of models might be based upon the growth in managerial awareness which is directly due to the modeling process. Often organizations find that the scrutiny which must be given operations in order to build models of them creates such enhanced understanding of those operations that the required insight into problems is obtained without completing the models. Obtaining insight may be just as important as saving money or increasing production.

A model may be judged to be successful if it demonstrably improves operations; it saves money; it makes more profit; it saves work; it reduces errors; it teaches management, technical, or operational personnel important lessons about their operations; it develops communication between different parts of the organization; or it creates an improved environment for problem solving. Not all of these results are readily measurable or free from dispute, so it is not always easy to determine whether a model is successful. Opinions as to the success of a model may be entirely subjective; no single quantitative criterion can be established.

## MISCONCEPTIONS ABOUT MODELS

The following are some of the common misconceptions about decision models:

1. Decision models are extremely complex—In reality, the most successful models are those that are simplest. Many models involve nothing more than a logical analysis or synthesis of available data.
2. Decision models eliminate the use of judgment and intuition—Many successful models employ the experienced judgment of the decision maker directly.
3. Decision models are built to use only quantitative criteria for decisions—Qualitative criteria can be incorporated into decision models. Models can provide more than numbers. They may be used to enhance the insights of the decision maker. In this respect the quantitative features of models can shed light on qualitative aspects of problems which cannot be modeled directly.
4. Decision models require expensive computers for execution—Many decision models do not need computers at all, although other models require

computer time and hardware. There are successful models built from string, marbles, soap bubbles, and cardboard.

5. Modeling experts are not trained in any aspect of business or administration, only in the technical details of model development—Modeling is in fact an important facet of diverse academic courses of study. Many successful models have been developed by people working in business or administration.

# REFERENCES

Byrd, Jack, Jr., and L. Ted Moore: "For Practitioners Only: A Case Study in Selling an OR/MS Project to a Nameless Company," *Interfaces*, vol. 8, no. 1, part 1, November 1977, pp. 96–104.

Churchman, C. West, and A. H. Schainblatt: "The Researcher and the Manager: A Dialectic of Implementation," *Management Science*, vol. 11, no. 4, February 1965, pp. B69–B87.

Fromm, Gary: *Federally Supported Mathematical Models*, Government Printing Office, Washington, D.C., 1975.

Geoffrion, Arthur M.: "The Purpose of Mathematical Programming Is Insight, Not Numbers," *Interfaces*, vol. 7, no. 1, November 1976, pp. 81–92.

Little, John D. C.: "Models and Managers: The Concept of a Decision Calculus," *Management Sciences*, vol. 16, no. 8, 1970, pp. B466–B485.

Martin, Michael J. S., and Shripad G. Pendse: "Transactional Analysis: Another Way of Approaching OR/MS Implementation," *Interfaces*, vol. 7, no. 2, February 1977, pp. 91–98.

Morris, William T.: "Matching Decision Aids with Intuitive Styles," in Henry S. Brinkers (ed.), *Decision Making*, Ohio State University Press, Columbus, 1972.

PoKempner, Stanley J.: *Management Science in Business*, Conference Board, Report Series, no. 732, 1977.

Schultz, Randall L., and Dennis P. Slevin: *Implementing Operations Research/Management Science*, American Elsevier Publishing Co., New York, 1975.

Skinner, Wickham: *Manufacturing in the Corporate Strategy*, Wiley, New York, 1978.

# QUESTIONS

1 What was the decision that MCEMS needed to make?

2 What were the attitudes of the various individuals in the MCEMS case toward the decision model effort.

3 How would you describe the timeliness of Baker's study with respect to the decision to be made?

4 What role did the model play in the final MCEMS decision? What influenced this role?

5 In retrospect, what could have been done to improve the model's effectiveness in the MCEMS case?

6 Were the conditions of the MCEMS decision effort conducive to the successful use of a decision model?

7 Why is the role of a model stated as "providing insights regarding the decision effort in such a way as to enhance the decision maker's overall intuitive abilities"? Do you agree with this philosophy?

8 Why is it important to adapt the model to the decision maker?

9 How can the following attributes of executive style influence the type of model to be developed?
   (*a*) Analytical patterns
   (*b*) Decision making speed
   (*c*) Boldness, audacity
   (*d*) Communication
   (*e*) Explicit rules of thumb

10 What do the four states in the Churchman-Schainblatt communications matrix mean? (Use your own words.)

11 Why are pilot studies useful devices in the development of decision models?

12 What does a user-directed, step-by-step approach mean with respect to the development of a decision model?

13 For which of the decision types described by PoKempner (operations versus planning) is the use of decision models likely to be the most successful?

14 Why is the amount of time available to make a decision an important consideration in the model's likely effectiveness?

15 Of the misconceptions about models, which do you think is the most difficult to overcome?

# EXERCISES

1 Discuss the potential role of decision models in the following decisions:
  (*a*) Replacement of a piece of manufacturing equipment
  (*b*) Hiring of a new employee
  (*c*) Establishing a work force assignment schedule
  (*d*) Determining the proper inventory level
  (*e*) Choosing a new office building site
  (*f*) Developing the best product mix
  (*g*) Building a new university student union
Classify the model by assigning it the description below that best describes its role:
  (1) Major role—limited decision maker input
  (2) Shared role—model and decision maker have significant role
  (3) Minor role—most input comes from the decision maker

2 Analyze the following personal decisions you have made or anticipate making. How would a decision model help you in each case?
  (*a*) Selecting a college       (*b*) Selecting a major
  (*c*) Buying a car              (*d*) Deciding on a job
  (*e*) Going to graduate school  (*f*) Buying a house
  (*g*) Changing a hair style     (*h*) Choosing a vacation
For each of these decisions, outline those factors which may restrict the use of a decision model.

3 For each of the attributes of executive style listed in Table 2.2, indicate which end of the spectrum would make a decision model effort most likely to be successful?

4 You have been given three potential projects for a term paper on the application of quantitative methods in management. The final grade will be based on how likely the client would be to implement your recommendations. What criteria would you use in choosing one of the three projects?

5 What are possible ways to achieve the "mutual understanding" state as described by Churchman and Schainblatt?

6 You and a group of your classmates have been asked to prepare an inventory management system for a local store. The store owner has agreed to pay you very well for your efforts, but has asked that you provide an outline of what you plan to do before he or she approves the project. The store owner has agreed to pay you for two days' time to prepare the proposal. The project offers many opportunities for future work. What specific pieces of information would you seek in preparing your proposal?

7 In a project for a consulting client, you have been asked to justify expenditures for a pilot study. Prepare your justification.

8 You are the manager of a manufacturing facility that is about to engage the services of a consultant to improve the scheduling of production in the plant. What *specific* criteria would you use to judge the proposal from the consultant?

9 In the situation described in Exercise 8, what steps, as decision maker, would you take to achieve the level of "mutual understanding" described by Churchman and Schainblatt? What would you expect the modeler to do?

10 After spending two years with an organization, you have been given the opportunity to head a high-level task force with the charge of examining the role of "computer aids to decision making." As one of the activities of this task force, you are trying to anticipate the resistance that might exist to this new approach to decision making. Prepare a list of perceptions that exist that are likely to contribute to this resistance.

11 For the list identified in Exercise 10, outline activities that need to be undertaken to reduce the anticipated resistance.

## CASELETS

1. Jim Wooster was preparing his first project briefing for Stanton Morris, his boss and the new chief of engineering at EVTECH. Wooster was anxious about the briefing. Since Morris had come to EVTECH, Wooster had been trying to figure out what Morris wanted to see in project summaries. Whenever Wooster tried to talk about his project, Morris seemed to be in a hurry. Wooster had prepared a briefing paper and presentation for Morris, but was unable to schedule two hours with Wooster to make his presentation.

   Morris had obtained the reputation of being a very successful project manager during his prior job at a larger company; however, Wooster had begun to have doubts about his performance as chief of engineering. Since coming to EVTECH a month before, Morris had seemed to spend all his time talking with people throughout EVTECH. It seemed to Wooster that his boss spent too much time with the directors of personnel and purchasing and the head of the fabrications shops. Although he had no general staff meetings, Morris had an annoying habit of dropping in on his staff members unexpectedly. Morris also had the habit of making snap decisions without giving them the due attention Wooster thought they deserved.

   Wooster was also concerned about the professional atmosphere being created by Morris. In the past, the office that Morris now occupied had been so neat it had been a showplace for visiting clients. Schedules of projects had been posted on the walls and had conveyed a very professional atmosphere. Since Morris had taken over the office, the project boards had not been updated, the library book shelves had been emptied, and Morris's desk was embarrassingly messy. Little pieces of paper were everywhere.

   What upset Wooster more than anything else was that Morris seemed to know everything that was going on.

   (*a*) Describe Stanton Morris's executive style.
   (*b*) What should Wooster do to gain Morris's attention?

2. William Ralston, manager of materials for the Jefferson Sand Company asked one of the company's management system staff to prepare an inventory control system for the company. This undertaking was potentially very

important to the management sytems group since it offered an opportunity to make substantial improvements in an area of the company that long had been considered a sacred cow.

Cheri Webster, one of the brighter members of the management systems group, was asked to head the project. She met Ralston in his office on the nineteenth floor of the corporate headquarters and from the moment she entered Ralston's office she was impressed by her surroundings. Shelf after meticulous shelf of "mix" books lined Ralston's wall. As soon as Webster entered the office, Ralston carefully put away the material he was working on. His language was precise, and his words were carefully chosen. The notes he took looked like they had been typed.

The inventory project Ralston had in mind was far less exciting than Webster had originally thought. All Ralston wanted was a computerized inventory forecasting system based on the existing manual system.

Webster thought about the system to be developed for Ralston very carefully. There seemed to be two general directions she could take:

*System 1*—An inexpensive system using an older teletype terminal with sixty columns for output. The output would be jumbled, but with experience it could be easily read. Some of the input data would probably have to be omitted from the output.

*System 2*—A more expensive system on a modern terminal with full 132-column reading. Both systems would accomplish essentially the same task in the same length of time, but System 2 would take one month more to set up.

(*a*) Which system should Webster propose in this case?
(*b*) What factors led to your choice?
(*c*) Are personality factors valid considerations in designing a decision system?

## CASE 2.1: AMPLER PRODUCTS

### Introduction

For several years, Ampler Products had not funded its general services department at a proper level. Salaries in the department were dangerously low compared with those of industries in surrounding areas. In order to raise salaries of existing employees, new hirings at the physical plant were reduced by not replacing those who quit or retired. Only in highly critical areas were staffing levels maintained.

The resulting understaffing caused Ampler's physical plant to deteriorate. Eventually problems became so severe that the production managers filed complaints over the deterioration of certain buildings. Reports of manufacturing areas with less than 50 percent of their lights in operation became common. Parking lots developed huge potholes, and the pavement surface within the plants began to crumble.

The complaints came to the director of general services, who, deciding to get more information as a first step, assigned Pete Anderson to the project. Anderson arranged a meeting with Frank Mason, director of buildings and grounds. At the meeting, Mason outlined the problem as he saw it.

"It's as simple as this. We don't have enough people. Each year we lose a couple more. I just attended a national conference of B&G directors. We're probably in the bottom quarter of the nation's industries in terms of the number of employees per thousand square feet of plant space. I haven't had any luck convincing the administration of that. We need more people though."

As they discussed the upcoming project, Anderson scanned Mason's impressive office. An entire wall was filled with plaques honoring Mason's work with the International Association of Buildings and Grounds Directors (IABGD). Mason was a past president of the association and had been designated as director of the year for the northeast section. When asked about the award, Mason expressed some regret at not having been designated as the national director of the year.

Mason seemed quite nervous throughout the meeting in contrast to the impression given by the plaques on the wall. He was insistent that all meetings with buildings and grounds employees be cleared through him. Although Mason was cordial, he seemed to have little confidence in the study.

## Initial Observations

Anderson began his analysis by reviewing the records of the buildings and grounds department. He found that there had been a loss of twenty-two people over the last five years. He also found that data on job requests was available from a job request ticket which accompanied each job. The ticket showed the time the job was submitted to the department, the start and finish times for each job, and the workers assigned.

In the prior two years, nearly 2500 job requests had been made. Anderson decided to study a small sample of tickets to gather some quick insights into the problem. He took a systematic sample of every fifth request. On computer cards he punched the date the job was first requested, the date the job began and ended, a code for each job type (e.g., replacing lights, mowing grass, repairing floor surfaces), and the cost of the job. There was one card for each job. Computer analysis of the data was the next step.

Anderson obtained printouts which showed how frequently different job conditions occurred. He was especially interested in jobs whose start had been delayed inordinately or which had taken a long time to finish.

Several facts were immediately revealed by the analysis. First, there was a distinct increase in the number of job requests during the months of May and June. After some thought, the reasons for this fact dawned on Pete. At the beginning of the fiscal year (April), money generally became available for maintenance projects. Therefore, administrators tended to submit several job requests at the beginning of the fiscal year. The impact of the sudden annual glut of job requests at the buildings and grounds department was compounded by two other factors:

(1) outside work which had been delayed during the winter was being scheduled now, and (2) vacations began to cut into the work force in June.

Although the overall average waiting time for jobs to be undertaken was about a month, the average waiting time for a job submitted during May and June was between two and three months.

Anderson also accidentally uncovered a productivity study that had been performed for the buildings and grounds department. The study, although five years old, contained useful information. For instance, the study had developed time standards for a large percentage of the jobs typically performed.

Using this information, Anderson analyzed the jobs in his sample to determine the efficiency of operation for the different jobs. Much to his surprise, the efficiency varied from 60 to 105 percent with a mean efficiency of 72 percent. His problem took on a new perspective as he began to question whether the long job delays were due to a worker shortage or to inefficient work methods.

To examine this aspect of the problem further, he determined the standard time for each job in his sample and computed the total standard time that would be needed for all the jobs in the sample. He then obtained an estimate of the total standard time which should have been needed over the past two years and compared this with the total time available over the past two years. He then defined a workload ratio as

$$\text{Workload ratio (WR)} = \frac{\text{total standard time}}{\text{total available time}}$$

$$= 1.08$$

Pete interpreted this to mean that the physical plant had 8 percent more work than it could reasonably handle. While the ratio indicated that there were not enough workers, the problems did not appear as critical as had been originally guessed.

Pete extended his analysis further by examining the standard costs which had been assigned to the jobs. Taking into account increases in wage rates, Anderson was able to compare the costs of actually doing the jobs with standard costs. As he expected, the actual costs were much higher, even higher than he had expected.

Anderson decided to ask Frank Mason at this point for his reactions. After making a few preliminary remarks, Anderson asked about the previous productivity study. Just at the mention of the study, Frank Mason went into a rage.

"Those fools that did that report don't know what they are talking about. How do they know who is and isn't productive just by looking at them working? We're no different now that we were twenty years ago when I came here. All that productivity stuff is a bunch of paperwork to keep clerks busy."

Although Anderson disagreed with Frank Mason, he decided to go on to other questions. As the meeting progressed, Anderson could tell that Frank Mason was becoming more and more reluctant to answer his questions. To avoid making the session even more hostile, Anderson concluded his questioning.

Anderson's next appointment was with Earl Davidson, a former assistant director of buildings and grounds. Pete didn't need to question him very extensively before Earl opened up with what seemed to be pent-up emotions about the problems of the department.

"Frank Mason thinks he's the director of a country club. Everything he does is to minimize the amount of time he has to spend on the job. No wonder the productivity is low. Those workers get no supervision at all. They aren't trained to do a job. His secretary is the one who keeps records on what's done, and even makes job assignments. Do you know why the costs are so high? For the most part, he's promoted his buddies in the physical plant to jobs they can't do. He lets them get their higher salaries for doing virtually nothing. I guess you noticed the amount of time you call and he's out of town. He actually spends most of his time at meetings of the IABGD. The problem is Frank Mason, pure and simple." This gave Anderson a different view of the physical plant. Without relying upon Davidson's comments entirely, Anderson followed his interview by making his own extensive observations along with additional interviews. He found Earl Davidson's comments to be valid. The work force clearly lacked motivation. Job performance never seemed to be rewarded nor did there appear to be any justification for employee promotions.

## Development of a Management Control System

Realizing that Frank Mason would fail to implement almost any suggestion to improve the productivity of the buildings and grounds department, Anderson decided to develop a management control system that would limit the number of management decisions available to Mason. A scheduling system was established for worker assignments. Another system was set up to assign priorities to the various job requests.

In effect, the management control systems developed by Anderson removed Mason from day-to-day decision making. The systems developed without consulting Mason were written up in a formal report and submitted to the director of general services, Walter Cook.

Cook was a shrewd veteran of organization politics and quickly realized what Anderson was trying to do. Cook called Anderson to his office and asked him how he thought Mason would react to the report. Pete decided not to mince words. He described his findings about Mason's management problems in detail. He suggested strongly that Mason should be replaced.

When asked if he had made every effort to work with Mason, Anderson related the hostile meetings they had on the project. Cook, aware of Mason's inattention to the job, was forced into a difficult decision. The systems proposed by Anderson were good but would never work without Mason's support. Mason had been good for the company. His work with the IABGD had brought considerable favorable publicity to Ampler. Recently, the plant had been displayed prominently in the *Buildings and Grounds Journal* along with a nice write-up of Mason's efforts. Cook realized that much of the article was fictitious, but it was good publicity. It took a week to make the decision about Mason.

## The Decision

Cook decided to replace Mason as director of buildings and grounds. He transferred him to an insignificant position in charge of a five-worker motor pool and garage. Mason took the decision very hard, complaining bitterly that Anderson had never considered him in any of his work on the management control systems. Cook did question the degree of Anderson's efforts at trying to work with Mason. However, Cook had no doubts as to the soundness of his decision to replace Mason.

## Postscript

A week after his demotion, Mason dropped dead of a sudden heart attack.

## Discussion Guide

1 What clues to Mason's personality were obtained from the initial meeting with Anderson?
2 Did Anderson do all he could to work with Mason? What would you have done?
3 What were the chances that a model could be successful in such a situation?

## CASE 2.2: WATSON POWER COMPANY

### Introduction

"POWER SHORTAGES OCCUR AGAIN IN JEFFERSON OVERNIGHT"

So read the headlines of the morning paper. The previous evening's problems had brought the number of outages for the month to eleven. A representative of the Watson Power Company was quoted in the morning paper making comments critical of the public service commission. The representative charged that the commission was not allowing rate increases to cover the costs of maintaining power lines and suggested that additional maintenance workers and more sophisticated equipment would solve the blackout problem.

The various electric power issues came to a head at the following Jefferson City Council meeting. Each council representative had a solution to the problem, one which reflected the biases of both representative and constituency. Charges and countercharges erupted and the discussion turned into a verbal brawl. No headway was made toward resolving the conflict, and the only note of consensus was a unanimous vote for adjournment. The council had accomplished essentially nothing.

Following the council meeting, the mayor and the director of the utility agreed to hire a consultant to determine what could be done to avoid local power outages. The mayor agreed that if the consultant felt that a rate increase was warranted to cover maintenance expenses, the mayor would personally support the increases before the public service commission.

The debate over the recent occurrence of power outages was only the latest instance of a series of conflicts between the Watson Power Company and the city of Jefferson. The power lines in Jefferson had been installed originally in the 1920s, and the city claimed that little maintenance work had been done since. Watson Power countered by saying that the allowed rate schedule was inadequate to support the maintenance work.

The offer by the mayor was the first acknowledgement by the city that rates might be low. The consulting firm of Marshall and Bender was hired to look into the problem. The firm assigned two of its best young employees, Cindy Hopkins and Andy Saoud, to the study.

## Initial Observations

The consultants began their study by making intensive observations of the utility maintenance department and how it responded to service calls. They spent several days at headquarters observing the processes of receiving calls, recording the necessary information, deciding upon the level of response, and assigning a respondent unit when it was necessary. They also kept track of the subsequent action and follow-up activities. The activities involved in handling service calls were easy to understand. When a call for assistance was received, the receptionist obtained basic information on the nature of the request. She decided whether the call was an emergency, and if not, the receptionist completed a data sheet which she gave to the dispatcher. If the call was an emergency, the dispatcher was notified immediately. The dispatcher determined the response needed and examined the status board to determine whether a unit assigned to the area of the request was available. The status of each unit was displayed on a magnetic board showing its present assignment and any backlogged assignments. During peak periods, the status board was not usually accurate or up to date, causing the dispatcher occasionally to lose track of calls that needed responses.

An analysis of the data sheets showed an average response time of twenty-seven minutes for emergency calls and three hours and twelve minutes for non-emergency calls. A more detailed statistical analysis showed that the time of day and location of a call had a significant effect on the response time in both the emergency and nonemergency cases.

Having acquired a basic understanding of the process of responding to a call, the consultants asked to accompany a maintenance unit for a day.

Hopkins and Saoud gained a better appreciation for the response process by observing a unit in action. They gained particular insights into what a typical line repairer felt about the long delays in getting to an emergency. The line repairers were fed up with paperwork. As one line repairer expressed their frustration: "We want to be technicians not secretaries. Look at what we have to do just to report our actions on that call we just investigated. I bet we spend thirty percent of our time filing out forms."

"One other thing I think we should mention," commented the first one's partner. "We have a lot of so-called emergencies that aren't really emergencies. For example, we never know when a call is a downed power line or just some crank who can't figure out that a fuse has blown."

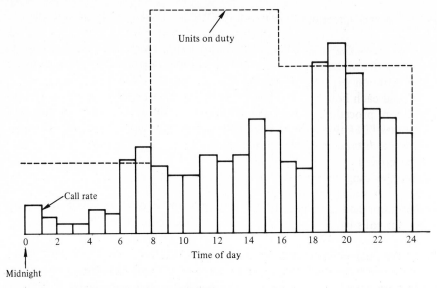

**Figure 2.1** Assignment of units versus call rate.

The experience with the line repairers began to show Hopkins and Saoud some operational improvements that were needed, and they began to make a list of such changes. However, a major problem remained unexplained. The allocation of line repairers seemed to exceed the number required by the frequency of calls. Data gathered on calls for assistance were plotted along with the assignment of personnel, as shown in Fig. 2.1.

The worker assignments were made in three shifts: 12 P.M.–8 A.M., 8 A.M.–4 P.M., and 4 P.M.–12 P.M. The 8 A.M.–4 P.M. shift had the greatest number of units assigned, but the calls during this shift were fewer than those during the 4 P.M.–12 P.M. period. The imbalance seemed due to management's habit in making assignments. In addition, the specific policy of making assignments in three shifts was causing problems because the call rate varied considerably over an eight-hour shift, and the third shift was not adequately staffed to be able to respond to the density of calls.

Preliminary analysis showed Hopkins and Saoud that their study should have two parts. First, a general set of operational improvements should be derived and suggested. Thus, one set of recommendations would center around changes in methods. The second phase of the study was more complex, and their major efforts were devoted to this phase, the development of a worker assignment procedure.

## Development of a Worker Assignment Procedure

The consultants decided that two procedures must be developed. First, some method of measuring the effect of unit assignments on service characteristics, such as the mean waiting time for service, had to be developed. They decided that a multiple-server queuing model* would be an appropriate tool for this aspect of the study.

Once the waiting time characteristics were developed, they expected to be able to find the minimum number of units needed each hour to meet some acceptable criterion (e.g., mean waiting time = ten minutes). Since the number of units needed each hour was likely to vary, the consultants decided to develop an optimization procedure which would minimize the number of line repairers needed but still allow continuous eight-hour shifts. Since the number of line repairers was a discrete quantity, they decided that an integer programming model† would be needed.

After spending considerable time and money on their procedure, a new approach to the waiting-time analysis was attempted. After six months of effort, the consultants had devised an elaborate procedure that would predict the waiting time for calls based upon the number of units assigned to each section of the city.

The eventual plan devised by Hopkins and Saoud involved extensive revision of the work schedules of the line repairers along with a redrawing of the boundaries assigned to the various units. There were few suggestions for operational improvements in the plan because the time and effort devoted to worker assignments had left little time to study basic operational improvements in how units responded to calls.

## Results of the Study

A report was written and delivered to the city and to Watson Power, and a briefing session for council and the utility was arranged. The suggested major changes in shift times and assignments were discussed at length at the briefing. The director of Watson Power emphasized that the workers would probably not support such a change. The mayor, anticipating this reaction, reiterated the long-standing position that productivity issues would be an important factor in deciding whether to support a rate increase. The mayor indicated personal support for the ideas presented in the consultants' analysis and pledged to see that they were implemented.

The utility director countered by charging that the consultants had not done their job. The analysis, the director claimed, looked at only a minor aspect of the utility maintenance problem. As the meeting dragged on for hours, it began to be clear to everyone present that the real maintenance productivity issues had not been discussed in the report.

Even after the long, inconclusive meeting, the mayor thanked the consultants for their report. However, the mayor left them with a sobering thought: "You know it's been six months since those power outages. Since the weather cleared up, we haven't had many problems. I had hoped that we could interest Watson

---

*Queing models will be discussed in Chap. 8.

†Integer programming models are a subset of procedures for resource allocation models as discussed in Chap. 6.

Power in doing something about this problem now. I'm afraid, though, that any changes in their operation have just been tabled until we're faced again with the same problem."

## Discussion Guide

1 What problem was addressed by the study? Was this the original problem? Why was it changed?

2 Comment on the appropriateness of the models used in this study. Did they address the true problem?

3 In view of the implementation problems caused by delays in completing the study, should a less sophisticated, quicker solution approach have been attempted?

4 Why do you believe such a complex solution procedure was used?

5 As the mayor of the city, what would you have done to have ensured that a better study was done?

6 Describe the communications process between the model builders and managers in this case.

7 What were the likeley chances of success for the modeling effort at the beginning of the study?

# PLANNING AND
# POLICY DECISIONS

# INTRODUCTION TO PART TWO
# PLANNING AND POLICY DECISIONS

The lessons from Part 1 of the text are several. It was shown that decision making is a complicated activity consisting in large part of interactions between people with widely differing attitudes. Models, formal or informal, often apply to or are the direct cause of decisions, but to be fully effective, they must be tailored to the people and the environment they must serve.

Building upon Part 1, Part 2 delves into the diverse world of organization-wide decisions. Such higher-level considerations usually deal with the future direction of the organizations, so these kinds of decisions are referred to generically as planning and policy decisions.

A distinction is drawn throughout this text between higher-level decisions and operational decisions, which are viewed as dealing with specific and limited areas of organizational concern. This distinction is to a degree arbitrary, since it is true that all organizational decisions are interrelated. However, the planning and policy issues discussed are those which are very likely to relate strongly to the organization's future well-being.

Part 2 is similar to Part 1 in that the topics of both parts are general enough that they equally well describe problems encountered in both public and private organizations, whereas some topics in Part 3 require a knowledge of cost trade-offs which may be difficult to identify in some public organizations.

Throughout this book an effort has been made to avoid topics which are well covered by courses in specific disciplines, such as marketing, accounting, and finance. This does not mean that such topics are unimportant, but it would have been unwise to diffuse the text material with technical topics from additional disciplines. The generalities which guide the use of the quantitative models presented can easily be extended to the use of techniques from specific fields of expertise.

The following are the dominant topics of Part 2: the kinds of decisions which must be made at the policy and planning level, models which may be applicable, and people considerations which must be a part of the models.

# THREE

## ANTICIPATING THE FUTURE

### SYNOPSIS OF THE CHAPTER

This chapter presents a variety of forecasting techniques and describes the process of implementing forecasts in management decision making.

Most organizations require that reasonable estimates of future conditions be developed from time to time. The methods of developing estimates may range from totally subjective to mechanically computational. In few instances can completely automated forecasts be expected to dictate organizational strategies without being tempered by managerial judgment. The materials of this chapter demonstrate this point.

Regression analysis, one of the most popular and at the same time most quantitative forecasting tools, is given detailed attention in the chapter's technical notes. Smoothing techniques and short-term forecasting procedures are presented, as are some of the more subjective techniques.

Forecasting is the prerequisite to planning in any organization. This chapter attempts to present managerial aspects of forecasting as they might commonly be encountered.

### MAJOR CONCEPTS PRESENTED IN THIS CHAPTER

1. Individuals react to future forecasting in different ways
   a. Some see forecasting as a useless, time-consuming exercise.
   b. Some see forecasting as a necessary evil for anticipating potential future problems.
   c. Some see forecasting as a way of anticipating what might happen in order to get ahead.
2. Forecasting offers information about the future to be used in decision making. In this respect, it is no different from any other data collection effort.

3. There are three general approaches to forecasting:
   *a.* Expert opinion
   *b.* Trends and historical data
   *c.* Causal models
4. Methods that rely upon expert opinions are very flexible in application but are greatly dependent upon the quality of the experts and the manner of achieving consensus.
5. Trend forecasts are perhaps the most common methods. They are generally simple to use but make a critical assumption that future conditions will behave in the same way as they did in the past.
6. Causal methods are the most sophisticated of the forecasting methods. Their strengths are the analytical relationships treated by the model. They suffer from a weakness of not being well understood and subsequently believed by decision makers.

## EXPECTATIONS OF THE STUDENT

The student, after studying this chapter, should be able to do the following:

1. Describe why forecasting is important for decision making
2. Describe why individuals and organizations are reluctant to think about the future
3. Describe the three major forecasting methods
4. Describe the following forecasting approaches:
   *a.* Delphi method
   *b.* Growth analogy
   *c.* Historical analogy
   *d.* Cross-impact analysis
   *e.* Scenarios
   *f.* Trend lines
   *g.* Moving averages
   *h.* Exponential smoothing
   *i.* Regression analysis models
   *j.* Product life cycle models
   *k.* Input-output models
5. Prepare a trend line forecast
6. Calculate a moving average
7. Determine an exponentially smoothed average
*8. Use a regression analysis computer package to make forecasts
*9. Analyze trend, seasonal, cyclic, and random patterns in data to be forecast
10. Select appropriate forecasting techniques to be used for a given situation

---

*These topics are discussed in technical notes and may be omitted at the instructor's discretion.

## MARTINSBURG TRUCK BODIES

In Martinsburg there was a small family-owned welding shop that went by the name of Marshall Welders. Bob and Ray Marshall, the coowners of the shop, were entrepreneurs constantly on the lookout for likely new business ventures. Their welding shop was very successful and generated cash that the Marshalls aimed to invest before the federal government "got its hooks into it."

In 1974, the right opportunity presented itself. The Arab oil embargo had stimulated a boom in the use of coal, and the railroads that traditionally had hauled coal to distant markets could not accommodate the increased coal demand. However, the proximity of power generation plants to the coal fields made the hauling of coal by trucks cheaper than by railroad.

The Marshalls saw the building of coal trucks as a natural diversification for their manufacturing facilities. They had previously made trucks, and this fact, coupled with their experience in welding, had prepared them to produce high quality trucks. Financing by a local bank enabled the Marshalls to complete their plans and erect a manufacturing facility to produce coal-hauling trucks and trailers. This new activity was incorporated under the name of Martinsburg Truck Bodies.

Three main products were designed by Bob Marshall, whose experience made him an expert on the strength and physical characteristics of welded metal. Although Bob had not been to college and had not studied engineering, the trucks he designed were thought to be among the highest quality trucks on the road. The trucks were often referred to by the name of MARTS.

Partly because of their experience and partly because of their early entry into the market, their new company increased its annual sales from $850,000 the first year to $8.5 million in less than five years. Plant employment grew from fifteen welders to seventy-five welders and assemblers. The Marshalls were dedicated to keeping the plant nonunion and had worked at maintaining the confidence of their employees. Although the United Auto Workers had made efforts to unionize the plant, the workers had rejected organizing efforts.

As the company grew, Bob and Ray Marshall gained respect from the Martinsburg business community. Bob was selected to serve on the board of a new bank, and Ray was appointed chairman of the state's economic and community development commission. To free their time for their new interests, the Marshalls turned over the routine financial management of the company to John Pepper. Pepper was a former bank executive who held an M.B.A. but had never before worked in a manufacturing business. One of the first tasks the Marshalls gave Pepper was the financial planning of a new truck plant near the western U.S. coal fields.

Although the company had adequate financial muscle to build the new plant, Pepper fretted over the future and prepared a memo containing questions outlining his qualms (Exhibit 3.1). When the Marshalls received the memo, Pepper could tell by their frosty reaction that his trepidations had not been received well. He was called into Bob's office for a discussion of the memo. As he sat there look-

### EXHIBIT 3.1 Memorandum

TO:          Robert and Raymond Marshall
FROM:      John Pepper
SUBJECT:  Future concerns on the Coyote plant
    After looking at the plans for the new Coyote plant, I have become concerned about our future planning. I have listed below several issues that we need to discuss before we make a definite commitment to the Coyote plant.

1. Is the future for coal as great as the federal government portrays it?
2. What effect will coal slurry pipelines have on the transportation of western coal?
3. What will our competitors do? Will GM, Freuhauf, and others enter this market?
4. What will be our competitive position in the industry? Will quality be the prime motivator for buyers, or will it be price?
5. How will government actions affect us? For example: subsidies to railroads, limits on generating plants in the West, and emission controls on trucks.
6. Is there skilled labor available in the West? Can we pay competitive wages?
7. Will there be restrictions on power generation plants in the West that would require the hauling of coal over longer distances, thus making truck hauling uneconomical?

    I think we need to hire someone to help us answer these questions Would you be receptive to inviting some consultants in to make proposals for a study of the future and its effects on Martinsburg Truck Bodies?

ing at a 10- by 15-foot mural of the Colorado Rockies, it suddenly dawned on Pepper that he was challenging the Marshalls on a personal issue. As their trophies showed, both Marshalls loved to hunt and fish in the West. The Coyote plant, as it would be called, offered an opportunity for the Marshalls to spend a good bit of time in the West not only at company expense, but nominally for the purpose of "business."

"Tell you the truth, John," Bob said, "I think you are trying to make this new plant too big an issue. Look, if we can make a go of a truck operation here, we can do it anywhere. Why all the fuss?"

Anticipating this reaction, Pepper was prepared with several case studies from his college courses. He illustrated how in case after case companies had gone bankrupt because of making unwise expansions. After several such examples, Ray Marshall became concerned. "Bob, I think we ought to consider what John has to say. Maybe we are being too hasty about this new plant."

"You were nervous when we expanded our Martinsburg plant. If the Coyote plant fails, it fails. We can still make a good income from this plant."

Arguments continued for another hour, becoming steadily more heated. Bob finally agreed to hire a consultant. His motivation was not one of a concern for the future of the business, but one of concern for the brotherly relationship that was being strained by the debate. Bob's primary hope for the future was that his son Greg would be named company president upon Bob's retirement. Ray had been agreeable on this point because his own son was younger than Greg and did not seem at all interested in the business.

Having obtained approval to do so, Pepper contacted a consultant with whom he had worked during his banking days. He was George Thompson, a principal consultant in a rapidly growing econometrics firm (Oracle Associates). The firm was noted for its sound forecasts of business activity. One of Oracle's brochures outlined the need for forecasting.

### WHY FORECAST?

The question "Why Forecast?" seems to be easily answered. For any organization to function, it must have a view of the future. The organization must have the lead time to react to anticipated future problems. The future may entail new customers or clientele, new products or services, new regulations or new competitors. Why then would any decision maker not be interested in the future as it affects his organization?

Perhaps the strongest reason for not examining the future is the subconscious fear stirred up by its scrutiny. For the same reasons that individuals avoid unpleasant feelings, so too do individuals shy away from an in-depth analysis of the future. Individuals are comfortable doing what they have done in the past, and the thought of change made necessary by the future is disturbing. To relieve this discomfort, individuals may retreat from the need to prepare for the future. Rationalization will replace forecasts, but the fact remains that a subconscious fear of change, a retreat from reality, is being served.

Another view of forecasting is that the whole process is "crystal ball gazing," something to be done in a bar on Saturday night and forgotten by Monday. Forecasting blunders are legendary and well remembered. Those who deny the value of forecasts typically point to some catastrophe and ask the forecaster how his methods could predict it.

Forecasts should be treated as input data for decisions similar to information from any source. Any observation may be in error; so too might be any forecast. Data may be ignored when common sense dictates. The same holds true for a forecast that appears to miss the mark. Forecasts are data describing the likely future. They do not override judgment. They can, however, provide valuable advance warning of future events.

As John Pepper read the document, he tried to relate it to the problems he was having with Bob Marshall. He tried to imagine what subconscious ploys he might use to change Bob's views. Before George Thompson ever appeared at the plant, Pepper briefed him on the problem as he saw it. He asked Thompson to prepare a brief outline of the forcasting techniques and how they might be used to address the needs of Martinsburg Truck Bodies. Thompson digested the information from Pepper and tried to see how various forecasting approaches might bear on the problem at hand.

## APPROACHES TO FORECASTING

Forecasting methods can be classified into three broad categories:

1. Forecasts based upon expert opinion
2. Forecasts based upon trends and historical data
3. Forecasts based on causal factors

In the first category are those forecasts based upon some expert or group of experts. These forecasts can vary from the "visionaries" that populate American talk shows in early January to those of a structured panel of experts reacting to each other's forecasts in a prescribed fashion. Of these latter methods, the most common is the *Delphi method.*

## METHODS BASED ON EXPERT OPINION

### Delphi Method

The Delphi method was developed by the RAND Corporation in 1969. (See Dalkey, 1969.) It requires the assembling of a panel of experts to share their expertise in preparing a forecast of future trends or events. The panelists are asked to make initial predictions. Then the predictions of the panel members are anonymously compiled and statistically summarized. Since the responses are anonymous, a panelist is neither influenced nor browbeaten by the other panelists. A person with an unpopular view can persist in that view and feel no pressure to change. A Delphi panel member may not even know who the other respondents are if anonymity has been properly assured.

Once statistical summaries of the first round predictions are complete, they are submitted to the panel, and the panelists are asked to cite reasons for varying from their original forecasts or for maintaining them. Again, the anonymity of response is maintained. A new statistical summary is prepared and distributed to the panel.

This process continues iteratively until the panel either reaches a consensus, or it becomes apparent that no consensus can be reached. The Delphi method is a useful device in those cases where past data are limited or where it is likely that past events are not good predictors of future events. As an example, suppose that the future of the nation's energy independence is dependent upon fusion power. The Delphi method might help predict the first successful commercial fusion power plant better than past data on conventional power plants.

In this specific instance, the procedure might be as follows. A panel of experts is assembled. In this case they would be physicists, engineers, environmentalists, and utility executives. They would be asked the question, "When will the first commercial fusion power plant be started?" Their initial responses would be summarized as shown in Fig. 3.1.

In Fig. 3.1, the range of first-round estimates is portrayed. Normally the range markings in such a depiction extend from the 25th to the 75th percentile. In this case, 25 percent of the responses estimate a start-up date of 2025 or earlier and 75 percent of the responses indicate a start-up of 2125 or earlier. The median date (the one in the middle of all responses) was the year 2100.

During the second round, panel members receive summaries of the first round, and new responses to the question, along with supporting justification, are solicited. As shown in Fig. 3.1, the range now extends from the year 2050 to 2115 with a median response of 2080. Responses are again summarized and presented to the panel. By this time, reports of encouraging technological developments at Princeton and in Russia appear. Also, a few negative views of large

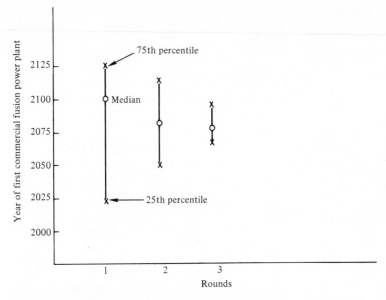

**Figure 3.1** Statistical summary of Delphi rounds.

amounts of capital required for a new plant have been heard. The panelists, after reflecting, are asked to provide a new round of forecasts.

The third round, also summarized in Fig. 3.1, shows considerable movement toward consensus, and the moderator of the panel may wish to conclude the session with this round. The year 2075 is the median forecast within a range from 2070 to 2090.

In the case of Martinsburg Truck Bodies, a Delphi panel could have addressed several issues raised by John Pepper. Each of these issues concerned situations about which little past data existed. In addition, future conditions could have been quite different from those of the past.

The Delphi method is adaptable to different purposes. Generally, it is more useful as a forecasting tool in the long range, ten years and beyond. The value of the Delphi method depends greatly upon the knowledge of the panel of experts chosen, and their sincerity and interest largely determine the value of the resulting forecasts. The phrasing of the initial questions can also be a crucial element in the accuracy of the Delphi forecasts. Studies of the effectiveness of the Delphi method and its variants can be found in the works of Linstone and Turoff (1975), Sackman (1975), and Ament (1970).

## Other Qualitative Forecasting Methods

Other qualitative forecasting methods include historical analogies, growth analogies, cross-impact methods, and scenarios. This list is not exhaustive, but it does include commonly applied methods.

An *historical analogy* is simply a forecast of some phenomenon based upon

**Table 3.1 Cross-impact table**

| If this development occurs | Then the probability of | | | | |
|---|---|---|---|---|---|
| | $E_1$ | $E_2$ | $E_3$ | $E_4$ | $E_5$ |
| $E_1$ | X | .... | ↑ | .... | .... |
| $E_2$ | .... | X | ↑ | ↑ | .... |
| $E_3$ | .... | .... | X | .... | ↑ |
| $E_4$ | .... | .... | .... | X | .... |
| $E_5$ | .... | ↑ | .... | .... | X |

historical trends of other phenomena. The growth rate of home computers may be related to a similar pattern of growth in electronic calculators, for instance.

A *growth analogy* attempts to predict the success of a new product or venture on the basis of a predefined relationship. Typical of such relationships is an S-shaped curve implying slow initial growth followed by rapid growth, trailing off as a result of eventual market saturation.

The success of either form of analogy is limited to the few categories of events to which historical or growth patterns can be applied. No attempt is made to include tested cause-and-effect relations in such analogies, making the validity of either form questionable.

*Cross-impact analysis* is a form of contingency analysis. As shown in Table 3.1, the occurrence of event 1 ($E_1$) implies an increase in the probability of event 3 ($E_3$). In a similar fashion, the occurrence of event 2 ($E_2$) will likely increase the probabilities of events 3 and 4.

From the cross-impact table, quantitative estimates can be made of the various probabilities. Events are then simulated by use of a simulation model built from the probability estimates. As an event occurs during the mathematical simulation, the probabilities of subsequent events are adjusted, and the process continues until all events have occurred. This process is then repeated many times to obtain a set of probability estimates that reflect the expected degree of interaction between the different events. Although the cross-impact procedure was successfully applied to predicting the progress of the federal Minuteman program, its general applicability has been limited because it involves a complex set of calculations which are highly dependent upon initial probability estimates.

A *scenario* is a written statement of a possible future which may be used to examine the repercussions of some plan. For example, scenarios may be prepared for the worst case, best case, and most likely case. An organization may wish to test a specific plan of action to see how it might be affected by the conditions of various scenarios. Scenarios have considerable value as planning tools. They are less specific than other forecasting methods but easier to understand.

# TREND METHODS

## Trend Lines

*Trend lines* are simple indicators of what has happened and what may be likely to happen. Trend lines are curves fitted to historical data. If a straight line or a

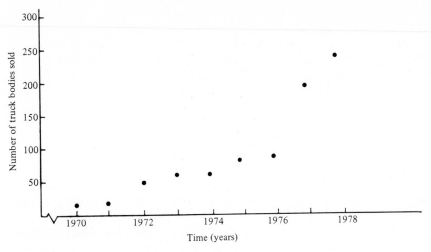

**Figure 3.2** Numerical plot of truck sales by MTB.

curve on a graph closely imitates the past data, then the line or curve is felt to have predictive properties. Consider the data plotted as points in Fig. 3.2, which shows the history of truck body sales by MTB.

The data points seem to show that, as time goes by, body sales increase. The natural temptation is to "fit" the data with a straight line which deviates little from the points. Such a line is shown in Fig. 3.3. Given the equation of such a trend line, the number of truck bodies expected to be sold in any future can be calculated by simply plugging in the year in question.

The advantage of the trend line as a forecasting method is its simplicity. It takes little advanced knowledge to plot a line through data points and extend this line into the future. In fact, trend forecasts are often cited by the news media in

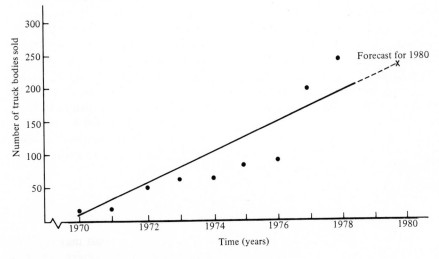

**Figure 3.3** Trend line of truck sales by MTB.

such comments as "If the current rate of inflation continues, the price of a pound of hamburger will be $10.00 by 1990." The primary criticism of a trend forecast is that it is no more than a naive projection of the past into the future. Trend line forecasts tend to ignore a range of external factors that may affect the future. For this reason, trend line forecasts should be applied only to very short-term forecasting (less than two years).

Trend lines may be nonlinear. For example, exponential trend lines are used to estimate continuously compounding growth rates. Quadratic, cubic, and logarithmic curves are all appropriate at times.

## Moving Averages

Data taken over time often have a cyclic or time-dependent character which interferes with the understanding of the basic trend the data follow. The removal of the cyclic nature is called *smoothing*, and a common smoothing technique is that of *moving averages*. The moving average technique of prediction consists of first averaging the data over several time periods then using this average to predict the value of the data from the next period. For example, shipments of trucks from Martinsburg Truck Bodies were observed over six months to be as shown in Table 3.2 in the column labeled "Actual shipments."

For the three-month moving average, the first three months' demands are averaged and are used as the forecast for the next time period. Thus, the actual demands for January, February, and March are used to forecast the demand for April:

$$\text{Forecast for April} = \frac{32 + 26 + 40}{3} = 32.7$$

This number appears as the "Three-month moving average" in Table 3.2.

As each new demand period passes, the forecast for the next time period is calculated. Since the actual demand for April was 28 units, the forecast for May will be

$$\text{Forecast for May} = \frac{26 + 40 + 28}{3} = 31.3$$

The same basic procedure is used in making predictions from a four-month moving average (as shown in the last column of Table 3.2) or from a moving av-

**Table 3.2 Moving average forecasts for steel truck bodies**

| Month | Actual shipments | Three-month moving average | Four-month moving average |
|---|---|---|---|
| January | 32 | ....... | ....... |
| February | 26 | ....... | ....... |
| March | 40 | ....... | ....... |
| April | 28 | 32.7 | ....... |
| May | 36 | 31.3 | 31.5 |
| June | 29 | 34.7 | 32.5 |

erage of any number of time periods. The moving average technique is attractive because it requires little data and can be easily calculated without a computer. However, the moving average sacrifices accuracy for simplicity and other methods of smoothing, such as exponential smoothings, are more commonly employed.

## Exponential Smoothing

The *exponential smoothing procedure* has almost the simplicity and computational ease of the moving average technique, but has more flexibility. The exponential smoothing procedure replaces the equal weighting of data for each time period (as in the case with the moving average technique) with a weighting factor $\alpha$. The forecast for the next time period is found from the relationship

$$F_{t+1} = \alpha X_t + (1 - \alpha)F_t$$

where $F_{t+1}$ = forecast of unknown $X$ for next time period
   $\alpha$ = weighting factor
   $F_t$ = forecast for last observed time period
   $X_t$ = observed value for $X$ for last time period

When no previous forecast is available, the first observed value is generally used as the forecast. To demonstrate, assume $\alpha = 0.2$ and use the actual shipments from Table 3.2. The forecast for February is

$$F_{t+1} = \alpha X_t + (1 - \alpha)F_t$$

$$F_2 = 0.2(32) + (0.8)32$$

$$F_2 = 32$$

For March, the forecast would be

$$F_3 = \alpha X_2 + (1 - \alpha)F_2$$

$$F_3 = 0.2(26) + (0.8)32$$

$$F_3 = 30.8$$

Forecasts for the entire six-month period are shown in Table 3.3.

**Table 3.3 Exponentially smoothed forecasts for steel truck bodies**

| Month | Actual shipments | Forecasts for various weighting factors | | |
|---|---|---|---|---|
| | | $\alpha = 0.2$ | $\alpha = 0.6$ | $\alpha = 0.8$ |
| January | 32 | ....... | ....... | ....... |
| February | 26 | 32 | 32 | 32 |
| March | 40 | 30.8 | 28.4 | 27.2 |
| April | 28 | 32.6 | 35.4 | 37.4 |
| May | 36 | 31.7 | 31.0 | 29.9 |
| June | 29 | 32.6 | 34.0 | 34.8 |

As shown in Table 3.3, the higher the value of $\alpha$ the more emphasis that is placed upon the most recent observation. Smaller values of $\alpha$ in the range of 0.1 to 0.2 are more commonly used. The basic exponential smoothing technique is one of the most frequently used forecasting techniques for short-term forecasting (generally less than one year).

## CAUSAL MODELS

### Regression Analysis Procedures

One of the more commonly used methods for forecasting is *regression analysis,* which develops a forecast of some variable from its past values and the values of other variables which appear to be related to the forecasting variable. Many variables can be studied at once.

There are several reasons for the popularity of regression techniques:

1. A curve, or a prediction equation, is produced by regression analysis, and this prediction form has the same appeal as that of the simple trend line mentioned earlier.
2. Easy-to-use computer software is available to do the lengthy arithmetic required by more complex sets of data.
3. There is a well-developed body of statistical theory which can be applied to regression analyses. As a result, estimates of the likelihoods of regression parameters can be made.
4. Out of many candidate variables, regression analysis can often identify those which have predictive power. This identification can sometimes indicate the nature of the cause-and-effect relations which explain why things happen as they do.

The future demand for steel truck bodies is influenced by the demand for coal. By recording past amounts of coal mined within the service area of Martinsburg Truck Bodies, a general relationship can be identified. Consider the data of Fig. 3.4 as an example.

Regression analysis in its simplest form attempts to relate one variable ($X$) to another ($y$). To do so, it estimates the slope ($b$) and the intercept ($a$) of a model in the general form

$$y = a + bX$$

In the case of MTB,

$y$ = truck bodies sold per year (the dependent variable)

$X$ = millions of tons of coal mined per year in service area (the independent variable)

$a$ = intercept of the linear model that best describes relationship between $y$ and $X$

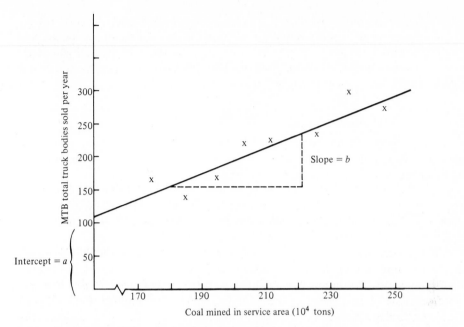

**Figure 3.4** MTB truck bodies as a function of coal mined.

$b$ = slope of the linear model that best describes relationship between $y$ and $X$

(A detailed discussion of how $a$ and $b$ are estimated appears in Technical Note 3.1.) If a good-fitting model can be found, forecasts of truck bodies sold can be made by estimating future tons of coal to be mined and substituting this estimate for $X$ in the model.

Mathematically, regression analysis is a set of procedures for describing relationships between one variable and several other variables. The predicted variable is called dependent, while the several variables are called independent. If there is a genuine causal relationship between the dependent and independent variables, then a specific choice of independent variable values should strongly predict the dependent variable. Such prediction is the goal of regression analysis. The relationship between coal mined and truck bodies sold had an identifiable causal nature and was, therefore, a candidate for regression analysis: the moving of coal required trucks which in turn required truck bodies.

In general, the causal relationships underlying regression equations may not be obvious. However, a nonobvious relationship may still provide a good predictive model. Regression analysis is a mix of art and science. Modelers or decision makers may be able to identify causally related variables intuitively, but they may not. In either case, computer programs offer a combination of techniques for identifying predictive models.

The more specialized the techniques required to obtain any forecasting model, the less susceptible the model is to intuitive judgment. To be an effective tool in decision making, the model ultimately requires an investment of trust by the decision maker, which in turn requires a technical understanding of the model. The quantitative analyst who prepares data for computational analysis and who interprets the computer output is the most likely individual to be able to explain the forecasting model so that it appears trustworthy.

## Decomposition Methods Applied to Time Series

Two simple ways for making forecasts from data taken over time are the moving average and exponential smoothing methods which base forecasts on the averaging of previous observations. More sophisticated procedures for modeling time series include the *decomposition methods*, which smooth data by breaking down the series of observations into components of seasonality, trend, cycle, and randomness. Each of these components (except randomness) is forecast separately and then combined into a composite forecast.

This procedure is aimed at isolating each of the components, but the steps used vary from one algorithm to another and can be very complex. Because of their complexity, decomposition methods tend to be restricted to cases in which large amounts of past data are available for analysis by sophisticated software. However, to demonstrate some of the ideas underlying the analysis of time series data, a procedure which combines smoothing with regression analysis is demonstrated in Technical Note 3.2.

## Autoregressive-Moving Average Methods

Perhaps the most advanced of the time series tools are those based upon a combination of autoregressive and moving average methods. *Autoregressive methods* are statistical procedures that forecast a variable's value from past values of the same variable.

The Box-Jenkins technique is best known of the autoregressive–moving average approaches. Although these approaches are the most accurate of those discussed, they are difficult to understand. The complexity of the procedures guarantees that they require a computer for execution. While it is possible that a lack of understanding of computers has prevented some decision makers from placing their trust in computer forecasting models, that situation is unlikely to last long. Competition and the generally growing acceptance of the most sophisticated forecasting tools will force most decision makers to become adept at interpreting standard computational forecasts.

## Other Causal Models

There are a wide variety of special purpose causal models that can be applied in restricted cases. Product life cycle models and input-output procedures are two examples of these.

The *product life cycle model* is a conceptual model of the process a product goes through from research and development through eventual phase-out. When carefully applied, the product life cycle model can be useful in forecasting future sales for an item. However, the life cycle approach is more applicable to an entire industry than to an individual company.

A typical product's life cycle is shown in Fig. 3.5. Investment is required to develop a product, test markets, initiate advertising campaigns, and begin distribution. Once a product catches on, it begins to make money. During its period of popularity, it becomes a commodity item, exciting competition. Eventually, it loses popularity and is ultimately obsolete, at which time it has been replaced by a new product.

Although this behavior is typical of many products, there are many others which never reach the break-even point. They never get off the ground. Other products become necessary and seem never to become obsolete. Also, the time span describing portions of the curve in Fig. 3.5 is highly variable. For some products a life cycle may be a few months; for others it may be many years. However, many companies, through experience, can predict with reasonable accuracy the duration of appeal of certain products.

Knowledge of a product's life cycle permits a company to spend money for the right reason at the right time. It also gives it a timetable for new product development, scheduling of sales campaigns, and capital budgeting.

In a university, if an academic department knew the life cycle of demands for various kinds of applied knowledge, it could gear its course offerings to those demands. Such a strategy would allow the department to maintain a constant or increasing number of students while other departments floundered in uncertainty.

A lack of understanding of the product life cycle can result in poor timing on the part of management, and in all human activities, timing is important.

*Input-output analysis* is a popular technique for modeling large sectors of an economy and studying the interrelationships of important economic units. This technique is excellent for governmental macroeconomic analyses, but far less adaptable to the aims of individual companies.

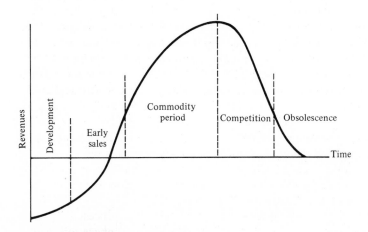

**Figure 3.5** The life cycle of a typical product.

**Table 3.4 Transactions between economic segments in 1970, in millions of dollars**

| Supplier | Purchaser | | | | |
|---|---|---|---|---|---|
| | Lumber | Steel | Fossil fuels | Consumers | Totals |
| Lumber | .... | 5 | 2 | 247 | 254 |
| Steel | 14 | ..... | 126 | 395 | 535 |
| Fossil fuels | 27 | 400 | ..... | 579 | 1006 |
| Consumers | 0 | 0 | 0 | ...... | 0 |
| Totals | 41 | 405 | 128 | 1221 | 1795 |

Input-output analysis begins with a matrix of transactions between large segments of an economy in a state, region, or country. The total dollar transactions are recorded in the matrix. The transactions matrix of a fictitious four-segment economy is shown in Table 3.4.

Table 3.4 represents such a small part of an economy that it is altogether incomplete, but it can be used to demonstrate several of the basic ideas of input-output analysis. Very large economic categories are listed. In fact, one difficulty presented by input-output models is that data from industries tend to be so highly aggregated that fairly large industries may not be identifiable in the data base.

The transactions are taken to represent the causal relationships between the purchasers and suppliers of goods and services. For example, it is implied by the table that for every $535 of demand for steel, $126 of that demand will be due to the fossil fuel market. Thus, all proportions and ratios that can be derived from the transactions table are taken to represent a fixed structure of relationships between the market segments. Two limitations become obvious rather quickly. The data in input-output analyses are usually several years old, due to the difficulty of obtaining the numbers, and the relationships are not likely to be as static as the input-output procedure must assume.

However, given its limitations, input-output analysis is still a valuable planning tool. It facilitates predictions of what might happen to one industry as a result of shifts in demands throughout an entire economy. Since the input-output model is built upon well-defined interrelationships, model results can be subjected to causal investigation, and rational explanations for results can be derived.

A governmental agency can use an input-output model to study the domestic effect of quotas on foreign imports, the effect of fuel prices on consumers, and the likely level of tax revenues in the next fiscal year. Despite limitations, input-output models have shown themselves to be effective planning tools.

## MARTINSBURG TRUCK BODIES REVISITED

Given an improved understanding of the available approaches to forecasting, John Pepper met with George Thompson to work out a set of objectives for the forecasting study at Martinsburg. They agreed upon a three-phase approach, described as follows:

*Phase 1*—Prepare a forecast of the future of coal production with specific emphasis on western coal.

*Phase 2*—Prepare a forecast of the ability of Martinsburg to compete in the coal hauling business.

*Phase 3*—Prepare a forecast of the material requirements at the Martinsburg plant.

The Phase 3 study sprang from a specific problem that had frustrated Pepper. The plant was forever either running out of supplies or having such a surplus that metal parts were stored outdoors and thus rusted.

For the Phase 1 study, Thompson convened a Delphi panel. Fortunately, the experts he needed were available at a mining conference being held at the local state university. The panel's consensus was that western coal did have a substantial future in view of the environmental problems eastern coal faced. The panel felt that most of the coal used would be hauled over long distance either by train or by pipeline. Demand for coal truck transportation in the West was expected to be less than that in eastern coal fields. The primary need for trucks in the West appeared to be for moving coal from surface mines to railroads or pipeline loading sites.

The Phase 2 study required a blend of special-purpose models. Product life cycles and learning curves were combined to give a picture of the future nature of competition in the truck hauling business. This study identified a serious future problem for Martinsburg Truck Bodies. The cost of trucks appeared to be the major determinant in a coal company's decision as to which coal-hauling truck to purchase. As the coal-hauling business became more profitable, major truck companies would find investments in the coal truck business attractive. With their capital base, they could afford investments in automatic welders and elaborate jigs and fixtures that would allow for substantial reductions in the cost and, therefore, the purchase price of a truck. If Martinsburg were to retain its position in the industry, it would have to make major investments in automated equipment to reduce its operating costs. These investments would consume all of Martinsburg's cash and require substantial loans in addition. The conclusion was that expansion into other areas of the country would endanger the very structure of the company by draining away capital investment resources.

The Phase 3 problem was effectively analyzed by use of an exponential smoothing model and an inventory control system (see Chap. 7). The solution provided by this phase of the study was accepted with negligible conflict, unlike the other phases.

As expected, Bob Marshall was enraged by the conclusions of the Phase 2 study. He disputed the importance of the cost factor in truck purchase decisions made by coal companies and gave several specific examples illustrating how important quality was in the mind of truck buyers. Since he did not believe the premise that price was the dominant purchase criterion, he disputed the entire study.

The report and subsequent discussions precipitated an emotional exchange between the brothers, one that had been building up during their entire business association. Bob Marshall was incensed that an outsider to the business would be allowed to question their planning, but Ray Marshall became fully convinced that the Coyote plant would be a mistake.

With no resolution of the dispute in sight, Bob Marshall halfheartedly agreed to buy out his brother's interest in the Coyote plant. What originated as an idle comment evolved into a formal arrangement by which Bob Marshall gained 100 percent control of the Coyote plant by giving his brother an additional 15 percent share in the Martinsburg facility. John Pepper was directed by Bob Marshall to restrict his activities entirely to the Martinsburg facility. George Thompson refused to forecast the fate of the business but he appeared skeptical.

## THE PRACTICE OF FORECASTING

Forecasting experiences are not always as traumatic as those experienced at Martinsburg; in many organizations, forecasting is a regular component of the decision making process. This fact is borne out by a survey by Wheelwright and Clarke (1976) of forecasting activities in over 125 companies. The study, although designed to study organizational commitment to forecasting, revealed that companies with annual sales up to $500 million spent $10,000 to $50,000 on forecasting. A staff of as many as five forecasting professionals was common in these organizations. Larger organizations showed a definite trend toward specialized forecasting staffs. A study by Dalrymple (1975) revealed that over 90 percent of firms sampled listed forecasting as either important or very important.

Not surprisingly, Wheelwright and Clarke found frequent communications problems between the user of the forecast and the forecaster. A majority of companies in their survey listed the identification of new forecasting situations as problems. Other significant problems encountered were understanding the management problem (15 percent) and identifying the important issues in a forecasting situation (29 percent).

Little seems to be known about the psychological forces that affect a forecast. However, Alvin Toffler's work *Future Shock* is a landmark study of the way people react to change. It shows that forecasts of change may bring about the same set of psychological and sociological reactions as does change itself.

Although there have been many efforts made to improve forecasting methods, little work seems to have been done on identifying hidden organizational barriers to the effective use of forecasting procedures. Many of these barriers undoubtedly result from the same forces that affect the use of decision models generally.

As the evidence of Wheelwright and Clarke and Dalrymple illustrates, those forecasting procedures that are based upon human input appear to be the most widely used. One way to interpret this fact is that organizations perceive a need to forecast but are not comfortable with purely mathematical approaches that remove human input from the forecast. Many individuals and organizations view forecasts as part reflection of past trends and part wishful thinking. An organization may not be willing to accept the results of a mathematical forecast if these results are negative. This fact may force adjustments to be made in the forecast to produce a more optimistic estimate of the future. Although such forecasts may not be scientific, they may be more readily accepted than the purely quantitative forecasts that predict a difficult future. As long as individuals and organizations are willing to accept subjective forecasts and develop plans to make them come true, the more subjective forecasting procedures may continue to be popular.

## REFERENCES

Ament, R. H.: "Comparison of Delphi Forecasting Studies in 1964 and 1969," *Futures*, March 1970, pp. 35–44.

Dalkey, N.: "The Delphi Method, An Experimental Study of Group Reaction," RAND Memorandum RM-5888-PR, RAND Corporation, Santa Monica, Calif., March 1969.

Dalrymple, D. J., "Sales Forecasting Methods and Accuracy," *Business Horizons*, December 1975, pp. 69–73.

Linstone, H. A., and M. Turoff: *The Delphi Method: Techniques and Applications*, Addison-Wesley, Reading, Mass., 1975.

Sackman, H.: *Delphi Critique*, Lexington Books, Lexington, Mass., 1975.

Wheelwright, S. C., and D. G. Clarke: "Corporate Forecasting: Promise and Reality," *Harvard Businesses Review*, vol. 54, no. 6, 1976, pp. 40 ff.

## TECHNICAL NOTE 3.1 REGRESSION ANALYSIS

If two variables, $X$ and $y$, are thought to be related to one another, the simplest relation to assume is linear, and the general form of the linear relation is given by the simple linear model

$$y = a + bX$$

The relation is determined by supplying values for the parameters $a$ and $b$.

Often past data exist of observations which can be represented as points on a graph. The process of estimating $a$ and $b$ is equivalent to determining which line through the points on the graph comes closest to points (as demonstrated in Fig. 3.6). The line chosen is called a regression line.

For the simple linear model $y = a + bX$ the coefficients $a$ and $b$ can be found from the following relationships:

$$b = \frac{n\Sigma Xy - (\Sigma X)(\Sigma y)}{n\Sigma X^2 - (\Sigma X)^2}$$

$$a = \overline{y} - b\overline{X}$$

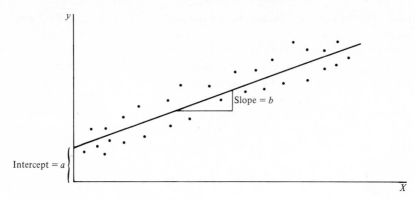

**Figure 3.6** Data points and regression line.

where  $b$  = slope of linear relationship
$a$  = intercept of linear relationship
$n$  = number of observations
$X$  = value of independent variable for each observation
$y$  = value of dependent variable for each observation
$\overline{y}$  = average of $y$ observations
$\overline{X}$  = average of $X$ observations

The data of Fig. 3.4 are summarized in Table 3.5.
The coefficient values are calculated as follows:

$$b = \frac{n\Sigma Xy - (\Sigma X)(\Sigma y)}{n(\Sigma X^2) - (\Sigma X)^2}$$

$$b = \frac{8(359,870) - (1440)(1685)}{8(350,580) - (2,073,600)}$$

**Table 3.5  Regression calculations**

| Truck bodies sold = $y$ | Coal mined, $10^4$ tons = $X$ | $Xy$ | $X^2$ |
|---|---|---|---|
| 160 | 178 | 28,480 | 31,684 |
| 130 | 183 | 23,790 | 33,489 |
| 150 | 193 | 28,950 | 37,249 |
| 220 | 202 | 44,440 | 40,804 |
| 225 | 200 | 45,000 | 40,000 |
| 230 | 225 | 51,750 | 50,625 |
| 300 | 235 | 70,500 | 55,225 |
| 270 | 248 | 66,960 | 61,504 |
| *Totals* 1,685 | 1,440 | 359,870 | 350,580 |

$$b = 0.619$$

$$\overline{y} = 1685/8 = 210.6$$

$$\overline{X} = 1440/8 = 180$$

$$a = \overline{y} - b\overline{X}$$

$$a = 210.6 - 0.619(180)$$

$$a = 99.2$$

A forecast for the number of truck bodies sold in any year could be obtained from the following equation.

Number of truck bodies sold $= 99.2 + 0.619 \times (10^4)$ tons of coal mined

If the coal tonnage is expected to be $220 \times 10^4$ tons, the estimated number of truck body sales would be

Number of truck bodies sold $= 99.2 + 0.619(220) = 235$

The correctness or validity of a regression model is measured by a number of criteria. Perhaps the most common of these measures is the coefficient of determination $R^2$. Essentially, $R^2$ is a measure of how much variation in observations is explained by the model. Discussions of the $R^2$ value appear in most statistics texts.

In most cases relations involve more complicated models, including non-linear models and those which have many variables. The methods for estimating the parameters for such models are naturally more complicated than those for the simple linear model, but these models are also described in detail in many statistics texts.

There are many computer software packages which make the long arithmetic required to calculate regression equations simple by allowing one to have the calculations done by a computer. Very large and complex models can be developed with little effort on computers.

## TECHNICAL NOTE 3.2 MOVING AVERAGE SMOOTHING AND TREND ESTIMATION FOR TIME SERIES DATA

In many forecasting situations, the available data have necessarily been gathered over time. Data obtained over time are called time series data and often must be interpreted and analyzed by special techniques. The reason for this special treatment is that there are occurrences which develop over time which may be reflected in time series data and which may interfere with a straightforward regression analysis of the data.

Time series data can be thought of as consisting of several likely components: trend, seasonal variation, cyclic variation, and irregular variation. Mathematically it is convenient to hypothesize a relation of the form

$$y = T \times C \times S \times I \tag{a}$$

or

$$y = T + C + S + I \tag{b}$$

where $y$ = variable to be forecast

$T$ = trend effect or that part of variation in $y$ explained by a trend curve

$C$ = cyclic effect, or that part of variation in $y$ explained by long term, regular variation

$S$ = seasonal effect, or that part of variation in $y$ explained by annual patterns of variation

$I$ = random effect, or that part of variation in $y$ which is completely irregular but significant in magnitude

For example, components might be similar to those in Fig. 3.7a to e.

Numerous techniques exist for analyzing time series data. One approach is to isolate each component and determine whether the model should be multiplicative as in Eq. (a) or additive as in Eq. (b). Isolated components can them-

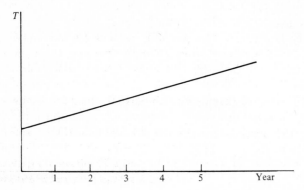

Figure 3.7a Trend component.

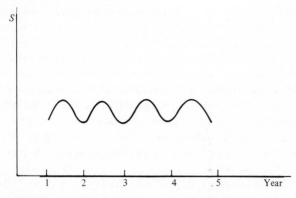

Figure 3.7b Seasonal component.

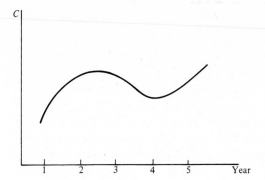

**Figure 3.7c** Cyclic component.

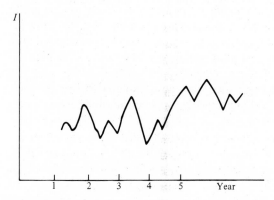

**Figure 3.7d** Irregular component.

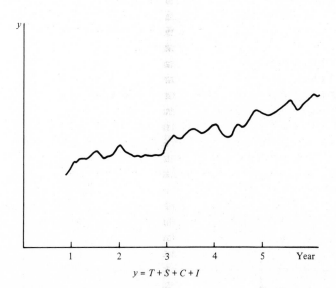

$$y = T + S + C + I$$

**Figure 3.7e** Combined components.

**Table 3.6 Regional truck sales**

| Year | 1961 | 1962 | 1963 | 1964 | 1965 | 1966 | 1967 | 1968 | 1969 | 1970 | 1971 | 1972 |
|---|---|---|---|---|---|---|---|---|---|---|---|---|
| Trucks sold, in 100s | 17 | 19 | 21 | 24 | 28 | 30 | 33 | 35 | 39 | 42 | 46 | 48 |

selves be used to anticipate future values of $y$. For example, if an additive cyclic component of $y$ with a five-year period were identified, one might be able to estimate $T$ and make predictions of $y$ based upon the cyclically adjusted model

$$y = T + C$$

A simple way to try to pick out the trend component is to "smooth" the data. Smoothing is simply the process of averaging out highs and lows due to the cyclic, seasonal, and irregular components prior to using the smoothed data as input to a regression analysis procedure. A simple smoothing method discussed in this chapter was that of moving averages, a modified version of which will be used in the example below.

MTB was interested in expanding its markets, so it gathered informaton on total sales of trucks in a region it was considering for penetration. The data were as found in Table 3.6.

Since data were obtained from complete years, no seasonal component of sales could be expected in this data. However, a plot of the data points shows that longer term components may exist in addition to a trend effect. (See Fig. 3.8.)

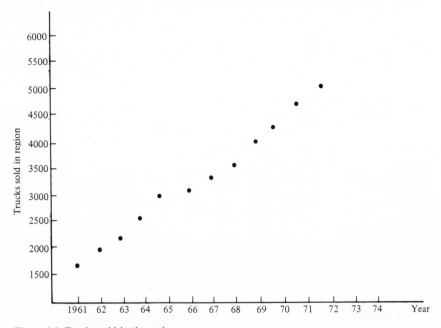

**Figure 3.8** Trucks sold in the region.

**Table 3.7 Centered moving average data**

| Year | 1962 | 1963 | 1964 | 1965 | 1966 | 1967 | 1968 | 1969 | 1970 | 1971 |
|---|---|---|---|---|---|---|---|---|---|---|
| Trucks sold, in 100s | 19 | 21.3 | 24.3 | 27.3 | 30.3 | 32.7 | 35.7 | 38.7 | 42.3 | 45.3 |

To eliminate the possible cyclic and irregular effects, the data were replaced by a three-year centered moving average. Each of the two components of the data points were averaged three at a time. The three points (1961, 17), (1962, 19), and (1963, 21) were replaced by (1962, 19) because

$$1962 = \frac{1961 + 1962 + 1963}{3} \quad \text{and} \quad 19 = \frac{17 + 19 + 21}{3}$$

The points from 1962 through 1964 were replaced by their average and so on, moving through the data set. The centered moving average data are shown in Table 3.7. The three-year averaging loses two points, but it smooths the data considerably.

The moving average data was used to calculate a simple linear regression equation, which was

$$\text{Trucks sold (100s)} = -5730.17 + 2.93 \text{ year}$$

This equation represents the trend $T$, and the fact that the slope of this line (that is, 2.93) is positive indicates that sales are generally increasing rapidly. MTB entered the regional market.

## QUESTIONS

1 What are the attitudes of Bob and Ray Marshall and John Pepper toward forecasting?

2 What general attitudes are likely to be encountered in forecasting business conditions?

3 What are likely arguments that a manager may give for resisting an effort to develop forecasts?

4 What arguments can be used to convince a reluctant manager of the value of forecasting?

5 What are the three general approaches to forecasting? Describe them.

6 How does the Delphi method differ from using forecasts from a group of experts and averaging the results?

7 What would be an historical analogy which might be used to predict future sales of large screen televisions?

8 What are weaknesses of the historical analogy and growth curve methods of forecasting?

9 What are the basic assumptions underlying the use of trend lines in forecasting?

10 Are trend forecasts, in general, better for short-term, or for long-term forecasts?

11 What is the basic reason for using the moving average method of forecasting?

12 How does exponential smoothing differ from the moving average procedure?

13 What is the impact of increasing the number of periods over which data are averaged in the moving average method?

14 How does regression analysis differ from simple trend line forecasting methods?

15 What basic assumptions would suggest the use of the product life cycle model in predicting events?

16 What are the situations for which the input-output method of forecasting might be appropriate?

17 What is meant by a "self-fulfilling" forecast? Describe one case in which you believe such a forecast was made.

## EXERCISES

1 Review newspapers and magazines for one week and describe the forecasts being reported. For each forecast, indicate as best you can the forecasting method.

2 An energy crisis was forecast for the entire decade in the 1970s, but a majority of Americans refused to believe the prediction. Why do you think this was so?

3 A forecast is to be prepared of the number of racquetball players there will be in the United States by 1990. If an historical analogy were to be used for making the forecast, what comparable phenomenon would you suggest for the analogy? Comment on the validity that could be expected of such a forecast.

4 An S-shaped growth curve has been proposed as a device for predicting the sales of home video recording devices. The curve is shown in Fig. 3.9. Do you believe that such a forecasting procedure would be accurate? Discuss the reasons for your answer. How could the time periods required for the shifts in the curve to occur be identified?

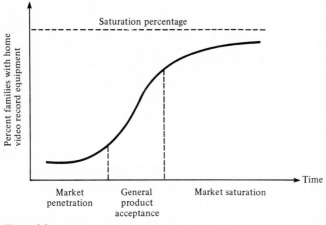

**Figure 3.9**

5 Prepare a best-case scenario and a worst-case scenario for one of your favorite sports teams for the next season.

6 The data in Table 3.8 represent the number of color television sets that were sold in the indicated year. Prepare a trend line forecast for the year 1974.

## Table 3.8

| Year | Color TV sales, in 1000s | Year | Color TV sales, in 1000s | Year | Color TV sales, in 1000s |
|------|--------------------------|------|--------------------------|------|--------------------------|
| 1954 | 5 | 1961 | 147 | 1967 | 5563 |
| 1955 | 20 | 1962 | 438 | 1968 | 5972 |
| 1956 | 100 | 1963 | 747 | 1969 | 5744 |
| 1957 | 85 | 1964 | 1404 | 1970 | 4729 |
| 1958 | 80 | 1965 | 2694 | 1971 | 6349 |
| 1959 | 90 | 1966 | 5012 | 1972 | 7908 |
| 1960 | 120 | | | | |

**7** From a company's sales data shown in Table 3.9, compute a three-month moving average.

**Table 3.9**

| Month | Sales, in 1000s | Month | Sales, in 1000s |
|---|---|---|---|
| January | 26 | July | 29 |
| February | 32 | August | 31 |
| March | 36 | September | 33 |
| April | 33 | October | 30 |
| May | 35 | November | 28 |
| June | 36 | December | 26 |

**8** For the data of Exercise 7, compute a table of exponentially smoothed averages using

(a) $\alpha = 0.10$
(b) $\alpha = 0.30$
(c) $\alpha = 0.50$

**9** The net proceeds from sales of refrigerators are shown in Table 3.10. Prepare a forecast for sales in 1978 by using regression analysis.

**Table 3.10**

| Year | Sales, in 100s | Households, in million |
|---|---|---|
| 1965 | 4930 | 57.6 |
| 1970 | 4286 | 64.0 |
| 1975 | 4582 | 72.7 |
| 1976 | 4817 | 74.1 |
| 1977 | 5705 | 76.8 |

**10** The sales of black and white television sets for the U.S. market are shown in Table 3.11. Develop a plot of sales versus year and compare the plot with the standard product life cycle curve. Does the plot correspond to that predicted by the product life cycle concept? What would you project as the sales in 1980?

**Table 3.11**

| Year | B/W TV sales, in 1000s | Year | B/W TV sales, in 1000s | Year | B/W TV sales, in 1000s |
|---|---|---|---|---|---|
| 1946 | 6 | 1956 | 7351 | 1965 | 8409 |
| 1947 | 179 | 1957 | 6388 | 1966 | 7189 |
| 1948 | 970 | 1958 | 5051 | 1967 | 5290 |
| 1949 | 2970 | 1959 | 6278 | 1968 | 5778 |
| 1950 | 7355 | 1960 | 5707 | 1969 | 5191 |
| 1951 | 5312 | 1961 | 6155 | 1970 | 4704 |
| 1952 | 6194 | 1962 | 6558 | 1971 | 4848 |
| 1954* | 7405 | 1963 | 7019 | 1972 | 5600 |
| 1955 | 7738 | 1964 | 8028 | | |

*1953 unavailable.

**11** You have been asked to provide a forecast of total passenger miles in a year for a major U.S. airline. What forecasting procedure would you select? Why?

**12** A forecast of total U.S. energy consumption is to be prepared. What procedure would you select? Why?

**13** A forecast is to be prepared of expected church attendance for each Sunday. What forecasting system would you recommend? Why?

**14** The jury of expert opinion (one version of the Delphi method) was ranked as the most frequently used forecasting method in both the Wheelwright and Clarke and the Dalrymple studies. Why do you believe this was so?

**15** For the forecasting methods listed in Table 3.12, rank the methods according to each of the criteria listed.

**Table 3.12**

| Criteria | Delphi | Historical analogy | Trend lines | Exponential smoothing | Regression analysis |
|---|---|---|---|---|---|
| Data requirements | | | | | |
| Short term accuracy | | | | | |
| Long term accuracy | | | | | |
| Use of qualitative factors | | | | | |
| Computational requirements | | | | | |
| Simplicity | | | | | |

Ranks: 1 = best; 2 = middle range model; 3 = worst model.

**16** Describe the potential organizational reaction to an uncomfortable forecast. What is your own reaction to such a forecast?

**17** "Forecasts are only accepted when they are positive." Do you believe this statement is true? Cite specific examples to support your belief.

## CASELETS

**1.** The College of Business of Bustler State University is faced with a potentially severe problem. In the late 70s, the college saw its undergraduate course load increase threefold. After several years of fighting the president's office to obtain additional faculty members, the college has received a promise that it will be authorized to hire more teachers. As a result, the dean has appointed a task force to establish a staffing plan for the next ten years.

The task force has decided to develop a prediction of the student course load as a first step toward drawing up its staffing plan. In order to predict loads, the task force believes it must forecast two numbers: the number of first-year students that will be entering the university, and the fraction of those students that will select business as a major.

(a) If you were a member of the task force, how would you prepare a forecast of the number of first-year students entering the university?

(b) How would you forecast the fraction of those students choosing to major in business?

**2.** API, a multinational chemical manufacturer, plans to investigate the pros and cons of producing polyvinyl chloride (PVC) in the United Staes. PVC is a very versatile plastic which is used in a wide variety of applications.

One major difficulty associated with PVC production, however, is that vinyl chloride monomer (VCM), from which PVC is made, is believed to be a cancer causing agent. This fact has made the API management skeptical of PVC's value because of its possible influence upon environmentally sensitive customers. On the other hand, sales of products made from PVC, such as plastic pipe and automobile trim are expected to accelerate because PVC is cheaper and lighter in weight than metal alternatives.

In the past, the API market group made PVC forecasts based upon projections of economic conditions and their own estimates of PVC consumption per unit of GNP. These gross forecasts were judged insufficient by the investment task force.

(*a*) Outline how you would make a ten-year forecast of PVC demand in the United States.

## CASE 3.1: ROCKINGHAM GLASS

### Introduction

Rockingham Glass, one of the nation's largest producers of glass bottles, faced uncertainties in the utilization of its facilities. A large part of Rockingham's sales was soft drink and beer bottles. Because of the seasonal nature of the sales of both types of bottle, Rockingham was forced to anticipate demands and produce in advance of actual orders.

For years the forecasts used by Rockingham had been based on the best guesses of the marketing staff. The vice president for production, Vince Ritchie, had become more and more vocal over the problems caused by the inaccuracies of the forecasts. His production operation had been plagued by the need for extensive overtime work in some months followed by layoffs in subsequent months. Ritchie suggested that the forecasting effort be turned over to Jason Turner's group. Ritchie obtained the approval of the company president and the forecasting responsibility was transferred to Turner's gorup.

Turner, the vice president for planning, had established a quantitative analysis group when he came to the company after serving as dean of engineering at a land grant university. Turner was excited at this new opportunity to show his group's value to the corporation. If accurate forecasts could be developed, the personal prestige of the quantitative group would be enhanced. More important, Turner saw this project as a great way to prove his value to the president.

### Previous Forecasting Work at Rockingham

In the past, the marketing staff at Rockingham had engaged the services of Econometric Resources, Inc. (ERI), to provide their forecasts. ERI had a staff of nearly thirty Ph.D. economists who were involved in economic forecasting. They devised forecasts of sectors of the economy from broad economic trends.

While the ERI work was sufficiently accurate to forecast national trends in the glass bottle industry and reasonably accurate at forecasting Rockingham's share of that industry, monthly demands were so far off that Ritchie's complaint was indisputable. It seemed to Turner that another approach must be taken if accurate monthly forecasts were to be made.

## Forecast Performance Criteria

Turner and his staff decided that the first step in the forecasting process was the development of performance objectives for the forecasting system. After extensive discussions with Ritchie's group, a decision was made to prepare a model that would forecast demand six months into the future. Any variables used in the model should be easily measured and should not themselves have to be forecast. Model accuracy was also discussed. After studying the effects of the forecast on production, Turner determined that forecasts of monthly demand should be within 7 percent of actual demand if the forecasts were to be useful.

## The Selection of a Forecasting Model

Before a forecasting model was attempted, Turner had one of his staff prepare a summary of past trends in demand for bottle shipments at Rockingham. Figs. 3.10a to 3.10c illustrate the extreme variation in demand for beer, soft drink, and all bottles for the period of time from 1972 to 1978. Earlier data was disregarded because of structural changes in the industry that would have invalidated older information as an accurate predictor of trends in the 1980s.

The shipment data showed two definite components, seasonal variation and an underlying trend. The trend effect was particularly evident in the warmer spring and summer months. The shipment data for the soft drink segment of the market demonstrated a modest upward trend, while the demand for beer bottles seemed relatively constant.

Because of the apparent seasonal variation in demand, a time series model was tested as a prediction tool. Exponential smoothing and Box-Jenkins forecasting methods were used to describe the data. Models were fit to the data of 1972–1976, and predictions were then made for the period 1977–1978. An attempt was made to forecast the total shipments of both beer and soft drink bottles.

Only six of the sixteen time series forecasts for shipments in the months from January 1977 to April 1978 fell within 7 percent of the actual demand figures. Turner and his staff were disappointed with the results and decided to employ another forecasting technique.

A fairly simple regression model was prepared that related total bottle sales to a set of variables that reflected economic conditions, industry conditions, seasonability factors and trend factors.

Since the planning horizon needed to be six months into the future, each of the variables used in the model had to lead total bottle shipments by at least six months. Economic variables included the new composite index of twelve leading indicators, the money balance deflated by the consumer price index, new orders of noncapital goods, and the leading indicator for new orders in capital goods industries.

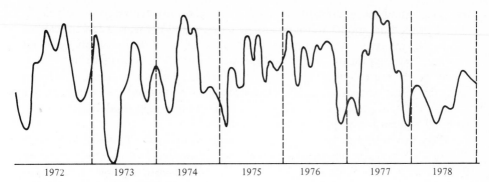

**Figure 3.10a** Beer bottle shipments.

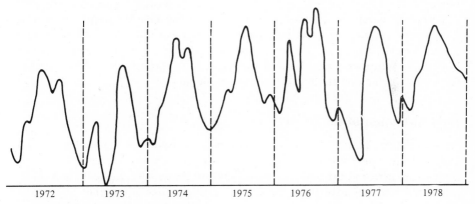

**Figure 3.10b** Soft drink bottle shipments.

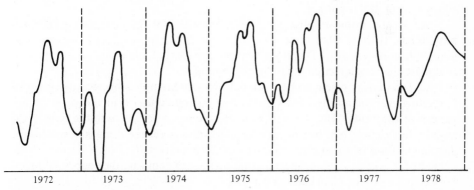

**Figure 3.10c** Total bottle shipments.

Industry variables included such quantities as soft drink bottles shipped, beer bottles shipped, and total bottles shipped during the previous six-month period. A trend variable was added to the model representing each year of data. Seasonal variables were added into the model to represent each month.

All together, thirty-two variables were tested in the model. Of these variables, ten were found to be statistically significant. The only economic variables included in the final model were the money balance and the new orders for capital goods. No industry variables were significant. Eight of the monthly seasonal variables were significant, but the overall trend variable was insignificant.

When the regression model was used to forecast the sixteen months of known data, the result was striking. The model predicted shipments that were within 7 percent of actual shipments for 60 percent of the months. The model accuracy was within 9 percent for 80 percent of the months.

Only one period of time revealed serious inaccuracy in the model. The summer of 1978 had demonstrated shipments much smaller than those predicted by the model. After looking into this situation, the forecasters found the explanation; a major customer had dropped his account with Rockingham during that time.

Since data representing each month were added into the model as soon as they were available, the effect of the lost customer was quickly absorbed into the model. Turner, feeling confident that the model could provide a solid basis for forecasting future shipments, asked the quantitative group to prepare a briefing for Vince Ritchie and the marketing vice president.

## Implementation of the Model

At the briefing, Turner emphasized two important aspects of the model. The first aspect of the model was that it was to be used in conjunction with other internal forecasts to arrive at the best judgment of future bottle sales. Since the sizes of the sales force and the advertising budget could likely affect the trends and market share factors, it was evident that such factors had to be weighed along with those factors identified by the model. Likely changes in major accounts had to also be considered in making forecasts.

The second point emphasized by Turner was that the model only reflected past trends. If there were basic changes in the bottle industry, the model would quickly lose its validity. Therefore, Turner proposed a plan that would be used to update the relationships inherent in the model.

As Turner was discussing the model, Wayne Stemple, the vice president of marketing, very carefully reviewed the forecasting equation included in the appendix of the study. The more he thought about the variables in the model, the madder he became. Not one of the forecast variables reflected marketing activity. The implication of the model was that marketing efforts had little impact on the demand for bottles. His feeling was that if the president saw the report, he might be inclined to reduce marketing's budget.

Vince Ritchie, however, was delighted with the model. He felt that at last someone would be able to give him a better guide to future production requirements. Given this information, Ritchie reasoned that he could reduce his production costs and avoid unpleasant layoffs.

Stemple raised a series of objections to the model once the briefing ended. He cited the recent "bottle-bill" legislation as a reason for his lack of faith in the model: "How are you going to account for the new trends in the bottle industry? For example, the bottle return laws or the use of plastic bottles?"

Turner explained to Stemple that the model was only one component of the forecast, and that marketing input would be needed for any forecast. Ritchie in turn was displeased at this prospect because he wanted to keep marketing out of forecasting entirely.

Turner, realizing the nature of the conflict, tried to satisfy both Ritchie and Stemple. He proposed that each month's forecast be reviewed by a task force consisting of designated representatives from the planning, marketing, and production divisions. This suggestion seemed to mollify both Ritchie and Stemple, and Turner agreed to write up the appropriate procedures for the task force.

## A Postscript

The forecasting procedure worked well from September 1978 through June 1979. In June 1979, a new derivation of the forecasting model was performed using the original set of thirty-two variables. Again, the same set of variables were found to be statistically significant, although the trend variable was also significant. The negative coefficient of the trend variable in the new regression equation reflected the declining use of glass in beverage containers and the reuse of glass containers through recycling.

## Discussion Guide

1 Discuss the prior forecasting activities at Rockingham and comment on why you believe this procedure was ineffective.
2 What forecasting procedure did Turner's group adopt? Why was this method selected?
3 Discuss the personal effects of the new forecasting system on the managerial positions of Jason Turner, Vince Ritchie, and Wayne Stemple.
4 How effective do you believe the forecast review task force will be in adjusting computer-generated forecasts?

# FOUR

## DEVELOPING PLANS

### SYNOPSIS OF THE CHAPTER

Developing plans is the process of designing both broad strategies and operational procedures for achieving ends.

The broad strategies of a company must focus the firm's activities and thus place it in a favorable competitive position. This chapter develops the concepts of experience curves, product life cycles, financial profiles, and displays of the competitive standing of product lines in order to make the bases for corporate planning clear.

The fundamental requirement of corporate planning is that the firm's management understand where the firm is now, where the management wants it to go, and what resources and competitive advantages the firm can use to advance itself.

The student should understand that corporate planning requires a fairly detailed knowledge of the firm's current financial status, of the firm's relation to its competitors, and of the market possibilities that planning can reasonably address.

A specific planning tool, PERT/CPM, is presented as one example of a tool used to plan individual projects which may be complex but fairly straightforward.

The management philosophy implicitly underlying the case of Spencer Industries, which dominates this chapter, is that a firm must focus its activities on those things it can do well. If profitable, it should do what it can do better than any competitor. This philosophy is that of the "focused organization."

### MAJOR CONCEPTS PRESENTED IN THIS CHAPTER

1. The process of planning (like forecasting) is viewed in three fundamental ways by individuals in organizations:
   a. As a waste of time
   b. As a necessary evil

   *c.* As an opportunity to anticipate future events and enhance the organization's ability to deal with the future
2. Planning is basically an effort to deal with uncertainty about the future.
3. The organizational planning process begins with and evolves around goals and objectives established by the organization. Most of these goals and objectives are concerned with the issues of growth and survival.
4. The development of a planning base is generally the second step in the planning process. Basically this process is a description of the current status of an organization from the financial, market position, and manufacturing perspectives.
5. Growth-share matrices and share-momentum graphs are useful ways of viewing an organization's overall competitive position.
6. Planning models, the third step in the planning process, are used in a vast majority of corporations in the United States but tend to be diverse in structure and are generally unique in application.
7. Before a planning model is developed, prerequisite conditions should be met in order for the planning process to be successful.
8. PERT/CPM models are methods of planning projects. Although not a general planning device, PERT/CPM models are useful in the managing of the interrelationships that exist in typical projects.

## EXPECTATIONS OF THE STUDENT

The student, after studying this chapter, should be able to do the following:

1. Describe the relationship of organizational missions and objectives to the overall planning process
2. Describe the eight types of organization objectives outlined by Drucker
3. Explain how the experience curve concept is used in planning and be able to plot simple experience curve data
4. Outline and explain the four steps in the general planning procedure
5. Describe the role of financial ratios in developing a planning base
6. Interpret and plot simplified growth-share and share-momentum displays for determining the competitive position of a business
7. Describe the factors that are conducive to the successful use of planning models
8. Apply PERT/CPM procedures for project management situations

## SPENCER INDUSTRIES

The board of managers of Spencer Industries was conducting another of its interminable Wednesday meetings. As usual, a debate was raging, and, again as usual, the argument was polarized along predictable lines. The old guard, consisting of men who had been with Spencer since its early days as the Spencer Com-

### TABLE 4.1 Board of managers

| Manager | Department | Age | Education | Years of experience at Spencer |
|---------|-----------|-----|-----------|-------------------------------|
| | | Old guard | | |
| S. R. Dennis | Marketing | 57 | B.B.A. | 35 |
| J. P. Olsen | Materials | 60 | High school degree | 37 |
| R. E. "Bub" Fleming | Purchasing | 59 | 11th grade | 36 |
| R. S. Barber | Methods and standards | 60 | B.S.I.E. | 40 |
| Bill David | Production | 63 | 9th grade | 43 |
| | | Young Turks | | |
| A. B. Miller | Comptroller | 27 | M.B.A. | 3 |
| I. S. Kendrick | Accounting | 28 | M.B.A. | 2 |
| Willy Wicker | Personnel | 25 | M.S. | 1 |
| Don Goeche | Forecasting | 32 | M.A. | 4 |
| J. E. B. Allison | Traffic | 31 | M.S.E. | 6 |

pany, was on one side of the question, and the Young Turks, all college graduates, were on the other. The breakdown of the board into the two groups is shown in Table 4.1.

Today's question was no more than a variation of every other question that had arisen for the past year. Fundamentally, all the debates were concerned with defining Spencer's goals and objectives. There were a few topics of genuine technical disagreement, such as the proper choice of accounting procedures, personnel policies, and distribution of keys to the executive washroom, but nearly every other argument had its roots in perceptions of where Spencer was headed and where it should go.

The five older, experienced members of the board had seen the firm start from almost nothing, expand, almost fail, restart, stabilize, and expand several times. They all owned substantial shares of Spencer stock and they were naturally very cautious. They had seen overcommitment by old John Spencer almost bankrupt the firm and throw them all into the streets in the late 40s. They had also seen the competition kill new product lines and territorial expansions. They had a keen sense of mortality. They perceived the young, college-educated board members as inexperienced and rash. It was a fact that not one of the five younger board members had ever done any of the production jobs in any of the plants of Spencer Industries.

The young board members, Miller, Kendrick, Wicker, Goeche, and Allison, were generally incensed at the do-nothing, antigrowth attitude they perceived on the other side of the table. No matter how high the projected return on investment they claimed as a support for a new capital investment, the old guard would sit on the appropriations request interminably. Sales forecast projections and market projections which were supported unquestionably by extensive computer printouts went unread by the older heads. The newer men wanted growth and felt it was necessary to the health of the company.

agreements on objectives were still fundamental. The only unifying factor was that each manager was intent upon "covering his own backside."

The central issue seemed to be whether Spencer should grow. The old guard was attached to high earnings per share (EPS) and was afraid that overextension would put the company back into the precarious position it had occupied shortly after the war. The younger managers, having little company stock in hand, were ready to gamble with company money and full of academic microeconomic theory.

As a devil's advocate, J. P. Olsen planted the seed, "But why grow at all?"

The 27-year-old college-educated A. B. Miller took up the challenge: "You can maintain the same operation only if you sell an unchanging product to a constant market and have no competition. We don't fit any of those criteria. Cooling systems and even mufflers change every few years. The market is not constant; it keeps growing. And even if the first two criteria were satisfied, we have more than twenty competitors. Tackett Products will run us out of business if we don't aggressively market cores. That's what Kendrick was telling us about experience curves. More businesses all the time are cutting into our radiator service and the same goes for our muffler business. If we don't both change and grow, we'll go under."

Spencer thought Miller's comments were surprisingly vehement but accurate. "Grow or die" was the business maxim which fit the situation, Spencer thought.

However, at this point the debate returned to questions which stemmed from long-standing fears of business reversal and the interest in remaining high returns on shares of company stock. The debate continued for some time with little resolution. Finally, Sam Kendrick, the manager of accounting, suggested that SI take action on developing some statement of objectives no matter how noncommittal the statements might be.

The board generated a series of objectives which Hiram Spencer thought were generally weak statements as bases for future action. As Spencer looked through the list (see Exhibit 4.1), it became apparent that the objectives were little more than a restatement of current policy. Although disappointed by the board's reticence to think beyond the current situation, Spencer felt it had made an important first step in doing some planning.

In an effort to encourage the planning process, Spencer asked Kendrick to prepare a study of the planning efforts of other companies.

**EXHIBIT 4.1  Initial objectives sought by Spencer Industries**

1. Increase sales at a rate of 5 to 10 percent per year on priority products.
2. Develop new product lines as warranted by market and technology.
3. Maintain a nonunion production facility.
4. Maintain total debt at no more than 40 percent of total assets.
5. Reduce costs of major product lines by 5 percent per year.
6. Provide a return on total assets of 20 percent.

## THE PLANNING PROCESS

Kendrick reported with an evaluation of how other corporations were doing their planning. He had found a survey of corporations in the United States, Canada, and Europe by Naylor and Schauland (1976) showing that 73 percent of the firms in the sample (346 corporations) were using some form of corporate planning model. Another 15 percent of the firms were in the process of developing a planning model at the time of the study (September, 1974). Few of these firms had truly integrated the financial, marketing, and production aspects of the corporation. The most frequent planning activities concerned financial activities, while marketing and production received less attention.

From his other research, Kendrick was able to summarize the usual planning process. Although the process of planning had become an established facet in the many organizations, the process itself differs from application to application. The general procedure that is used seems to follow these four steps:

1. Develop a planning base.
2. Develop a planning model.
3. Evaluate alternatives and make recommendations.
4. Develop an implementation plan for the preferred alternative(s).

The planning base is a description of the organization's current status. The base should include statements from the financial, market, and manufacturing sides of the organization. The planning base represents a set of benchmarks that can be used to measure the organization's performance from year to year.

The planning model, although different in each application, is a set of relationships that link the parts of the organization. Most of the relationships are deterministic in that an input to one part of the organization is assumed to produce a set of outputs from the given input that do not vary. For example, a specific increase in capital spending for manufacturing capacity is assumed to produce a fixed increase in units manufactured. Few corporate planning models include risk as a component of the model itself. The intent of the model is generally to provide a quick means of integrating models of the components of the organization.

The evaluation of alternatives is done in most cases by means other than the use of model. Few planning models are designed to derive optimal plans. Planning models usually answer "what if" questions. For example, what would happen if manufacturing capacity were increased by 10 percent this year? The model provides numerical consequences of such an action, but the evaluation of its desirability is left to responsible individuals in the organization.

The final step in the planning process is the development of a plan to implement the derived recommendations. This plan can be highly structured, giving detailed attention to the specific steps of the implementation process, or it can be more general, establishing only broad lines of responsibility.

## DEVELOPING A PLANNING BASE

Planning in most organizations consists of reviewing and evaluating last year's plan and generating a new plan for the next year. In profit-making organizations, the planning base evolves from data describing financial performance. Standard business reporting forms such as balance sheets and income statements can be used to generate such data. For example, financial ratios derived from such forms give quick indications as to a company's financial health. Although only a full picture of a corporation's activities can indicate its health and promise, financial ratios are valuable as guides for initial planning.

The balance sheet shown in Table 4.2 and the income statement shown in Table 4.3 served as a planning basis for Spencer Industries.

*Liquidity ratios* are used to test whether a company is in immediate danger of failing to meet its financial obligations. The higher these ratios, the better the short-term status of the company's finances. The usual ratios are the *current ratio* and the *acid-test ratio*. These ratios are defined as follows

$$\text{Current ratio} = \frac{\text{current assets}}{\text{current liabilities}}$$

### Table 4.2 Spencer Industries balance sheet for 1979–80

| Assets | December 31, 1980 | December 31, 1979 |
|---|---|---|
| Current assets: | | |
| Cash and marketable securities .............. | $ 1,823,419 | $ 1,517,332 |
| Accounts receivable ...................... | 6,211,376 | 6,317,737 |
| Inventories: | | |
|     Finished products and parts .............. | 41,668,367 | 34,217,798 |
|     Work in process ...................... | 2,356,558 | 1,985,335 |
|     Raw materials and supplies | 15,273,482 | 13,179,173 |
| Prepaid expenses .......................... | 1,067,034 | 834,762 |
| Accumulated income tax prepayments ........ | 237,128 | 185,221 |
| Total current assets ......................... | $68,637,364 | $58,337,358 |
| Plant and equipment: | | |
|     Land .................................... | $24,315,434 | $12,663,215 |
|     Buildings and improvements .............. | 14,229,873 | 14,103,415 |
|     Machinery and equipment .................. | 12,656,718 | 8,321,779 |
| | $51,202,025 | $35,088,409 |
| Less accumulated depreciation ............... | 20,712,665 | 18,343,957 |
| Net plant and equipment .................... | $30,489,360 | $16,744,452 |
| Total assets ................................ | $99,126,724 | $75,081,810 |

| Liabilities | December 31, 1980 | December 31, 1979 |
|---|---|---|
| Current liabilities: | | |
|     Accounts payable ........................ | $14,825,100 | $10,887,668 |
|     Notes payable .......................... | 7,654,123 | 7,710,138 |
|     Accruals ............................... | 8,345,665 | 7,833,051 |
|     Provision for federal tax .................. | 1,871,326 | 1,753,221 |
| Total Current Liabilities .................... | $32,696,214 | $28,184,078 |
| Long-term debt ............................ | 6,547,665 | 7,312,778 |
| Stockholders' equity: | | |
|     Common stock ......................... | 8,365,888 | 8,243,197 |
|     Retained earnings ...................... | 51,516,957 | 31,341,757 |
| Total stockholders' equity ................... | $59,882,845 | $39,584,954 |
| Total liabilities ............................ | $99,120,724 | $75,081,810 |

### Table 4.3 Spencer Industries income statement for 1980

|  | 52 weeks ended December 31, 1980 |
| --- | --- |
| Net sales | $56,060,331 |
| Cost of goods sold | 12,814,776 |
| Gross profit | $43,245,555 |
| Less operating expenses: |  |
| Selling | 1,215,815 |
| G&A | 3,343,083 |
| Gross operating income | $38,686,657 |
| Depreciation | 3,456,789 |
| Gross income | $35,229,868 |
| Less interest expenses | 832,028 |
| Net before taxes | $34,397,840 |
| Federal income tax | 14,250,175 |
| Net income after tax | $20,147,665 |

$$\text{Acid-test ratio} = \frac{\text{current assets} - \text{inventory}}{\text{current liabilities}}$$

Spencer's 1980 ratios were

$$\text{Current ratio} = \frac{\$68,637,364}{\$32,696,214} = 2.10$$

$$\text{Acid-test ratio} = \frac{\$9,338,957}{\$32,696,214} = 0.29$$

In this instance the current ratio is probably the better measure of Spencer's ability to cover short-term debts; since the bulk of inventories are finished products, which can usually be sold, although perhaps at a loss, in a crisis.

Kendrick contended that the two ratios indicated that an inordinate amount of assets were tied up in inventories, but that the company in general was in good shape in meeting its financial obligations. Kendrick suggested that SI might plan an effort directed at reducing inventories. Since the issue of inventories was not directly discussed in its list of objectives, the board of managers decided that no drastically revised operations would be devised just to maintain liquidity. The board next turned to *leverage ratios* which are used to measure whether the company is using too much of its own assets to finance operations. The usual leverage ratio is of the general form

$$\text{Leverage ratio} = \frac{\text{owner's financing}}{\text{creditor's financing}}$$

and this ratio should be low. A typical leverage ratio is the *debt ratio*.

$$\text{Debt ratio} = \frac{\text{total debt}}{\text{total assets}}$$

Spencer's debt ratio was

$$\frac{\$39,243,879}{\$99,126,724} = 0.396$$

The industry average for the debt ratio was about 0.33 for manufacturing concerns; however, Spencer could easily shift the ratio lower by stocking inventories of finished goods more slowly. In fact, management of inventories would appear to allow Spencer to shift this ratio substantially, since 1980 sales far exceeded the finished product inventory. This fact, and the increase in finished product inventory from 1979 to 1980, implied that stocks were being built at a prodigious rate, to levels which should be readily reducible.

The isolation of finished product inventory as a strong component of current assets accidentally pointed up an important fact. The company had demonstrated the ability to overproduce products, which meant that it had existing capacity to serve a larger market. The clear implication was that capital expenditures for greater productive capacity would not be required to meet higher product demand.

If higher demand for product could be developed, greater revenues could be generated without the need for correspondingly greater capital investment. In short, higher profits seemed to be accessible to more aggressive marketing.

For once the board seemed to agree on an issue. The old guard agreed with the implications that expansion of capacity was not necessary. The younger group was so overjoyed at the acceptance of quantitative measures that they were willing to support the philosophy of no expansion.

Kendrick next presented to the board his analysis of the profitability of Spencer. Numerous financial ratios for measuring profitability had been suggested, including the net profit margin and the return on total assets.

A net profit margin ratio can be defined as

$$\text{Net profit margin} = \frac{\text{net profit after taxes}}{\text{total sales}}$$

which in Spencer's case in 1980 was

$$\text{Net profit margin} = \frac{\$20,147,665}{\$56,060,331} = 0.36$$

Kendrick explained that the net profit margin implied that 36 percent of Spencer's sales were profit, a very good percentage. Unfortunately, this measure of profitability does not relate profits to investment and thus may be less than a conclusive ratio.

A better ratio might be return on total assets, defined as

$$\text{Return on total assets} = \frac{\text{net profit after taxes}}{\text{total assets}}$$

The 1980 value of this ratio was

$$\text{Return on total assets} = \frac{\$20,147,665}{\$99,126,724} = 0.20$$

Kendrick again explained that the return on total investment was 20 percent, a very handsome figure. But even this number was deceptive.

Accounting data include investments made at different times with differing values of the dollar. Thus, dollar values are not good measures of intrinsic values. In addition, assets may lead the profits for which they are responsible. For example, if Spencer were to bring some of its other ratios in line by reducing finished product inventories, the return on total assets would shoot up in 1981.

Kendrick explained that the above ratios were only a few of many which could have been used to assess a company's past performance and to plan its future. The last ratios discussed, those relating to profit, have such a diversity of values and interpretations that more consistent methods of assessing the effectiveness of planned investments were sought.

Financial ratios, while they give a picture of a company's financial performance, are not clear indications of a company's competitive posture. Using financial data reported by government agencies and trade associations, a company's competitive position can be measured through the use of growth-share matrices and share-momentum graphs.

## THE COMPETITIVE PICTURE

A growth-share matrix plots the relative market share of a product in a company's product line versus the overall market growth for that particular product. Relative market share for a specific company is defined as the ratio of the sales for that company's product to the sales of the leading company in the industry. When the company is the leader in sales, the second leading company in the industry is used for the ratio. The relative market share is plotted against the projected annual growth of the product for a period of several years. Since relative market share is generally a good indication of accumulated experience and in turn unit cost, the growth-share matrix describes the cost positions of products with different growth opportunities. The growth-share matrix for Spencer is shown in Fig. 4.2. The size of a circle in the figure is proportional to sales volume. Relative market share is typically plotted on a logarithmic scale.

Products in quadrant A represent cash generators. The market growth rate is stable, indicating a mature product, which means that the company can hold down its costs of marketing and R&D for products in this quadrant. At the same time, the company has a high market share on these products which gives it lower costs and a competitive edge in pricing.

Products in the B quadrant are dogs. Having both low market share and low annual growth, the company can expect little return from investments in this quadrant.

Products in the C quadrant are question marks. Although the company has a low market share, the annual market growth is strong, offering a chance for future earnings. The trick is to move the products from quadrant C to quadrant D.

Products in quadrant D are stars. They represent strong market share in rapid growth products. The market is still fluid in this quadrant and, because of this, earnings are not as great as they might be in quadrant A.

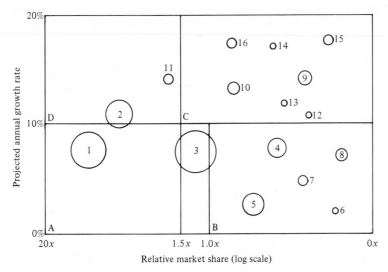

**Figure 4.2** Growth-share matrix of Spencer Industries.

A portfolio strategy evolves from this analysis. Cash from the products in quadrant A are used to stimulate sales for the question marks in quadrant C. It is hoped that the question marks will become stars, given the additional investment. As the market matures, the stars become cash generators. The dogs might be liquidated.

When applied to Spencer, this view of markets brought into question its product policies. As shown in Fig. 4.2, five of the company's twelve products fell in the dog quadrant. Although Spencer had six prospects in the question mark quadrant that could be developed into stars, its policy of promoting all products equally was shown to be inappropriate. No single product was being given the resource base it needed to improve its market share. Only one star (product 2) existed with the sales volume necessary to be a future cash generator. Two cash generators (products 1 and 3) existed, but the cash from these products was being used unwisely. The portfolio of Spencer's leading competitor, Tackett Products, looked much different (see Fig. 4.3).

The strategy of Tackett seemed to be prune and focus. The products in the dog category were being liquidated while the products in the question mark category were limited in number. The huge earnings of products 3, 4, and 5 were being invested in only two question marks. Aggressive attention was being given to products 9 and 15 to make them future stars, just as products 10 and 16 had become. Tackett had also decided not to compete with Spencer in the markets for products 1 and 2, thus saving its competitive resources.

The two growth-share matrices gave Spencer a revealing look at the weakness of its current planning approach. It became clear that little attention had been given to where Spencer was going. Another view of this problem was provided by way of share-momentum graphs prepared by Kendrick.

The share-momentum graph (see Fig. 4.4) illustrates the long-term company growth versus the long-term market growth. The 45° line shown separates those

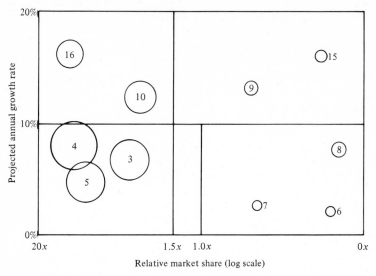

**Figure 4.3** Growth-share matrix for Tackett Products.

products for the company which are growing faster than the market from those products for the company which are growing slower than the overall market. The dotted line represents an arbitrary separation of high-growth products (above 10 percent) from low-growth products. Whereas the growth-share matrix provides a short-term assessment of a company's competitive position, the share-momentum display is a useful device for looking at the long-term position of the company.

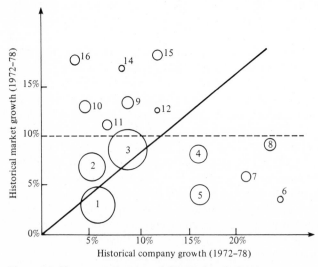

**Figure 4.4** Share-momentum graph for Spencer Industries.

As seen in the share-momentum graph, Spencer was in a state of full-scale retreat from the high-growth business. At the same time, it was aggressively promoting products that had limited market growth potential. Tackett was following a different strategy (see Fig. 4.5).

The strategy of Tackett resembled a blitzkreig. Through its focused strategy, Tackett was destroying Spencer. It was clear to the entire board that Spencer's days were numbered if something was not done. The strategy seemed to be obvious. Spencer needed to do three things:

1. Consolidate its resources on fewer products
2. Liquidate the low-growth products that had limited earnings potential
3. Become much more aggressive in seizing high-growth opportunities

The financial ratios had shown that Spencer had the cash and productive capacity to be more aggressive. The old guard now saw that a much more aggressive strategy was not only important for growth but for survival. Finally, Kendrick had the board's attention.

"One final thing," said Kendrick, "we are in trouble from the standpoint of our manufacturing position. If Tackett continues its current growth pattern, it will destroy our manufacturing advantage. If Tackett maintains its current growth rate, its progress down the experience curve will overtake us in two to four years on every major product we have. Once it has the lowest-cost position in the industry, it will be hard for us to gain ground."

Kendrick illustrated his points with a set of graphs of experience curves. By doing some crude estimating it was seen that Spencer was in just as much trouble from the manufacturing perspective as it was in marketing. The financial data had looked attractive, but was not reflective of the problems which would soon face Spencer.

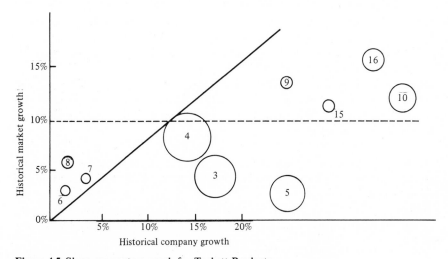

**Figure 4.5** Share-momentum graph for Tackett Products.

"I think we had better get moving on these problems fast," replied Barber; "I think we should get some computer help to aid us in generating and evaluating a plan."

The rest of the board was amazed. Barber was known as the most stoic member of the management team. If he got excited enough to do something, the problem had to be severe.

## DEVELOPING A PLANNING MODEL

Kendrick was asked by the board to review the various corporate planning models that existed to make a recommendation for an appropriate system to use at Spencer. He was also appointed to investigate computer assistance. As soon as he had made initial contacts with software groups, he was deluged with salesmen. Every planning organization seemed to have its own system and techniques for developing a planning model. Most of the models were developed around linear programming,* simulation,† or special-purpose procedures. Presented with such a divergent set of software systems, Kendrick was at a loss.

Acting on the suggestion of a friend, Kendrick reviewed an article written by Hammond (1974) that outlined the organizational climate conducive to successful corporate planning model development. As he reviewed each factor in such a climate, Kendrick evaluated the position of the Spencer organization with respect to that factor.

1. *Operations should be well understood and data should be available.* Spencer has a relatively simple process that should not be hard to model. Gathering accurate data, however, was a problem. Little formal data had ever been collected. However, there were experts in the company that could probably guess most of the necessary information.
2. *The data should be accessible.* Although Spencer had no data bank that could be accessed for much of the necessary data, Kendrick felt that the internal experts could generate the data rapidly enough for it to be useful. He doubted that the data would be voluminous enough to prevent it from being entered into the computer quickly.
3. *Budgets, plans, and control systems should be well defined and quantified.* Spencer was primitive in this regard. Hiram Spencer treated the annual budget as his private domain. There was no formal system for budgeting nor was there a system for management control of budgets.
4. *Corporate planning models should have top management support.* The board had become concerned about preparing for the future; there was no consensus on how to plan. Therefore, management support for a formalized model was not strong.
5. *Management scientists should be held responsible for successful implementation.* Spencer had no management science staff. Any model that was to be

---

*This technique will be presented in Chap. 6.
†This technique will be presented in Chap. 5.

prepared would have to be purchased outside of Spencer, and consultants would have to be hired to run it.
6. *There should be a history of successful model use in the organization.* This would be the first modeling effort at Spencer.
7. *The management team and modeler should share the same status and background.* If outside services were acquired, Spencer would have to be sure that the consulting group obtained familiarity with the business.

After reviewing Hammond's list, Kendrick was concerned that a formalized planning model purchased from an outside vendor might not work at Spencer. He decided that Spencer should first make a crude attempt at developing a simplified planning process that could be refined later if necessary. A simple procedure was then established as outlined in Fig. 4.6.

A computerized planning model derived from the simple model was next built upon a data base that consisted of costs, market share, and manufacturing data for each product. Industry data were also part of the data used in the model.

Planning the model required that SI specify a number of parameters, such as its desired growth rate relative to the rest of the industry. The parameters required by the model are shown in Exhibit 4.2. The model itself determined the total number of additional units of the product that would have to be produced to meet the goal. From the information in the data base, projections of additional manufacturing capacity requirements could be made. As shown in Exhibit 4.2, a 12 percent increase in manufacturing capacity was required to achieve the desired sales growth for the case illustrated.

The experience curve for each product was applied by the model to determine the relative reduction in production costs that Spencer could hope to achieve compared with its closest rival. Using price elasticity estimates, Spencer then determined the additional sales it could obtain by cost reduction efforts alone. In the case illustrated in Exhibit 4.2, the sales generated by the cost reduction were estimated to be 2.8 percent.

The remaining sales necessary to meet the market share goal were next calculated. The model hypothesized that these sales would have to be achieved through more aggressive marketing and additional cost reductions.

The last item calculated by the model was the overall profit improvement which meeting the desired growth goals would generate. To make the model easy to use, an interactive version was developed which could be operated from a terminal in Kendrick's office. Kendrick, Dennis, and David were given the responsibility of generating alternatives to be evaluated. Specific attention was given to alternatives that would improve the market position of established products 1, 2, and 3. High priority was also given to studying projects aimed at boosting Spencer's share in high-growth products (1, 10, 11, 14, 15, and 16).

The list of specific alternatives proposed by the three was as follows:

1. Develop western market areas by building a new regional warehouse and aggressively marketing high-profit products (products 9, 10, 11, 14, 15, and 16).
2. Build a factory to produce mufflers (product 3).

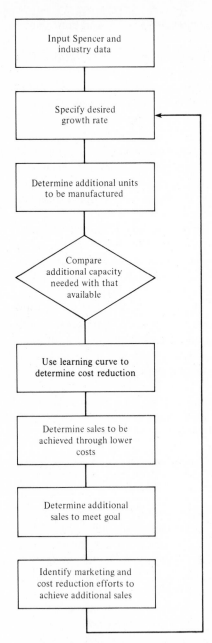

**Figure 4.6** Simplified planning process.

3. Expand the Moore City factory's production of radiators (products 1 and 2).
4. Liquidate products in the dog category of Fig. 4.2.
5. Develop home repair kits as a consumer sales item.

For each of these alternatives, return on investment (ROI) was calculated (see Table 4.4.). For each alternative, the board examined not only the projected

**EXHIBIT 4.2 Sample management report developed from the planning model**

| *Input parameters* | | | | | | | | | | | | | | | | |
|---|---|---|---|---|---|---|---|---|---|---|---|---|---|---|---|---|
| Product | 1 | 2 | 3 | 4 | 5 | 6 | 7 | 8 | 9 | 10 | 11 | 12 | 13 | 14 | 15 | 16 |
| Desired growth rate, % | 9 | 15 | 9 | 2 | 2 | 0 | 0 | 0 | 15 | 10 | 20 | 0 | 0 | 2 | 5 | 0 |

*Requirements to achieve goals*

Capacity expansion necessary—12 percent increase
Capacity investment requirements—$8.2 million
Estimated overall sales growth from expected cost reductions—2.8 percent
Estimated return on total assets—18 percent
Total debt ratio—42 percent

ROI but also the effect the investment option would have on the market position of Spencer's products. The Utah sales center project appeared attractive on two fronts. Not only did it have a high ROI, but it also improved Spencer's market position across a broad line of products.

Subsequently the board recommended to Hiram Spencer that the Utah sales center be built and accompanied by an aggressive advertising campaign. After considerable objection from Dennis, the board also agreed to the liquidation alternative. In reality, Kendrick thought that much of the appeal of this alternative was that it meant less work for most of the board members.

The home repair kit was the one idea that Hiram Spencer was particularly attracted to. Ever since its beginning, Spencer Industries had sold its products through parts dealers and large automotive repair shops. Assuming the company mission was to provide repair service, Hiram Spencer began to be excited by the growing do-it-yourself business in automotive parts. It seemed clear to him that Spencer needed to be aggressive in this phase of business. Consequently, he adopted the home repair kit option as a company activity. This caused Spencer Industries to exceed its desired debt ratio, but Spencer felt the time had come to be aggressive.

**Table 4.4 Economic comparison of alternatives**

| Alternative | ROI, % | Initial investment |
|---|---|---|
| Utah sales center | 24 | $3,132,000 |
| Muffler factory | 16 | $2,000,000 |
| Expansion | 6 | $1,200,000 |
| Liquidation | 28 | $ 800,000 |
| Home repair kits | 25 | $5,261,000 |

# PLANNING A SPECIFIC PROJECT—PERT/CPM METHODS

The choice of the Utah Sales Center was the centerpiece of the board's response to the president's list of requests. The board managed to successfully respond to the entire list, and Hiram Spencer cheerfully agreed to the proposed expansion. The commitment was made; plans had to be laid.

A task force of personnel drawn from the staffs of several of the company managers was put in charge of the project. The task force reported directly to President Spencer.

The company had never expanded into a market in this fashion. The New Orleans expansion was more typical of its procedures. In that case Spencer had simply bought out a warehouse and adapted activities to the capabilities of the facility. However, the Utah warehouse was to be built from the ground up. As a result, planning for the Utah center was meticulous.

The land for the building was already owned by Spencer, so no acquisition delay would occur. Funding was expected to be routine. Therefore, the main order of business facing the task force was whether to have a general contractor do the entire building or to let parts of the job to different bidders.

Members of the task force experienced in construction projects argued that the latter course was preferable because a general contractor would always have other jobs that a worker, say an electrician, could be working on. But if a smaller electrical firm was contracted for a job requiring its full-time effort, the schedule for that portion of the project would be more reliable.

It was decided to let bids for the several parts of the job to selected firms in the Salt Lake City area. However, it was felt that constantly sorting out the interrelations between the various work forces, including Spencer crews, would require services of a full-time, on-site project coordinator. The person chosen for this responsibility was Tad Dunbar.

Tad had worked for a large general contractor for five years as a project supervisor, and he was fully familiar with procedures and the likely range of building codes and regulations.

"I will need two things right away," he said. "I'll need all of the applicable building codes for that area, and I will need a detailed time schedule for the project components."

The first request was felt by the task force members to be easily answered and it was submitted to Bub Fleming's executive secretary. The second request had them scratching their heads a bit until Barbie Pettley from Allison's office cleared the air.

"Let's use PERT," she said.

PERT (Project Evaluation and Review Techniques) and CPM (Critical Path Method) were both developed in the late 1950s as effective methods of estimating project times and controlling project costs. Although these methods had some original differences, they are often thought of today as one technique, and are called PERT/CPM.

The basic process in any PERT/CPM effort follows an eight-step procedure:

1. Define activities to be performed as a part of the project.
2. Establish precedence relationships between the activities.
3. Develop a project network.
4. Estimate the activity times.
5. Determine the project completion time.
6. Determine the critical activities.
7. Establish the project schedule.
8. Develop the management control system.

The first step seems so simple that many may question why such an accepted step is any different from what any project manager would do normally. Yet, when a conscious effort is made to list all activities that must be done to complete a project, it becomes evident that the step that seems so simple is in fact difficult. In fact, many project managers consider defining activities to be the most beneficial in the entire PERT/CPM process.

Whenever possible, this step should involve representatives from all phases of a project. All too often, project activity lists are incomplete because activities that simultaneously overlap several groups are left out. By involving all groups in the activity generation process, the gaps in the project list will be minimized.

The step which establishes relationships requires the identification of predecessors for each activity. The question is asked: What activities must immediately precede each activity *i* in order for *i* to begin? A sample of activities and their precedence relationships is shown in Table 4.5.

The third step is the development of a project network displaying the activities and predecessors as shown in Fig. 4.7. This network is a useful display of the project. In this format, the network can give the nontechnical manager a better concept of the interdependencies of the activities that make up a project. The network is also useful in the identification of the activities which are critical to the early completion of the project.

**Table 4.5 Sample
activities and their
predecessors**

| Activity | Immediate predecessor |
|----------|-----------------------|
| A | None |
| B | None |
| C | A |
| D | A |
| E | B, D |
| F | C |

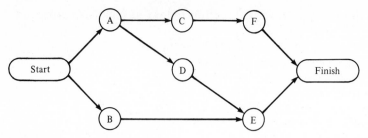

**Figure 4.7** Sample activity network.

Before the critical activities can be identified, however, time estimates must be made for each activity. The original PERT developers based time estimates on three separate times:

$a$ = optimistic time—one of best times encountered in past

$m$ = most likely time—most frequent time encountered in past

$b$ = pessimistic time—one of worst times encountered in past

From these time estimates, an overall time estimate can be developed from a theoretical relationship such as

$$T_e = \frac{a + 4m + b}{6}$$

where

$$T_e = \text{expected time for activity}$$

In many cases, a project may consist of activities for which little previous experience exists. For these cases, the expected time ($T_e$) is estimated directly by asking those involved in the activity how long they think it will take to complete the activity. Although this may appear to be a highly subjective process, the accuracy of the estimate can be improved during subsequent observations. For the project of Fig. 4.7, the times estimated are shown in Table 4.6.

The total project completion time can be estimated calculating the times of

**Table 4.6 Sample activities and their estimated durations**

| Activity | Estimated duration, days |
|----------|--------------------------|
| A        | 3                        |
| B        | 2                        |
| C        | 3                        |
| D        | 4                        |
| E        | 4                        |
| F        | 4                        |

all the possible paths through the network. From the activity network of Fig. 4.7, three possible paths connect the start of the project with the finish.

Path 1: ACF   Time = 3 + 3 + 4 = 10 days
Path 2: ADE   Time = 3 + 4 + 4 = 11 days
Path 3: BE    Time = 2 + 4 = 6 days

Since ADE takes the longest time, it is the critical path. The total project time is thus estimated to be eleven days. If ADE becomes longer, so does the entire project. On the other hand, if BE becomes as long as eleven days, the project duration is unaffected. Thus, BE is said to have slack, in fact, five days of slack.

Three facts are implied by the PERT/CPM diagram and by the identification of the critical path:

1. ADE must be monitored carefully to keep the project from requiring more than eleven days.
2. If resources committed to B, C, or F can be shifted to A, D, or E without significantly lengthening ACF or BE, the project might be able to be shortened.
3. In any event, a schedule of the project can be derived which shows the expected flexibility in starting and finishing times of each of the activities.

For the sample project, a schedule has been prepared by using the procedure described in Technical Note 4.1. The schedule is shown in Table 4.7 and shows the flexibility available to those activities not on the critical path.

The schedule shows that there is no flexibility in scheduling any of the critical activities, A, D, or E, but that there is flexibility for every other activity. For instance, activity B could start any time during the first five days and end at any time up to the end of the seventh day.

The project monitor must observe whether the activities are on schedule, and, if critical activities are lagging, must either reschedule them or shift resources to put them back on time. Noncritical activities can be delayed as a result, causing them to become critical. This, too, would require rescheduling.

Rescheduling the remainder of a project consists of doing a PERT/CPM analysis for the activities remaining. In the example, if A and B were complete, then C, D, E, and F would constitute the remaining project to be rescheduled.

### Table 4.7 Sample activities schedule

| Activity | Earliest start, day | Latest start, day | Earliest finish, day | Latest finish, day | Slack time, days |
|----------|---------------------|-------------------|----------------------|--------------------|------------------|
| A | 0 | 0 | 3 | 3 | 0 |
| B | 0 | 5 | 2 | 7 | 5 |
| C | 3 | 4 | 6 | 7 | 1 |
| D | 3 | 3 | 7 | 7 | 0 |
| E | 7 | 7 | 11 | 11 | 0 |
| F | 6 | 7 | 10 | 11 | 1 |

As was mentioned, activities may be able to be shortened by reallocating resources. However, there usually is no simple way to relate resources to the expected duration of an activity. Assigning two workers instead of one to a job may not cut the required time to do the job in half. However, if one is willing to assume simple time-resource trade-offs, then computer programs can be used to determine the resource allocation which would theoretically result in the shortest project time.

One other point about PERT/CPM must be stressed. The times assigned to activities are *expected* times, which means they are uncertain. Therefore, PERT/CPM time estimates may be quite inaccurate. Some PERT/CPM procedures attempt to establish likely ranges of times by use of a simple probabilistic reasoning, but the value of obtainng such ranges is questionable, since a schedule derived from a PERT/CPM analysis must be constantly monitored in any event.

The management project control system developed is generally a function of the organization itself. No general management control system can be proposed that will serve all organizations. In each organization there should be standard procedures for answering the following questions:

1. How are activity delays to be identified?
2. What should be done about these delays?
3. Who should be responsible for follow-up on delays?

One general premise can be suggested for all management control systems. The system should not be punitive. If a control system is established that punishes those who report delays, it will quickly become ineffective. Control systems must be designed with attention to diplomacy.

## THE UTAH SALES CENTER CONSTRUCTION SCHEDULE

Since the task force had decided to adopt the procedure of hiring multiple contractors, Dunbar ascertained that the schedule for each contractor would be required before he could prepare a detailed schedule. It was clear that there would be considerable interaction between the activities, as is shown in the network diagram of Fig. 4.8. On this diagram, he assigned the expected required time for each activity.

The PERT/CPM diagram describing the process was elementary, but, even so, it was a valuable aid to Tad Dunbar. It forced him to evaluate how difficult each step in obtaining a schedule would be. He not only drew upon his own experience, but also interviewed experienced construction people to obtain reasonable time estimates for the activities shown in Fig. 4.8.

The critical path includes obtaining the main construction schedule. The entire initial schedule appeared to require at least twenty-three weeks. Dunbar believed that it was unlikely that any activity other than main construction would need to start before twenty-three weeks were up, but he knew the importance of keeping this scheduling process under control. He therefore decided to

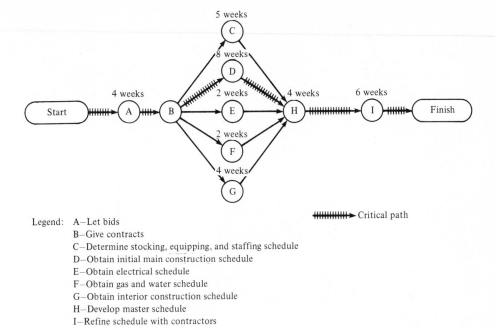

Legend: A—Let bids
B—Give contracts
C—Determine stocking, equipping, and staffing schedule
D—Obtain initial main construction schedule
E—Obtain electrical schedule
F—Obtain gas and water schedule
G—Obtain interior construction schedule
H—Develop master schedule
I—Refine schedule with contractors

**Figure 4.8** PERT/CPM Network for initial scheduling process.

try to expedite the process of obtaining the main construction schedule. He knew from experience exactly how to do it.

He waited five weeks until the main construction contract had been assigned to Sky Building Co. and caught the next flight to Salt Lake City. He met with Sky's owner, Bill Kemp. He explained that he had worked in construction himself for a long time and felt that unexpected delays due to problems with outside suppliers were the biggest causes of headaches. Kemp agreed and was well pleased with Tad's next statement.

Tad said, "I want to offer you the services of an expediter who will help you remove any roadblocks to getting your work done. The expediter will be stationed right here in Salt Lake City just to help you."

Kemp did not know what to think. At first he was happy, but then be became suspicious. Tad read his face and said, "And it won't cost you anything."

Tad had achieved three objectives at once. He had assured the expediting of a critical activity. He had placed a watchdog to keep up with the progress of the main construction process. And he had gotten on the good side of the contractor, a fact which would pay off when he was coordinating schedules.

After he had been to Sky, Tad stayed in Salt Lake City and visited each contractor in turn when the other contracts were awarded. He made the offer of an expediter to each of the smaller contractors. He saw no point in informing anyone that each company had the same expediter. Tad had only two people assigned to him, and one had to be left at Spencer to expedite the parent company's responsibilities on the project.

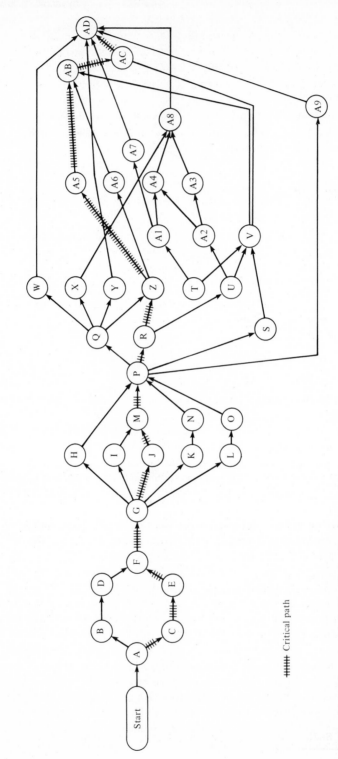

**Figure 4.9** Project network for the Utah sales center.

╫ Critical path

The full project network (see in Fig. 4.9) was prepared from conferences with the home office and with the Utah contractors and local licensing offices, such as those of plumbing and electrical inspectors. The explanations of the codes, precedence relations, and anticipated activity times used in this network are shown in Table 4.8.

The activities decided upon were only a small subset of the most complete possible list of activities, but Dunbar believed that the activities he had listed were the most significant ones over which to maintain tight control. The activities

**Table 4.8 Utah sales center activities**

| Activity code | Activity description | Immediate predecessor | Expected duration, weeks |
|---|---|---|---|
| A | Site preparation | . . . . . . | 13 |
| B | Water and sewer line laying | A | 4 |
| C | Gas line laying | A | 5 |
| D | Water and sewer inspection | B | 2 |
| E | Gas line inspection | C | 2 |
| F | Foundation work | D,E | 9 |
| G | Walls and roof construction | F | 14 |
| H | Insulation | G | 2 |
| I | Telephone wiring | G | 3 |
| J | Wiring and lighting installation | G | 5 |
| K | Plumbing fixture installation | G | 3 |
| L | Gas fitting installation | G | 2 |
| M | Electrical inspection | I,J | 2 |
| N | Plumbing inspection | K | 2 |
| O | Gas inspection | L | 2 |
| P | Interior walls | H,M,N,O | 12 |
| Q | Bringing in security crew | P | 1 |
| R | Painting | P | 5 |
| S | Office door installation | P | 1 |
| T | Loading bay door installation | R | 1 |
| U | Garage door installation | R | 1 |
| V | Telephone installation | S,T,U | 1 |
| W | Roads and lot paving | Q | 5 |
| X | Fencing of truck lot | Q | 2 |
| Y | Sign installation | Q | 2 |
| Z | Office construction | Q,R | 10 |
| A1 | Warehouse rack installation | T | 8 |
| A2 | Garage fittings | U | 7 |
| A3 | Stocking of garage | A2 | 2 |
| A4 | Stocking of maintenance area | A1, A2 | 2 |
| A5 | Stocking of office supplies | Z | 3 |
| A6 | Furnishing of offices | Z | 4 |
| A7 | Stocking of warehouse | A1 | 7 |
| A8 | Purchasing of trucks and forklifts | A, A3, A4 | 5 |
| A9 | Utility Hookups | P | 3 |
| AB | Hiring of staffs | V, A5, A8 | 5 |
| AC | Computer installation | V, AB | 4 |
| AD | Startup | A11 | 8 |

began with site preparation, which was considerably later than some other required steps, such as acquisitions of permits, but by the time Dunbar was able to obtain reasonable time estimates from all parties, the next major activity was site preparation.

As a planning tool, the PERT/CPM schedule turned out to be a godsend. The original critical path was A–C–E–F–G–J–M–P–R–Z–A5–AB–AC–AD for a project duration of ninety-seven weeks.

A glance at the PERT/CPM network prepared by Pettley showed Dunbar that the important activities to monitor were F and P and their predecessors. Throughout the project, Dunbar and Pettley constantly updated the network and the expected schedules, shifting expediter efforts as necessary.

As a result of Tad Dunbar's fine work, the entire project was completed early, in ninety-six weeks, three months earlier than the time limit he had been allowed. To reward Dunbar, Hiram Spencer made him manager of the planning department, a brand new department in the company. Tad, recently wed to Barbie Pettley, gratefully accepted the job. Hiram's move was not entirely without additional reasons. Dunbar, he had determined, was not philosophically aligned with either faction of the board of managers, and he expected that Dunbar's addition might be sufficient to break the usual ties. Hiram was right.

## REFERENCES

Drucker, Peter F., *Management, Tasks, Responsibilities, Practices*, Harper & Row, New York, 1973.

Hammond, J. S., III: "Do's and Don'ts of Computer Models for Planning," *Harvard Business Review*, March–April 1974, pp. 110-123.

Naylor, T. H., and H. Schauland: "A Survey of Users of Corporate Planning Models," *Management Science*, vol. 22, no. 9, 1976, pp. 927–937.

Perspectives on Experience, Boston Consulting Group, Boston, 1968.

## TECHNICAL NOTE 4.1 TABULAR PROCEDURE FOR PERT/CPM CALCULATIONS

The critical path is essentially the longest time path from the start of a project to its completion. While it is possible to determine the critical path by enumerating all of the possible paths and determining the path that takes the longest time, such a procedure becomes cumbersome as the project network becomes more complex. An alternative tabular procedure for determining the critical path is illustrated in Fig. 4.10.

A table is constructed with the activity times recorded for each activity. The earliest start and earliest finish are then calculated for each activity.

$$ES_i = \text{earliest start for activity } i$$

$$EF_i = \text{earliest finish for activity } i$$

$$t_i = \text{time necessary to perform activity } i$$

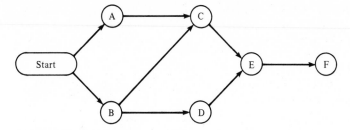

**Figure 4.10** Sample network.

These are calculated as follows:

$ES_i$ = maximum of earliest finish times of activities preceding activity $i$

$EF_i = ES_i + t_i$

For the network of Figure 4.10, the earliest start and finish times would be as shown in Table 4.9. The project is assumed to begin at time = 0. Therefore both the earliest start times for activities A and B would be zero. The earliest finish times for activities A and B would be

$$EF_A = ES_A + t_A$$

$$= 0 + 2 = 2$$

$$EF_B = ES_B + t_B$$

$$= 0 + 6 = 6$$

For activity C, the earliest time would be the maximum of the earliest finish time of activities preceding C. Since activities A and B precede C, the earliest start for C will be

$$ES_C = \text{maximum } (EF_A, EF_B)$$

$$ES_C = \text{maximum } (2, 6)$$

$$ES_C = 6$$

**Table 4.9 Earliest start and finish calculations**

| Activity | Activity times | Earliest start | Earliest finish |
|---|---|---|---|
| A | 2 | 0 | 2 |
| B | 6 | 0 | 6 |
| C | 3 | 6 | 9 |
| D | 1 | 6 | 7 |
| E | 4 | 9 | 13 |
| F | 7 | 13 | 20 |

The earliest finish time would then be

$$EF_C = ES_C + t_C$$

$$EF_C = 6 + 3 = 9$$

The remaining computations are performed in the same fashion as shown in Table 4.9. The project completion time is the largest time in the earliest finish time column (20 in this case).

The next step is to find the latest start and latest finish times for the project. In this case, the latest finish time for the last activity in the network is set equal to the overall project completion time. Thus, the project time of 20 is set equal to the latest finish time for activity F. The latest start time is then found by subtracting the activity time from the latest finish time. In the case of activity F, the latest start would be $20 - 7 = 13$.

In general, the latest finish time for an activity is found as follows:

$$LF_i = \text{latest finish time for activity } i$$

$$LS_i = \text{latest start time for activity } i$$

$$LF_i = \text{minimum of latest start times for all activities following } i$$

$$LS_i = LF_i = t_i$$

For activity E, the latest finish time is equal to the latest start time of the following activity (F in this case):

$$LF_E = LS_F$$

$$LF_E = 13$$

The latest start is then:

$$LS_E = LF_E - t_E$$

$$LS_E = 13 - 4 = 9$$

The remaining LS and LF values are shown in Table 4.10.

The flexibility between the earliest and latest start times is identified as the slack for the activities. For activity A, the slack is equal to $LS_A = ES_A = 4 - 0 = 4$. The remaining slack values are shown in Table 4.10.

**Table 4.10 Critical path calculations**

| Activity | Activity time | Earliest start | Earliest finish | Latest start | Latest finish | Slack |
|----------|---------------|----------------|-----------------|--------------|---------------|-------|
| A | 2 | 0 | 2 | 4 | 6 | 4 |
| B | 6 | 0 | 6 | 0 | 6 | 0 |
| C | 3 | 6 | 9 | 6 | 9 | 0 |
| D | 1 | 6 | 7 | 8 | 9 | 2 |
| E | 4 | 9 | 13 | 9 | 13 | 0 |
| F | 7 | 13 | 20 | 13 | 20 | 0 |

Those activities with zero slack represent the critical activities. In this case, the critical activities B–C–E–F form the critical path.

## QUESTIONS

**1** What is your evaluation of the past planning efforts at Spencer Industries?

**2** What was the major issue facing Spencer Industries that prompted the planning study?

**3** What was Hiram Spencer's view of the company's mission? How might the mission statement change the operations at Spencer Industries?

**4** As a member of the Spencer Industries management group, what specific objectives would you consider important?

**5** What is the critical question to ask when determining an organization's mission?

**6** What are the various types of objectives that need to be considered in developing plans for an organization?

**7** What is the experience curve concept? Why does the company which has the greatest amount of experience generally have the greatest profitability?

**8** What can the following items tell a company about its business? (Use your own words.)

(*a*) Current ratio

(*b*) Acid-test ratio

(*c*) Debt ratio

(*d*) Net profit margin ratio

(*e*) Return on total assets

**9** What information do the growth-share and share-momentum displays contribute to the planning process?

**10** What specific information did the growth-share matrix and the share-momentum graph provide about Spencer's business?

**11** No generally accepted planning model exists. Why do you think this is so?

**12** What are the conditions that are important to establish before considering the development of a planning model?

**13** How can an organization be sure that it has considered all viable alternatives in the planning process?

**14** How does the PERT/CPM model differ from the more general-purpose planning models?

**15** What is a critical activity?

**16** The planning process is sometimes considered to be more important than the plan itself. Why is this the case?

**17** What differences in planning processes are likely to exist between private industry and governmental organizations?

## EXERCISES

**1** For some organization which you are familiar with, describe the probable attitudes of the various key members of the organization with regard to a planning exercise.

**2** For your university department, develop what you would consider to be appropriate missions and objectives.

**3** Data in Table 4.11 show the cumulative volume of electric power. Plot an experience curve for this data on regular graph paper as well as log/log paper.

**Table 4.11**

| Year | Cumulative volume, billion kWh | Price per kWh | Year | Cumulative volume, billion kWh | Price per kWh, $ |
|------|------|------|------|------|------|
| 1939 | 600 | 0.0499 | 1955 | 4,713 | 0.0183 |
| 1941 | 859 | 0.0401 | 1957 | 5,801 | 0.0169 |
| 1943 | 1,204 | 0.0290 | 1959 | 6,997 | 0.0165 |
| 1945 | 1,596 | 0.0287 | 1961 | 8,399 | 0.0161 |
| 1947 | 2,005 | 0.0237 | 1963 | 10,006 | 0.0153 |
| 1949 | 2.495 | 0.0233 | 1965 | 12,054 | 0.0147 |
| 1951 | 3,094 | 0.0205 | 1967 | 14,620 | 0.0143 |
| 1953 | 3,821 | 0.0199 | | | |

**4** From an annual report given to you by your professor, compute the following ratios:

(a) Current ratio

(b) Acid-test ratio

(c) Debt ratio

(d) Net profit margin ratio

(e) Return on total assets

**5** TAB Electronics, a major producer of electronic appliances, is trying to assess its competitive position. It has accumulated the data shown in Table 4.12 on its major product lines.

**Table 4.12**

| Product line | TAB sales in millions of dollars | Sales of next leading competitor | Projected growth rates, % | Market growth rate, % (last 5 years) | Company growth rate, % (last 5 years) |
|------|------|------|------|------|------|
| Color TV | 36.2 | 18.9 | 2.1 | 2.8 | 2.4 |
| B/W TV | 8.1 | 12.3 | 0.5 | .6 | 3.6 |
| Microwave oven | 18.9 | 10.6 | 6.3 | 7.9 | 5.7 |
| Video cassettes | 3.6 | 4.2 | 8.9 | 12.2 | 10.2 |
| Large-screen TV | 1.2 | 5.6 | 7.3 | 6.8 | 5.3 |
| Quadraphonic stereo | 0.8 | 2.4 | 5.2 | 4.7 | 2.8 |
| Laser stereo | 0.2 | 0.8 | 6.1 | 2.1 | 1.7 |

(a) From these data, develop the growth-share and share-momentum displays.

(b) Analyze the competitive position of TAB Electronics.

**6** A company has a share-momentum graph as shown in Fig. 4.11.

Describe the apparent strategy in running this business.

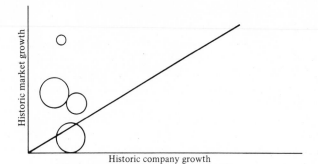

Figure **4.11**

7 From an article provided by your professor, analyze the use of planning models in the organization.

8 A student organization that you belong to is planning to host a student conference. As a part of this effort it must raise funds for the conference. Develop a list of activities that would be involved in a project to raise funds through the sale of some promotion item.

9 For the activity relationships shown in Table 4.13, develop a project network and identify the critical path. Specify the project's expected duration.

## Table 4.13

| Activity | Depends on | Estimated time |
|----------|-----------|----------------|
| A | None | 3.8 |
| B | A | 2.0 |
| C | A | 3.3 |
| D | A | 2.2 |
| E | B | 2.8 |
| F | B | 8.2 |
| G | F | 2.0 |
| H | C,E | 12.2 |
| I | G,H | 4.2 |
| J | I | 8.3 |

10 For the activity relationships shown in Table 4.13, develop a project network and identify the critical path. Specify the project's expected duration. Also, prepare a schedule for the activities.

## Table 4.14

| Activity | Depends on | Estimated time |
|----------|-----------|----------------|
| A | None | 2 |
| B | None | 4 |
| C | A | 3 |
| D | A,B | 4 |
| E | D | 6 |
| F | D | 1 |
| G | F | 2 |
| H | E,G | 4 |

## CASELETS

1. Polynomial Plastics, a small ($12 million sales) producer of quality plastic resins, has reached a critical point in its corporate growth. Polynomial began as an R&D facility developing new plastics concepts for larger plastics producers. Harrison Norton, the president of Polynomial Plastics, will reach retirement age in five years and wants the business to achieve a firm financial basis before that time. The largest single stockholder in Polynomial (with 22 percent of the shares) has indicated a desire to sell the stock if the company does not soon show significant growth. Norton personally would like to keep the business at the existing level and devote his major activities to research projects. Middle-level management at Polynomial has grown with the company and is generally apathetic about growth.

   The issue that must be resolved is whether to pursue a path of sales growth. If this direction is not adopted, Polynomial is likely to lose the financial backing of its major stockholder, which could lead to its acquisition by a conglomerate.

   You have been asked to help Polynomial Plastics decide on its future directions.

   (*a*) What additional information would you need to help Polynomial?

   (*b*) Outline the approach you would take in working with Polynomial.

2. Ajax Contractors, a construction firm, has been plagued recently by a series of difficulties in submitting bids for construction projects. Typically, Ajax receives a request for a bid one month in advance of the bid closing date. When Ajax was a smaller firm, it had a good record of meeting the bid closing dates, but as the business grew the company began to lose control of its bid submissions. As a result, Ajax hired three additional bid coordinators to help ensure that bids were submitted on time. This worked for a while but the problem of late bids again resurfaced.

   The new problem seemed to be more one of coordination than one of human power. Each bid coordinator was responsible for getting the bid through the system, using any feasible method. When bids required technical input, the coordinator had to seek it from one of the firm's engineers. Coordinators would compete for an engineer's time, causing the engineer to work on several bids at once.

   (*a*) What do you see as the major problems in getting the bids submitted on time?

   (*b*) What planning techniques should Ajax consider using to reduce the number of late bids?

## CASE 4.1: THE HATCHER ENERGY RESEARCH GROUP

### Introduction

The town of Hatcher was the home of the local university and several research centers. For years, a local energy research center concerned itself with "pork-barrel" projects oriented toward the utilization of coal. However, the advent of the Arab oil embargo brought the nation to a greater awareness of its energy needs, energy research was given top federal priority, and a degree of urgency was imposed on the work at the nation's energy research centers. The director of the Hatcher center answered this challenge by trying to improve the center's operation by demanding that project leaders become better at project management.

While the director was successful in making the various project leaders aware of project planning and management shortcomings, the goal, the stimulation of improved research management, was not met. The director was partly to blame. A career bureaucrat who saw research management as a process of "brow-beating" underlings whenever their work was not accomplished as planned, the director gave lip service to project management concepts but did not give them the organizational support they needed. In fact, the Hatcher Energy Research Group (HERG) had no real mission other than to spend all the funds available.

The Hatcher Center continued to flounder for nearly a year until the old director retired. A new research director took over and provided a different perspective. The new director, William Sherbourne, was fresh from several years of occupying similar positions in private industry. As he reviewed the management of the organization, he was amazed to find that no formal research planning and no systematic program of management were in existence.

Project management authority had been assigned according to a three-level management structure as outlined in Fig. 4.12. Project leaders were responsible for the actual conduct of the research work. These project leaders reported to project supervisors who were responsible for worker assignments, establishment of priorities, and miscellaneous activities. The project supervisors then reported to the research director, who had the general management responsibilities for the center.

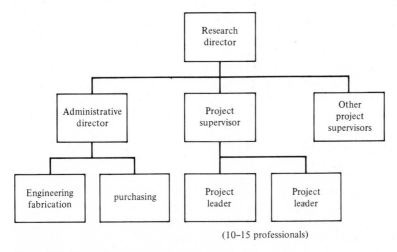

(10–15 professionals)

**Figure 4.12** Research management organization.

Sherbourne could see several shortcomings of the management structure immediately. First, the projects being worked on were not high-priority research topics. He could not see how the flow of bubbles through different ceramic materials was a project vital to the national interest. Sherbourne was also struck by the selfish attitudes of the project supervisors. There was constant bickering over the allocation of time in the fabrication shops, the analytical labs, and the computer center. None of the project supervisors appeared to realize that the group should function as a unit, not as a set of separate entities.

Sherbourne was puzzled by the lack of managerial expertise. The staff was technically competent, but it managed high-priority projects poorly. In order to alleviate these problems, Sherbourne brought in a former colleague of his (David Miller) as an outside consultant. He asked Miller to help develop better planning and management at HERG.

## Development of Research Missions

Throughout their long professional association, Sherbourne and Miller had held the same philosophy of management. When Miller suggested that HERG needed to develop a better focus for its research activities, Sherbourne was in perfect agreement. A task force of HERG employees was assembled to develop a mission statement and to prepare objectives for HERG.

Miller met with the task force and explained the objectives to be achieved. Miller asked the group to develop a planning structure for HERG which would contain the following:

1. A statement of missions—essentially the general direction of the group
2. A statement of ends goals—a list of specific accomplishments for the group over the next five years
3. A statement of means goals—a list of specific procedures for the group over the next five years
4. A statement of research priorities and recommendations for resource allocation
5. The development of action plans for each research project

The task force was stunned by the request. Not only had they never participated in such an effort, they did not believe such an approach would work in a research environment. Each member in one way or another expressed doubts that the "business" approach to product development would work in a government research setting.

Although many meetings were held, the task force was making no progress in its planning effort until one of its members, Joseph Peters, presented his ideas about mission statements, ends goals, and means goals to the group. The other members of the task force seemed relieved that something specific had been proposed but disagreed with Peters's views, which they criticized. However, the resulting debate ended in the preparation of the statements shown in Exhibit 4.3.

When the overall missions and goals statements were presented to Sherbourne, he was overjoyed. Finally, some sense was being made of the research

**EXHIBIT 4.3 Missions and goals statements for the Hatcher Energy Research Group**

---

**Mission Statements:**

1. To be the nationally recognized research leader in coal gasification and liquefaction efforts
2. To be one of the top five organizations in the nation in the area of enhanced oil and gas recovery
3. To support other research groups in the areas of coal extraction and coal processing

**Ends Goals:**

1. To produce the technological developments that will make coal gasification and liquefaction economically, environmentally and technically feasible by the year 1990
2. To produce technological developments that will boost secondary and tertiary recovery by 10 percent by the year 1985

**Means and Goals:**

1. To have completed a computer simulation of the synthex gasification process by 1982
2. To have pilot projects on enhanced oil and gas recovery in operation in three different oil and gas fields by 1982
3. To have a mobile computerized test van for oil and gas flow measurements by 1981
4. To have a working pilot plant for coal gasification and liquefaction by the year 1985
5. To have collected data on basic coal combustion characteristics in the synthex process by 1984
6. To have developed a decision model for enhanced recovery techniques by 1981
7. To provide outside support to other agencies equivalent to 15 percent of the HERG personnel budget (1980–85)

---

effort at HERG. Sherbourne sent a memo to his task force. He indicated that research plans would be based on how research projects fit the planning criteria.

The professional staff received the planning statements apathetically. A typical comment from a twenty-five year veteran was: "It looks like we are going through another management fad. We got rid of PPBS, MBO, and ZBB and we'll get rid of this fad as well."

Miller knew Sherbourne to be strong on follow-through and was sure the attitudes of the professional staff would change as soon as they saw funds being withdrawn when a specific project did not serve the missions of the organization. Now that the general framework of a planning system was in place, Miller turned to the operational problem that Sherbourne had described to him.

## The Reorganization Plan

Miller reviewed the organization at some length and decided to recommend a matrix form of management. This system as outlined in Fig. 4.13 established

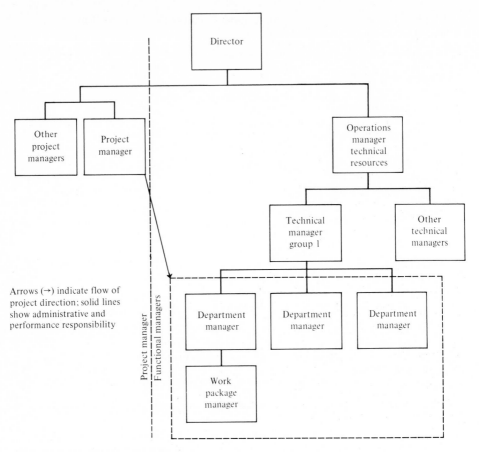

**Figure 4.13** The revised organization.

two groups. A group of project managers was to be designated as responsible for the management control of the different projects. This group would have no specific staff, but would contract for staff as needed from the various departments in the technical resources division of the organization.

A technical professional would report to a department manager but would be assigned project duties by a project manager. In this way, Miller felt that resources would be better utilized. Technical support could be shared between all of the projects, and the narrow focus of the various parts of the organization could be alleviated.

The reorganization proposed by Miller was a major change from that in existence at HERG, but he had seen it work effectively in his previous industrial experience. Miller went into considerable detail with Sherbourne discussing the effect such a change would have on the staff.

Even though the new organization would disrupt the existing organization, Sherbourne decided to obtain the approval of the plan from his superiors. He was willing to "take the heat" from disgruntled staff members in return for what he hoped would be long-term improvement at HERG.

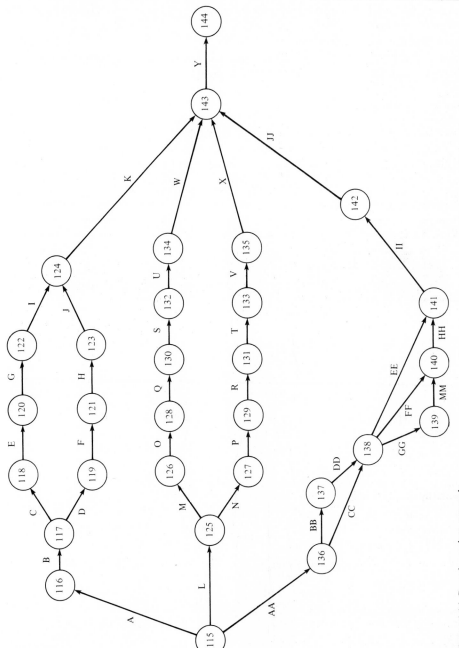

**Figure 4.14** Sample project network.

Project managers were carefully selected for their potential managerial skills. Technical managers were selected for their expertise in their technical specialties. Both groups were given extensive, secret briefing on the new organization and the improvements in planning expected as a result.

When the total organization was unveiled, "all hell broke loose." Project leaders under the previous system who now found themselves as technical support were incensed. Several resignations resulted.

## The Project Planning System

After the dust had settled, five high-priority projects were selected for funding. A project planning specialist was selected to give each of the project groups the technical expertise it needed to properly manage and control its projects.

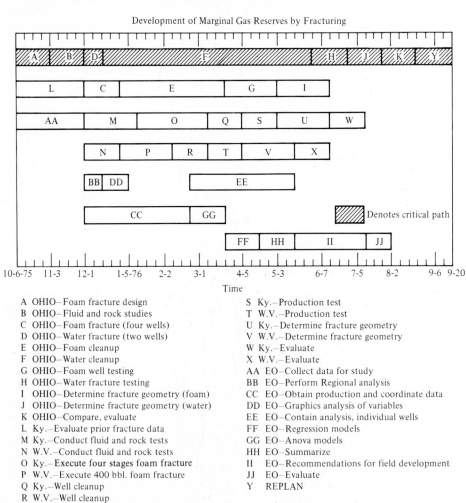

Development of Marginal Gas Reserves by Fracturing

| A OHIO–Foam fracture design | S Ky.–Production test |
| B OHIO–Fluid and rock studies | T W.V.–Production test |
| C OHIO–Foam fracture (four wells) | U Ky.–Determine fracture geometry |
| D OHIO–Water fracture (two wells) | V W.V.–Determine fracture geometry |
| E OHIO–Foam cleanup | W Ky.–Evaluate |
| F OHIO–Water cleanup | X W.V.–Evaluate |
| G OHIO–Foam well testing | AA EO–Collect data for study |
| H OHIO–Water fracture testing | BB EO–Perform Regional analysis |
| I OHIO–Determine fracture geometry (foam) | CC EO–Obtain production and coordinate data |
| J OHIO–Determine fracture geometry (water) | DD EO–Graphics analysis of variables |
| K OHIO–Compare, evaluate | EE EO–Contain analysis, individual wells |
| L Ky.–Evaluate prior fracture data | FF EO–Regression models |
| M Ky.–Conduct fluid and rock tests | GG EO–Anova models |
| N W.V.–Conduct fluid and rock tests | HH EO–Summarize |
| O Ky.–Execute four stages foam fracture | II EO–Recommendations for field development |
| P W.V.–Execute 400 bbl. foam fracture | JJ EO–Evaluate |
| Q Ky.–Well cleanup | Y REPLAN |
| R W.V.–Well cleanup | |

**Figure 4.15** Sample project schedule.

PERT/CPM systems were established for each of the five projects as shown in Figs. 4.14 and 4.15. A reporting system was established based upon a summary called the "Activity Delay Report" as shown in Exhibit 4.4. Each of the project leaders was briefed on the system, and it was installed at the beginning of the fiscal year.

## Postscript

The new management system worked fairly well during the first year of operation. A few personnel changes were made as it became evident that some individuals would not accept the system. In the middle of the fiscal year, President Carter imposed a hiring freeze on the agency that allowed only one replacement for every two resignations. The new matrix management system functioned well as the group began to do more outside contracting. Sherbourne felt very strongly that HERG was in a better position than sister research groups to continue functioning even though financial pressure was being applied from Washington.

As Sherbourne left his office one day, he heard one of the twenty-five year veterans showing a group of visitors the mission and goal statements displayed

**EXHIBIT 4.4 Activity delay report**

Project: _____

Activity: _____

Scheduled start and finish times: _____

Revised start and finish times: _____

Reason for the delay: _____

_____

_____

Responsibility for the delay: _____

_____

_____

Corrective actions taken or needed: _____

_____

_____

Anticipated effect of the delay on the rest of the project: _____

_____

_____

_____

Need for rescheduling the project: _____

_____

**EXHIBIT 4.4 (Continued) Progress reporting system instructions**

Once a month each project team will report to the research director on the progress made during the previous month. This report will consist of an indication on the project schedule of the activities completed that month. When an activity is only partially completed, an estimate will be made of the amount of the activity completed and noted accordingly.

For those activities which are more than four weeks behind schedule, a brief explanation will accompany the report detailing the reasons for the delay. The attached sheet illustrates the information needed for these activities. For activities which are two weeks behind schedule, a memorandum should be sent to the project manager informing him of the delay.

The project and activity lines are simply verbal descriptions of the particular task in question. These should conform with the titles on the project schedule sheet.

The scheduled start and finish times are those listed on the project schedule.

The revised start and finish times are the projected times which reflect the activity delay.

The reason for the delay segment of the report is a brief description of why the activity has been delayed.

The responsibility for the delay should detail the factors causing the delay (lack of materials, not enough people, etc.).

The next section of the report will outline what corrective actions have been taken or those that are needed (reassignment of personnel, expediting shop work, etc.).

The anticipated effect of the delay on the rest of the project will be a brief description of what subsequent activities will be delayed. Since a delay may affect the entire project, it is sufficient to examine only those activities which immediately follow the delayed activity.

In some cases, an unforeseen event may affect the project so severely as to require a new project schedule. In these cases, an indication of this fact at the bottom of the report will initiate a new schedule.

in the lobby. As the HERG employee proudly told his visitors about the importance of organization, Sherbourne considered his efforts a success.

## Discussion Guide

1 Describe the apparent planning process before the arrival of Sherbourne.

2 Describe the interaction between the organization at HERG and the planning process. Can any generalization be derived?

3 How does planning differ at HERG from that at Spencer Industries? How are they similar?

4 Were the prepared missions, ends goals, and means goals adequate in your view?

5 Describe the effect of the reorganization on the individuals involved. If you were Sherbourne would you have introduced the organization plan differently? What impact did Sherbourne's quick approach to reorganization have on the planning process?

6 Comment on the progress reporting system. Would you say the system was designed as a punitive measure or in the spirit of cooperation toward meeting planned schedules?

7 Why do you think the employee in the lobby had changed his attitude?

# FIVE

## EVALUATING RISKS

## SYNOPSIS OF THE CHAPTER

All decision making is uncertain. No matter what choices are adopted, the possibility exists that these choices will have unfavorable repercussions. Alternatives not chosen may prove in time to have been the best. Managers are conscious of these extreme possibilities and would like to avoid them.

One tool for analyzing alternatives before choosing one is the decision model. Risk analysis can take numerous forms and may employ modeling techniques discussed elsewhere in this book, but the models discussed in this chapter are well suited to predicting the effects of choices in an environment of risk.

Three primary modeling tools are presented: (1) probabilistic simulation, (2) deterministic simulation, and (3) decision trees. These tools differ primarily in the amount of detailed knowledge required for their use. Probabilistic simulation requires knowledge of the relations between events along with a considerable body of past data. Deterministic simulation requires a good knowledge of cause-and-effect relationships between events. Decision trees require good guesses as to the likelihood of events and their repercussions.

Each of these techniques can be applied to a reasonable range of data. Inputs can be varied to study their effects on model predictions. Probabilities and even causal mechanisms in the models can be changed to reflect different opinions about the future.

The student should come away from this chapter with a feeling for the levels of information required for each modeling technique and an appreciation of the difficulty of estimating risks. An additional point stressed in the main body of the chapter and in its case studies is that risk is difficult to define, and different people will likely have different opinions about risks and their consequences.

## MAJOR CONCEPTS PRESENTED IN THIS CHAPTER

1. Individuals accept risk conditions in different ways. Some individuals view uncertainty as a means of enhancing the value of a decision to their administrative careers. Other individuals view uncertainty as a threat.
2. Decision models in risk situations attempt to measure the risk conditions in order to evaluate alternative decision options.
3. Monte Carlo simulation models evaluate risk conditions by describing the various events influencing the decision as a series of probability distributions. The events affecting the decision are then generated from the probability distributions in order to test different alternatives.
4. Decision trees can be used to evaluate risk conditions by describing the sequence of the decisions that are to be made and the events that may occur. Probability estimates for each event are used to evaluate the expected consequences of each decision option.
5. Deterministic simulation models are useful devices for evaluating risks when limited data is available for evaluating probabilities. The goal of the deterministic simulation model is to measure the likely outcome of applying a specific set of input conditions to the system being modeled.

## EXPECTATIONS OF THE STUDENT

The student, after studying this chapter, should be able to do the following:

1. Distinguish between the risk taker and the risk avoider with respect to the following variables:
   a. Value of the decision
   b. Level of information about the decision
   c. Development of the decision model
2. Outline and discuss the following modeling procedures with respect to the level of information known about the uncertainty and the approach taken to model uncertainty:
   a. Monte Carlo simulation
   b. Decision trees
   c. Deterministic simulation
3. Outline, discuss, and apply the six-step development process of Monte Carlo simulation models
4. Outline, explain, and apply the five-step development process of decision tree models
5. Outline, explain, and apply the three-step development process of deterministic simulation models

## SUNSET BANK

The management of Sunset Bank was suffering nervous distress, caused by recent changes in the banking industry. Banking's prior disregard of customer wishes was quickly changing because of competition for customers. Banks were trying to provide better service. The choice of which services to provide constantly bedeviled the Sunset management.

Sunset over the years had been the premier bank in the community. It had all the best families on its board. Because of substantial support in the state legislature, it had been able to defeat branch banking provisions every year they had been proposed. Its hand-picked banking representative on the state banking commission, Coleman Turloff, also protected its interests by ensuring that no new banks were allowed to enter the community.

Trouble began when Coleman Turloff died unexpectedly of a heart attack at a basketball game featuring the state's two universities. The governor, in revenge for the banking industry's lack of support during the last campaign, selected an avowed consumer advocate as Turloff's replacement. The governor then threatened the legislature's banking committee with withdrawal of local highway funds (in committee members' home districts) if it did not approve the appointment.

The new banking commissioner instituted a vast change in the state's banking industry. New banks were approved in virtually every city. Sunset suffered the incursion of four new banks into its service area alone. The new banks were operated by a new breed of managers, aggressive in the pursuit of business.

The new banks introduced drive-in facilities, express checking, after-hours check cashing, and a host of other features designed to attract additional customers. Sunset's response to each new service was to wait and see. It eventually adopted each new concept but only after several months of debate.

The result of Sunset's wait-and-see attitude was a gradual decrease in customers. Its competition would advertise each new advance with great fanfare, while Sunset could only respond with a lukewarm advertisement when it eventually imitated the service.

Austin Kincaid, the vice president of operations for Sunset, was under pressure to be more responsive to new service concepts. He was given total authority to institute any new concept which would reverse the flow of customers away from Sunset.

Kincaid, from his very beginning in banking, had been known as a conservative manager. In fact, he had chosen banking as a career because of its perceived stability. His personal style of decision making was to avoid any decision until the outcome of the decision was known with virtual certainty. This style had served him well in the past, but increasing pressure for change had forced him to rethink it.

Montgomery Ashton, the president of the bank, was emphatic that Sunset must adopt a more aggressive approach to customer services. He had secretly purchased land along one of the community's busiest streets for the purpose of locating a drive-in facility there. The facility was at the very limit of the bank's allowable range for a drive-in facility. The building of any ancillary facility more than one-half mile from the bank was prohibited by law. Customarily, all drive-ins were directly adjacent to the parent banks; so not only was this a unique idea, but the drive-in's location in the heart of town would give the bank a major competitive edge.

Ashton decided to delegate the operational design of the facility to Austin

Kincaid. He also made it clear to Kincaid that his future with Sunset rested on how well he did this job. Kincaid was terrified by the responsibility given him by Ashton. Lying awake one night worrying, he thought of an idea that might save him.

Cindy Myers, a young M.B.A. recently hired to be director of the bank's data processing section, was constantly bombarding Montgomery with management journal articles on the value of decision models. It occurred to him that one of these models could remove from him the burden of evaluating all the operational decisions in planning the new drive-in facility.

However, instead of turning over to Myers the operational analysis of the new drive-in facility, Kincaid decided on a more cautious approach. He decided to give Myers a problem with which to test her skill. Guidelines for operation of the after-hours checking facility had been difficult to establish. A decision had to be made as to the amount of money to be left in the check cashing machine each weekend. Too much money in the machine meant that the bank was tying up funds it could invest for the weekend period. Too little money resulted in customers not receiving the funds they expected.

The computer controls on the machine allowed it to limit the amount of money a customer could receive whenever the supply of cash dropped below a given level. Originally the bank had limited each customer to $20 whenever the total cash reserve dropped to $300.

Solving the operational problem of the after-hours facility seemed to Kincaid an ideal test of Myers's ability to help him in the eventual design of the new drive-in facility. He still had doubts, however, and decided to give Myers low visibility until he could determine whether she could be of help.

## DECISION MAKER ATTITUDES TOWARD RISK CONDITIONS

Individuals approach uncertainty from different perspectives. Figure 5.1 illustrates how two types of individuals might approach uncertainty.

Risk takers look upon decisions as a way of establishing their worth to an organization. Making good decisions with limited information is a rare talent

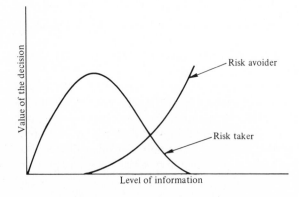

**Figure 5.1** Decision value as a function of level of information.

that can bring reward to those who possess it. Since these individuals' reputations are based on their decision making ability, they must have some information before they have a chance to make decisions. However, a high level of information about the decision is of little value to these individuals. When abundant information exists, risk taking decision makers feel that others should have already made the decision.

Models developed for risk takers should provide quick insights. They should not attempt to be comprehensive. The models themselves may not even need to be completed. The process of structuring the models may be sufficient to provide the insights needed.

Risk avoiders look upon decisions as necessary evils. They would like to avoid making decisions until they are reasonably sure of making the correct decision. Risk avoiders would not consider making a decision based upon the limited information base sought by risk takers.

Models developed for risk avoiders should be detailed and validated with great precision. All aspects of uncertainty should be modeled. Risk avoiders frequently ask for more and more detail in the model as they subconsciously avoid making the decision.

The above descriptions of risk takers and risk avoiders are exaggerated, but they define the extremes that may be required of models in risky situations.

## DECISION MODELS FOR EVALUATING RISKS

Risks attendant upon certain decisions can be analyzed by systematic models of the decision process. Models cannot remove risks, but they can be useful aids to understanding risks. Models offer the decision maker the opportunity to test numerous alternatives and thereby anticipate future problems before they happen.

Models used for evaluating risks take the same basic approach: a systematic description of the factors affecting the decision is prepared and put into mathematical form. In the instance of banking, such a model allows an abstract transaction to flow through the mathematical system and experience the same phenomena as a real-life transaction would. Data are collected on the relative frequencies and strengths of relevant events and are subsequently used to generate a synthetic record of transactions as they flow through the system.

In another example, it is possible to process an insurance application through a synthetic model of the application process. The model would contain descriptions of each of the processing steps the application encounters. Operational features of the system can then be altered, and the model can be run again to evaluate the consequences of the changes.

The obvious advantage of using this modeling approach to analyzing risk is that many operational changes can be investigated prior to making those changes in the physical system. Although the models available are very flexible in their range of applications, their accurate usage requires extensive data collection on

**Table 5.1 Approaches to modeling uncertainty**

| Information known about the uncertainty | Approach taken to model uncertainty | Appropriate modeling procedure |
|---|---|---|
| Probability distribution of past history | Use probability distributions as basis for generating events to test alternatives | Monte Carlo simulation |
| Probability estimates | Use probability estimates to determine "expected" results of following each alternative | Decision trees |
| Scenarios of likely events | Use scenarios to identify what would happen if the scenario were valid | Deterministic simulation |

the system being analyzed. Table 5.1 describes the model options that exist according to the type of information available.

In the first instance, sufficient data exist to provide a basis for generating abstracted events to examine alternatives. For example, demands for cash on a particular banking day can be reasonably predicted from past distributions of demand. Monte Carlo simulation can then be used to predict the consequences of future actions from past data.

In the second instance, data is limited to estimates of the likelihood of certain events. For example, an estimate of selected future growth possibilities for an investment can be made, but data may be too limited to provide more than probability estimates for each level of growth. The decision tree approach utilizes these probability estimates to determine the expected consequences of different decisions.

In the third instance, no estimates of probabilities are available, but scenarios can be developed which describe possible future events. A deterministic simulation model is then used to assess the performance of the system being studied under the conditions of the scenario. The decision maker must determine the likelihood of each scenario before making a decision.

Models for evaluating risks have been used in virtually every variety of management decision. Production flows, distribution systems, and scheduling systems are but a few of the operational areas in which risk assessment models have been useful.

## THE CHECK CASHING DECISION

Kincaid called Myers to his office to outline the check cashing decision in question. Myers was pleased at the opportunity to do more than write COBOL programs. She immediately began to develop the model and found that two pieces of information were required—the number of customers using the after-hours facility and the amount of cash ordinarily requested. Myers could see that the banking industry provided substantial advantages to the modeler; detailed records were kept on virtually every phase of the business. In particular a magnetic tape record of all transactions at the after-hours facility was readily accessible.

After a full day of struggling with bit strings, logical record lengths, and parity, Myers learned how to read most of the tape. She wrote a small program to obtain information on the number of customers using the facility per hour and on the amounts of cash required. Data were summarized for twenty weekends.

The data clearly showed that usage varied considerably throughout the weekend. From 5 P.M. to 11 P.M. Friday, demand was heavy. The times from 11 P.M. Saturday to 7 A.M. Sunday and the times from 11 P.M. Sunday to 9 A.M. Monday displayed low usage rates. Saturday from 7 A.M. to 11 P.M. had a usage pattern similar to that of Friday evening, while Sunday from 7 A.M. to 11 P.M. showed lower demand than either Friday or Saturday. The amount of money requested did not seem to depend strongly on the time of request.

Myers summarized the frequency of occurrences as shown in Tables 5.2 to 5.5.

In order to use the past data to simulate the check cashing machine's operation, Myers decided to use Monte Carlo simulation. She first assigned random numbers to each distinct event in each of the Tables 5.2 through 5.5. Random numbers were assigned according to the relative frequency of events for the purpose of later imitating the process being studied.

### Table 5.2 Time period A (5 P.M. to 11 P.M. Friday and 7 A.M. to 11 P.M. Saturday)

Check cashing requests per hour

| Number of requests | Frequency | Percent of occurrences |
|---|---|---|
| 0 | 2 | 1 |
| 1 | 16 | 11 |
| 2 | 44 | 30 |
| 3 | 58 | 40 |
| 4 | 20 | 14 |
| 5 | 4 | 3 |
| 6 or more | 2 | 1 |

### Table 5.3 Time period B (11 P.M. Saturday to 7 A.M. Sunday and 11 P.M. Sunday to 9 .A.M. Monday)

Check cashing requests per hour

| Number of requests | Frequency | Percent of occurrences |
|---|---|---|
| 0 | 120 | 81 |
| 1 | 20 | 13 |
| 2 | 8 | 5 |
| 3 | 1 | 1 |

### Table 5.4  Time period C (7 A.M. to 11 P.M. Sunday)

Check cashing requests per hour

| Number of requests | Frequency | Percent of occurrences |
|---|---|---|
| 0 | 5 | 3 |
| 1 | 25 | 12 |
| 2 | 120 | 59 |
| 3 | 40 | 20 |
| 4 | 10 | 5 |
| 5 | 2 | 1 |

### Table 5.5  Distribution of amount requested

| Amount, in dollars | Percent of occurrences |
|---|---|
| 0–20 | 26 |
| 20–40 | 46 |
| 40–60 | 19 |
| 80–100 | 9 |

Assignment of random numbers can be demonstrated for the events of Table 5.2. In this table, 40 percent of the hours during the times cited showed three requests for cash. Thus, 40 percent of the random numbers assigned to this table should be assigned to the event "three requests in an hour." One hundred random numbers (00 through 99) were assigned to Table 5.2, and "three requests" was assigned the forty-number subset, 42 through 81. The entire set of random number assignments is shown in Table 5.6.

### Table 5.6  Random numbers assigned to requests per hour from 5 P.M. to 11 P.M. Friday and from 7 A.M. to 11 P.M. Saturday

| Number of requests | Relative frequency | Random numbers |
|---|---|---|
| 0 | 0.01 | 00 |
| 1 | 0.11 | 01–11 |
| 2 | 0.30 | 12–41 |
| 3 | 0.40 | 42–81 |
| 4 | 0.14 | 82–95 |
| 5 | 0.03 | 96–98 |
| 6 or more | 0.01 | 99 |

During the execution of a simulation model, the events in each sample period are generated through the use of a random number generator. The model selects the number of requests for cash during each simulated hour by choosing a random number, so called because it is selected through a process designed to guarantee that past selections of numbers do not affect later selections.

If a model were simulating the number of requests during the hour from 6 P.M. to 7 P.M. on Friday, it would select a random number. Let us say the number is 48. Since 48 is among the numbers assigned to three requests, the computer would record three requests for cash during the simulated hour.

Random numbers were also assigned to the events of Tables 5.3 through 5.5 and are listed in Tables 5.7 through 5.9.

Note that in simulating events one must generate a random number for each event being generated. It would bias the simulation experiment to do otherwise. For example, one might be tempted to use the same random number for the time the requests for funds is made and for the amount requested. However, this misuse of random numbers would result in such peculiarities as small amounts of money always being requested by each customer whenever few requests were made and large amounts always being requested by each customer when a large number of requests were made.

**Table 5.7 Random numbers assigned to requests per hour from 11 P.M. Saturday to 7 A.M. Sunday and from 11 P.M. Sunday to 9 A.M. Monday**

| Number of requests | Relative frequency | Random numbers |
|---|---|---|
| 0 | 0.81 | 00–80 |
| 1 | 0.13 | 81–93 |
| 2 | 0.05 | 94–98 |
| 3 | 0.01 | 99 |

**Table 5.8 Random numbers assigned to requests per hour from 7 A.M. to 11 P.M. Sunday**

| Number of requests | Relative frequency | Random numbers |
|---|---|---|
| 0 | 0.03 | 00–02 |
| 1 | 0.12 | 03–14 |
| 2 | 0.59 | 15–73 |
| 3 | 0.20 | 74–93 |
| 4 | 0.05 | 94–98 |
| 5 | 0.01 | 99 |

**Table 5.9 Random numbers
assigned to amounts requested**

| Amount, in dollars | Relative frequency | Random numbers |
|---|---|---|
| 0–20 | 0.26 | 00–25 |
| 20–40 | 0.46 | 26–71 |
| 40–60 | 0.19 | 72–90 |
| 60–80 | 0.00 | ........ |
| 80–100 | 0.09 | 91–99 |

Table 5.10 shows a set of random numbers that will be used for the examples in this text. In selecting numbers from this table, any row or column can be used. Column 5 will be selected arbitrarily for the first example.

The bank's original policy was to start the weekend with $3000 in the check cashing facility. Controls were also set to limit a customer to $20 whenever the cash on hand dropped below $300. Myers decided to simulate this policy to see whether her simulation model imitated reality. Table 5.11 contains a hand-calculated version of the model which was presented to Austin Kincaid to demonstrate the principles of the simulation model.

Table 5.11 begins the simulation at 5 P.M. on Friday. The random number 63 is selected from column 5 of the random number table. The time period 5 P.M. to 6 P.M. on Friday is referred to in Table 5.6, and the number 63 falls in the interval, 42–81, corresponding to three requests for the hour.

Three additional random numbers are generated to determine the amount of money requested by each customer. The selected numbers, 89, 92, and 20, correspond to check amounts of $50, $90, and $10. The total cash request of $150 is honored since the cash balance in the facility is above $300. The new cash balance of $2850 ($3000 − $150) is available for the next hour.

The next hour is simulated in the same way. The random number 29 is generated, representing two customers for the hour. Two random numbers, 17 and 05, are then selected which generate a $10 request for each customer. Each request is honored, leaving a cash balance of $2830.

The number of assignments of Table 5.6 are used until the 11 P.M. to 12 P.M. time period, when data from time period B (Table 5.7) are used. The same process continues until each weekend hour has been simulated.

During the 8 P.M. to 9 P.M. time period on Sunday, the cash balance drops below $300. For the remainder of Sunday and for early Monday morning, customers are restricted to $20. This limit reduces eight customer requests. A balance of $120 remains at the end of the weekend.

Once Myers was sure the basic procedure would work, her next step was to computerize the operation. A FORTRAN program was prepared to produce output similar to that in Table 5.11. Myers then ran the computer model for a total of 100 weekends.

For each weekend, Myers recorded the number of customers who had their check requests reduced and the number of customers who received no cash at all.

**Table 5.10 Random numbers**

| Row | 1 | 2 | 3 | 4 | 5 | 6 | 7 | 8 | 9 | 10 |
|-----|-----|-----|-----|-----|-----|-----|-----|-----|-----|-----|
| | | | | | Column | | | | | |
| 1 | 03 | 33 | 57 | 74 | 63 | 17 | 62 | 39 | 05 | 91 |
| 2 | 74 | 33 | 43 | 10 | 89 | 15 | 52 | 73 | 73 | 88 |
| 3 | 09 | 00 | 20 | 95 | 92 | 45 | 09 | 88 | 16 | 51 |
| 4 | 42 | 12 | 87 | 14 | 20 | 01 | 64 | 31 | 86 | 29 |
| 5 | 16 | 08 | 20 | 41 | 81 | 65 | 74 | 56 | 00 | 67 |
| 6 | 21 | 40 | 29 | 96 | 29 | 21 | 15 | 34 | 33 | 06 |
| 7 | 21 | 57 | 02 | 89 | 17 | 37 | 47 | 42 | 97 | 48 |
| 8 | 55 | 78 | 83 | 33 | 05 | 24 | 86 | 60 | 16 | 03 |
| 9 | 44 | 66 | 99 | 51 | 84 | 60 | 79 | 93 | 68 | 25 |
| 10 | 91 | 84 | 46 | 81 | 37 | 61 | 43 | 15 | 80 | 43 |
| 11 | 91 | 21 | 31 | 27 | 84 | 05 | 35 | 14 | 29 | 68 |
| 12 | 50 | 38 | 66 | 19 | 72 | 09 | 12 | 06 | 91 | 18 |
| 13 | 65 | 05 | 72 | 28 | 81 | 39 | 25 | 48 | 42 | 45 |
| 14 | 27 | 96 | 83 | 41 | 10 | 68 | 64 | 73 | 36 | 05 |
| 15 | 37 | 94 | 39 | 89 | 00 | 16 | 65 | 49 | 39 | 17 |
| 16 | 11 | 70 | 51 | 38 | 19 | 66 | 71 | 05 | 12 | 78 |
| 17 | 37 | 30 | 06 | 54 | 04 | 53 | 62 | 95 | 78 | 11 |
| 18 | 46 | 70 | 85 | 38 | 57 | 15 | 97 | 17 | 45 | 61 |
| 19 | 30 | 81 | 42 | 58 | 21 | 30 | 32 | 86 | 05 | 07 |
| 20 | 63 | 64 | 46 | 09 | 44 | 78 | 83 | 42 | 92 | 83 |
| 21 | 82 | 84 | 99 | 67 | 43 | 50 | 21 | 64 | 51 | 88 |
| 22 | 21 | 32 | 92 | 09 | 64 | 51 | 64 | 62 | 26 | 05 |
| 23 | 60 | 98 | 07 | 53 | 13 | 59 | 26 | 29 | 85 | 41 |
| 24 | 43 | 46 | 24 | 25 | 86 | 33 | 25 | 54 | 71 | 15 |
| 25 | 97 | 63 | 89 | 16 | 07 | 92 | 21 | 18 | 47 | 20 |
| 26 | 03 | 01 | 05 | 38 | 55 | 92 | 26 | 86 | 21 | 98 |
| 27 | 79 | 06 | 03 | 17 | 07 | 76 | 79 | 25 | 83 | 88 |
| 28 | 85 | 68 | 47 | 03 | 65 | 11 | 02 | 26 | 99 | 68 |
| 29 | 18 | 14 | 61 | 06 | 12 | 46 | 32 | 74 | 64 | 00 |
| 30 | 08 | 15 | 60 | 36 | 65 | 16 | 53 | 09 | 07 | 41 |
| 31 | 79 | 29 | 04 | 16 | 15 | 12 | 66 | 38 | 22 | 73 |
| 32 | 92 | 82 | 27 | 32 | 17 | 27 | 98 | 63 | 11 | 34 |
| 33 | 23 | 25 | 40 | 67 | 12 | 02 | 14 | 23 | 35 | 99 |
| 34 | 09 | 96 | 05 | 97 | 28 | 14 | 00 | 80 | 70 | 75 |
| 35 | 59 | 33 | 26 | 62 | 69 | 76 | 50 | 43 | 86 | 70 |

The average number of customers affected by the check cashing policy was determined and plotted as a function of the number of weekends simulated (see Fig. 5.2).

Figure 5.2 showed that averages began to stabilize after forty simulation iterations. Therefore, Myers decided that any subsequent simulation of alternatives should be run at least forty weekends. Stable results are important in simulation models because averages that fluctuate wildly from trial to trial do not lend credence to the model.

## Table 5.11 Simulation analysis of check cashing facility

Original cash available = $3000
Limit of $20 per check when supply drops below $300

| Time | Day | Cash available | Random number | Number of clients | Random number for check amounts | Check amounts | Total cash request | Total cash delivered | Remaining cash available | Total number of clients receiving reduced amounts | Total number of clients receiving no cash |
|---|---|---|---|---|---|---|---|---|---|---|---|
| 5 P.M.– 6 P.M. | Fri. | $3000 | 63 | 3 | 89, 92, 20 | $50, $90, $10 | $150 | $150 | $2850 | 0 | 0 |
| 6 P.M.– 7 P.M. | Fri. | $2850 | 29 | 2 | 17, 05 | $10, $10 | $ 20 | $ 20 | $2830 | 0 | 0 |
| 7 P.M.– 8 P.M. | Fri. | $2830 | 84 | 4 | 37, 84, 72, 81 | $30, $50, $50, $50 | $180 | $180 | $2650 | 0 | 0 |
| 8 P.M.– 9 P.M. | Fri. | $2650 | 10 | 1 | 00 | $10 | $ 10 | $ 10 | $2640 | 0 | 0 |
| 9 P.M.–10 P.M. | Fri. | $2640 | 19 | 2 | 04 | $10 | $ 10 | $ 10 | $2630 | 0 | 0 |
| 10 P.M.–11 P.M. | Fri. | $2630 | 57 | 3 | 21, 44, 43 | $10, $30, $30 | $ 70 | $ 70 | $2560 | 0 | 0 |
| 11 P.M.–12 P.M. | Fri. | $2560 | 64 | 0 | ......... | ......... | 0 | 0 | $2560 | 0 | 0 |
| 7 A.M.– 8 A.M. | Sat. | $2550 | 15 | 2 | 17, 12 | $10, $10 | $ 20 | $ 20 | $2540 | 0 | 0 |
| 9 P.M.–10 P.M. | Sun. | $ 290 | 68 | 2 | 88, 79 | $50, $50 | $100 | $ 40 | $ 250 | 2 | 0 |
| 10 P.M.–11 P.M. | Sun. | $ 250 | 47 | 2 | 76, 95 | $50, $90 | $140 | $ 40 | $ 210 | 4 | 0 |
| 8 A.M.– 9 A.M. | Mon. | $ 120 | 43 | 0 | ......... | ......... | $ 0 | $ 0 | $ 120 | 8 | 0 |

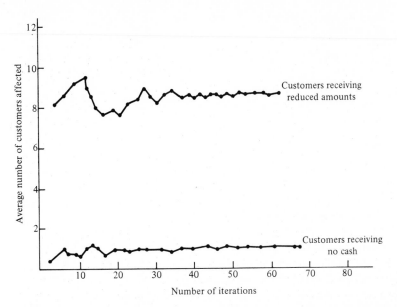

**Figure 5.2** Plot of average number of customers affected as a function of number of iterations of simulation model.

Having obtained stable averages, Myers checked the validity of the model. She could read check requests and amounts received from the tape of the bank's actual transactions. The number of requests that were limited during a weekend because the cash reserve of the machine fell below $300 averaged 8.6 (reduced amounts) and 0.4 (no cash). The model predicted these values to be 7.9 and 0.2. Myers felt that these values were close enough to demonstrate the validity of the model and began testing alternative check cashing policies.

The bank could control three operational variables: the initial cash reserve, the cash level (called the safety level) which triggers the reduced cash policy, and the limit on the check amount during low cash periods. These three variables are interrelated, making the task of identifying a proper operational strategy difficult. The higher the initial cash reserve, the longer it takes for cash to drop to the safety level, which means that fewer customers receive reduced cash. Thus, raising the cash reserve leaves fewer customers disappointed. Myers decided to use a trial-and-error process to arrive at an equitable compromise between customer satisfaction and cash committed to the machine. The results of her trials are shown in Table 5.12.

The result of the existing policy was that an average of $148 remained at the end of the weekend and that an average of almost eight customers received reduced amounts.

A simulation reducing the safety level to $200 (alternative A) lowered the average number of customers receiving reduced amounts from 7.9 to 6.5. However, the customers receiving no cash at all increased from 0.2 to 2.8, and the cash at the weekend's end dropped from $148 to $92. Since this alternative would

**Table 5.12 Alternative check cashing strategies**

| Alternative | Initial cash reserve | Safety level | Cash limit | Average number of customers receiving reduced amounts | Average number of customers receiving no cash | Remaining cash |
|---|---|---|---|---|---|---|
| Existing | $3000 | $300 | $20 | 7.9 | 0.2 | $148 |
| A | $3000 | $200 | $20 | 6.5 | 2.8 | $ 92 |
| B | $3000 | $300 | $30 | 4.1 | 1.6 | $ 99 |
| C | $3200 | $300 | $20 | 3.8 | 0.1 | $216 |
| D | $3200 | $250 | $20 | 2.9 | 0.1 | $208 |
| E | $3200 | $250 | $25 | 1.8 | 0.2 | $196 |

make 2.6 more people very angry, Myers tried raising the cash limit while keeping the safety level at $300 (alternative B).

Alternative B showed an improvement in both customer-related performance measures while keeping the same initial cash level. The next alternative to be investigated raised the initial cash level to $3200 while keeping the safety level and cash limit at their original amounts. As expected, this alternative significantly improved customer performance measures. Fine-tuning the strategies eventually led to alternative E, which included a $3200 initial cash stock and a $250 safety level and a cash limit of $25.

Alternative E appeared to Myers to be the best, since it limited the bank's loss in interest while improving the customer satisfaction measures. Myers could not understand why the bank had not followed this plan originally.

Myers wrote a report describing her results and presented it to Austin Kincaid. As usual, Kincaid postponed any action, but he was clearly impressed with the study. Kincaid promised Myers he "would get back to her."

Two days later, Myers found a copy of a memo in her mailbox from Austin Kincaid to Montgomery Ashton detailing the "progressive management analysis techniques being used in evaluation of operational strategies." The memo showed the analysis that Myers had done and indicated that alternative E had been selected. Kincaid further assured the president that the bank had the management capability to ensure that the new Sunset facility would be a model of operational efficiency.

Myers was happy that her study had been well received by Kincaid but was disappointed that she had received no credit for doing the work. She decided that women's liberation advocates might be right about the misuse of women in business, and she vowed that the president would know about the next study she did.

## THE MONTE CARLO METHOD

The Monte Carlo method, as demonstrated by the check cashing study, consists of the following steps:

1. Collect data on system performance.
2. Represent uncertainty by preparing distributions of data.

3. Assign random number ranges to each distribution.
4. Develop a computational model imitating the flows of the system.
5. Generate system conditions from the random number assignments.
6. Compute measures of system performance for the generated conditions.

In the check cashing decision, system performance data were collected from the operation of the check cashing system. The number of check cashing requests per hour for different time periods and the amounts of money requested were uncertain. Random number assignments were then made, as shown in Tables 5.6 through 5.9, and a model was designed to show the cash amount each hour and the cash requests being made. Random numbers were used to simulate the operation of the after-hours facility as shown in Table 5.11.

Although each application of the Monte Carlo method is unique, the basic process is the same as that outlined above.

## THE DRIVE-IN FACILITY MODEL

When the president responded to Kincaid's memo with glowing praise of the simulation study, Kincaid aggressively undertook the planning study for the drive-in facility. He sent a memo to Myers indicating that he wanted a complete analysis of the new facility. He specifically wanted to know the consequences of installing each alternative number of drive-in bays.

Along with his memo, Kincaid sent Myers three architectural drawings of possible layouts for the drive-in site. The configuration with the easiest highway access could accommodate only three service bays. A total of twelve cars could enter the system in this configuration. Another configuration would accommodate six bays but would require that the entrance to the facility be on a side street. This alternative could accommodate a limit of ten cars. A compromise between these extremes was another configuration which would allow up to four bays but which would limit the total cars in the facility to eight. A pneumatic tube system for exchanging money and communications between the car and the drive-in tellers was to be installed with the same operational design as that at the drive-in now in place adjacent to the bank.

In order to evaluate the service provided customers at the facility, Myers found that she needed information on the arrival rate of customers and the service rate of the tellers.

The service rate was easy to obtain from observations of the existing drive-in at the bank. Myers felt that the time it would take to process a banking request would not change at the new site, since the same technology and procedures would be used.

The arrival pattern was a different matter. Estimating the use of the new drive-in would require a knowledge of how many customers would use it instead of the older, less convenient one. Another complicating factor was the need to determine the design period, that is, the period of time for which a system was to function most effectively.

If the new site's capacity were based upon demand represented by 10 A.M. middle-of-the-week traffic, its design would be different than it would be if it

### Table 5.13 Processing times for banking requests

| Service time, min. | Percent of observations | Random number assignments |
|---|---|---|
| 0–1 | 14 | 00–13 |
| 1–2 | 22 | 14–35 |
| 2–3 | 28 | 36–63 |
| 3–4 | 19 | 64–82 |
| 4–5 | 11 | 83–93 |
| 5 and longer | 6 | 94–99 |

were based upon the demand resulting from a local industry's payday. The final choice of the design period for the facility was left to Kincaid. Myers knew Kincaid's aversion to taking risks, so she decided to give him maximum flexibility by developing a model for studying different design periods and customer demand ranges. Myers felt that such an approach would give her a larger role when the results were presented, since she believed that Kincaid would not want to make such an open-ended presentation by himself. Kincaid would be forced to share the credit with her.

Once the general modeling approach was formulated, Myers began her data collection. She assigned a clerk to record the amount of time the tellers took to service customers at the existing drive-in window. These observations were summarized, and Myers assigned random numbers to them, shown in Table 5.13, for use in later simulations.

To obtain a description of the customer arrival pattern, Myers assigned another clerk to record the time between arrivals at the existing drive-in. Both peak and off-peak periods were observed, and graphs were prepared showing the distributions of arrivals under both conditions (see Figs. 5.3 and 5.4).

Myers noted that the data patterns were similar from day to day. Thus, by using her knowledge of probability theory, she was able to construct a complicated simulation model to describe this process of arrivals and services.

Myers ran the simulation model for three design configurations (3, 4, and 6 bays) and for four representative arrival rates. For each run she tabulated the utilization percentage of the facility, the length of the maximum waiting line and the average waiting line, the average waiting time, and the number of cus-

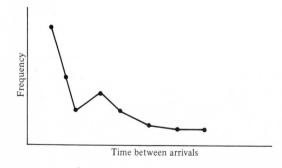

Figure 5.3 Arrival pattern (peak period).

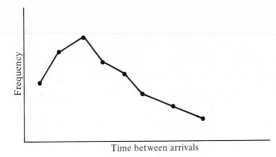

**Figure 5.4** Arrival pattern (off-peak period).

tomers unable to enter the facility. These results, as presented to Austin Kincaid, are shown in Table 5.14.

When she presented the results to Kincaid, she could tell they disturbed him. Kincaid had expected to have one specific answer he could send to the president. Instead, he was faced with a range of options. Although he had measures of effectiveness for each option, there was risk associated with the selection of any of them. Without having done any study, Kincaid could have pleaded ignorance in making a decision, but with the study in hand, he could be held accountable for an incorrect design decision.

Kincaid's initial response to the study was to delay making a decision. Finally, after several weeks of indecision, he received a curt memo from the presi-

**Table 5.14 Results of simulation runs**

| Daily Statistics | Peak–off-peak arrival rates | | | |
|---|---|---|---|---|
| | 120 customers/ hour–40 customers/hour | 90 customers/ hour–30 customers/hour | 80 customers/ hour–27 customers/hour | 60 customers/ hour–20 customers/hour |
| **Three Bays** | | | | |
| Percent utilization | 72 | 60 | 52 | 45 |
| Maximum queue | 12 | 12 | 12 | 7 |
| Average queue | 2.8 | 1.8 | 1.7 | 0.4 |
| Average wait time, min | 3.3 | 2.4 | 2.9 | 0.9 |
| Customers turned away | 44 | 24 | 9 | 0 |
| **Four bays** | | | | |
| Percent utilization | 59 | 48 | 46 | 34 |
| Maximum queue | 9 | 9 | 9 | 4 |
| Average queue | 1.7 | 0.7 | 0.7 | 0.1 |
| Average wait time, min | 1.9 | 0.9 | 1.1 | 0.2 |
| Customers turned away | 37 | 6 | 1 | 0 |
| **Six bays** | | | | |
| Percent utilization | 43 | 31 | 32 | 24 |
| Maximum queue | 5 | 3 | 4 | 2 |
| Average queue | 0.3 | 0.02 | 0.05 | 0.01 |
| Average wait time, min | 0.3 | 0.03 | 0.08 | 0.02 |
| Customers turned away | 1 | 0 | 0 | 0 |

dent reminding him of the urgency of the decision as to the number of bays. Architects had been retained and awaited instructions to begin their work. Kincaid faced a crisis; he wished that Myers had never done the study.

Kincaid decided to ignore the study entirely and adopt the full complement of six bays. He destroyed his copy of Myers's report as well as all correspondence concerning it, and he gambled that no one would remember that the study had been performed.

Myers began to suspect something was amiss, because Kincaid never asked for clarification of the model. She surreptitiously investigated to find out what had happened to her study.

In the meantime, Kincaid presented his recommendation to the president. When asked about the study that was to have been performed on the design options, Kincaid told the president that the effort "hadn't paid off." The president was unhappy with the unsupported nature of Kincaid's recommendation and decided to pursue the design decision on his own.

Myers, suspecting that Kincaid had not presented her study to the president, decided to force the issue. She sent a note to the president asking whether he thought it appropriate for her to present a talk on her drive-in facility model to an upcoming banker's meeting.

The president responded as Myers had hoped by immediately calling her about her question. He asked that Myers bring her report to his office. When the president saw the results of the study, he was impressed. The report gave him a clear picture of the options facing the bank.

The option of four bays appeared to be more than adequate for the expected customer load (80 per peak hour). Even if the load increased by 50 percent to 120 customers per peak hour, the facility still appeared adequate. The four-bay option would also permit the entrance to the facility to remain on the main highway. Guided by these considerations, the president decided to proceed with a four-bay design.

Once the decision was made, the president called Kincaid into his office and confronted him with the Myers study. Kincaid made an effort to discredit the work by attacking Myers. The more Kincaid explained his actions, the angrier the president became. The meeting ended abruptly as the president asked Kincaid to leave. The president then immediately dictated a termination letter to Kincaid.


## THE MORTGAGE LOAN DECISION

After Myers's successes with models became known, other vice presidents of the bank become interested in upgrading decision making in their functional areas. When Montgomery Ashton praised the work of Cindy Myers, there was a scramble for the services of the computer group. Horace Crabtree, vice president for consumer services, was among the first to seek out Myers for help with a decision that had been plaguing his operation.

Prospective home mortgages submitted to Sunset were evaluated and assigned a numerical risk index ranging from 1 to 60. In the past, any application with a risk index of 30 or higher was granted a loan; whereas indices of 29 or less led to rejection of the application. It cost the bank $200 to evaluate an application.

Because of the limited availability of mortgage money, the bank had considered raising its loan standards. Horace Crabtree was considering increasing the acceptable credit risk index to 35, but he was unsure what impact such a standard would have on the bank.

Money could be raised to satisfy the expected mortgage demand within the 30 to 35 risk index range, but the profitability of these loans would be small. Depending upon the default rate of the loans in the 30 to 35 category, the bank could lose money on them.

Although the bank generally recovered its loan for any default, it cost the bank an average of nearly $2000 in legal fees and short-term interest losses. On the other hand, the bank earned an average profit of approximately $4000 on any loan in the 30 to 35 risk category which was uneventfully repaid.

One option Crabtree was considering was the use of the more detailed financial analysis provided by a credit rating service for further screening of the applications with credit ratings in the 30 to 35 range. The service would cost $500 per application but Crabtree felt it might be a worthwhile investment, considering the speculative nature of the loans. Summarizing figures from applications at other banks, the Manhattan Group provided Sunset with their accuracy rates for loans in the range being reviewed by Sunset. These are shown in Table 5.15.

Myers modeled Crabtree's decision by use of a decision tree (see Fig. 5.5). Her model consisted of a tree upon which each decision option was a branch. Each branch, representing a possible outcome of the decision to be made, includes the probability (P) of that outcome. Expected costs for each outcome are then calculated so that options can be compared.

For each branch of the tree, Myers prepared a cost estimate. If the applications were rejected and the loan were to have been a good risk (branch A), the cost would have been $200 for the financial evaluation plus $4000 in lost income due to not making the loan.

For branch B, the cost would have been simply the charge for the financial evaluation itself ($200). No opportunity loss was assigned this branch since the loan would have been adjudged a bad risk.

## Table 5.15 Manhattan Group credit rating accuracy rates

| Manhattan Group rating | Actual risk | Percent |
|---|---|---|
| Good risk | Good | 54 |
| Good risk | Bad | 6 |
| Bad risk | Good | 4 |
| Bad risk | Bad | 36 |

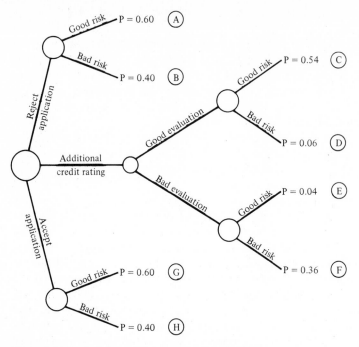

**Figure 5.5** The decision tree for mortgage loan decisions.

The cost of branch C was more complicated, since the additional credit survey was taken at a charge of $500. The only other charge was that for the financial evaluation.

The costs of the remaining branches were developed similarly as is shown below:

Branch D: Cost of financial evaluation + cost of credit survey + cost of lost investment = $200 + $500 + $2000 = $2700

Branch E: Cost of financial evaluation + cost of credit survey + cost of lost investment = $200 + $500 + $4000 = $4700

Branch F: Cost of financial evaluation + cost of credit survey = $200 + $500 = $700

Branch G: Cost of financial evaluation = $200

Branch H: Cost of financial evaluation + cost of lost investment = $200 + $2000 = $2200

The next step in the decision tree procedure was the determination of expected costs for each decision option. This step consisted of multiplying the cost of each branch by the probability of that branch. The expected costs of each branch corresponding to an option were then added to obtain the total expected cost of each decision option.

For the option of rejecting all applications with a risk index in the range of

30 to 35, the expected cost was found to be

$$\text{Expected cost of reject option} = 0.60(4200) + 0.40(200)$$
$$= \$2600$$

The expected cost of the other decision options were found in the same manner as shown below:

Expected cost of more information option

$$= 0.54(700) + 0.06(2700) + 0.04(4700) + 0.36(700)$$
$$= \$980$$

$$\text{Expected cost of accepted loan option} = 0.60(200) + 0.40(2200)$$
$$= \$1000$$

The interpretation of these expected costs requires some explanation. The expected cost of an option has little meaning when applied to a single loan application. However, if the expected cost is viewed as the anticipated average cost over a large number of similar applications, this is a reasonably accurate interpretation.

Based upon her analysis, Myers determined that the option of engaging the credit survey group was expected to be the best for the bank. However, the cost difference was so small ($980 versus $1000) that Myers decided to investigate the sensitivity of the decision to the assumed lost investment cost ($4000). As interest rates fluctuated, the amount of money that could be made on a typical home loan was expected to vary considerably. To analyze this sensitivity, all other assumed values were held constant.

By setting the expected cost of the "more information" option equal to the cost of the "accept loan" option, Myers could find the profit rate which would make the two options equally attractive. The calculation for identifying the break-even profit was as follows:

Expected cost of more information option

$$= \text{expected cost of accepted loan option}$$
$$0.54(700) + 0.06(2700) + 0.04(x + 700) + 0.36(700)$$
$$= 0.60(200) + 0.04(2200)$$
$$x = \$4500$$

Whenever the expected profit rate was greater than $4500, Sunset's best strategy was to accept loans in the 30 to 35 risk index range. A similar formulation established $1107 as the lower range for the profit rate at which loans in the 30 to 35 financial index range should be rejected outright.

Expected cost of more information option

$$= \text{expected cost of reject loan option}$$

$$0.54(700) + 0.06(2700) + 0.04(x + 700) + 0.36(700)$$

$$= 0.60(200 + x) + 80$$

$$x = \$1107$$

The results of the sensitivity analysis indicated that additional information on loan applicants in the 30 to 35 index range should be sought as long as the profit on a home mortgage was in the range between $1107 and $4500.

Her analysis completed, Myers prepared a report for presentation to Horace Crabtree. The report was received with great interest. Not only did it formulate the decision options in a concise fashion, it gave the bank an operating strategy. Since the Manhattan Group was to be hired on a loan-by-loan basis, the current profit rate could easily be evaluated before a specific credit rating was sought.

## DECISION TREE MODELS

Decision tree models have the same basic objectives as do Monte Carlo models: the reduction of uncertainty in decision making. The use of decision trees is motivated by having insufficient information about uncertainty to describe it by a probability distribution. The only information about uncertainty required in the decision tree model is a subjective estimate of the probability of certain events. The way this estimate is used in a decision tree is as follows:

1. List the decision alternatives for the decisions to be made.
2. For each of these alternatives, describe the likely events that may result from each of the alternatives. Assign probability estimates to each event.
3. Subsequent decisions arising from each alternative are outlined in the same way and given probability estimates.
4. The consequences of each sequence of alternatives is then evaluated according to the appropriate criteria.
5. The expected consequences of each of the first-stage decisions is then evaluated by weighting each consequence by probability estimates.

## THE PENSION PROGRAM

No sooner was the mortgage decision model completed than another vice president came to Myers to ask for her help. The successes of the modeling activities had become so well known throughout Sunset that different groups were seeking help from Myers as a matter of organizational face-saving. Myers's group was the hottest force to hit Sunset in some time. The bank had gone so long without giving analytical attention to decisions that Myers found the bank full of opportunities for success. Almost anything she did worked well and led to further requests for help.

Louis Baxter, vice president for institutions, had been given a problem concerning the pension program to solve for the state's board of regents. Tenured faculty at the state's universities and colleges were provided with a pension program based upon a percentage of their annual salary. The state legislature had become conscious of the finanical commitment it was making to the pension program and asked the board of regents to examine these obligations more closely.

The board of regents in turn asked the Sunset Bank to prepare the financial analysis of the program. Louis Baxter was perplexed and turned to Cindy Myers's group for help. Myers had become much more aware of her strategic position in the bank and was able to obtain an agreement that she would be the main contact with the board of regents. She saw this study as another chance to strengthen her position in the bank and hoped to move up in the bank organization by demonstrating an ability to deal effectively with one of the bank's larger clients. She began to collect background data for the study.

After several meetings with the board of regents administration staff, she had ascertained most of the important factors that she needed to model. The goal of the study was formulated: Develop a model which will show the pension fund commitments as a function of such key policy variables as annual salary increase, pension fund percentage, and staffing policies. The model was to apply only to those faculty members with a rank of assistant, associate, or full professor.

Myers collected past data on the existing staffing levels, salaries, pension fund rates, and hiring policies summarized in Table 5.16.

She also obtained data on the movement of the faculty from one rank to another rank or status from one year to the next as shown in Table 5.17.

One other piece of information needed was the enrollment estimate for the period to be studied. Since demographic data existed for the state's population, Myers decided to base her enrollment forecasts on the anticipated percentage change in the number of 18-year-olds in the population each year. The forecast was visualized as follows:

$$N_{t+1} = N_t P_{t+1} K$$

## Table 5.16 Background data for the pension fund model

| Faculty level | Average salary | Current staff | Percent new positions |
| --- | --- | --- | --- |
| Assistant | $16,280 | 2260 | 80* |
| Associate | $22,320 | 1340 | 12 |
| Full | $29,560 | 1290 | 8 |

*80 percent of all new faculty hired are assistant professors.

## Table 5.17 Transition rates for faculty positions

| Faculty level | Resign | Assistant | Associate | Full | Retire |
|---|---|---|---|---|---|
| Assistant | 0.10 | 0.83 | 0.05* | ...... | 0.02 |
| Associate | 0.08 | ...... | 0.84 | 0.03 | 0.05 |
| Full | 0.02 | ...... | ...... | 0.93 | 0.05 |

*5 percent of all assistant professors are promoted to associate each year.

where

$N_{t+1}$ = enrollment in year $t + 1$
$N_t$ = enrollment in year $t$
$P_{t+1}$ = percentage change in 18-year-olds from year $t$ to year $t + 1$
$K$ = empirical proportionality constant

Once the data were collected, Myers constructed a model that would fore-cast enrollment for each of the next twenty years, prepare staffing plans to meet projected needs, update salary levels and pension fund requirements for each year, and then accumulate the total requirements. A diagram of the model's logic is shown in Fig. 5.6. The flowchart of Fig. 5.6 was translated into a mathematical model.

The mathematical model of this case was a deterministic simulation which simply worked through a set of calculations according to a prescribed set of rules. The intent of the model was to measure as accurately as possible the likely out-come of applying a specific, predetermined set of input conditions to the system being modeled. A probabilistic simulation, such as that used earlier for the drive-in facility, works on the principle of generating system inputs from historical frequency distributions to determine the response of the system to various input conditions. The deterministic simulation also describes system outputs for a range of input conditions, but assumes no knowledge of distributions and no un-certain quantities. The probabilistic simulation yields a more generalized descrip-tion of the system but may require more historical data than are sometimes available.

As she had done before, Myers prepared a sample set of calculations by hand to illustrate the modeling procedure to Louis Baxter (Table 5.18). This study in-vestigates the year 1981. The percentage change in enrollment was the driving force in the model. Assuming a 1 percent drop in enrollment from 1980, the en-rollment in 1981 was projected to be 67,365 students. Assuming a faculty-to-student ratio of 1 to 15, the 1981 faculty needs were found to be 4491 positions. According to the historical pattern of transition rates for faculty (Table 5.17) the number of assistant professors available in 1981 was found to be 83 percent of those available in 1980 or 0.83 (2260) = 1876. Similarly the retention rate for as-sociate professors in 1981 was found to be 84 percent of the 1980 supply. How-ever, the number of assistant professors [0.05(2260)] promoted to associate were

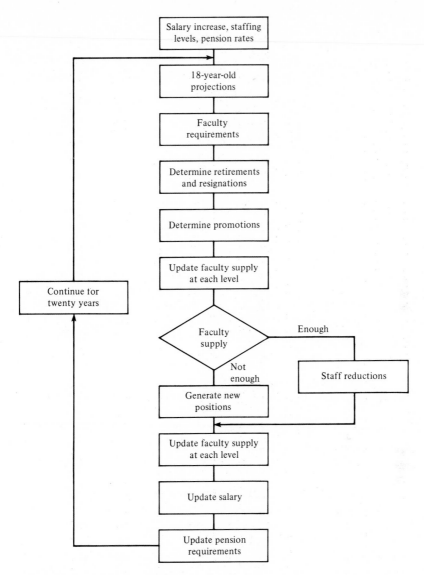

**Figure 5.6** Pension fund model logic.

also added to the 1981 figures, giving a total of 1659 associate professors. Full professors in 1981 were found in similar manner.

The total supply of 3860 faculty was found to be 631 short of the 4491 needed. Using the new position patterns of Table 5.17, the 631 positions were allocated as shown in Table 5.18. The total faculty in each category was then found and, by assuming a 7 percent annual rate of increase, total faculty salary payments were calculated. A 6 percent pension rate was then applied to the total salary payments

**Table 5.18 Sample pension fund model calculations**

| Year | Percent change in enrollment* | Total enrollment | Total faculty requirements† | Faculty supply | | | | New faculty require- ments | New positions | | | Total salary payments, in dollars‡ | Pension fund requirements, in dollars§ |
|---|---|---|---|---|---|---|---|---|---|---|---|---|---|
| | | | | Assistant | Associate | Full | Total | | Assistant | Associate | Full | | |
| 1981 | −1 | 67,365 | 4491 | 1876 | 1659 | 325 | 3860 | +631 | 505 | 76 | 375 | 94,773,165 | 5,686,390 |
| 1982 | −2 | 66,018 | 4401 | 1976 | 1576 | 401 | 3953 | +448 | 358 | 54 | 437 | 99,945,837 | 5,996,758 |
| 1983 | −2 | 64,698 | 4313 | 1937 | 1486 | 455 | 3878 | +435 | 348 | 52 | 490 | 105,369,454 | 6,322,167 |
| 1984 | −3 | 63,757 | 4183 | 1897 | 1406 | 501 | 3804 | +379 | 303 | 46 | 531 | 110,003,927 | 6,600,235 |
| 1985 | −2 | 61,502 | 4100 | 1826 | 1330 | 538 | 3694 | +406 | 325 | 49 | 570 | 115,916,589 | 6,954,995 |

*1980 enrollment = 68,045.
†Staffing level = 1 faculty member per 15 students.
‡Salary increase = 7 percent per year.
§Pension fund note = 6 percent of annual salary.

158

to derive the pension fund commitments. The computational process was then repeated for four years, assuming small enrollment decreases, to obtain the total pension fund commitment through 1985.

Myers presented her tentative model to the board of regents. The vice-chancellor for administration, Clyde Wacker, was very pleased with the simple description of the model and gave it his approval. However, his initial belief that the pension fund would increase at the same rate as salary increases appeared to be refuted. If student enrollment declined, the number of faculty positions would decline, resulting in smaller pension fund commitments. Wacker was also surprised by the gradual shift toward a higher percentage of full professor positions. Since the higher salaries were paid in these positions, Clyde was concerned both about the future salary budget and about eventual pension fund commitments.

Myers asked about the validity of the transition rate assumptions. It seemed to her that as national enrollments dropped, there would be a continually smaller percent of resignations. Criteria for promotion would undoubtedly tighten, resulting in a slower rate of promotion. Wacker agreed with her assessment and asked that the model be run under assumptions of different sets of transition rates.

Myers wrote a FORTRAN computer program to do the model computations. Several cases were run, assuming various staffing levels, salary increases, and pension fund rates in addition to a range of transition rates. The results effectively illustrated the interrelationship among the variables. Myers scheduled a special presentation to a group consisting of the board of regents, selected legislative leaders, and the governor's administrative assistant.

The presentation was well received. The administrative assistant to the governor was afterwards heard to remark to the senate president. "Those clowns at the board of regents have finally gotten their act together."

## DETERMINISTIC SIMULATION MODELS

Deterministic simulation models are the most general and perhaps the simplest of the models for resolving uncertainty. They also provide the least evaluation of the overall risk involved in the decision. The process of developing deterministic simulation models is as follows:

1. Develop a model of the system treating all consequences of events as certain.
2. Prepare scenarios of possible future events.
3. Execute the model for each scenario.

All relations in deterministic models are causal, i.e., output is a direct consequence of input. No attempt is made to model risk or uncertainty. However, by using a deterministic model to study a range of likely scenarios, a feeling for uncertainties can be gained.

The result of the deterministic simulation is not an evaluation of the expected consequences of different decisions, but rather an estimate of what would happen if these events occur. It is up to the decision maker to judge the relative likelihoods of the scenarios.

## A POSTSCRIPT

Several weeks later Cindy Myers met with the board of regents in a follow-up session. She was shocked when Clyde Walker abruptly offered her a job as the director of special projects. This position was a newly created administrative assignment that would allow her to be the chief administration problem solver of the board of regents in a wide variety of problem areas.

She told Montgomery Ashton about the offer to see whether the bank would offer a promotion and a raise if she would stay. Ashton, now realizing the value of Myers's talents, offered to make her his assistant administrator. This was the highest position ever offered to a woman at Sunset Bank. It also represented the fastest movement upward in the organization in the history of the bank. Myers was gratified by the offer but postponed a decision until she had considered the alternatives objectively.

## QUESTIONS

1 How effective were the past planning efforts at Sunset Bank?
2 What was the major issue facing Sunset Bank that prompted the planning study?
3 Why does the risk taker view high levels of information as of limited value?
4 What are the different ways of reducing uncertainty through the use of decision models?
5 What test can be used to tell when enough iterations have been conducted by a simulation model?
6 What are the steps involved in developing a Monte Carlo simulation model? Describe them.
7 How does the decision tree approach differ from that of a Monte Carlo simulation model? Which method should generally be more accurate?
8 How does the deterministic simulation model differ from the Monte Carlo simulation model?
9 Do risk evaluation models provide optimal solutions?

## EXERCISES

1 Evaluate three decisions that you have made that involved an evaluation of risks. For each of these comment on the following:
  (a) The amount of information available about the decision alternatives
  (b) Your ability to estimate either implicitly or explicitly the probabilities of various events affecting the decision
  (c) The differences in risk aversion attitudes you demonstrate in making a job-related decision versus making a personal decision
  (d) The confidence you would have in using a decision model in making each of the three decisions
2 Identify a decision maker that you know, and comment on the following:
  (a) Where the person is on the risk taker–risk avoider continuum
  (b) Whether the person seeks additional information from others in making decisions involving risk

3 Outline the approach taken to evaluating risks by the five decision maker coping patterns discussed in Chap. 1:
    (*a*) Unconflicted change             (*d*) Hypervigilance
    (*b*) Unconflicted adherence      (*e*) Vigilance
    (*c*) Defensive avoidance

4 A manager is noted for decision making ability. This individual always seems to be able to take an ambiguous situation and pull out of it the key factors in making a decision. When considerable uncertainty exists, the manager seems to always make the right decision. Colleagues feel that the manager has been very lucky but do not dispute that talent has led to promotions. How would such a manager likely view the use of a decision model in a critical decision involving considerable uncertainty?

5 How would you expect a risk avoider to react when making a decision to use a decision model? Would a risk avoider tend to view the model as an important aid in making decisions, or would such a person see the model as a rival in an area in which he or she feels uncomfortable?

6 A nursing schedule is to be prepared for a hospital. On any given day, the number of absences to be expected is as shown in Table 5.19.

**Table 5.19**

| Number of absent nurses | Probability |
|---|---|
| 0 | 0.10 |
| 1 | 0.40 |
| 2 | 0.20 |
| 3 | 0.20 |
| 4 | 0.05 |
| 5 | 0.05 |

A group of six nurses live in the area that can be called out in case of absences on the regular staff. The probability of a nurse being available when called is 0.20. A proposal has been made to pay some of these nurses to be on call. According to this proposal the nurses would receive $10 per day for on-call duty but would also guarantee the hospital that they will work when called.
    (*a*) Compare the existing system with the on-call proposal (assuming three on-call nurses out of a group of six). Simulate for ten days.
    (*b*) How many on-call nurses should the hospital hire? Simulate each alternative for ten days.

7 John Baxter would like to improve his decision making in using his new checking account. The account automatically transfers money from his savings account to his checking account whenever he overdraws his checking account. A $5 service charge is assessed every time a transfer is made and the bank automatically transfers $5 in excess of his overdraft. The bank pays an effective interest rate of 0.5 percent per month on savings on money that has been in savings for the entire month. Baxter has kept a record of his check amounts for each month as summarized in Table 5.20.

**Table 5.20**

| Check amount, $ | Relative frequency |
|---|---|
| 5 | 0.10 |
| 10 | 0.25 |
| 15 | 0.30 |
| 20 | 0.20 |
| 25 | 0.10 |
| 30 | 0.05 |

Checks for amounts greater than $30 can usually be planned for in advance and amounts are placed into checking just to cover them. The time between check cashing varies as shown in Table 5.21.

**Table 5.21**

| Days between checks | Relative frequency |
|---|---|
| 0 | 0.10 |
| 1 | 0.40 |
| 2 | 0.30 |
| 3 | 0.10 |
| 4 | 0.10 |

Occasionally Baxter receives checks which he deposits in checking. The monthly total of these checks varies as shown in Table 5.22.

**Table 5.22**

| Total check receipts, $ | Relative frequency |
|---|---|
| 0 | 0.60 |
| 50 | 0.30 |
| 100 | 0.10 |

Assume that the checks enter the bank on the tenth banking day and that there are twenty banking days per month.

   (a) Evaluate Baxter's policy of depositing $300 in checking and $200 in savings whenever the levels are low.

   (b) Evaluate an improved strategy of your own selection and show why it is better.

**8** A company has a quality control program which is designed to identify defective products before they are shipped. If the defective level is 10 percent, the company would like to be able to detect this condition at least 90 percent of the time. A sampling plan has been set up as follows:

   Take a sample of five items from a lot. If two or more defectives are found, reject the shipment. If one defective is found, take another sample of five items and reject the shipment if a defective is found. Otherwise, ship the lot.

   (a) If the defective level is actually 10 percent in a lot, will the sampling plan perform as intended?

   (b) Propose a sampling plan of your own and evaluate it.

**9** The U.S. Forest Service needs to make a decision on a budget request for a program to suppress forest fires. It is estimated that eighteen fires will occur during the main fire season in its national forests. The costs of suppressing fires are a function of time of day and day of the week, since the regular fire suppression forces are most easily available from 6 A.M. to 6 P.M. on weekdays. Overtime and other compensation is calculated on hours other than these. The estimated costs are shown in Table 5.23.

**Table 5.23**

| Time | Cost per fire |
|---|---|
| 12 P.M.– 6 A.M. | $10,000 |
| 6 A.M.–12 M. | $ 4,000 |
| 12 M.– 6 P.M. | $ 3,000 |
| 6 P.M.–12 P.M. | $ 8,000 |

In addition, costs are 1½ times those shown in the table if the fire occurs between 6 P.M. Friday and 6 A.M. Monday. Last year's budget has allowed only $100,000 for the fire fighting effort. According to the historical data in Tables 5.24 and 5.25, how much money should be budgeted? Assume the fire is put out in the time period generated (e.g., 12 P.M. to 6 A.M.).

**Table 5.24**

| Year | Number of fires per day | | | | | | | |
| | Mon | Tues | Wed | Thur | Fri | Sat | Sun | Total |
|------|-----|------|-----|------|-----|-----|-----|-------|
| 1974 | 4 | 3 | 2 | 6 | 4 | 12 | 6 | 37 |
| 1975 | 3 | 4 | 2 | 2 | 6 | 7 | 14 | 38 |
| 1976 | 3 | 3 | 2 | 3 | 6 | 3 | 12 | 32 |
| 1977 | 3 | 2 | 2 | 2 | 6 | 4 | 8 | 27 |
| Totals | 13 | 12 | 8 | 13 | 22 | 26 | 40 | 134 |

**Table 5.25**

| Year | Number of fires per time of day | | | | |
| | 12 P.M.–6 A.M. | 6 A.M.–12 M. | 12 M.–6 P.M. | 6 P.M.–12 P.M. | Total |
|------|---------------|--------------|--------------|----------------|-------|
| 1974 | 3 | 8 | 18 | 8 | 37 |
| 1975 | 2 | 8 | 18 | 10 | 38 |
| 1976 | 0 | 4 | 11 | 17 | 32 |
| 1977 | 0 | 2 | 21 | 4 | 27 |
| Totals | 5 | 22 | 68 | 39 | 134 |

**10** A personnel office has had trouble with long lines of applicants registering for employment. Forms are processed in two stages. When the forms at the first stage are complete, the forms are sent directly to the second stage. The director has proposed that a second clerk be added to the second stage while a single clerk remains at the first stage. Applicants arrive at the rate shown in Table 5.26.

**Table 5.26**

| Time between arrivals, min | Relative frequency |
|----------------------------|--------------------|
| 2 | 0.20 |
| 4 | 0.30 |
| 4 | 0.30 |
| 8 | 0.15 |
| 10 | 0.05 |

The processing times for the first and second stages are shown in Tables 5.27 and 5.28.

**Table 5.27  First stage**

| Processing times, min | Relative frequency |
|-----------------------|--------------------|
| 2 | 0.30 |
| 4 | 0.20 |
| 6 | 0.20 |
| 8 | 0.20 |
| 10 | 0.10 |

### Table 5.28 Second stage

| Processing times, min | Relative frequency |
|---|---|
| 4 | 0.30 |
| 6 | 0.30 |
| 8 | 0.20 |
| 10 | 0.20 |

(a) Investigate this proposed staffing plan. Determine the average waiting time per client.

(b) Make any suggestions you think will improve the system.

11 Kalkreuth Brothers, an industrial roofing contractor, is considering submitting a bid for a major roofing job. They estimate that the roof could be completed at a cost of $125,000 by using the conventional hot tar method. They believe that a new cold tar process could do the job at a cost of $96,000. However, the cold tar process has not been entirely proven and has only an 80 percent chance of success.

John Kalkreuth, Sr., president of the company, is considering two different bid packages: one for $150,000 and the other for $125,000. He feels that the $150,000 proposal has a 25 percent chance of acceptance while the $125,000 bid has a 60 percent chance. John Kalkreuth, Jr., has researched the cold tar process and estimates its chances of working to be 70 percent. If the cold tar process were used and did not work, hot tar would have to be used at an additional expense of $34,000.

    (a) Which bid should be submitted, and what process should be used?

    (b) John Kalkreuth, Jr., has been known to be a little careless with his figures. Over what range of probability estimates (of the cold tar process being successful) would the $125,000 bid be the most attractive?

12 The United States is faced with a need to expand its coal resources. Suppose the coal production capacity in 1980 is 200 million tons per year. This capacity consists of the mines shown in Table 5.29.

### Table 5.29

| Age of mine, years | Tonnage capacity |
|---|---|
| 0–5 | 80 |
| 5–10 | 50 |
| 10–15 | 50 |
| 15–20 | 20 |

Mines that have been open for up to five years can be expected to increase 10 percent in capacity by the five- to ten-year period while mines that are ten to fifteen years old will decrease in capacity by 30 percent by the fifteen- to twenty-year period. Mines are retired after twenty years in operation.

What will the country's mining capacity be in the year 2000 if the new mine capacity is increased by 10 percent during each five-year period?

13 Agony Airlines needs an improved method for making flight cancellation decisions during the winter months. If a forecast of bad weather is encountered, the airlines can cancel the flight as early as twelve months prior to scheduled departure or it can cancel later. The impact of cancellation is that some passengers schedule a replacement flight on Agony and some do not. The mix of these passengers is shown in Table 5.30.

**Table 5.30**

| Policy | Action taken | Percent of cancelled passengers who reschedule on Agony |
|---|---|---|
| Early cancellation | Cancel twelve hours prior to departure | 52 |
| Late cancellation | Cancel at flight time if necessary | 34 |

Agony has found from experience that 72 percent of the flights it cancels early would have to be canceled later if the decision is postponed. The average plane load is fifty-six passengers, and the average ticket price is $80 per passenger.

    (*a*) Which of the two policies, early or late cancellation, is the best?

    (*b*) What effect does the passenger load have on the decision?

**14** Evaluating risks involves an assessment of probabilities of different courses of action. Frequently, these probability estimates are very subjective. How can the impact of the probability estimates be measured?

**15** A gas station owner would like to make a decision about converting the station's pumps to self-service operations. What information must be collected to make such a decision?

**16** A restaurant manager would like to determine the best number of table servers to staff. Would a simulation model be an appropriate decision model for such a situation? What information would be needed for a simulation model in this case?

**17** The Amalgamated Building Trades Union (ABTU) has a policy of training its own artisans who are then certified to work on construction projects. The apprenticeship program lasts two years and passes through four phases. The percent of trainees that go from one phase to the next is shown below:

| | |
|---|---|
| Percent of trainees from phase 1 to phase 2 | 70 percent |
| Percent of trainees from phase 2 to phase 3 | 80 percent |
| Percent of trainees from phase 3 to phase 4 | 85 percent |
| Percent of trainees from phase 4 to certification | 95 percent |

Each year approximately 5 percent of the certified work force leaves the labor pool. The existing labor pool consists of 1200 craftspersons. Since the training program only accepts high school graduates, the ABTU is concerned about the number of trained workers it will be able to provide in the future as the number of 18-year-olds declines. The training program currently attracts 1 percent of the graduates within a 100-mile radius of the center. The total number of local high school graduates is 100,000 per year and is expected to decline by 5 percent per year. There are currently 900 phase 1, 650 phase 2, 500 phase 3, and 450 phase 4 trainees.

    Calculate the number of craftspersons and the number of trainees in each category for the next five years.

# CASELETS

1. Homewood Products, a producer of consumer goods, has just developed a new form of toothpaste that it believes has the potential for substantial sales to the "mature" segment of the market. Since the population is growing older, Homewood has begun to deemphasize the "social" aspects of its products and has begun to stress cost and health value. The new toothpaste (Regal) has been

test marketed within the Homewood organization and has received mixed, but generally favorable, reviews.

Homewood must now make the next major decision about Regal. The company could introduce the product into a test market—their normal procedure. To do this would postpone Regal's introduction to the national scene for at least two years. Homewood could shorten the test phase by using a special consumer panel. This step would give a less accurate indication of the product's potential but could lead to Regal's full scale introduction to markets in less than one-and-one-half years. A decision to place Regal on the market immediately would have the product distributed nationally within half a year. Any delay in introducing the product would lessen Regal's chance to achieve its full potential market share. If Regal is not successful, however, Homewood could lose substantially on unused stock and on lost opportunities.

(*a*) What are the sources of risk in this decision?
(*b*) How much information is known about the risk conditions?
(*c*) What are the likely adverse consequences of the various decision alternatives?
(*d*) What risk evaluation model would be best to use in this case?

2. A rural state had seen its highway deaths increase in recent years. A study of the problem revealed a major problem to be the long time required to move a victim from the accident site to a hospital. The roads in many parts of the state were just two-lane highways over difficult terrain. Janet Courson, the director of the state health department, has been interested in the possibility of using helicopters as medical ambulances since the Vietnam war and has been advocating that the state try this idea.

The state legislature has been approached to provide $5 million in funding to initiate the program. Sam Jurgenson, the chairman of the state health department, has been very cool to the proposal. During the past legislative season, Jurgenson tabled the budget request until Courson could support her proposal with an estimate of the lives saved by the airborne emergency system. Courson has asked her staff to make suggestions on how to convince the legislature of the proposal's merit.

(*a*) What are the sources of risk in this decision?
(*b*) How much information is known about the risk conditions?
(*c*) What are the likely adverse consequences of the various decision alternatives?
(*d*) What risk evaluation model should be used?

3. Clarkson Associates, a growing management consulting business, has decided to apply its management talents to its own future. George Clarkson, principal owner and president of the consulting firm, has decided to look at its future over the next twenty years. He has developed an outline of five investment options the company might adopt, including investments in expanding the business itself. While the business is growing and well respected, Clarkson is

afraid that with a larger staff Clarkson Associates may saturate the market. Clarkson has discussed this problem with his officers and has asked them to help develop an analytical procedure for studying the investment decision.

(*a*) What are the sources of risk in this decision?
(*b*) How much information is known about the risk conditions?
(*c*) What are the likely adverse consequences of the various decision alternatives?
(*d*) What risk evaluation model should be used?

## CASE 5.1: WESCON CONCRETE COMPANY

### Background

Western Concrete Company (Wescon) was one of the world's largest producers of concrete and brick products. With plants throughout the United States, Wescon was able to dominate the market for brick and other formed concrete products. Its R&D effort was noted for excellence throughout the industry.

As the market began a shift to unformed products, Wescon began to experience difficulties. Unformed materials were generally produced in a loose, granular form that was either bagged or placed in a drum. The difficulty in marketing the unformed line of products was that the type of customer and the market for this line were both new to Wescon. While the consumers of Wescon's formed materials were often willing to wait three months for an order, the customers for unformed materials behaved much differently. The unformed materials required little special equipment, and, as a result, a great number of small businesses existed to supply regional needs. The long lead time (ten weeks) typical of Wescon's operations was causing a decline in its market share of the formed product market also.

Kovach and Turner, a pair of consultants, had worked with the corporate staff of Wescon on several projects addressing the operations of company plants. As a result of one project, the consultants recommended that Wescon buy a storage shed for its unformed finished products at its Notluf plant. By doing this, Wescon could develop inventories of its high-volume unformed products. Its sales representatives could then promise next-day delivery on the more popular brands. The shed was estimated to cost $250,000.

The president of the company, an opponent of high inventory charges, vetoed the shed but did agree to let the plant stack its formed products outdoors. The plant manager decided to use the employees' parking lot for the outside storage, thus freeing space for storing 5000 tons of unformed product within the plant. The manager hoped that the resulting inconvenience to corporate offices in parking their cars would prompt them to view a storage shed with greater favor.

Tom Rush, director of plant operations at the eastern corporate office, supported the plant manager on this issue, but he realized that an appropriations request for such a facility would receive the president's blessing only if a strong justification could be found for it. He turned to the consultants Jim Kovach and Roger Turner for help since their original recommendations had been responsible for the inventory policy at Notluf.

## Developing a Justification Strategy

The consultants met with Rush to outline a justification for the storage facility. Rush described the president as being very cautious in agreeing to any new building proposals, although receptive to the new inventory policy. The president supported the latter because the availability of ready-to-ship stocks was having a positive impact on the sales of unformed products.

Rush, knowing the president's decision style, felt that the only way a new building could be justified was if the existing storage space could be shown to be insufficient. Rush asked the consultants to do a study to determine whether 5000 tons of storage space for unformed products was sufficient.

From prior experience with Rush, the consultants knew that he wanted a serious study of the inventory needs. Although Rush personally wanted the new warehouse, he was also a conscientious executive who did not play games with the president's office. If the new facility were not justified, Rush would accept that conclusion.

## Reviewing the Existing Inventory Policies

Before the consultants began the development of a decision model, they met with Dick Leggett, director of materials management, to gain an understanding of the inventory control policies that were in force at Wescon. Leggett had devised a MAX/MIN policy for Wescon. Whenever the inventory level for a product dropped to the MIN level, an inventory order was initiated for enough stock to bring the level up to the MAX point. The MIN level was set at a value equal to one month's peak demand. The MAX level was set at three months' peak demand. By using peak demands to determine his MIN levels, Leggett was in effect maintaining safety stocks of products.

The inventory policies were applied to the top twenty-one products, and Leggett, a meticulous individual, had complete records of past demand for each product. Demand data was recorded at biweekly intervals. Each individual order in each time period had even been recorded.

## The Decision Model

In this case, a decision model has to answer the following questions:

1. Are proposed MAX/MIN levels adequate?
2. Will total inventory that needs to be in storage each month exceed the 5000-ton storage capacity?

The consultants decided to use a probabilistic stimulation as a model. This approach would allow for a test of various MAX/MIN policies for each product but would at the same time show the combined effects of all MAX/MIN levels. The probabilistic approach was also selected because sufficient data existed to generate the demand experience such a model would require.

The model performed the following operations for each month of simulated experience:

1. Demands for each product were generated from the previous year's demand experience.
2. The inventory level was checked for each product to see whether its MIN level had been reached.
3. Where necessary, production was initiated to bring inventory up to the MAX level.
4. The total inventory level of all products before and after the production of additional stock was determined.

## Use of the Decision Model

The model was run for several cases which reflected different operating conditions and assumptions.

Case A—The original MAX/MIN levels were investigated, assuming demands to be at historical levels.

Case B—The MAX/MIN levels were revised so that no product would be out of stock more than 5 percent of the reorder periods.

Case C—The inventory policy was applied only to the top ten products. The revised inventory levels from case B were used.

Case D—Demands were increased by 30 percent. The revised inventory levels from case B were used.

The results of the simulation runs for each case are shown in Table 5.31.

The most striking result of the simulation runs was that the average inventory level reached capacity in only case D. The MAX/MIN levels generally applied reasonable controls. Three products had out-of-stock conditions that were outside acceptable limits, while four products reached inventory levels which were higher than desired. Case B resolved these slight discrepancies with little expansion of the total inventory level. Case C, originally thought necessary to meet the capacity limit, turned out to be of little interest. If the demand were to increase by 30 percent, Case D indicated that the in-plant storage would still be sufficient, although tight.

## Table 5.31 Case Summary

|  | A | B | C | D |
|---|---|---|---|---|
| Average inventory level, tons | 3,643 | 3,880 | 2,489 | 5,043 |
| Percent of times inventory exceeds 4000 tons | 12 | 34 | 0 | 100 |
| Percent of times inventory exceeds 4500 tons | 0 | 1 | 0 | 97 |
| Average inventory investment | $468,231 | $514,288 | $368,829 | $668,574 |
| Average production, tons | 1,568 | 1,567 | 1,154 | 2,037 |
| Average demand, tons | 1,570 | 1,569 | 1,157 | 2,041 |

## Discussion of the Results

The consultants met with Tom Rush and Dick Leggett to present their results. Rush, as expected, was disappointed. He had looked forward to establishing a warehouse precedent and thought this situation offered an excellent opportunity. Although Rush was willing to go along with the results of the model, he spent considerable time reviewing the simulation procedure, hoping to find a flaw. Unable to challenge the model successfully, Rush seemed resigned to accepting the results of the study.

While Rush was unhappy, Leggett was impressed. The model confirmed that his operating policies were sound. Following the meeting, Leggett asked the consultants to help with an inventory updating problem he had been facing for months.

The president of the company was also impressed. The consultants' project had confirmed the president's own beliefs about the lack of need for a warehouse. This was one of the few cases in his memory that a definitive study had been done at Wescon on the effectiveness of a capital expenditure. The president planned to ask for similar studies on all future appropriation requests.


## CASE 5.2: THE CITY OF FLATTS

### Introduction

The city of Flatts constructed a primary sewage treatment plant in 1965. The plant, designed for a population of 60,000, was capable of removing 61 percent of the suspended solids and 34 percent of the biochemical oxygen demand (BOD). However, this degree of treatment no longer met the effluent standards ordered by the state department of health, requiring 85 percent BOD removal. In addition, the federal Environmental Protection Agency (EPA) requirements of secondary treatment included a requirement for control of BOD and suspended solids that the system could not meet.

In light of these stricter standards, the Flatts Sanitary Board asked a consultant to prepare an analysis of available secondary treatment alternatives. A "bio-surfs" plan was recommended with a total estimated project cost of $3,722,725. Of this amount, $2,680,725 was estimated to be available from federal funds administered by the EPA under Public Law 660.

The additional annual operating costs incurred by this plan were estimated to be $44,300. When bond indebtedness was taken into account, the annual revenue required to run the secondary plant was estimated to be $144,797. This revenue would have to be obtained by levying a 26 percent increase in sewer rates.


### City Council Action

The sanitary board presented the findings of the consultant to the city council and asked for approval to initiate the develcpment of a secondary sewage treatment plant. The city council was split into three factions over the question. Strong opposition was led by Jake Ling, the longest-tenured member of the council. Jake

Ling was noted for his opposition to almost any spending proposal and for his incessant bickering with public officials who did not meet his approval.

He was particularly incensed by this proposal since many of his constituents were living on limited, fixed incomes. Jake Ling began his opposition to the sanitary board's proposal by lecturing the council: "We have a proposal before us which is of the most nefarious nature. We are being told a blatant lie by this group of so-called public servants. How can they expect us to believe that we are required by law to build a secondary treatment plant when our neighbors down the river from us don't even have a primary facility? Clearly, we are not being told the truth when they claim that state law requires such a facility. I ask my fellow council members to consider the effect of a 26 percent increase in sewer rates on their constituents' budgets. Many of our residents are hard pressed to meet their expenses now. This rate increase would drive them into bankruptcy."

Jake Ling's not-so-friendly antagonist, Louella Miller, representing the city's most affluent ward, responded with equal vehemence: "We've just witnessed some more of Jake Ling's hysterics. He wouldn't admit that we needed sewage treatment even if his own children were dying from the filth that is dumped into our river. Is it too much to ask that we return our river to the condition that we found it? If we don't start cleaning up our environment, we may pass the point of no return. We've all heard about Lake Erie's problems and the mess that the Cuyahoga and Hudson rivers are in. Surely, no one wants a situation like that here."

The third faction of the council, representing a majority of the membership was less dogmatic in its reactions to the secondary treatment plant proposal. These members wanted more information before making a decision.

The mayor, in response to the controversy, proposed that a subcommittee of the council be established to gather additional data before the council was asked to make a definite decision. He said: "I am going to ask an ad hoc committee to look into this problem for us. If we need to hire professional help in this matter, I think the severity of the problem warrants expenditure of funds for some technical advice."

With approval from the council for this action (over Jake Ling's opposition), the mayor established a subcommittee of council members from the uncommited majority to delve further into the issue. At the same time, the mayor met with a sanitary engineering consultant to solicit his technical support. The sanitary engineer, Bill Poke, was president of a small consulting firm dealing with pollution studies. Three of his staff were to be included in the study. Don C. Corsi, a part-time employee and operations research analyst, was asked to see what could be done to help in this decision making situation. At the same time, Poke asked a recent civil engineering graduate, Julie Wheeler, to help with the project. A third member of the team was Sam Poke, Bill Poke's son and a public administration graduate.

## The Decision Model Development

After its preliminary study of the situation, the project team began the development of a model for the analysis of alternatives. Don Corsi was given the task of developing a usable decision process.

His proposed analytical device was a decision tree. As Corsi explained the situation: "We have a series of alternatives which must be evaluated. However, the performance of each of these alternatives depends upon what the future population of the area might be. If the area doesn't grow, a decision to delay secondary treatment may be best. However, increasing growth may suggest the building of the plant now. A decision tree is useful in cases like this. I have outlined what this approach looks like on this sheet of paper (Fig. 5.7).

"Initially, there are three options—build now, delay, or make a commitment of funds. Depending upon the growth rate of the community, the effectiveness of the decision will be evaluated on the basis of its cost and the degree of environmental protection provided. I've labeled these $V_1$, $V_2$, $V_3$, etc."

"Wait a minute," interrupted Sam Poke. "You're not saying that we're going to put a dollar amount on pollution levels so that we can add this to the plant costs to get your $V$ values?"

"Not necessarily," answered Corsi. "However, we do need to put the two values on some equal basis."

"How are we going to do that?" asked Poke.

"As I see it, we can develop a numerical index for the pollution level. At the same time we could set up a similar index for the costs and then combine the two index values to get our values for $V$."

"Don, isn't something like that procedure used by highway departments when they evaluate different highway locations?" asked Julie Wheeler.

"I'm not sure," responded Don, "but I've seen reports of different cases where such indices have been used."

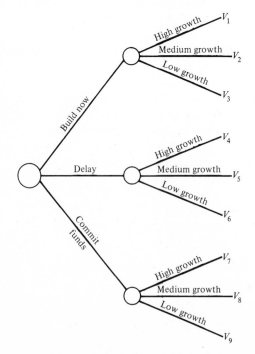

**Figure 5.7** Decision tree outline.

"I'm not so sure that the index values will be very meaningful," commented Poke. "I've another question: What weight do we give cost as opposed to pollution?"

"We'll have to study that problem," replied Corsi. "I would imagine that we'll have to conduct a survey of citizen opinions. Sam, do any of your survey research friends have procedures for doing something like this?"

"I believe that I could develop some sort of questionnaire to see what public attitudes are on this matter," replied Sam Poke.

"If I were to develop the decision model, Julie, could you develop a pollution index for BOD and suspended solids which we could combine with our cost index and Sam's weighting factors?"

"I think so, Don, but I'm a little confused. What does this procedure tell us once we have the $V$ values?"

"I forgot to go into that," replied Corsi. "Once the $V$'s are determined we'll take the probability of high, medium, and low growth and from these determine which decision option gives the minimum expected value for the pollution-cost index."

"I hate to be such a pessimist," interrupted Poke, "but how are you going to measure the *probability* of high, medium, and low growth?"

"Actually, I thought you could help us on that, Sam. Doesn't the county development authority have that kind of information?"

"I'm sure that some kind of information exists," responded Poke. "But I'm not sure how precise it is. I imagine that any probability estimates will be very hard to come by."

"I realize that," said Corsi. "We'll try to conduct a sensitivity analysis of the probability estimates. That way we'll have some idea of the relative importance of the probability estimates. What do you two think? Should we approach the project this way?"

"Your approach sounds find to me," responded Wheeler.

"I still have my doubts about all the hocus-pocus that we seem to be doing," replied Sam Poke. "However, any approach to this problem seems to be plagued with a lot of uncertainty. I guess this method is as good as any."

Having agreed to the approach, the three team members began their phases of the study.

## Development of the Cost-Pollution Indices

Don Corsi and Julie Wheeler began their work by trying to develop an index for pollution levels. After extensive discussion, they decided that a scale of 0 to 5 should be used. Separate scales were set up for BOD removal, suspended solids, and costs. The relative scale values for each decision option were then determined. For example, the do-nothing option was eveluted as

$$\text{BOD index} = 4.2$$

$$\text{Suspended solids index} = 4.6$$

$$\text{Cost index} = 0.5$$

for a future of high growth in the community.

Sam Poke's responsibilities were to arrive at relative weighting factors for cost versus pollution considerations. The intent of this phase of the study was to develop some method of combining the cost and pollution indices into a single weighted index. Poke prepared a questionnaire which was to be circulated to a sample of citizens from Flatts and the surrounding county. The survey was conducted for 200 families selected from the telephone directory.

## Development of Probability Estimates of the Community's Growth

Poke's efforts were aimed at estimating growth probabilities for the community. To accomplish this task, he met with Cindy Warman, head of the county development authority. After explaining the purpose of the study, Poke asked if the county development authority had made growth estimates; no estimates were available. Having anticipated this problem, Poke asked Warman if she would participate in a survey of community leaders to help estimate the growth probabilities; she agreed.

After five interviews, Poke made estimates of the growth probabilities as shown in Table 5.32. After this phase of the work, Poke reported back to the group.

## Completion of the Decision Model

The team was now ready to put the information into the decision model. Originally, the model was formulated as a single-stage model. However, the team decided upon a two-stage model and chose a set of decisions substantially as shown in Fig. 5.8. The second stage was designed to explore the consequences of delaying the project. At a later date, pollution problems, court rulings, or legislation might require the building of the plant. In a similar fashion, a formal commitment might be reviewed later if the level of pollution did not seem to warrant the building of the plant.

The values for $V$ were then calculated for each decision option, and using the growth probability estimates, the expected effectiveness of each option was found. The second-stage probabilities associated with whether a treatment plant would be required were developed by Julie Wheeler.

The outcome of the decision tree analysis showed the measure-of-effectiveness (MOE) for each alternative to be as shown in Table 5.33.

Since the lowest MOE value was the best, the "build now" alternative appeared to be the most attractive. However, due to the amount of subjectivity in the decision process, the team decided to perform a sensitivity analysis. The

**Table 5.32 Growth rate probabilities**

| Alternative | High | Medium | Low |
|---|---|---|---|
| Build | 0.5 | 0.4 | 0.1 |
| Delay | 0.3 | 0.5 | 0.2 |
| Formal commitment | 0.35 | 0.55 | 0.1 |

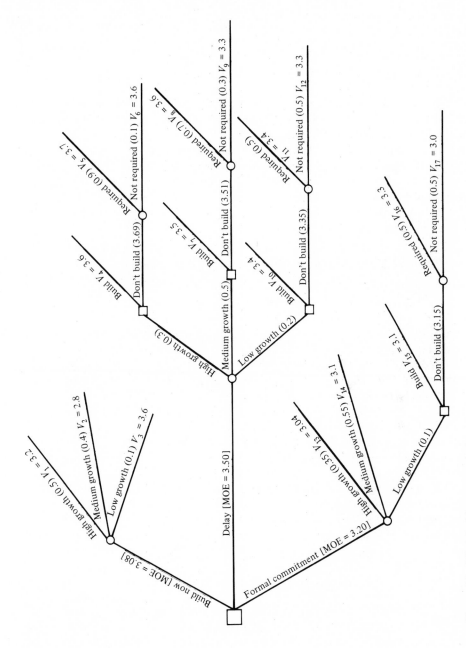

**Figure 5.8** Final decision tree analysis.

**Table 5.3. Evaluation of the alternatives**

| Alternative | Measure-of-effectiveness value |
|---|---|
| Build now | 3.08 |
| Delay | 3.50 |
| Formal commitment | 3.20 |

probability estimates were examined to see what influence these might have on the eventual decision. For a reasonable range of growth rate probabilities, the "build now" alternative still remained the most attractive. The analysis, however, was sensitive to the $V$ values used. Small alterations in these values made the "build now" and "formal commitment" alternatives appear comparable. However, since the most reasonable $V$ values favored the build now alternative, the group decided to recommend the "build now" alternative. The project team began the preparation of their report and arranged a meeting with the subcommittee to present it.

## The Political Environment of the Secondary Sewage Plant Decision

While the study was being conducted, the issue of the secondary treatment plant had become more and more heated. Louella Miller released to city council a letter advocating strict pollution control that she had received from the state department of natural resources. Jake Ling was irate at the tone of the letter and voiced his disapproval of the state's interfering in local matters. He was incensed at Louella Miller for her actions in bringing the issue before the state. By implication, Jake Ling charged Louella Miller with the responsibility for any legal action which the state took against the city.

During the debate, George Pulice, the head of the Concerned Taxpayers of Mountaineer County, added fire to the debate by contending that the sanitary board had exceeded its authority in hiring consultants at all. He charged the committee with trying to gain the approval for a secondary plant without consent of the council.

The debate raged for weeks, resulting in extreme polarization of council opinions. Frequent shouting matches highlighted council sessions. In many cases, the debate had ignored relevant issues and had evolved into attacks on personalities. Consequently, many council members had fixed viewpoints rooted in superfluous arguments.

## Presentation of the Study Results

The project group met with the subcommittee and presented their report. They described their procedures in general terms and explained the reasoning behind their recommendation to begin building the secondary treatment plant. The subcommittee quickly decided that the team should make a report to the entire council. On such an emotional issue, the subcommittee was unwilling to go on record as supporting or rejecting the recommendation. A meeting of the group and city council was arranged, and copies of the report were distributed to the remaining members of the council.

The group met with the city council in special session. Don Corsi was in charge of the presentation. Although he made a concerted effort to reduce the amount of technical detail to a simple level, it became apparent that most members on the council failed to comprehend the procedure being used. There was a vague understanding concerning the $V$ values, but the technique used to find them was not understood. When Corsi presented the group's recommendation, the opposing factions on the council quickly began their heated debate.

Louella Miller began by stating: "Here we have the latest in a long series of valid points in favor of the secondary treatment. Economic, legal, and environmental considerations all point to the necessity of building the plant now. I believe that these experts have provided us with a valuable service in putting this issue into proper prespective."

Jack Ling responded in a very irritated fashion, "All that I've seen tonight is a lot of mathematical garbage that I'm sure none of us understands. You can talk all you want to about $V$'s and probabilities, but that doesn't pay for sewer bills. Try to explain this stuff to people who have had their sewer bills doubled."

Sam Poke tried to explain their study further by stating: "Mr. Ling, we varied the probabilities and we found the same result. We also took into account the increase in sewer rates. If you delay the plant construction, the city will be paying 12 to 15 percent more each year for it. There's no doubt that you will have to have a plant in a few more years. The law will require it."

"I don't care what you so-called experts say. You don't pay sewer bills. No state or federal government is going to force us to go bankrupt to pay for a sewage treatment plant. It's time we took a stand on the increasing centralization of government."

The debate at this point turned more acrimonious than any that the council had experienced in years. Lost in the name calling, the shouting, and the threats of political retaliation was the project report. It appeared that no council member understood the report well enough to use it in either a positive or negative manner in the debate.

The debate finally ran its course and a motion was presented by Jake Ling to restrict the sanitary board from any further efforts with regard to a secondary sewage treatment plant. The vote of 7 to 5 in favor of the motion effectively terminated the city's participation in a regional solid waste program. The project team was given a brief note of thanks from some of the members of the council, but it was clear that their report had had little impact on the decision.

## Postscript

Following the council decision, the name-calling and bitterness continued. The seven dissenting council members were sued by a local environmental group. Communities surrounding Flatts saw the hopes of their participation in a regional solid waste program dwindle and were faced with the difficult decision of how to provide for sewage treatment.

The city was also sued by the EPA in what was expected to be a landmark decision on separation of rights in governmental disputes.

## Discussion Guide

1 Do you believe that the general approach used was satisfactory? If not, what approach should have been used?

2 Where does the failure to implement the study lie? With the city council? With the study itself? With other factors?

3 What improvements could have been made to have achieved a better implementation of the study?

4 Comment on the approach taken with regard to the decision model. Could improvements have been made?

5 Do you feel that the questionnaire gave accurate results?

6 Comment on the role decision models should take in such controversial political issues.

## RESOURCE ALLOCATION DECISIONS

## SYNOPSIS OF THE CHAPTER

The most common general problem in organizations is that of allocating scarce resources to competing activities. This chapter develops the application of a common technique, linear programming, to this problem.

Linear programming (LP) is a popular modeling tool because it can be used to study a large number of diverse problems reliably. It has been used to study very large problems and has been credited with saving many organizations huge sums of money. Linear programming is equally valuable to profit and nonprofit concerns and ranks with simulation and regression analysis as one of the most popular quantitative models in decision analysis.

This chapter presents many of the ideas associated with LP which are of paramount interest to management. Such ideas include how to interpret the economic trade-offs that allocations of resources imply and how to evaluate the effects of uncertain conditions.

As is the case in each chapter of this book, the vagaries of data and the influence of nonquantitative realities upon model implementation are emphasized.

The technical note contains a variety of modeling situations and demonstrates models which fit those situations. Students should be able to obtain some feeling for LP modeling from these examples.

## MAJOR CONCEPTS PRESENTED IN THIS CHAPTER

1. Resource allocation is a major organizational concern, since the control of resource allocation decisions is a major source of managerial power.

2. Linear programming models view resource allocation decisions as a process of optimizing an objective subject to a series of constraints.
3. Resource allocation decisions in many cases involve multiple objectives which must be balanced to achieve an acceptable solution.
4. The impact of constraint limits on the achievement of an objective can be measured through the use of shadow prices.
5. The number of alternatives receiving allocations is limited by the number of constraints placed on the decision.

## EXPECTATIONS OF THE STUDENT

The student, after studying this chapter, should be able to do the following:

1. Describe the factors that would influence a manager's use of a decision model to allocate resources
2. Formulate simple decision situations as linear programming models
3. Solve simple linear programming models using the graphical method
4. Use a computer package to solve linear programming models
5. Interpret the results, including shadow prices, from a linear programming model

## MARLINTON METALS

Marlinton Metals (MM), a small metal business, was the largest employer in a predominantly rural county. Its competitive advantage was a cheap, dependable source of labor. Since it was also the major industry in Hiawatha County, it enjoyed an absence of environmental pressures.

The president of MM, Harry N. Kline, was a blacksmith by trade, but in fifty years of business he had seen his business diversify into production of several dissimilar products. Harry was also a member of the state legislature and used his political contacts to improve his business prospects. A contract for boiler tubing was awarded to MM shortly after Harry had obtained an air pollution variance from the state air pollution control commission. Rumors throughout the state told of Harry buying this deal, but there was no evidence, only hearsay. Distracted by his legislature and marketing activities, Harry turned over the day-to-day operations of MM to Jim Johnson, his plant manager.

Jim Johnson had been hired by MM from the automobile industry two years earlier. He was originally from Hiawatha County and had welcomed the chance to return home. In order to entice Jim to MM, Harold Kline had offered Jim a profit sharing plan including a 1 percent share of the company's profits, and Jim Johnson had accepted after convincing the president that the 1 percent share should be based on operating profits alone.

Operating profits in this case consisted of sales revenues minus costs of labor, raw materials, and electricity. Since overhead costs were out of Jim's control, he managed to convince Harold Kline that his profit share should not be reduced by these costs.

Promised a base salary of $20,000 and a 1 percent share of the approximately $1.2 million profits per year, Jim Johnson took the job. At the end of his first two years as plant manager, Jim asked for a meeting with Harold Kline to discuss a raise in salary. The president was disturbed by the request and indicated to Jim that any salary increase would have to be derived from improved profits. He angrily told Jim to do something about MM's inadequate profit margin.

Irritated by the president's attitude, but still rational, Johnson called upon two local consultants, Sam Webster and Ed Barnes, to see whether they could suggest means of increasing profits.

After a thorough review of procedures at the plant, Webster and Barnes were convinced that operating costs were reasonably well controlled, but that product mix was not. The simple fact was that MM was not producing its most profitable product line. They discussed with Johnson the profit opportunities at MM and suggested a method of studying the plant to discover the optimum line of attack.

Johnson thought about their proposal for some time. Although Johnson was primarily concerned with improved profits (especially his), he realized that several other issues were involved. Would the use of a mathematical model to allocate plant resources result in his relinquishing authority? How would his staff react to such an approach?

## ISSUES INVOLVED IN ALLOCATING RESOURCES

A major decision faced by any administrator is how to allocate scarce resources such as workforce, capital, raw materials, energy, and machine capacities. Intuition is characteristically the main guide in making such decisions, and, when in doubt, the loudest "squeaking wheels" are greased the most. Resource allocation is a major area of organizational politics because control over resource allocation is a major exercise of power which can be directed toward gaining strategic advantages inside the organization. Why, then, would a Jim Johnson turn over such an important political tool to the caprices of a decision model? While there may be no general answer to this question, decision models are used in resource allocation for several reasons.

Large organizations may make resource allocation decisions involving thousands of variables. Canadian Forest Products, Ltd., a producer of wood products, must decide on the grades of lumber to use, the veneer thicknesses to peel, the veneer preparation options, the plywood manufacturing options, and the markets to concentrate on. The possible combinations create up to 50 million decision options. The decision task is so *complex* that it requires mechanized assistance. In such a case an administrator may have little choice but to sacrifice some authority in order to solve a difficult problem.

Similarly, the *time* required to make a decision may prompt an administrator to relinquish some of this authority. For example, a coil slitting decision at the Hawthorne works of the Western Electric Company required hours to make when the decision was made without any analytical support. A decision model reduced this time to less than ten minutes. Since each shift's production depended upon the coil slitting decision, the increased production implied by a reduction in decision time was a major inducement to the use of a decision model.

The potential organizational benefit of a decision model may outweigh any advantages administrators may feel they have in making the decision intuitively. If administrators can show a substantial improvement in decision performance by using a model, they may make more of an impression on the organizational hierarchy than they could by stubbornly exercising their resource allocation authority. National Airlines has been able to save several million dollars in fuel costs by its use of a decision model for fuel management, while fuel costs at other airlines have increased. In such a case, the need for cost improvement leads management to favor the use of a model.

A decision model may also be used to support administrators' personal preferences for a particular policy direction. In the Citron Company example of Chap. 1, the marketing director felt that a reduction in the number of brands was necessary to increase profits. He used a decision model to demonstrate his beliefs about this marketing policy decision. This shows how decision models may be used to *support personal viewpoints* when such support is needed to effect a specific resource allocation policy.

Decision models can also be valuable in *training*. Administrators may be willing to relinquish part of their control to a model but insist that they remain the final authority in the decision. An effective compromise may be the use of a model to augment the human decision process. In this case, the function of the model would be to provide administrators with the insight they otherwise would have lacked.

Finally, administrators may wish to employ an objective, dispassionate decision model to *avoid complaints of subjectivity*. Decision models have been developed to allocate football seating, parking spaces, and places in medical schools and to reapportion political districts. In each case, a model was used primarily for its *objective value* in removing bias, replacing faulty intuition, and avoiding litigation.

In the case of MM, Jim Johnson decided that the profit potential was a sufficient inducement for him to relinquish part of his resource allocation authority to an analytical model. In reality, product mix decisions did not represent a large power source to him, and he felt that a model could do much of the work involved in this time-consuming and often complicated decision. He contracted Webster and Barnes to proceed with the study of MM's product mix, but in their contract he stipulated that two conditions must be met:

1. The consultants had to explain whatever model they chose in a simplified fashion that Johnson could understand. (Johnson felt this condition to be very important, since he eventually had to sell the model to Harold Kline.)
2. The consultants were also instructed to develop a model that would give Johnson some options to pursue rather than giving him a single "optimal"

results. Flexibility was to be built into the model to explore ranges of conditions.

# CONCEPTS OF RESOURCE ALLOCATION MODELING

When managers turn to an analytical model to help them in decision making, they are looking for some method of quantifying their choices. They would like to have a procedure which can compare alternative choices and rank them. The procedure should automatically consider any conditions that must be met as a part of the evaluation of alternatives. These concepts must guide the modeler's efforts.

The first step in developing an analytical model is determining the controllable and noncontrollable variables. In the Marlinton Metal case, Jim Johnson had control over how many units of each type of product should be manufactured; so the number of units was controllable. The raw materials required to make one unit of product is generally a noncontrollable variable. While raw material requirements may be controllable from a design or manufacturing viewpoint, they represent fixed inputs per unit and cannot be changed capriciously. Controllable variables represent possible decisions, while noncontrollable quantities describe the process being modeled.

Once the nature of the variables is known, the next step in the modeling effort is to determine the objectives to be satisfied. While the usual objectives are maximizing profits or minimizing costs, these are occasionally overruled by other less apparent objectives. For instance, take the case of Harold Kline, who was a politician and businessman. His political career would be hurt if his plant suddenly fired half of its workforce; so he would not make such a move, even if it might increase plant profits.

A model must be capable of looking at both explicit and implicit objectives. In many cases, implicit objectives are the keys to implementing the solution; so the model must be flexible enough to deal with quantitative *and* qualitative aspects of resource allocation decisions.

The modeling of system constraints is the third step in the process. Maximum profit is clearly limited by factors such as plant capacity, worker-hours available, raw material supplies, and other constraints. The model must be able to quantify these constraints and model their limiting effects on production alternatives.

Two analytical procedures are commonly used in resource allocation decisions: linear programming and ranking schemes. Linear programming is a procedure for finding "optimal" levels of controllable variables satisfying specific objectives and constraints. Ranking processes, on the other hand, are loosely structured procedures that involve the assignment of numerical weights to a selected group of alternatives.

Linear programming works best in those allocation cases which are easily quantifiable, which allow numerous alternatives, and which have a single, clear-cut objective. On the other hand, ranking processes are best applicable to qualitative judgments concerning few alternatives but multiple objectives. Ranking procedures are the basis of most purely intuitive decisions.

## LINEAR PROGRAMMING AS A RESOURCE ALLOCATION MODEL

The consultants decided that the resource allocation decision at MM was sufficiently quantifiable to justify the use of linear programming. An LP model consists of a linear objective function to be optimized subject to linear constraints. That is, no variable in an LP model appears with a power differing from 1.0.

The potential number of reasonable production alternatives was large and primarily determined by product mix; therefore, the consultants set out to produce a linear programming model that would tell MM the product mix which would maximize profit. Prior to looking at the full-blown model, a study of a simpler LP example was developed for MM by the consultants to illustrate the principles of linear programming. (Several modeling situations and their LP models appear in Technical Note 6.1.)

## AN INTRODUCTORY EXAMPLE

This example deals with resource allocation at a small plant owned by Universal Alloys. A high-grade product and a low-grade product can each be made from a ton of raw material. However, weekly low-grade production can exceed high-grade production by no more than 40 tons because of processing limitations. The only stringent constraint on total production is that no more than 80 tons of raw material is available per week. High-grade product sells for $200 a ton, and low-grade product sells for $100 a ton. Management must make a decision as to how to allocate its production for the next week.

Since two decisions must be made, two variables will be used to designate the decisions:

$$x_1 = \text{tons of low-grade product per week}$$

$$x_2 = \text{tons of high-grade product per week}$$

Revenue is calculated by adding the revenue from sales of low-grade and high-grade product. In this case

$$\text{Revenue} = \$100x_1 + \$200x_2$$

and revenue is the objective function. The goal of the analysis is to

$$\text{Maximize } 100x_1 + 200x_2$$

Notice that no units appear in an LP formulation, so the modeler must check the implied units carefully. Checking units is especially important in large models.

The limitation on raw material is expressed as

$$x_1 + x_2 \leqslant 80$$

The units match up. Activities $x_1$ and $x_2$ are in units of tons per week, and the number 80 represents a capacity limitation in tons per week.

The other constraint on production is that production of the low-grade product ($x_1$) cannot exceed production of the high-grade product ($x_2$) by more than 40 tons. Altogether, the problem is:

$$\text{Maximize } 100x_1 + 200x_2$$

Subject to: $x_1 + x_2 \leqslant 80$
$\qquad\qquad x_1 - x_2 \leqslant 40$
$\qquad\qquad x_1, x_2 \geqslant 0$

Including the nonnegativity requirements, the problem has four constraints. The nature of the four constraints can be better understood by looking at graphical representations of them. These appear in Figs. 6.1 through 6.7.

The nonnegativity constraints limit the potential solution points to the area shown in Fig. 6.1.

The display of the other two constraints is only slightly more complicated. A two-variable inequality is satisfied by all the points on one side of a boundary line and no points on the other side. The boundary line equation is obtained by simply replacing the inequality sign in the constraint with an equality sign. Thus, the resource constraint's boundary is

$$x_1 + x_2 = 80$$

This line is graphed in Fig. 6.2. The portion of the area which satisfies the constraint is shaded. Combining the solution sets (allowed points) from Figs. 6.1 and 6.2 produces the set shown in Fig. 6.3. The boundary line for the last constraint is

$$x_1 - x_2 = 40$$

**Figure 6.1** The portion of the ($x_1$, $x_2$) plane to which nonnegativity constraints restrict the solution (shaded portion).

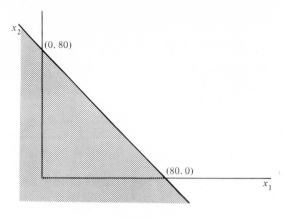

**Figure 6.2** The boundary line and the solution set for the inequality $x_1 + x_2 \leqslant 80$.

This line and the solution set for the corresponding inequality are shown in Fig. 6.4. It is easy to verify that the solution sets for the inequalities do lie where they are indicated by substituting a point not on the inequality's boundary line into the inequality. For example, if (0, 0) is substituted into

$$x_1 + x_2 \leqslant 80$$

it becomes

$$0 + 0 \leqslant 80$$

which is true; so (0, 0) is on the side of the boundary line which is in the solution set. Figure 6.5 shows the overall solution set to the inequalities in the LP region. This set is called the "feasible set." A theorem of linear programming says that a problem's solution is always a vertex (or extreme point) of the feasible set for the prob-

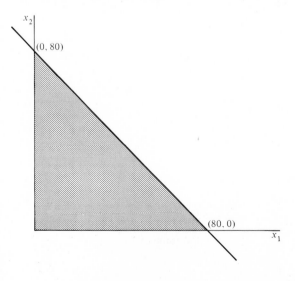

**Figure 6.3** Solution set for $x_1 \geqslant 0$, $x_2 \geqslant 0$, and $x_1 + x_2 \leqslant 80$.

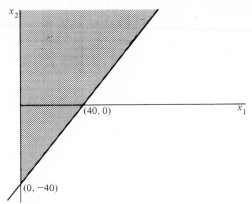

**Figure 6.4** Boundary line and solution set for $x_1 - x_2 \leqslant 40$.

lem. The extreme points in Fig. 6.5 have been labeled A, B, C, and D. Table 6.1 lists the coordinates of these points and the corresponding values of the objective function. Table 6.1 shows the optimum solution to the problem to be as follows:

The plant can make a maximum profit of $16,000 per week by making no low-grade product and 80 tons of high-grade product per week.

The geometric approach to solving LP problems is not a good general algorithm, but it serves well as an introduction to the ideas of linear programming. Geometric displays also clarify the role of the objective function. The objective function can be thought of as representing a family of lines. The optimal line has the equation

$$16,000 = 100x_1 + 200x_2$$

This line and others in the family are sketched in the feasible set in Fig. 6.6.

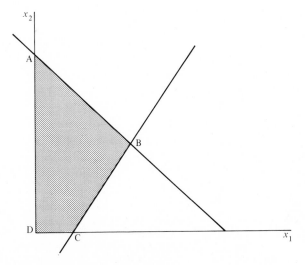

**Figure 6.5** The feasible set.

## Table 6.1 Extreme points and objective function values

| Point | Coordinates $(x_1, x_2)$ | Objection function $100x_1 + 200x_2$ |
|-------|--------------------------|--------------------------------------|
| A | (0, 80) | $16,000 |
| B | (60, 20) | $10,000 |
| C | (40, 0) | $ 4,000 |
| D | (0, 0) | $    0 |

Figure 6.6 makes it clear that the "most extreme" point in the feasible set are at (0, 0) and (0, 80) when the set is viewed along the direction of the family of parallel objective lines.

The solutions which occur at points A, B, C, and D are called basic feasible solutions to the LP problem, and, geometrically, they can be recognized as being all of the intersections of the constraint boundaries which satisfy all constraints. That is, only those four vertices satisfy all of the constraints. The only points of interest in solving an LP problem are basic feasible solutions. As a result both the minimum and the maximum of the objective function of an LP problem occur at basic feasible points.

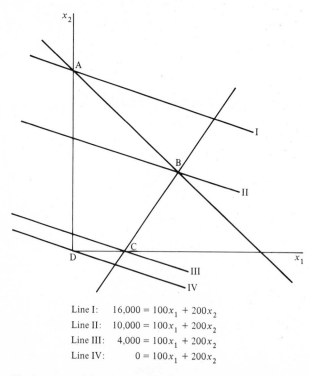

Line I:   $16,000 = 100x_1 + 200x_2$
Line II:   $10,000 = 100x_1 + 200x_2$
Line III:   $4,000 = 100x_1 + 200x_2$
Line IV:   $0 = 100x_1 + 200x_2$

**Figure 6.6** Four lines from the family of lines of the form $z = 100x_1 + 200x_2$.

It is evident that whenever the number of variables in an LP problem exceeds two, the graphical approach to solution becomes very difficult. For instance, if four variables are involved, one must be able to draw pictures successfully in four-dimensional space to adequately depict the feasible set. Since this represents a considerable limitation, a more general solution procedure must be used.

The implied procedure of the geometric solution is to find all intersections of all constraint boundaries and then test the objective function value of each feasible intersection, but the guiding principle of any LP solution technique can be seen. If a mathematical procedure can produce basic feasible solutions and compare them, regardless of the number of variables, then it is a general solution algorithm.

At this point, it would be useful to return to the Universal Alloys example and comment on some of the decision-related aspects of modeling. Notice that the optimum result indicated that none of the low-grade product should be produced. While this solution is mathematically optimal, it may not be desirable to management. The implications of not producing a specific product may be a shift in business policy which management abhors. Perhaps the low-point product is a "loss leader" which is used to stimulate sales on the high-grade product. There may be other reasons to examine the optimum solution carefully. An "optimum" solution is not necessarily an acceptable solution. Later in this chapter, suggestions will be given for making LP models more compatible with decision making realities, but before exploring this point further, let us renew the discussion of Marlinton Metals.

## MARLINTON METALS REVISITED

Once the consultants had sold Jim Johnson on the linear programming approach, their next step was to prepare the plant model. In previous discussions they had decided upon a model that would keep up with resource utilization while determining the best mix of products to manufacture.

Although MM produced over fifty products altogether, the consultants found that six of these products accounted for over 90 percent of MM's sales. To reduce data collection efforts, the model was set up for the top six products. (Names used in the LP model are in parentheses.)

1. #3 conveyor rollers (ROLLERS)
2. Special duty 3-inch pipe (threaded) (PIPES)
3. Blue steel 30-caliber rifle barrels (RIFBS)
4. One-inch waterwall boiler tubing (BOILTUB)
5. Steel refractory brick casings (BRICK)
6. One-inch commercial retarder tubing (RETUB)

The next step for the consultants was to gather the following information:

1. Prices of the products
2. Labor requirements for the products
3. Time requirements for making the products

**Table 6.2 Product requirements**

| | Rollers | Pipes | Rifbs | Boiltub | Brick | Retub | Total available resources |
|---|---|---|---|---|---|---|---|
| Prices | $6/roller | $4/pipe | $6/barrel | $5/foot | $6/casing pair | $4/foot | |
| Labor requirements | 0.13 hours/roller | 0.25 hours/pipe | 0.2 hours/barrel | 0.4 hours/foot | 0.2 hours/pair | 0.3 hours/foot | 4800 hours/week |
| Plant time requirements | 0.0067 hours/roller | 0.0075 hours/pipe | 0.01 hours/barrel | 0.02 hours/foot | 0.01 hours/pair | 0.01 hours/foot | 140 hours/week |
| Raw material requirements | 5.333 pounds/roller (steel bars) | 4 pounds/pipe (iron piping) | 2.6 pounds/barrel (rolled steel) | 1.2 pounds/foot (tubing alloy #1) | 3.1 pounds/pair (plate steel) | 1.4 pounds/foot (tubing alloy #2) | |
| Electricity requirements | 1.57 kWh/roller | 3 kWh/pipe | 2 kWh/barrel | 2 kWh/foot | 5 kWh/pair | 3.5 kWh/foot | |

4. Raw material requirements for the products
5. Raw material costs
6. Raw material availability
7. Electricity requirements for the products
8. Electricity costs

These data seemed necessary to the consultants, but were extremely difficult to collect. No standard time estimates had ever been made for the products; in fact, no industrial engineer to do such estimates was even employed by the company. The use of production logs to gather data proved useless since the data were not accurate. As a result, the consultants were forced to rely upon estimates provided by the supervisor in each section.

Raw material requirements were equally difficult to collect, in part because of uncertain scrap losses. In this case, however, inventory records were better kept and some estimate of raw material requirements could be made from them.

Even the prices of the products were difficult to measure, since Harold Kline made a habit of discounting prices for "special" friends. "Book" prices were finally agreed upon as the most appropriate for the model.

After a data base was in hand (as described in Tables 6.2 and 6.4) the next step was putting together the plant model. The objective to be satisfied was chosen:

Maximize profit = revenues − costs

Essentially, profit was treated as revenues obtained from sales of the six products less the costs of raw materials, labor, and electricity. In mathematical form this objective function was written as follows:

Maximize: Profit = 6 ROLLERS + 4 PIPES + 6 RIFBS + 5 BOILTUB

+ 6 BRICK + 4 RETUB − 1.0 STBARS − 0.17 IRONB

− 0.45 ROST − 0.21 ALL1 − 0.25 ALL2 − 0.60 PLTST

− 6.12 LABOR − 0.05 ELEC1 − 0.01 ELEC2 − 0.01 ELEC3

**Table 6.3  Raw material data**

| Raw material | Cost | Availability |
|---|---|---|
| Plate steel (PLTST) | $0.60/pound | 1 ton/week |
| Tubing alloy #1 (ALL1) | $0.21/pound | 1.6 tons/week |
| Tubing alloy #2 (ALL2) | $0.25/pound | 3 tons/week |
| Rolled steel (ROST) | $0.45/pound | 6 tons/week |
| Iron piping (IRONB) | $0.17/pound | 10 tons/week |
| Steel bars (STBARS) | $1.00/pound | 4 tons/week |
| Electricity (ELEC) | $0.05/kWh | Unlimited |

## Table 6.4 Definitions of mathematical variables used in the model

**ROWS**

OBJ—profit in $
LABOR—total labor used in worker-hours
ELEC—total electricity used, kWh
STBR—steel bars used, pounds
IRON—iron pipe used, pounds
ROLSTL—rolled steel used, pounds
ALLOY1—amount of alloy #1 used, pounds
ALLOY2—amount of alloy #2 used, pounds
PLANTIME—limit on plant time availability, hours
STLBRLM—limit on steel bar availability, pounds
ROLSTLIM—limit on rolled steel availability, pounds
PLATSTL—plate steel used, pounds
ALLOY2LM—limit on availability of alloy #2, pounds
PLATSTLM—limit on plate steel availability, pounds
LABLIM—limit on labor availability, worker-hours
ALLOY1LM—limit on availability of alloy #1, pounds
IRONBL—limit on availability of iron pipe, pounds

**COLUMNS**

ROLLERS—rollers produced
PIPES—pipes made
RIFBS—output of rifle barrels
BOILTUB—feet of boiler tubing produced
BRICK—number of brick casing pairs made
RETUB—feet of retarder tubing made
STBARS—steel bars used, pounds
IRONB—iron piping used, pounds
ROST—rolled steel used, pounds
ALL1—alloy #1 used, pounds
ALL2—alloy #2 used, pounds
PLTST—plate steel used, pounds
LABCOST—labor used, worker-hours
ELEC—electricity used, kWh

After the objective function was formulated, the next step was the development of the constraint equations.

The total labor used could not exceed 4800 hours. Therefore, this constraint was written as

$$\text{LABOR} \leqslant 4800$$

Since the model had to cost out LABOR, another equation was added to the model to define LABOR as a function of the products. Therefore, the equation

$$\text{LABOR} = 0.13 \text{ ROLLERS} + 0.25 \text{ PIPES} + 0.2 \text{ RIFBS} + 0.4 \text{ BOILTUB}$$
$$+ 0.2 \text{ BRICK} + 0.3 \text{ RETUB}$$

was added to the constraint set as well.

The consumption of electricity was defined in a similar manner:

ELEC = 1.57 ROLLERS + 3.0 PIPES + 2.0 BOILTUB + 5.0 BRICK

+ 2.0 RIFBS + 3.5 RETUB

The remaining equations were straightforward. For example, the amount of steel bars used was

STBARS = 5.3 ROLLERS

The limit on steel bars was 8000 pounds. Therefore, the equation

STBARS ≤ 8000

was added to the model.

Table 6.5 illustrates the data for the LP model in a tableau format. Most LP problems are solved on a computer, and Table 6.5 is organized in the form appropriate for computer output. The row name is the labor assigned to the row, and the row type is listed according to the following code:

N = nonbinding row (usually the objective)

L = less-than-or-equal-to constraint

G = greater-than-or-equal-to constrant

E = equality constraint

Each column in Table 6.5 is headed by the name of the variable that column represents. The last column contains the right-hand-side (RHS) entry for each row. The names of rows and columns are as defined in Table 6.4.

To illustrate the data format in Table 6.5, consider the following equation:

ELEC = 1.57 ROLLERS + 3.0 PIPES + 2.0 BOILTUB + 5.0 BRICK

+ 2.0 RIFBS + 3.5 RETUB

The first step in translating the coefficients of this constraint into those in the tableau is to transfer all variables to the left of the equals sign:

ELEC − 1.57 ROLLERS − 3.0 PIPES − 2.0 BOILTUB − 5.0 BRICK

− 2.0 RIFBS − 3.5 RETUB = 0

The row name of ELEC is given the row, and, since it is an equality row, E in the row type. The coefficients are then recorded as shown in Table 6.5.

The consultants ran the resource allocation model on a computer and obtained a solution showing that $30,207 per week in profit could be made by producing the following (rounded to whole numbers):

| | |
|---|---|
| 0 rollers | 645 brick casing pairs |
| 3077 rifle barrels | 4268 feet of retarder tubing |
| 1121 feet of boiler tubing | 5000 pipes |

## Table 6.5 Tableau of Coefficients

| Row name and type | ROLLERS | PIPES | RIFBS | BOILTUB | BRICK | RETUB | STBARS | IRONB | ROST | ALL1 | ALL2 | PLTST | LABCOST | ELEC | RHS |
|---|---|---|---|---|---|---|---|---|---|---|---|---|---|---|---|
| OBJ, $ <br> N | 6.0 | 4.0 | 6.0 | 5.0 | 6.0 | 4.0 | −1.0 | −0.17 | −0.45 | −0.21 | −0.25 | −0.60 | −6.12 | −0.05 | |
| LABOR, worker-hours <br> E | −0.13 | −0.25 | −0.2 | −0.4 | −0.2 | −0.3 | | | | | | | 1.0 | | |
| ELEC, kWh <br> E | −1.567 | −3.0 | −2.0 | −2.0 | −5.0 | −3.5 | | | | | | | | 1.0 | |
| STBR, pounds <br> E | −5.333 | | | | | | 1.0 | | | | | | | | |
| IRON, pounds <br> E | | −4.0 | | | | | | 1.0 | | | | | | | |
| ROLSTL, pounds <br> E | | | −2.6 | | | | | | 1.0 | | | | | | |
| ALLOY1, pounds <br> E | | | | −1.2 | | | | | | 1.0 | | | | | |
| ALLOY2, pounds <br> E | | | | | | −1.4 | | | | | 1.0 | | | | |
| PLANTIME, hours <br> L | 0.00667 | 0.0075 | 0.01 | 0.02 | 0.01 | 0.01 | | | | | | | | | 140 |

(Continued to the next page)

quirement did not have an extreme effect on profit, it was left unchanged. No lower limit was placed on labor, but the limit on electricity was allowed to vary from 35,000 kWh to 50,000 kWh to study the effect of electricity limits on profit margin.

Figure 6.7 shows the results of the additional analysis studying the electricity limit. In each case roller production was fixed at 1500 rollers with a selling price of $6.50 per roller. The peak electricity needed for full production was nearly 43,000 kWh giving a profit margin of $29,532. When a 35,000-kWh limit on electricity was imposed, the profit margin decreased to $28,518.

Given these additional results, Jim Johnson felt he had enough information to make a recommendation to the president. His recommendation entailed several changes in the organization:

1. Limit electricity consumption to 41,000 kWh.
2. Reduce employment by twenty-eight people—Only 3645 worker-hours were needed when electricity was limited to 41,000 kWh.
3. Keep roller production at 1500 and raise the price to at least $6.50.
4. Seek a more profitable product line to occupy the roller department.

As Jim Johnson expected, the president was very concerned over the proposed reduction in workforce. Jim reminded the president of his request for improved profitability and further demonstrated that his recommendation would save over $6850 per week in direct labor charges. The president would agree to the other recommendations but was hesitant to approve any reduction in workforce.

After a week had passed, Harold Kline called Johnson into his office to tell him of his decision with regard to the workforce reduction. The president had checked with personnel and had found that twelve employees were due for retirement that year. The president suggested a policy of not replacing them or any

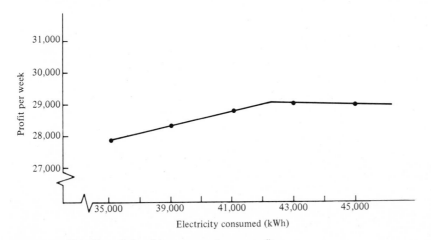

**Figure 6.7** The effect of electricity consumption on profits.

other employees until the full reduction of twenty-eight persons was achieved. He understood the loss in incentive this would represent to Johnson and offered a $2000 bonus as compensation. After additional discussion on long-term strategy for MM, Jim Johnson returned to his office with the euphoric feeling that improved management practices might eventually arrive at MM.

# TECHNICAL NOTE 6.1 EXAMPLES OF LINEAR PROGRAMMING MODELS

It is difficult to educate people to the general principles of modeling, but it is not difficult to allow them to acquire the principles inductively by studying models that have already been built. In this spirit, several modeling situations and their accompanying LP models are shown below.

For each situation the data are displayed, variables are defined, the objective is specified, the objective function is shown, and the constraining conditions are expressed as equations or inequalities.

Although the situations described are fairly simple, the alert student could easily extend the implied principles to other situations.

## 1 A BLENDING PROBLEM

A chemical company must make a decision as to the allocation of three feedstocks to four different products. Table 6.10 gives data on the manufacturing of the products:

**Table 6.10**

| Product | Required composition of raw material, % | | | Minimum demand, barrels | Maximum demand, barrels |
|---|---|---|---|---|---|
| | 1 | 2 | 3 | | |
| A | $\geqslant 20$ | $\leqslant 30$ | ....... | 1000 | 5000 |
| B | $\geqslant 10$ | $\geqslant 20$ | $\leqslant 40$ | 2000 | 6000 |
| C | $\leqslant 30$ | ....... | ....... | 2000 | 7000 |
| D | ....... | $\geqslant 20$ | $\leqslant 50$ | 4000 | 8000 |
| Raw material availability, barrels | 2000 | 3000 | 5000 | | |

The selling prices per barrel for products A, B, C, and D are $100, $200, $250, and $175, respectively. The costs of raw materials 1, 2, and 3 are $60, $70, and $90, respectively.

### The decision variables

$$x_{A1} = \text{amount of raw material 1 in product A}$$

$$x_{B2} = \text{amount of raw material 2 in product B}$$

$$\vdots$$

$$x_{D3} = \text{amount of raw material 3 in product D}$$

### The objective

Maximize revenues − costs

Maximize $100(x_{A1} + x_{A2} + x_{A3}) + 200(x_{B1} + x_{B2} + x_{B3}) + 250(x_{C1} + x_{C2} + x_{C3})$

$+ 175(x_{D1} + x_{D2} + x_{D3}) - 60(x_{A1} + x_{B1} + x_{C1} + x_{D1})$

$- 70(x_{A2} + x_{B2} + x_{C2} + x_{D2}) - 90(x_{A3} + x_{B3} + x_{C3} + x_{D3})$

### The constraints

Maximum and minimum demand: $1000 \leqslant x_{A1} + x_{A2} + x_{A3} \leqslant 5000$

$$2000 \leqslant x_{B2} + x_{B2} + x_{B3} \leqslant 6000$$

$$2000 \leqslant x_{C1} + x_{C2} + x_{C3} \leqslant 7000$$

$$4000 \leqslant x_{D1} + x_{D2} + x_{D3} \leqslant 8000$$

Raw material availability: $x_{A1} + x_{B1} + x_{C1} + x_{D1} \leqslant 2000$

$$x_{A2} + x_{B2} + x_{C2} + x_{D2} \leqslant 3000$$

$$x_{A3} + x_{B3} + x_{C3} + x_{D3} \leqslant 5000$$

Raw material composition: $x_{A1} \geqslant 0.20(x_{A1} + x_{A2} + x_{A3})$

$$x_{A2} \leqslant 0.30(x_{A1} + x_{A2} + x_{A3})$$

$$x_{B1} \geqslant 0.10(x_{B1} + x_{B2} + x_{B3})$$

$$x_{B2} \geqslant 0.20(x_{B1} + x_{B2} + x_{B3})$$

$$x_{B3} \leqslant 0.40(x_{B1} + x_{B2} + x_{B3})$$

$$x_{C1} \leqslant 0.30(x_{C1} + x_{C2} + x_{C3})$$

$$x_{D2} \geqslant 0.20(x_{D1} + x_{D2} + x_{D3})$$

$$x_{D3} \leqslant 0.50(x_{D1} + x_{D2} + x_{D3})$$

## 2 THE PRODUCT MIX PROBLEM

A company has four products to which it must allocate its scarce resources. The selling prices of products A, B, C, and D are \$100, \$110, \$150, and \$90, respec-

**Table 6.11**

| Department | Production requirements, hours/units | | | | Hours available | Cost, $/hour |
|---|---|---|---|---|---|---|
| | A | B | C | D | | |
| 1 | 2.1 | 3.2 | 2.8 | 1.7 | 800 | 10 |
| 2 | 1.6 | 2.8 | 4.1 | 2.3 | 600 | 12 |
| 3 | 1.8 | 2.1 | 3.7 | 1.8 | 1200 | 18 |

tively. Each product must be sent through three departments as shown in Table 6.11.

All products are manufactured for storage, but the total storage space cannot exceed 10,000 ft². The storage requirements for products A, B, C, and D are 1.2, 1.8, 1.6, 2.0 ft² per unit. The minimum demand to be met for products A, B, C, and D should be 50, 60, 40, and 20, respectively.

*The decision variables*

$x_A$ = number of units of product A to manufacture

$x_B$ = number of units of product B to manufacture

$x_C$ = number of units of product C to manufacture

$x_D$ = number of units of product D to manufacture

*The objective*

Maximize revenues — costs

Cost of product A = sum of production costs in each department

$$= 10(2.1) + 12(1.6) + 18(1.8)$$

$$= \$72.6/\text{unit}$$

Maximize $27.4x_A + 6.6x_B + 6.6x_C + 13.0x_D$

*The constraints*

Minimum demand: $x_A \geqslant 50$

$x_B \geqslant 60$

$x_C \geqslant 40$

$x_D \geqslant 20$

Production capacity: $2.1x_A + 3.2x_B + 2.8x_C + 1.7x_D \leqslant 800$

$1.6x_A + 2.8x_B + 4.1x_C + 2.3x_D \leqslant 600$

$1.8x_A + 2.1x_B + 3.7x_C + 1.8x_D \leqslant 1200$

Storage space: $1.2x_A + 1.8x_B + 1.6x_C + 2.0\ x_D \leqslant 10,000$

**Table 6.12**

| Time of day | Minimum number of policemen needed |
|---|---|
| 6 A.M.–10 A.M. | 8 |
| 10 A.M.– 2 P.M. | 12 |
| 2 P.M.– 6 P.M. | 16 |
| 6 P.M.–10 P.M. | 18 |
| 10 P.M.– 2 A.M. | 10 |
| 2 A.M.– 6 A.M. | 4 |

# 3 THE WORKFORCE ASSIGNMENT PROBLEM

A city would like to have an efficient way to schedule its routine patrol duty. After observing calls for different periods of time, the police chief has estimated that the workforce needs to be as shown in Table 6.12.

*The decision variables*

$x_1$ = number of policemen beginning work at 6 A.M.

$x_2$ = number of policemen beginning work at 10 A.M.

$x_3$ = number of policemen beginning work at 2 P.M.

$x_4$ = number of policemen beginning work at 6 P.M.

$x_5$ = number of policemen beginning work at 10 P.M..

$x_6$ = number of policemen beginning work at 2 A.M.

*The objective*

Minimize policemen needed

Minimize $x_1 + x_2 + x_3 + x_4 + x_5 + x_6$

*The constraints*

Minimum demand: $x_1 + x_2 \geqslant 12$

$$x_2 + x_3 \geqslant 16$$

$$x_3 + x_4 \geqslant 18$$

$$x_4 + x_5 \geqslant 4$$

$$x_5 + x_6 \geqslant 8$$

# 4 THE TRANSPORTATION PROBLEM

A city must collect garbage in four different zones of the city. It has two disposal sites which it can use to dispose of the garbage. Data on the operation of the sanitation department are shown in Table 6.13.

**Table 6.13**

| Zone | Transportation time to disposal site, min | | Volume to be collected, truckloads |
|---|---|---|---|
| | 1 | 2 | |
| A | 40 | 28 | 4 |
| B | 36 | 41 | 6 |
| C | 20 | 27 | 3 |
| D | 18 | 20 | 5 |
| Capacity of disposal site per week, truckloads | 10 | 18 | |

The city would like a disposal plan which minimizes total time lost due to transportation.

### The decision variable

$$x_{A1} = \text{number of truckloads sent to site 1 from zone A}$$

$$x_{A2} = \text{number of truckloads sent to site 2 from zone A}$$

$$\vdots$$

$$x_{D2} = \text{number of truckloads sent to site 2 from zone D}$$

### The objective

Minimize total transportation time

Minimize $40x_{A1} + 28x_{A2} + \cdots + 20x_{D2}$

### The constraints

Waste to be collected: $x_{A1} + x_{A2} = 4$

$$x_{B1} + x_{B2} = 6$$

$$x_{C1} + x_{C2} = 3$$

$$x_{D1} + x_{D2} = 5$$

Disposal site capacity: $x_{A1} + x_{B1} + x_{C1} + x_{D1} \leqslant 10$

$$x_{A2} + x_{B2} + x_{C2} + x_{D2} \leqslant 8$$

## 5 THE FACILITY PLANNING PROBLEM

The Western Water Company must expand its capacity to meet anticipated increased demand because of an energy consumption boom. The company's objective is to have its water processing capacity as large as possible by the end of the year.

Each 10,000 gallons of water produced in a day requires $10 (for the purchase of chemical treatment materials and the payment of wages); it yields $1200 of utility revenues per day at the beginning of the next period.

In each year, the company can use either or both of two construction techniques to expand its plant. Each requires cash in the period the expansion is initiated, and one takes more time than the other. Specifically, building a unit of capacity by expansion method 1 requires $1 million when the construction activity is started and yields the added capacity by the beginning of the following year. Building a unit of capacity by expansion method 2 requires $0.5 million when the construction activity is started and yields the added capacity by the beginning of the year after the following one.

The company has 10 million tax dollars to finance its production and expansion in year 1, but requires that the subsequent production and expansion activities be self-funding (that is, no supply of cash will be forthcoming from *outside tax sources* after the first year). The plant capacity at the start of year 1 is 2 million gallons per day.

### The decision variables

$x_t$ = amount of water that can be produced in year $t$

$u_t$ = expansion in capacity by method 1 in year $t$ (measured in 100,000 gallons/day)

$v_t$ = expansion in capacity by method 2 in year $t$ (measured in 100,000 gallons/day)

$w_t$ = unused cash at the end of year $t$

$z_t$ = unused plant capacity at end of year $t$

### The objective

Maximize plant capacity at end of sixth year

Maximize $x_4$

### The constraints

Cash available for expansion:

Year 1: $u_t + 0.5v_t + w_1 = 10$

Year 2: $u_t + 0.5v_t + w_2 = w_1 + 1190x_1$

Year 3: $u_3 + 0.5v_3 + w_3 = w_2 + 1190x_2$

Year 4: $u_4 + 0.5v_4 + w_3 = w_3 + 1190x_3$

Production level:

Year 1: $x_1 = 20$

Year 2: $x_2 = x_1 + u_1$

Year 3: $x_3 = x_2 + u_2 + v_1$

Year 4: $x_4 = x_3 + u_3 + v_2$

# 6 THE INVESTMENT PROBLEM

A pension fund has two options for investing the contributions to the fund during a year. At the end of the year long-term investments are to be made; so all cash invested during the year must be available at the end of the year. Investment option A is a two-month investment which yields a return of 1.6 percent. Investment option B is a four-month investment which yields a return of 3.8 percent. A decision must be made as to the level of investment in each option. Approximately $20,000 in payments is available in every two months for investment.

*The decision variables*

$x_{At}$ = amount of money invested in option A at beginning of three-month time period $t$

$x_{Bt}$ = amount of money invested in option B at beginning of three-month time period $t$

$y_t$  = uninvested cash in three-month time period $t$

*The objective*

Maximize pension fund investments until end of year

Maximize $y_6 + 1.016x_{A6} + 1.038x_{B5}$

*The constraints*

Cash available for investment:

Time period 1: $x_{A1} + x_{B1} + y_1 = 20,000$

Time period 2: $x_{A2} + x_{B2} + y_2 = 20,000 \ y_1 + 1.016x_{A1}$

Time period 3: $x_{A3} + x_{B3} + y_3 = 20,000 + y_2 + 1.016x_{A2} + 1.038x_{B1}$

Time period 4: $x_{A4} + x_{B4} + y_4 = 20,000 + y_3 + 1.016x_{A3} + 1.038x_{B2}$

Time period 5: $x_{A5} + x_{B5} + y_5 = 20,000 + y_4 + 1.016x_{A4} + 1.038x_{B3}$

Time period 6: $x_{A6} + x_{B6} + y_6 = 20,000 + y_5 + 1.016x_{A5} + 1.038x_{B4}$

# QUESTIONS

1 What resource allocation decisions has Marlinton Metals been making in the operation of its plant?

2 Why was Jim Johnson interested in having help in allocating Marlinton's resources?

3 In the Marlinton Metals case, what are the decision variables which Johnson can control in running the plant? What is the objective he is pursuing? What are the constraints limiting his choices?

4 What factors may lead a manager to use a decision model for allocating resources?

5 What is the meaning of each of the following?
(a) Controllable variables
(b) Objectives
(c) Constraints
(d) Feasible solution
(e) Basic feasible solution

6 How is it possible to get more than the usual unique solution to a linear programming model? (Show graphically.)

7 How may some constraints in a model be redundant? (Show graphically.)

8 Why does the optimum solution occur at the extreme point of the feasible solution set? (Explain intuitively.)

9 What is the economic logic used in the Marlinton Metals model?

10 What information does the shadow price provide for a decision maker?

11 How does the number of constraints in a linear programming model affect the number of alternatives receiving resource allocations?

12 What are the management styles of managers that might make those managers receptive to the use of a resource allocation model? Describe them.

13 Linear programming considers only one objective at a time. How can more than one objective be incorporated into a model? How was this done at Marlinton Metals?

14 In which of the areas listed below would management generally be most inclined to use a model? Least inclined?
(a) Anticipating the future
(b) Developing plans
(c) Evaluating risks
(d) Allocating resources

15 Linear programming models are used less frequently in government and service industries to allocate resources. Why do you think this is so?

# EXERCISES

1 For the decision areas listed below, outline the decision variables (or options) available, the objective(s) considered, and the constraints affecting the decision.
(a) Deciding on the funds allocated from monthly income
(b) Deciding upon the mix of recreation activities to pursue
(c) Deciding on the amount of time to be devoted to different activities during a typical work or school day

2 Describe the functional areas (e.g., manufacturing, personnel, purchasing) of an organization that you believe would be the most receptive to the use of a resource allocation model.

3 Describe the likely organizational impacts caused by use of a resource allocation model in determining the mix of products to be made at a manufacturing facility.

4 A company is going to use linear programming to schedule its daily production for each shift. The operating conditions of the plant change each shift, so the model must be run for each shift. What

operational conditions must be placed on the model? In particular, discuss each of the following:
(*a*) Who should be responsible for the model?
(*b*) How should data be collected?
(*c*) What reporting criteria must be met?
Do you think such a model will be successful?

5 You are an active gardener who must decide what to do with your tomatoes. You can either can them for consumption during the winter or you can convert them into soup. Although you prefer soup, it is much more expensive to produce and takes much more time. On the other hand, canned plain tomatoes provide greater flexibility for use during the winter. After considerable thought, you have decided that the relative value of soup to plain tomatoes is 3 to 2.

You have a total of 100 pounds of tomatoes to can. You have decided that you would like to have at least 20 quarts of soup and 10 quarts of tomatoes. A quart of soup requires 2 pounds of tomatoes while a quart of plain tomatoes requires 4 pounds. What is the best way to use your tomatoes?

6 An insurance agency processes claims of two different types. Each claim must be processed through three office sections. The time requirements in each section are shown in Table 6.14.

**Table 6.14**

| Section | Application time, hours | | Time available, hours/week |
| | A | B | |
|---|---|---|---|
| 1 | 5 | 8 | 80 |
| 2 | 8 | 4 | 80 |
| 3 | 12 | 4 | 120 |

Each application must go through each section to be completed.
(*a*)How many completed applications of each type should be processed per week if an application of type A is twice as important as one of type B?
(*b*) If you were given the opportunity to hire one more person, which section should be given that person?

7 West Chester, a small city of 15,000 people, requires an average of 300,000 gallons of water daily. The city is supplied from a central waterworks, where the water is purified by conventional methods such as filtration and chlorination. In addition, two different chemical compounds, a softening chemical and a health chemical, must be added to soften the water and for health purposes. The waterworks plans to purchase two popular brands of products that contain these chemicals. One barrel of the Chemco Corporation's product gives 2 pounds of the softening chemical and 4 pounds of the health chemical. One barrel of the American Chemical Company's products contains 3 pounds and 1 pound of the chemicals.

To maintain the water at a minimum level of softness and to meet a minimum in health protection, experts have decided that 60 and 40 pounds of the two chemicals that make up each product must be added to the water daily. At a cost of $3 per unit for Chemco's product and $4 per unit for American Chemical's product, what is the optimal quantity of each product that should be used weekly to meet the minimum level of softness and a minimum health standard?

8 A builder is trying to maximize the profit from a tract on which brick and frame houses are being built. A brick house yields a profit of $1200, while a frame house produces only an $800 profit.

There are a number of things which constrain the builder from making the greatest possible profit:
(*a*) The FHA has specified that at least five brick houses and five frame houses be built on the tract.
(*b*) Labor is in short supply for finishing the interiors. Each house requires 500 worker-hours and a total of only 15,000 worker-hours are available.

(c) Finish lumber is in short supply. The brick house requires 200 board feet of finish lumber and the frame house requires 400 board feet. The builder can only acquire 4000 board feet.

(d) The brick makers are on strike and the builder can only acquire 150,000 bricks. Each brick house requires 15,000 bricks. Frame houses require none.

Determine the number of brick and frame houses that the builder can construct to yield the maximum profit within the specified constraints. What is this profit?

9 A farmer receives $0.35 per pound of okra, $0.27 per pound of squash, $0.25 per pound of purple onions, $0.12 per pound of beans, and $0.40 per pound of watermelon. The farmer wants to plant crops from the choices listed above on 22 acres. The farmer has the seed necessary to plant all the acreage with any one of the crops, but wants to mix crops in order to achieve the optimum financial benefit (assuming that all crops earn as expected). Over the growing season the farmer can count on 80,000 gallons of irrigation water. Water costs $0.05 per 1000 gallons. Cash reserves permit an expenditure of as much as $2000 to get the crops in and to the buyers. Extra cash can be borrowed at a 12 percent interest rate.

An acre produces 5200 pounds of okra with a requirement of 10,000 gallons of water and 200 pounds of fertilizer. Ten acres of okra requires 3 worker-days of labor to harvest and get the produce to the buyers. Fertilizer costs $18 per 100 pounds and labor runs $30 per worker-day.

Ten acres of squash produces about 80,000 pounds of squash, which requires a total of 100,000 gallons of water and 3000 pounds of fertilizer. Harvesting and getting 10 acres of squash to buyers requires 3.5 worker-days of labor.

Purple onions by the acre amount to about 6500 pounds at a cost of 15,000 gallons of water and 50 pounds of fertilizer. Harvesting 10 acres of these onions and getting them to market requires 1.5 worker-days.

Ten acres of beans produces a crop of 90,000 pounds and requires 800 pounds of fertilizer and 140,000 gallons of water. Harvesting and transporting requires 3 worker-days of labor.

Finally, an acre will produce 300 pounds of watermelon, which requires 125,000 gallons of water and 800 pounds of fertilizer. Harvesting and transplanting of 10 acres' worth requires 5 worker-days of labor.

(a) Calculate the activities and write the LP problem in algebraic form.

(b) Define all variables used in the problem statement. Produce a table listing (1) row names, (2) row identification, (3) row units, (4) column names, (5) column definitions, and (6) column units. For each row indicate its type.

(c) Produce a matrix tableau of coefficients representing the LP model.

(d) Code and run the problem using the computer.

(e) Write a letter to the farmer explaining exactly what should and should not be grown, how many acres should be used to grow which crops, how much of each required resource the farmer should be prepared to obtain, and how finances should be managed. Tell the farmer what profit can be expected from following your advice.

(f) How much could the farmer make from an additional acre of land?

(g) How much is additional free water worth to the farmer?

10 A machine shop has begun to expand and wishes to develop a five-year plan for adding on to its numerical control capacity. It is estimated that one machine is needed for every 500 units in monthly demand. The projected monthly demands for the next five years are 30,000, 50,000, 70,000, 80,000, and 90,000 units. Any machine purchased in one year does not become available until the following year. If machine capacity is not available, leased equipment can be provided at an annual cost of $10,000 per machine per year. Permanent machines cost $15,000. The inflation rate is expected to be 10 percent per year. Any permanent capacity purchased above the company's needs are estimated to incur an opportunity cost of $2000 per year. The board of directors has promised equipment budgets of $400,000, $600,000, $600,000, $600,000, and $400,000 for the next five years. Lease costs come out of a separate budget of $600,000 per year which must also be used for other operating expenditures. The lease is for two years. The company currently has 40 machines.

(a) Determine a building program for the machine shop that minimizes costs.

(b) Analyze the acceptability of the original plan.

**11** The analysis in Table 6.15 has been completed for a resource allocation decision aimed at maximizing profits.

**Table 6.15**

| Resource | Resources used | Resources surplus | Shadow price |
|---|---|---|---|
| Raw materials | 1262 tons | 0 | $122/ton |
| Storage space | 500 ft² | 100 ft² | 0 |
| Labor time | 3200 worker-hours | 0 | $4.10/worker-hour |
| Plant time | 120 hours | 20 hours | 0 |

(*a*) Which resources are the actual contraints on the solution?

(*b*) If additional labor can be bought at a rate of $4.50/hour, should the plant work overtime?

(*c*) If raw materials cost $110/ton, would it be worthwhile to purchase them?

**12** A linear programming model will allocate resources to no more variables than there are constraints in the model. Give an intuitive explanation of why this is so.

**13** An emission discharge restriction has been imposed on the operation of a chemical unit. The impact of the restriction is a limit on production time, since the unit must be shut down whenever the discharge reaches the allowable limit. An LP model designed to maximize the profits for the company has given a shadow price value for the discharge limit. What does the shadow price value tell the company with regard to the opportunity costs of abiding by the discharge limit?

**14** How can linear programming be used to establish prices for products that reflect the total cost of the product (both explicit and implicit).

**15** You have been asked to make a presentation to a manager to convince him that a linear programming model should be used to help make resource allocation decisions. What important points would you stress in this presentation?

## CASELETS

1. Barker and Smith, a contract pharmaceutical manufacturer, produces generic drugs for larger and more famous companies. For years Jim Barker, president of the company, has been concerned about the earnings of the business. Although drugs differ in specific ways, most drugs go through a similar sequence of manufacturing steps: raw material preparation, batching of raw materials, mixing of the batch, forming of the drug, coating, and packaging.

   Time estimates are available for the steps required in making most generic drugs. Once an order is received, a process sheet is prepared and a manufacturing cost estimate is produced. The cost estimate is then used to prepare a price quote for the product. The price can be set to give a minimum return above costs, but higher prices are negotiated whenever possible. Because Jim Barker has long been concerned about keeping established clients, Barker has agreed to produce small, difficult orders for some favored clients.

   In the past, Barker has set the price of these special product runs at what he considered to be a fair return, but he has begun to wonder whether this policy is wise. Barker has decided to rethink his mode of accepting and pricing orders. He has decided to appoint a task force to look at the following:

1. The production capabilities of the facility
2. The most desirable orders for the facility
3. The determination of a rational price for potential orders which can be used as a basis for negotiations
4. The advisability of the continued acceptance of small, difficult orders for favored customers
5. The price that should be charged for these small runs if they are accepted

You have been asked to head up this task force and have developed the following questions to give to the task force:
(*a*) What effect does the production of low-volume orders have on the company's profitability?
(*b*) What contributions can linear programming make in the following?
    (1) Evaluating plant capacity utilization.
    (2) Developing a rational pricing system
(*c*) What information would be required for a linear programming model?

2. Over time, the U.S. government has initiated twenty-three early childhood development programs. In a recent budget session, a decision was made to grant the package of programs a 5 percent funding increase for the next fiscal year. The question to be resolved by the Office of Management and Budget is how much additional funding should be granted to each of the twenty-three programs.

    After debating the relative merits of each program, no resolution could be reached as to what funding level should be approved. At the suggestion of one of the younger budget analysts, a linear programming approach to the problem was attempted. The decision variables were chosen as the amounts of funding to allocate to each program. Thus, there were twenty-three variables. The model was to maximize the educational achievement of the students measured by before-and-after tests.

    Constraints were established to reflect budget restrictions. Four additional constraints were added to ensure that the funding would be at least at minimum levels for the different groups receiving the funds.

    The model was then run and the results presented to the chief of the budget section responsible for educational programs. The chief was concerned that only five programs had received additional funding. He suggested that additional restrictions be added to the model to guarantee that each program receive some minimum level of increase.

    (*a*) Why did the original model provide allocations for only five variables?
    (*b*) What effect would the additional constraints have on the overall objective of maximizing educational achievement?
    (*c*) Do you think the additional constraints were appropriate?

## CASE 6.1: BREATHLESS TOBACCO COMPANY

### Introduction

Hack N. Cough, president of Breathless Tobacco Company (BTC), had become increasingly concerned over high costs of cigarette production at this firm's manufacturing facilities. According to industry trade publications, BTC's costs were 20 percent higher than those of its main competitors.

BTC was a small, independent tobacco firm specializing in exotic cigarettes for a small but growing market of smokers who were disappointed with the standard cigarette offered by the larger manufacturers. While some of the higher costs at BTC were attributed to the limited scale of operations, the president felt that cost reductions were feasible and necessary in order to increase market share.

The president appointed the chief of industrial engineering, David Thacker, to solve the problem of cost control. Thacker promptly assigned his top analyst, Toni Mengoli, to work on the problem full time.

### Cost Analysis

The first step Mengoli and Thacker took was to make a detailed analysis of the costs of cigarette manufacture. Of these costs, only those of raw materials appeared to be in line with costs experienced by other companies in the industry. There appeared to be no way to lower these costs. Manufacturing and transportation costs appeared to present the greatest opportunities for cost reduction, and a detailed analysis revealed that this was indeed true. For example, plants designed for menthol cigarettes also produced regular and extra-long brands. Such mixed production was inefficient and appeared to result from a careless decision process. Armed with this insight, Mengoli and Thacker were able to prepare a plan of action to submit for the president's approval.

### The Plan of Action

Mengoli and Thacker agreed that an allocation procedure guaranteeing manufacturing efficiencies through the assignment of production to the proper plants was necessary. Their initial studies had shown that enough information was available to build a model for use in allocating production. Since the model would only need to be applied yearly, the time available for data collection was sufficient to make linear programming a practical approach to modeling allocation. A linear programming model of the requisite decisions was therefore constructed.

BTC operated five production facilities and produced over 130 different varieties of cigarettes. The resource allocation decisions that were to be made would determine how much of each cigarette type to produce at each plant.

The objective of the resource allocation effort was decided upon as

Maximize sales revenues less costs

The model would make resource allocation decisions subject to limitations in plant capacities, product demand constraints, and limits on tobacco availabilities.

Once the structure of the model was outlined, Thacker met with Bob Viola, the vice president for manufacturing, who had been asked by the president to oversee the modeling project. Viola was an aggressive manager in his early forties. He had received an M.B.A. from a prestigious school and was obviously on a "fast-track" at BTC. Viola was remotely familiar with linear programming from his M.B.A. program. Unfortunately for both Thacker and Mengoli, Viola's business professor had impressed upon him the difficulty of applying linear programming to practical situations. Two facts had stuck in Viola's mind: that he had hated the pain-in-the-neck procedure that he had learned for solving linear programming problems and that the linear programming was strictly a numerical procedure that did not account for qualitative factors.

Viola listened to the presentation patiently but skeptically. "How many variables does this model involve?" he asked. Thacker had not anticipated such a detailed question but had fortunately made a prior estimate of model size.

"One thousand variables and nearly 300 constraints," Thacker answered, rather proud of the size of the model he and Mengoli were about to undertake. Much to their chagrin, the vice president appeared shocked.

"What did you say? My God, that will take forever to do," Viola responded.

"No, sir," Mengoli interjected. "The new computer systems are so efficient that they can take care of a problem like this in no time."

Not convinced, Viola asked about the data. "Have you estimated how long it will take to collect the data?"

"We can write programs for generating the data base," Mengoli responded.

"How long will that take?" the vice president continued.

"We checked with the data processing group and they think we can get the data in six months."

"What!" Viola shouted. "Hack has to do something about this decision before next month's board meeting."

Several minutes of silence elapsed as Thacker pondered this dilemma. All of a sudden the picture of Christopher Columbus hanging on the vice president's wall beside his Italian-American League certificate generated an idea. Who was that Italian mentioned in the OR/MS literature? Pareto! That was the guy's name. He said something about a concentration of value in a limited portion of the total universe.

Suddenly Thacker asked, "How many products does it take to make up 80 percent of our sales?"

"A few, I'm sure," Viola responded. "Let me check. The latest figures I have show that twelve brands make up 87 percent of our sales."

"I think that's our answer. Let's model the top twelve products. We can collect that data by hand."

"How long will the model take?"

"I think we can get something to you in three weeks," Thacker responded.

"That's more like it. Remember, we have a major problem here that needs to be solved in a short period of time. I can't impress on you enough the critical nature of this problem. No ivory tower stuff."

Somewhat chastened by the last remark, Thacker and Mengoli left the office with mixed emotions. This was their big moment to aid in an important decision. It was also an assignment that could ruin them if they failed to do it right.

## Development of the Allocation Model

After gaining the blessing of the vice president, Thacker and Mengoli began fleshing out the model and completed it fairly quickly. Aided by the high level of corporate sponsorship, Thacker was able to gather data from the various departments much more quickly than normal; the accounting group acted civilized for the first time in Thacker's experience. After a limited amount of debugging, the analysts were able to make a test run. The results of the model seemed reasonable, so Thacker arranged a meeting with Viola.

## Results of the Model

The results presented to Viola are summarized in Table 6.16.

The allocation plan would cost approximately $30.5 million, which was about $2.1 million less than that of the current allocation procedure. Thacker

**Table 6.16  Cigarette production allocations**

| Cigarette type* | Burlington | Sanford | Roanoke | Fayetteville | Peterstown |
|---|---|---|---|---|---|
| 1–R | 1,200,000† | | | | |
| 2–R | 800,000 | | | | |
| 3–M | | | 2,600,000 | | |
| 4–M | | 1,100,000 | 1,900,000 | | |
| 5–M | 2,700,000 | | 2,300,000 | | |
| 6–FT | | 450,000 | | 850,000 | |
| 7–FT | | 2,400,000 | | | |
| 8–FTM | | 1,800,000 | | | |
| 9–FTM | | | | 2,200,000 | |
| 10–XL | | | | 3,000,000 | |
| 11–XLM | 500,000 | | | | |
| 12–XLM | 838,500 | | | 161,500 | |

*Code: R = regular, M = menthol, FT = filter tip, FTM = filter tip menthol, XL = extra long, ELM = extra long menthol
†All figures are in cartons per month.

was pleased with the results of the model and gleefully anticipated his meeting with Viola.

When the results were presented to Viola, his reaction was different from that expected. "This solution is absurd. Thacker, you should know better. You know how many fires we have in producing cigarettes. What would happen if a fire breaks out in Burlington? You would wipe out three brands that you have only being produced at Burlington. It would take over six months to get back into production, and we would run out of stock of those three brands entirely."

Embarrassed that he had not considered the fire situation in the model, Thacker quickly pointed out that constraints could be added that would not allow more than a given percentage of certain types of cigarettes to be produced in any one plant. Viola seemed content with this provision and suggested that a limit be placed on production preventing more than 60 percent of any one brand being made at any one plant. A new run of the model was made and the results summarized as shown in Table 6.17.

The new results were presented to Viola before a report on the model was written. Again Viola expressed concern. "Look, we can't run a plant producing only 270,000 cartons per month. That's what you allocated to Peterstown."

Returning to the model, Thacker decided to leave the Peterstown plant out of the model entirely. Another run was made and new results obtained. Then another meeting with Viola.

"These results look a lot better. How much did we save?"

**Table 6.17 Revised cigarette production allocations**

| Cigarette type | Burlington | Sanford | Roanoke | Fayetteville | Peterstown |
|---|---|---|---|---|---|
| 1–R | 650,000 | | 5,500,000 | | |
| 2–R | 400,000 | 300,000 | | | 100,000 |
| 3–M | | | 1,200,000 | 1,400,000 | |
| 4–M | | 1,100,000 | 1,800,000 | | 100,000 |
| 5–M | 2,700,000 | | 2,300,000 | | |
| 6–FT | | 450,000 | | 780,000 | 70,000 |
| 7–FT | 960,000 | 1,440,000 | | | |
| 8–FTM | 520,000 | 1,228,000 | | | |
| 9–FTM | | | 880,000 | 1,320,000 | |
| 10–XL | | | 1,200,000 | 1,800,000 | |
| 11–XLM | 300,000 | | | 200,000 | |
| 12–XLM | 838,500 | | | 161,500 | |

Thacker, somewhat saddened, reported, "We saved $1.3 million. That's $800,000 less than the original solution."

"I'll assure you that $800,000 is a cheap price to pay for the fire insurance we have built into the model. Let's go see Hack."

## Postscript

The president was pleased but somewhat miffed by the report. He had been plant manager at Peterstown at one time and knew what an effect the plant closing would have on the town. After giving some thought to the problem, he decided to go along with the report, but he asked that Peterstown be converted into a regional warehouse to save the jobs in the community.

Each student in Thacker's collegiate OR/MS class had been promised a diamond for any study credited with certified savings of more than $1 million. A certified audit of the savings from the study led to Thacker receiving the promised diamond pin.

## Discussion Guide

1 Describe the changes necessary in the model. Should these problems have been anticipated by Thacker and Mengoli?

2 Was Viola's statement about the $800,000 fire insurance valid?

3 To what extent should an allocation model include qualitative considerations such as the Peterstown plant closing?

4 Could equivalent results have been obtained by any other process?

5 How often should these results be reevaluated? Was the Peterstown closing a wise decision?

## THREE

## OPERATING DECISIONS

# INTRODUCTION TO PART THREE
# OPERATING DECISIONS

Operating decisions can be big or small. They tend to dominate daily decision making. They require answers to questions about who, when, where, and how much but rarely about why. Operating decisions are usually of a restricted nature and are limited to a well-defined domain, thus permitting models to play an important role in making them.

Operational decisions described in this chapter are chosen from the most dominant ones encountered in practice. Service decisions have received special emphasis because of their growing importance. As in prior chapters, cases have been chosen and described so as to avoid overt reference to specific disciplines such as accounting, marketing, and finance.

Operating problems occur more often in large enterprises than in small ones. A small organization providing a limited array of goods and services from a single site is unlikely to encounter many of the problems described. To avoid complicating factors, however, the scope of the decisions in this part has been restricted to the lowest level of activity at which the problem would be encountered. As a result, most cases deal with smaller organizations, individual offices, or small assemblages of plants. Although large organizations are deemphasized by the adoption of this strategy, the operational units described are small enough to display the topical specificity implied by the chapter titles.

The nature of the operating decisions described and how they are likely to manifest themselves in organizations are topics which are addressed in each chapter of Part 3. In addition, specific operating problems are detailed in the chapters, and the uses of decision models in dealing with these specific problems are explained. The reader should acquire a good, general introduction to operating decisions from Part 3.

# SEVEN

## MATERIALS AND INVENTORY DECISIONS

## SYNOPSIS OF THE CHAPTER

Management of inventories is one of the most difficult of organizational problems, made more difficult by the fact that many organizations devote little attention to it except during bad economic conditions.

Inventories are necessary to all but the most primitive operations, but they are costly. The comfort of having large inventories of necessary items must be balanced by the pain of paying for the privilege of holding them.

This chapter describes the three dominant types of inventories: raw materials, components, and finished products. Although no perfectly applicable inventory management rules can be given, these three categories of inventories must usually be viewed differently.

Material requirements planning (MRP) is discussed as it applies to components in the production of finished products.

Systems which can be used to apply rough information to inventory control are discussed.

The most commonly referenced inventory control procedure, the economic order quantity (EOQ) is also explained.

The characteristics of effective inventory management are discussed, as are some of the drawbacks to effective control which are common to management structures. The difficulties inherent in assigning costs to inventories are also detailed.

## MAJOR CONCEPTS PRESENTED IN THIS CHAPTER

1. The role of inventory is to facilitate production and to fill orders without undue delays.
2. Inventories occur at numerous points in the organization from raw materials through to finished goods.

3. Inventory control models must consider the following variables:
   a. The structure of the organization
   b. The types of items in inventory
   c. The most important items to control
   d. The mechanism for replenishing the inventory stocks
4. The following major cost categories are involved in inventory control:
   a. Maintaining the inventory investment
   b. Resupplying the inventory
   c. Running out of stock
5. Intuition-based inventory systems are designed to structure inventory decisions in the following situations:
   a. Limited cost data is available.
   b. Analytical support is unavailable.
6. In economic order quantity models, there is an analytical trade-off between holding costs and order costs. These models function best when the following conditions are met
   a. The demand for the item can be predicted.
   b. The item is independent of other items in inventory.
7. Material requirements planning systems are information and decision systems that are best used in production where demands for components of various levels of production are dependent upon the demand for finished goods.

## EXPECTATIONS OF THE STUDENT

The student, after studying this chapter, should be able to do the following:

1. Tell about the origin of inventories, give the reasons for different inventory policies, and describe the uses of inventories
2. Discuss considerations involved in developing a scientific inventory plan with respect to the following:
   a. Organizational structure
   b. Types of inventory
   c. Mix of items in inventory
   d. Triggering mechanisms for production runs or orders
3. Evaluate the appropriate cost components for:
   a. Inventory holding costs
   b. Setup costs
4. Discuss and apply intuition-based inventory systems
5. Discuss and apply economic order quantity systems for a simple situation
6. Discuss and apply material requirements planning systems.

## FAIRMONT HOUSEHOLD PRODUCTS, INC.

Fairmont Household Products, Inc., was a small company making specialty products such as ice buckets, place mats, and related products. The main consumers of these products were trading stamp redemption centers and regional retail chains. Although Fairmont also maintained its own showroom, marketing of the products was done by a sales service company that handled similar products for a group of companies. Fairmont Household's products were marketed under the brand name Fairhouse.

As orders arrived at Fairhouse, they were entered in the production schedule as soon as the production manager, Hank Conforti, was assured that the necessary materials were available. In the case of ice buckets, production would proceed when cardboard cylinders and plastic coverings were available. Metal handles, a plastic bottom disc, and assorted decorative features comprised the other material necessary to produce a bucket. Other products in the Fairhouse line required cardboard sheets and plastic coverings as their major materials.

Orders varied in size from 50 units to 5000 units and had lead times which mysteriously ranged from two to six weeks. When an order was received, the ordered units were added to the production schedule. Frequently, Hank Conforti had to revise the schedule to expedite an order. In these cases, partially completed items were stored beside the workbench until they could be worked on again. Even so, overtime production was common and nearly 10 percent of the orders were falling behind schedule. When an order was expedited, the plastic coverings prepared for the order being interrupted were frequently damaged or unaccountably lost.

Previously, Hank Conforti had encountered difficulty in maintaining supplies of materials and had compensated by stocking as much as six months' worth of supplies. Inventory reviews were informal and supply orders were placed whenever stocks appeared to be low.

Demand was generally constant throughout the year except for a 10 to 20 percent increase in monthly demand during the Christmas production period from September through early November.

Most of the work was performed by women who used the income from the job to supplement their husbands' wages. Since most of the women had husbands who worked full time, their income from Fairhouse tended to be used for luxuries. The marginal nature of this income had two effects. There was considerable absenteeism; on the other hand, the women complained little if layoffs were necessary during slack demand periods.

Fairhouse decided to hire a consultant to clean up its inventory and production control problems after a long series of late deliveries had been experienced. Hank Conforti contacted a local management consultant, Samuel Isaacson, about solving the problems.

Arriving at the plant, Isaacson had difficulty finding the entrance. The door which he thought was an entrance was virtually inundated by piles of cardboard. On the second circuit of the plant, a dingy red door yielded to a push, and he shuffled through the dust to find the office. The entire plant seemed to be several layers deep in cardboard, plastic, and other items. However, he became lost in a maze of cardboard and happened upon an overall-clad man in a broom closet who was polishing a five-iron, a seven-iron, and the metal plate on a three-wood. Estimating that this person was a maintenance man, Isaacson asked him for directions to Hank Conforti's office whereupon the man laid down his irons, dusted

## Table 7.1 Fairmont Household Products, Inc.

Income Statement
For the Year Ended December 31, 1980

| | | |
|---|---:|---:|
| Sales revenue | | |
| Sales | | $2,089,673 |
| Returns and allowances | $5,300 | |
| Sales discounts | 8,700 | 14,000 |
| Net sales revenue | | $2,084,673 |
| Cost of goods sold | | |
| Finished goods inventory, January 1, 1980 | $ 23,300 | |
| Cost of goods manufactured (Schedule A) | 643,845 | |
| Cost of goods available for sale | $667,145 | |
| Finished goods inventory, December 31, 1980 | 19,650 | |
| Cost of goods | | $ 647,495 |
| Gross margin on sales | | $1,437,178 |
| Operating expenses | | |
| Selling | $42,873 | |
| General and administrative | 37,911 | |
| Total operating expense | | $ 80,784 |
| Net income before taxes | | $1,356,394 |
| Income tax expense | | 483,133 |
| Net income after income taxes | | $ 873,261 |

## Table 7.2 Fairmont Household Products, Inc.

*Schedule A*
Schedule of Cost of Goods Manufactured
For the Year Ended December 31, 1980

| | | | |
|---|---:|---:|---:|
| Materials used | | | |
| Materials inventory, January 1, 1980 | | | $275,833 |
| Materials purchased | | $568,779 | |
| Purchases, returns and allowances | $3,100 | | |
| Purchases discounts | 4,250 | 7,350 | |
| Net cost of materials purchased | | | 576,129 |
| Cost of materials available for use | | | $851,962 |
| Materials inventory December 31, 1980 | | | 338,421 |
| Cost of materials used | | | $513,541 |
| Direct labor | | | 87,341 |
| Manufacturing overhead | | | 43,747 |
| Total period manufacturing costs | | | $644,629 |
| Work-in-process inventory, January 1, 1980 | | | 36,395 |
| Work-in-process inventory, December 31, 1980 | | | 37,179 |
| Cost of goods manufactured | | | $643,845 |

off one tennis shoe, and said, "I'm Hank Conforti." Somewhat embarrassed, Isaacson introduced himself.

Conforti and Isaacson made their way to the manager's office and found Mrs. Shortlet, the secretary to the owner of the company, waiting for them. She had come all the way to the plant from Metroburg to meet with the consultant Hank had invited to look into the plant's costs. She had brought balance sheets from the three previous years and income statements for the same period.

It was clear from the income statements and the schedules of costs of goods that raw material costs had increased substantially over the past three years. Transportation charges had also risen and it eventually became evident that these costs were due to the increasing number of special delivery orders. Discussion with Hank and Mrs. Shortlet revealed to Isaacson that inventory charges had also increased by over 30 percent per unit sold in three years. Inventory control appeared to be the central problem impairing the plant's cost control. The income statement and schedule of costs of goods for 1980 in Tables 7.1 and 7.2 demonstrate the high contribution of materials to overall costs.

After discussing some procedural details, Hank Conforti and the consultant agreed on a project outline and decided that Isaacson should review the inventory procedures at Fairhouse and suggest some way to reduce inventory costs.

## THE ORIGIN AND PURPOSE OF INVENTORIES

Inventories originate from the primordial fear of shortage. To a large extent, attitudes on inventories are still primarily irrational, although the day is probably past when such attitudes are blamed on childhood training. There are rational reasons for holding or avoiding inventories, and effective management should base its inventory policies on reason. Inventories of finished goods are kept in order to satisfy customer demand quickly. Inventory between two production stages can be used to guarantee ease of production.

An early instance of the conscientious use of inventories as an element of organizational strategy came from the business mind of J. C. Penney (1931). He established a central warehouse to supply his numerous stores. Penney wanted to use the warehouse to gain volume discounts and to keep consistent storeroom supplies. However, the warehouse concept failed because the store managers were independent souls who were incensed by the idea that their supplies should be ordered by someone else.

In the manufacturing environment, the use of inventories as a part of a manufacturing strategy has a long but uncertain history. Frederick Taylor, the "father of scientific management," was one of the early advocates of manufacturing planning as a means of reducing costs. The use of mathematics in the determination of inventory levels can be traced back to 1915 in a publication by Ford Harris (1915).

Inventories today have a multitude of uses. The most obvious of these is in retail stores which must have stocks from which to supply customer needs. Wholesale inventories are used to supply retail stores in both a timely and consistent fashion. Long production runs, which are used to build inventories, reduce unit production costs by spreading setup costs over a larger volume of products. In-process inventories ensure that all production stages are kept fully supplied.

Various other efficiencies and cost reductions motivate the holding of inventories. For example, inventories can consist of extra product generated while operating important equipment, such as furnaces or kilns, which are costly to shut down. Similarly, problems incurred by short production runs can be avoided by stockpiling critical raw stocks needed to ensure that longer runs can be made.

Not every instance of building inventory stocks is aimed at costs or efficiency. For instance, labor conditions can result in overstocking. A good example is a union factory which experiences low demand on one product line. Management can lay off workers, but if it does so, there will be a chain reaction of "bumping" wherein workers with seniority will take jobs on other product lines. The result of bumping is that layoffs are spread throughout the plant and workers experienced on the various product lines are replaced by workers experienced only on the closed line. To avoid this problem and other labor problems, management may adopt "level loading," the policy of keeping constant production levels without regard to demand or inventory levels.

Irrational or sloppy procedures may result in expensive, useless inventories. Inventories have a way of getting lost; once large quantities of items have been in a warehouse long enough, they seem to become invisible. Sometimes salespersons attain inordinate control over production, and a nervous salesperson often opts for large safety stocks of items with high profit margins.

Irrational and sloppy reasons for overstocks and understocks must routinely be questioned. Inventories are expensive to hold, but missing the opportunity to make a sale is also costly. Costs must be balanced, and rational policies must be applied if possible.

Upon reviewing the inventory situation at Fairhouse, Isaacson discovered that inventories were needed for at least three purposes:

1. To keep a reliable supply of raw materials
2. To achieve economies in setup costs
3. To keep production stages fully utilized

The next question to be answered was what inventory decisions would have to be made to lower costs effectively in these three areas.

## INVENTORY DECISIONS

Several of Hank Conforti's routine decisions were actually inventory decisions. These were: (1) when should an order or a new production run be initiated, and (2) how much should be purchased or produced? *When* and *How much* are questions common to all inventory decisions. The question Isaacson considered was whether a manager such as Hank Conforti could successfully rely on intuition or whether the objective assistance provided by a decision model was needed.

This question is difficult to answer to the satisfaction of an individual manager due to the "doctrine of accountability." This doctrine states that no supervisors can be held accountable for that over which they have no control. Inventories are unlikely to be under the total control of any individual; therefore, an individual manager will likely prefer the policy which minimizes personal risk.

Inventory decisions generally involve few organizational rewards, but considerable organizational risks. In Hank Conforti's case, his recognition as a good plant manager did not come from successes in inventory control. On the other hand, unsuccessful inventory decisions could have been a highly visible financial indicator of Hank Conforti's lack of managerial talents. Therefore, he may have had a strong incentive to use an aid which lessened the risk of expensive inventory problems.

As was mentioned, inventory decisions can affect many parts of an organization, including each stage of production and the marketing and purchasing functions. Consequently, different members of the organization may make conflicting inventory decisions based upon perceptions of their own organizational well-being, and only a unified inventory policy handed down by upper management can avoid frequent and disruptive organizational conflicts. Objective decision models can help produce such a unified system.

Inventory control can be too complex to approach without a model. Even in smaller businesses, inventory decisions may involve thousands of items. To control stocks of all such items, a manager, through necessity, may turn to some form of analytical guide. A model may be able to consider the many facets of inventory control, at least assuring that all of the interrelationships between products and components are considered.

The bottom line of inventory control is that it offers opportunities for significant cost reductions. Inventory cost may be one of the largest components in a product's total cost. An inventory model that can cut inventory costs by as little as 1 percent may make a significant impact on profits.

In reviewing the situation at Fairhouse, Isaacson felt that Hank Conforti's reason for turning to a model for inventory control was his desire to reduce costs. However, as he observed the plant manager's absorption in his daily golf game, Isaacson felt that Hank Conforti only wanted some system that would require a minimum investment of his own time and that Conforti was not really interested in day-to-day operations at Fairhouse. Isaacson mapped his plans for developing a model that Conforti would use. The first step was to study the inventory problems at hand.

## INITIATING THE INVENTORY CONTROL STUDY

In order for a specific inventory plan to be developed, several inventory characteristics must be identified:

1. The organizational structure's relation to inventory
2. The types of inventory

3. The relative quantities of inventory items
4. The triggering mechanism for production or ordering

## Organizational Structure

Inventory control functions often enter into organizational structure as shown in Fig. 7.1.

An arrangement such as this inherently causes conflicts because purchasing and inventory control are not directly under the same manager. While the purchasing manager is responsible for the control of raw materials inventory, the inventory control manager is generally responsible for in-process and finished goods inventory. In a financial statement, however, the cost of inventories is generally reported as one figure. Thus, divided responsibility exists for inventory cost control, but accountability may not be divided equitably.

Ammer (1969) argues that a materials manager's position should be established and given the centralized function of purchasing, production control, and materials movement, as shown in Fig. 7.2.

The inventory control system must be designed to fit the required organizational structure. If an inventory control function has authority to cut across several prior lines of accountability and jurisdiction, then the organizational structure will be effectively redefined.

At Fairhouse, Hank Conforti was solely responsible for inventory, and Isaacson decided that an extremely simplified system would have to be developed to satisfy Conforti's requirements. In addition, Isaacson realized that something had to be done to counter the "sloppy" attitudes of the entire Fairhouse organization toward inventory control.

One important ally that Isaacson hoped to recruit in his inventory control activities was Conforti's son, Henry. Conforti had insisted that his son get a business degree and afterwards had hired him into the production department. Henry Conforti was a shy young man who naturally took to accounting as his collegiate

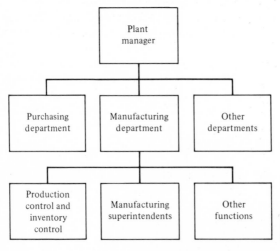

**Figure 7.1** Typical organization structure.

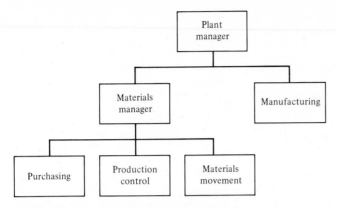

**Figure 7.2** A centralized inventory organization.

major. He liked to work with numbers and was uncomfortable in managerial situations at Fairhouse. Isaacson saw Henry Conforti as the logical person to take a role in inventory control at Fairhouse. Having acquired an understanding of the organizational factors at Fairhouse, Isaacson next turned his attention to the various types of inventory that need controlling.

## Types of Inventory

In most companies until the early 1960s, all types of inventory were treated as requiring only one type of inventory control system. In-process and raw material inventories were controlled in the same fashion as finished goods. As a result, inventories often did not match requirements. With the introduction of material requirements planning (MRP) systems, a new approach was initiated for dealing with dependent demands. An item with dependent demand is one that has its demand level fixed by some other item. Inventory for the dependent item is dictated solely by orders. For example, the demand for handles for ice buckets was directly determined by the overall demand for ice buckets. In such a case, it makes no sense to maintain an inventory control system for handles separate from the control system for buckets.

In general, raw materials and in-process inventories must be treated in a fashion different from that of finished goods. In the case of Fairhouse, finished goods inventories were largely determined by the marketplace. The demand for components, such as cardboard cylinders, handles, and plastic wrap, was a function of both finished goods and of in-process inventories and raw materials; yet, each type of inventory had its own peculiar control mechanism.

## The Mix of Items in Inventory

In virtually every organization, the distribution of inventory quantities follows an "80-20" relationship. That is, 20 percent of the items in inventory comprise over 80 percent of the total inventory value. While the specific numerical values may

**Table 7.3 Distribution of inventory value at Fairhouse**

| Inventory class | Items in inventory | Percent of items | Inventory value | Percent of inventory value |
| --- | --- | --- | --- | --- |
| A | 23 | 10.3 | $610,263 | 86.6 |
| B | 69 | 30.9 | 51,387 | 7.3 |
| C | 131 | 58.8 | 42,671 | 6.1 |
| Totals | 223 | 100.0 | $704,321 | 100.0 |

differ from situation to situation, it is generally true that a small number of inventory items comprise a large part of the inventory investment. Special strategies should be established for the 20 percent items since these offer the greatest opportunities for inventory cost reduction.

With these ideas in mind, Isaacson investigated the previous year's sales. He discovered that if he divided items into rough categories A, B, and C, their relationship to inventory costs could be understood easily with the help of Table 7.3.

This table convinced Isaacson to concentrate his attention on the production of class A items and to reduce the attention he gave to the class B and C items. His next step was to analyze the order initiation system at Fairhouse.

## The Triggering Mechanism for Production Runs or Orders

Production runs in an operation are generally triggered either by orders received or by the occurrence of low inventory levels. The higher the price or the more unusual an item, the more likely it is that a call for its production is triggered only by a customer order; in this case, management is primarily concerned with completing the product on time. Sufficient availability of raw materials inventories is required to ensure that production of such items can meet promised due dates.

Production of low-priced, high-volume items is likely to be triggered by a need to replenish inventory. Inventories, from raw materials through finished goods, are important to the smooth functioning of this type of production system.

The appropriate inventory control system, then, depends upon the production triggering mechanism. In the case of Fairhouse, production was usually initiated by actual orders received from its marketing organization.

## ASSESSMENT OF COSTS IN INVENTORY CONTROL

One of the most difficult facets of inventory control is the identification of the appropriate costs, including inventory holding costs and order or setup costs. Cost estimation is difficult for several reasons. In many cases, the accounting system may not be flexible enough to provide an estimate of these costs. In other cases, there are philosophic differences of opinion as to how such costs should be derived.

## Inventory Costs

The inventory holding cost is the cost of carrying an item in inventory. Generally this cost is expressed as an annual percentage of the nominal product value. The major component of this cost is the cost of capital invested in inventory. Other charges for holding inventory include the following:

1. Warehouse costs, including facilities, labor, and utilities
2. Inventory losses due to theft, spoilage, or obsolescence
3. Taxes and insurance
4. General and administrative costs

The annual rate charged for capital investment in inventory is a controversial figure. Some organizations use the going rate on invested securities as this number, since the money invested in inventories could have been invested in interest-bearing opportunities. Other organizations argue that the overall rate of return on the organization's net worth should represent the true cost of capital. Another view advocates that the carrying cost's capital-related component should be the rate at which future incomes and expenses are discounted to present value. An assumption made in each of these cases is that the inventory investment is liquid and risk-free. Although this assumption is not generally valid, it is used to justify the use of standard return-on-investment criteria for the cost of capital in inventory. If the inventory capital is much less liquid than that of other capital investments, a higher charge on inventory capital is appropriate.

The type of inventory also affects liquidity and, thus, the capital charge associated with that type. Raw materials are generally more liquid than finished goods. In-process inventories are probably less liquid than are raw materials or finished goods. Retail and wholesale inventories, since they involve a segmented market, are less liquid than are finished goods at the plant. The organization may wish to consider fitting different capital charges to different types of inventory.

Once the cost of capital is determined, the remaining inventory charges need to be determined. It should be emphasized that these costs should be variable, not fixed, charges. In other words, these costs should only include elements that vary with the inventory level, so-called direct costs.

## Setup Costs

The second major component of costs of producing to inventory is setup cost. This cost is incurred by the setup of a production line. Jigs and fixtures need to be put in place, models need to be changed, patterns need to be altered, and other adjustments may be required in changing from one product to another. For purchased items, the corresponding cost is an order cost, since it costs money to execute an order. Costs may include such items as clerical and computer expenses.

What constitutes the order cost is often in dispute. The purchasing department clearly exists for the purpose of processing orders, but the question is whether it is legitimate to factor the entire cost of this department into order costs. In answering this question, it is important to recall the role of the order cost in the inventory decision. Basically, an analysis must be made of the extra costs directly attributable to an order. There are some fixed costs of purchasing which are independent of the number of orders. These should not be considered in the inventory cost analysis. Exactly what does or does not constitute valid order costs is controversial and may only be resolved according to the organization's accounting philosophy.

A similar controversy with respect to production setup cost is whether to include the loss of production time during setup as an opportunity cost component. If the facility is operating at full capacity, the loss in profits during downtime is generally considered a legitimate expense to be added into the setup cost.

Focusing on Fairhouse, Isaacson found that no detailed cost records existed on either the carrying cost or the setup cost. He did find that the lead operator performed the setups and that Hank Conforti did the ordering of raw materials. A rate of return of 25 percent was generally required of capital investments, and inventory was stored anywhere at all throughout the plant. Isaacson was also able to find the history of lead times for raw material orders. He decided that his next step should be to go to the very start of the production process and do an analysis of raw material inventories to see whether obvious improvements could be made.

## INVENTORY ANALYSIS—INTUITION-BASED SYSTEMS

In many organizations, lack of cost data is cited as a reason for not using any form of inventory cost analysis. Cost data may not have been collected or may not be in a usable form. Inventory levels might also be so fluid as to make *any* rigorous inventory procedure inaccurate. However, even in such cases fairly simple procedures can be used for estimating appropriate inventory levels.

Hank needed a "quick and dirty" inventory analysis procedure and Isaacson suggested one based upon Table 7.4. The first requirement of a rapid, simple procedure is a minimal set of qualitative and quantitative data. Table 7.4 is an outline of a data analysis form that was adapted for collecting and displaying the minimal data at Fairhouse.

Table 7.4 illustrates the type of data that is likely to exist in any organization, large or small, public or private. The trade-off between order costs and inventory costs is implicit in the table but is not treated explicitly since these costs are difficult to estimate. The review necessary to prepare such a table could take place at any fixed time intervals; in this case it was done every week. The order decision for each item in the table will be reviewed to illustrate the table's use.

It can be seen that embossed handles were a noncritical item and that 1200 units were on hand. Since yearly demand was 20,000 units, or 400 units per week, the time required to exhaust this inventory level was only three weeks. Since lead time was four weeks, Hank saw that he should have placed an order the prior week. He made a decision to place an expedited order for twelve weeks of supply. The order quantity was subjective, reflecting Hank's desire to balance the cost of carrying the $1.50 items in inventory against the cost of frequent orders.

**Table 7.4 Inventory analysis worksheet for 5/23**

| Previous order | Item | Demand per year* | Item cost | Critical item? | Lead time, weeks | Estimated supply on hand or on order | Time to exhaust current supply, weeks | Decision |
|---|---|---|---|---|---|---|---|---|
| 3/14 | Embossed handles | 20,000 | $0.50 | No | 4 | 1200 | 3 | Reorder now—expedite 3/21 |
| 12/20 | Cardboard cylinders | 10,000 | $8.25 | Yes | 2 | 4000 | 20 | Don't order |
| 3/21 | Plastic sheet, alligator pattern | 12,000 | $2.75 | No | 2 | 800 | 3.3 | |
| 10/11 | Knobs | 8,000 | $0.20 | No | 3 | 500 | 3.1 | Reorder now |

*50 weeks = 1 year

233

On the hand, cardboard cylinders were a critical and costly item. An earlier decision had been made to keep a large stock of this item on hand because of its critical nature. A stored cylinder is 10 feet long prior to cutting, each cylinder being equivalent to ten buckets. During Hank's inventory review, he decided that too many cylinders had been stocked in the past. Twenty weeks of supply were currently on hand and it had been twenty-two weeks since the last bucket order. Since the cost of the item was substantially more than that of other items, he suddenly realized that this item must be a major component of his raw material inventory cost. The lead time of two weeks also indicated that the need for a large supply did not exist.

Plastic sheet with an alligator pattern was one of the more popular coverings for the ice buckets. In his review of this item, Hank Conforti found that 3.3 weeks of supply was on hand. Since the lead time was two weeks and the item was not critical, he decided to hold off ordering additional quantities for another week.

Knobs for the ice bucket lids were another item reviewed. The supply of this inexpensive item's inventory was adequate only to carry it through the order period. Therefore, a new order was placed for additional units. Since the unit cost was low, Hank decided to order a nine months' supply of knobs. His decision was influenced by the small size of the item and its ease of storage, in addition to the availability of discounts from the supplier on large purchases.

The worksheet in Table 7.4 demonstrates an easy-to-use, easy-to-implement procedure. Its advantage over more formal systems is that the required data are usually available; the only periodic number necessary is a count of the items on hand. Although the system does not weigh the direct trade-offs between ordering and carrying costs, it does provide a decision framework the manager can use in a logical manner.

Isaacson, with Henry Conforti's assistance, set up the inventory system exemplified in Table 7.4 for seventeen of the eighty-six different items held in raw material inventory. These seventeen items comprised 89 percent of the total raw material inventory in the previous year. The remaining sixty-nine products were to be managed informally, as before. At the start of the implementation, Hank Conforti discovered that he had over $90,000 in excess inventory. After three months of implementation, the average inventory investment dropped by 38 percent. Having gained control of raw material inventory, Conforti looked around for new problems and asked Isaacson to start work on the inventory carried in his display shop.

# INVENTORY ANALYSIS—
# ECONOMIC ORDER QUANTITY SYSTEMS

A cursory look at the retail display room inventory revealed an entirely different inventory situation than had been encountered in the raw materials stockroom. But again, the 80-20 principle described the stocks; approximately 150 items were kept on the shelves, while only 23 made up the bulk of total sales.

The existing inventory policy dictated that a production order go to the plant whenever stock ran out. Hank Conforti had little time to devote to the display room and rarely had inventory counted. He based his production quantity decisions on some mixture of shelf space availability and his feelings about future demand.

Isaacson began his investigation by estimating inventory costs. He discovered that Fairhouse's return on net worth during the previous year had been 22 percent. He decided to use this figure as the carrying charge for retail inventory, since the additional costs of holding inventory appeared to be minimal.

The cost of setup for a production run was more difficult to assess. Isaacson observed the actual setup of a job and found the lead operator to be the main person performing the job. The setup he observed took twenty minutes, but no additional workers were idled during that time. Using the wage rate of the lead operator, he was able to obtain a labor cost for setup.

Since Fairhouse was not performing at full capacity, Isaacson decided not to include an opportunity cost for profits lost during setup in his setup cost.

After reviewing several inventory control plans, Isaacson decided that a "Q" type of system would operate best. In this system, the inventory is reviewed on a continuing basis. A simplified description of such a system follows. When the inventory drops to a given level (called the reorder point), an order is placed for a fixed number of units (called the economic order quantity or EOQ). This system is graphically shown in Fig. 7.3. Orders arrive instantaneously, and inventory is depleted at a constant rate, resulting in orders being made at fixed intervals.

In order to use the Q system, Isaacson had to determine both the reorder point (RP) and the order quantity (EOQ). The order quantity, he reasoned, would be influenced by the costs of carrying inventory, the cost of setting up the production line, and the demand rate for the product. In general, the reorder point should be influenced by the amount of time it takes to replenish the inventory and the consequences of running out of stock.

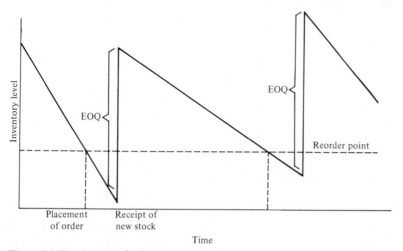

**Figure 7.3** The Q system for inventory control.

## Cost Components

At any given time, the inventory cost will be the amount of inventory on hand times the inventory carrying charge $h$. Given an expected maximum inventory equal to the EOQ and an expected minimum level of zero, the average inventory level throughout the year will be EOQ/2. Thus, the total inventory cost will be $h(EOQ/2)$.

The other cost required is the order cost. Given a demand of $D$ (units per year) and a production quantity of EOQ, the number of orders in a year will be $(D/EOQ)$. If the setup charge is $S$, the total charge will be $S(D/EOQ)$.

If the minimum total cost is to be achieved, the total cost of inventory should be set equal to the total setup cost. Thus

$$h(EOQ/2) = S(D/EOQ)$$

$$EOQ = \sqrt{\frac{2DS}{h}}$$

It is interesting to note that this formulation represents a balancing of both the marketing and financial forces in an organization. Marketing policy is directed toward maintaining inventory levels at a sufficiently high level to prevent running out of stock and long delivery delays. The finance department on the other hand would like to keep inventory costs at a minimum in order to reduce overall costs. Thus, the formulation presented above amounts to a balancing of two forces within the organization.

In order to illustrate the concept of an economic order quantity, Isaacson selected a high-volume item for analysis. The showroom demand for a plain black ice bucket was found to be 1200 units per year. The item sold for $10.50 and took an average of one hour to set up on the production line. Using the previously determined numbers, appropriate costs were then calculated to be

$$h = (\$10.50 \text{ per unit}) \times (0.22 \text{ per year})$$

$$h = \$2.31 \text{ per unit per year}$$

$$S = (1 \text{ hour per setup}) \times (\$8.50 \text{ per hour})$$

$$S = \$8.50 \text{ per setup}$$

From these calculations, Samuel found the economic order quantity to be

$$EOQ = \sqrt{\frac{2DS}{h}}$$

$$EOQ = \sqrt{\frac{2(1200)\ (8.50)}{2.31}}$$

$$EOQ = 94 \text{ black ice buckets}$$

The order policy is stated thus: Order 94 buckets whenever the reorder point is reached.

The reorder point was the next quantity to be calculated. Since a formal replacement policy did not exist at Fairhouse, Isaacson asked for guidance from Hank Conforti. After some discussion, they agreed that enough stock should be available to allow three weeks for replenishing stocks. Checking the past year's sales slips, Isaacson was able to calculate the standard deviation of demand during lead time. The reorder point was then formulated as

$$RP = D_{LT} + KS_{LT}^{*}$$

where

$RP$ = reorder point
$D_{LT}$ = demand during lead time
$S_{LT}$ = standard deviation of demand during lead time
$K$ = protection constant

Before Isaacson could apply this formula, he needed to know the amount of protection that Hank Conforti wanted to provide for the items in the showroom. Isaacson explained that a $K$ value of 1.0 should provide enough stock to get through approximately 68 percent of the reorder time periods without shortages.

A $K$ value of 2.0 would have provided protection during 95 percent of the previous year's reorder periods; whereas, a $K$ value of 3.0 provided protection for 98 percent of the reorder periods.

Hank decided to use a $K$ value of 1.0, since a customer would generally select another item if the preferred one was out of stock. Isaacson found the standard deviation of demand to be thirty-two items and calculated the reorder point to be

$$RP = D_{LT} + KS_{LT}$$

$$RP = 3(1200/50) + 1(32)$$

$$RP = 104 \text{ ice buckets (black)}$$

Isaacson then explained the policy to the retail manager, "When your stock drops to 104 units, place an order for 94 units."

When he presented the analysis to Hank Conforti, the plant manager seemed impressed by the inventory control system.

"I do have one concern, Sam. Do I have to keep a running count of inventory for each item?"

Isaacson responded by illustrating the use of the two-bin inventory system. He suggested that the inventory representing the reorder point (e.g., 104 black buckets) be placed away from the main shelf area of the storeroom. When the supplies on the main shelf ran out, a new production order would be placed, and the reorder stock would be brought forward and placed on the shelf.

Hank Conforti liked the idea of the two-bin system, but seemed to be concerned. "I'm really worried about these calculations you did. I trust you, but what happens when you leave? What should I know about the assumptions you

---

*Where the standard deviation of demand ($S$) is calculated for a week's unit of time, the standard deviation of demand for the lead time can be found approximately as $S_{LT} = (\sqrt{LT})S$.

used in the equation? Why didn't you do the same thing for raw materials inventories? What about intermediate products we use in making our final merchandise? Could you tell me again why you used different inventory methods for different stages of production?"

## Limitations on the Use of EOQ Models

The economic order quantity model is a simple approach to a large variety of inventory conditions, but, since it is a simplified model, it must be used carefully. Several limitations of the model and its assumptions must be weighed before using the model.

The model assumes that demand is uniform over a long time period. For example, if the demand is sixty units per month, the model assumes that the daily demand will be approximately two units. This condition might not be true for inventories that have "lumpy" demand. A monthly magazine, for instance, has its greatest demand at the beginning of the month.

In its pure form, the EOQ approach to inventory assumes that the demand is totally known. The model presented in the previous section allows for variation in demand in that it provides for safety stock in the determination of the reorder point. However, the formula does not consider the possibility of permanent shifts in demand.

Economies of scale in production and volume discounts in purchased orders are not considered in the basic EOQ model. Consider the setup cost (or order cost). It is influenced by the order size: it may be more economical to produce or order in larger batches.

The basic EOQ model does not consider possible obsolescence of an item. Even though the EOQ model suggests a six-month order be produced, it would be unwise to follow that advice if the item may become obsolete during that six-month period. Goyal (1973) discusses this problem as it applies to greeting card production.

In many production (and ordering) situations, complementary products are produced or ordered together. Once a production line is set up for one product, the setup of others may be inexpensive. In the case of Fairhouse, once the line is set up for a standard ice bucket, changes in pattern result in only minor setup costs.

The same principle applies to ordering items. If a hospital pharmacy places an order for one type of drug from a supplier, the increase in order cost of ordering additional drugs in the same order is minimal. As discussed earlier, the basic EOQ model assumes the order cost to be constant and does not consider the effect of complementary products requested on the same order.

The EOQ model may be inappropriate if production is constrained to fixed batch sizes. For example, a mixing container used in the production of chocolate candy may produce batches of only one size. An EOQ requiring a fraction of a batch to be made may not be feasible.

Other constraints limiting the applicability of the EOQ approach are those imposed by the influence of other products: there may not be enough warehouse space to produce all products at EOQ levels. In this case the problem is one of "constrained mixed inventory." Similarly, there may not be enough production time to produce one product at its EOQ level because other products cut into available time. There may be a company policy limiting the total dollars allocated to inventory, and in the case of mixed inventory this problem becomes especially complicated.

Although the above limitations imply that the EOQ model is an ineffective inventory control tool, it is an effective approximation for many types of inventory. Wilson (1977) provides a simple set of rules of thumb for dealing with most of the mentioned limitations on the EOQ model. Brown (1977) also offers practical suggestions for dealing with the shortcomings of the classic EOQ model.

## INVENTORY ANALYSIS-MRP SYSTEMS

One severe restriction on the use of EOQ models stems from products whose demand is dependent upon other stages of production. The demand for the vinyl used in ice bucket coverings is entirely dependent upon the demand for ice buckets. If a customer places an order for 1000 ice buckets of a particular design, it does not make sense to base the production level of vinyl coverings of that design on an economic order quantity. Instead, the production of the vinyl coverings must be subordinated to the production of the buckets. To derive the levels of production of items that make up an assembled product requires a special approach different from that of the EOQ model. This approach is material requirements planning.

Material requirements planning (MRP) systems had their origins in the early 1960s and sprang from the need for an inventory control procedure which could coordinate the production of the subassemblies that go into a final product.

MRP systems are effective inventory management tools for controlling availability of any items whose demands are determined by the production level of a final, assembled product. Examples of dependent items include the various levels of subassemblies, purchased components, and raw materials. EOQ systems are effective in dealing with independent demands such as finished goods. Thus, while an EOQ model may be used to specify the total number of finished goods to produce at any one time, MRP systems are used to govern production of the components that go into a finished good.

In order to use MRP systems, the following requirements must be met:

1. A correct bill of materials exists for each finished good.
2. An accurate production schedule is available for a reasonable production planning horizon (generally four to sixteen weeks).
3. There is a high degree of integrity in inventory record keeping, i.e., records are fairly accurate.

The availability of a computer is often listed as a requirement for MRP systems; computer needs will be discussed at the appropriate point.

Isaacson found that not one of the above requirements existed at Fairhouse. Since Hank Conforti had "grown up" with the business, he had never felt it necessary to prepare a parts list (bill of materials) for any of the items sold. There were no operations procedures or other documentation for any product. Fortunately, the product structure was simple, and Isaacson believed he could generate a bill of materials for the major products on his own.

Orders arriving at Fairhouse typically requested a four- to six-week delivery schedule. At any time, the next four weeks' schedule was fairly well determined, and schedules for the fifth and sixth weeks could be predicted with reasonable accuracy. Schedules beyond the sixth week were generally unavailable.

The question that had concerned Isaacson most throughout the inventory project at Fairhouse was that of the integrity of the inventory records. Hank Conforti was a seat-of-the-pants manager; he was a freewheeling manager who did not like detail work. As long as his golf game did not suffer, he was happy. But, if an order was late, he gladly took on the challenge of getting it out the door on time. He took considerable satisfaction in running a "crisis-oriented" facility. As a result, when he was away, the plant failed to operate as well. In fact, Hank Conforti blamed his son Henry for the company's problems during Hank's absences. The business background that Henry had obtained along with his accounting degree had not seemed to give him the preparation he needed at Fairhouse.

Isaacson discussed the inventory problems at Fairhouse with a colleague who agreed with Isaacson's earlier idea of making Henry Conforti an integral component of the plant inventory systems. The colleague suggested involving Henry in MRP.

"Henry understands the necessity of rationalizing the production system, since he has had problems coping with it. The MRP system will not only give Henry a way of earning his father's respect but will also provide him with a method for reducing the crisis atmosphere that he deplores."

Isaacson decided to follow his colleague's advice and began to develop an MRP system for Fairhouse that would involve Henry Conforti in its operation. To minimize the system installation problems, Isaacson decided to concentrate his attention initially on the ice bucket product line. His first step was to develop the bill of materials.

A bill of materials is generally broken down into levels: level 0 representing the finished product; level 1, major components in the final assembly; level 2, subcomponents of the major components; and so on until the final level, which usually consists of raw materials. A bill of materials for the ice bucket is shown in Fig. 7.4.

Having drawn up a bill of materials, Isaacson's next step was to establish lead times for the various production stages and a master schedule for the next six weeks. The lead times were difficult to obtain because some of the previous records represented expedited orders, while others were influenced by abnormal delays. Using his own judgment, Isaacson arrived at values he hoped were representative. His next step was to examine the demand forecast for ice buckets as shown in Table 7.5.

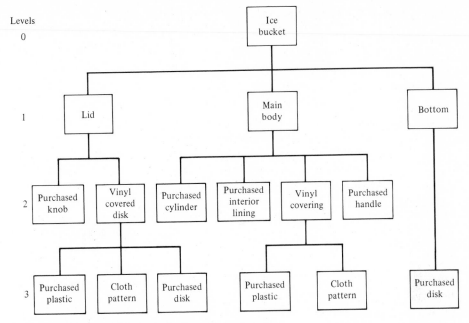

**Figure 7.4** Bill of materials for ice bucket with level coating.

From this schedule, Isaacson attempted to devise a master schedule reflecting the order release dates for a time horizon of six weeks. A first attempt at the development of a master schedule is shown in Table 7.6.

As shown in Table 7.6 sufficient inventory exists in week 1 to supply projected requirements for that week. In week 2 no orders are projected, so enough supply exists for that week. In week 3, an order of 200 units is due for shipment. Since only 50 units remain in inventory from the previous week, an order of 150 units must be received during week 3 to accommodate the order. Since lead time is 2 weeks, an order must be made during week 1 to provide the material for week 3. Similarly, orders must be released in weeks 2 and 3 to accommodate demands during weeks 4 and 5.

One value of an MRP system is its enhancement of planning, which can be useful in achieving economies as compared with conventional job order production. For example, it may be more economical to combine the orders of 50 and 40 units in weeks 2 and 3 into one order. After looking at the setup and inven-

**Table 7.5 Requirements forecast for
conventional ice bucket**

|  | Week | | | | | |
|---|---|---|---|---|---|---|
|  | 1 | 2 | 3 | 4 | 5 | 6 |
| Projected requirements | 50 |  | 200 | 50 | 40 |  |

### Table 7.6 Master schedule for conventional ice bucket*

|  | Week | | | | | | |
|---|---|---|---|---|---|---|---|
|  | 0 | 1 | 2 | 3 | 4 | 5 | 6 |
| Projected requirements |  | 50 |  | 200 | 50 | 40 |  |
| Inventory | 100 | 50 | 50 |  |  |  |  |
| Planned order release |  | 150 | 50 | 40 |  |  |  |

*Lead time = two weeks

### Table 7.7 Revised master schedule for conventional ice bucket*

|  | Week | | | | | | |
|---|---|---|---|---|---|---|---|
|  | 0 | 1 | 2 | 3 | 4 | 5 | 6 |
| Projected requirements |  | 50 |  | 200 | 50 | 40 |  |
| Inventory | 100 | 50 | 50 |  | 40 |  |  |
| Planned order release |  | 150 | 90 |  |  |  |  |

*Lead time = two weeks

tory costs, Isaacson did in fact decide to combine the orders for weeks 2 and 3, thus producing the master schedule of Table 7.7.

Once this revised master schedule was prepared, Isaacson examined the scheduling of components. The lead times for lids and bottoms were each one day, while the lead time for the main body was one week. Master schedules for each of these assembled items are shown in Tables 7.8 to 7.10.

Similar schedules could be formulated for the components making up the lid, main body, and bottom. At each level, a decision must be made as to whether consolidation of orders would be desirable. For example, it may be economical to combine the 150- and 90-unit orders for lids into one order. On this point, Orlicky (1975) offers several methods for determining the appropriate lot size to use in MRP systems.

### Table 7.8 Master schedule for ice bucket lid*

|  | Week | | | | | | |
|---|---|---|---|---|---|---|---|
|  | 0 | 1 | 2 | 3 | 4 | 5 | 6 |
| Projected requirements |  | 150 | 90 |  |  |  |  |
| Inventory |  |  |  |  |  |  |  |
| Planned order release |  | 150 | 90 |  |  |  |  |

*Lead time = same week

**Table 7.9 Master schedule for main body***

|  | Week | | | | | | |
| --- | --- | --- | --- | --- | --- | --- | --- |
|  | 0 | 1 | 2 | 3 | 4 | 5 | 6 |
| Projected requirements | 150 | 90 | | | | | |
| Inventory | | | | | | | |
| Planned order release | 150 | 90 | | | | | |

*Lead time = same week

Once the master schedule is set up for each level of production, the next MRP step is to implement production based upon the schedule. However, there are inevitable changes in orders, in inventory counts, in costs, in lead times, and in other elements of the control system that influence the master schedule prepared for the MRP system. Two options available for reflecting these changes are regeneration of the schedule and incremental adjustment.

In the regeneration approach, all changes are accommodated at fixed time periods, generally one week from the previous generation of a schedule. In the incremental approach, changes are accommodated continously.

It is in the adjustment operation that MRP systems generally require computer assistance. When numerous products are involved, the process of changing the master schedule can be so cumbersome that it is impossible to react quickly enough to changes without computer assistance. However, industrial inventory managers suggest that MRP systems should be done by hand before being computerized, and then the manual and computer systems should be operated in parallel during an extended checkout period. In this way, the peculiar features of that industry can become understood and incorporated into the computer systems, and important errors in data can be located.

Once Isaacson had outlined the MRP system for the ice bucket line, he became concerned about implementation problems incurred by such a complex system. He realized that it would take some time to sell the idea of a computer to Hank Conforti, even though it would be relatively inexpensive. He realized that the amount of time it would take to keep the MRP system in operation could be prohibitive, but from previous plant experience, Isaacson also knew

**Table 7.10 Master schedule for ice bucket bottom***

|  | Week | | | | | | |
| --- | --- | --- | --- | --- | --- | --- | --- |
|  | 0 | 1 | 2 | 3 | 4 | 5 | 6 |
| Projected requirements | | 150 | 90 | | | | |
| Inventory | | | | | | | |
| Planned order release | | 150 | 90 | | | | |

*Lead time = same week

how visual aids for production planning might be used. He therefore designed a master schedule display board.

The display consisted of the master schedule charts of Tables 7.7 to 7.10 mounted on a movable track. The track made it possible to position the master schedule under the proper week as one week ended and the next one began (Fig. 7.5). Pegs were provided for recording the appropriate requirements, inventory, and order release information for each level of production. As additional information became available, an updated index card was prepared and placed upon the appropriate peg.

Isaacson prepared an operational description of the display board and showed it to Henry Conforti. Isaacson could tell from Henry's instant attraction to the display that it constituted an inanimate ally in the implementation of the MRP system. The bookkeeping aspects of the MRP system seemed to match Henry's personality. Isaacson guessed that Hank Conforti would go along with the system if for no other reason than it would take less of his time away from golf. Once the MRP system became a regular component in production control at Fairhouse, Isaacson anticipated that more products would be added to the system and that eventually computer support would be purchased. Samuel had one final task, the writing of a summary report for Fairhouse describing the work he had done.

| Legend | 0 | 1 | 2 | 3 | 4 | 5 | 6 |
|---|---|---|---|---|---|---|---|
| Finished ice bucket: | | | | | | | |
| Requirements | | 50 | | 200 | 50 | | 40 |
| Inventory | 100 | 50 | 50 | | 40 | | |
| Order release | | 150 | 90 | | | | |
| Lid: | | | | | | | |
| Requirements | | 150 | 90 | | | | |
| Inventory | | | | | | | |
| Order release | | 150 | 90 | | | | |
| Main body: | | | | | | | |
| Requirements | | 150 | 90 | | | | |
| Inventory | | | | | | | |
| Order release | | 150 | 90 | | | | |
| Bottom: | | | | | | | |
| Requirements | | 150 | 90 | | | | |
| Inventory | | | | | | | |
| Order release | | 150 | 90 | | | | |

Fixed slide holder

Movable schedule cards which are shifted one position to the left as each week passes

A new card is added at the end of each week

**Figure 7.5** The master schedule display board.

**5** Identify the out-of-stock consequences in the following cases:

    (*a*) A hospital running out of a commonly used antibiotic

    (*b*) A family running out of blank checks

    (*c*) A supermarket running out of a sale item

    (*d*) A computer center running out of paper for its printers

**6** A gem merchant produces high-quality jewelry from imported stones. The merchant has a line of rings, bracelets, necklaces, pins to which the gems are added. The setup of a jewelry line generally requires two people, a salaried artist who designs the appropriate artistic features for the items and an hourly setup person who determines the tooling required for the production run. The line is ordinarily shut down for two hours for any setup. Its ten employees are idle during the setup even though the plant is at full capacity. The cost per item varies considerably according to the quality of the gem. Little space is required for storage but insurance rates are high. A tax is incurred on the stones as they are brought into the country, and another tax is assessed once all stones are sent to the wholesale jewelry brokers. The gem merchant has an accepted standard rate of return to be used in economic comparisons.

    For this situation, outline the cost components to be included in both the production setup cost and the inventory cost.

**7** The foundation office of a major university has in the past had an inventory problem. The supplies it uses are stored in a basement room where various clerical personnel have access to the supplies they need. One of the clerks has been designated as the supply manager and has been given the duty of reordering when the supplies get low. The problem has been that no one notifies the supply manager about low supplies until it is too late. The bulkiness of the supplies prohibits them from being stored in the supply manager's office, although a limited amount of storage space does exist there.

    Available data on monthly demand and order lead times is shown in Table 7.13.

**Table 7.13**

| Supply | Supplies (units) | | Lead time, weeks | Critical | Item cost |
|---|---|---|---|---|---|
| | On hand | Monthly demand | | | |
| Printed envelopes | 3800 | 1500 (boxes) | 2 | No | $1.50/box |
| Printed checks | 500 | 1100 (checks) | 6 | Yes | $0.05/check |
| Scholarship checks | 600 | 150 (checks) | 6 | Yes | $0.06/check |
| Dental fund checks | 780 | 350 (checks) | 6 | Yes | $0.06/check |
| Medical corporation checks | 1290 | 1200 (checks) | 4 | Yes | $0.06/check |
| Tax deductible receipts | 600 | 400 (boxes) | 4 | Yes | $2.00/box |
| Non-tax deductible receipts | 380 | 400 (boxes) | 4 | Yes | $2.00/box |
| Envelopes—gold | 500 | 600 (boxes) | 2 | No | $1.00/box |
| Envelopes—white | 700 | 1700 (boxes) | 2 | No | $1.00/box |
| Travel advance forms | 300 | 200 (sheets) | 1 | No | $3.00/sheet |
| Salary advance forms | 100 | 300 (sheets) | 1 | No | $3.00/sheet |
| Campus envelopes | 560 | 1000 (boxes) | 0.5 | No | $1.75/box |
| Foundation checks | 820 | 2000 (checks) | 6 | Yes | $1.50/box |

    (*a*) Outline the general structure of an inventory control system for this organization, including a description of how reorder decisions should be made.

    (*b*) Describe the operating system which might be implemented to make the inventory control system work.

**8** A retail store stocks a line of office supplies which have a relatively stable monthly demand. One of the products, legal pads, has been selected for an in-depth inventory analysis as a possible pilot study for an inventory control system for the rest of the supplies. The monthly demand of 2620 units has a standard deviation of 56 units. The cost of the item to the retail store is $0.26. The inventory charge rate has been established as 28 percent of product cost per year. The order cost has been prorated to $5.20 per order. The lead time generally is two weeks.

(a) Prepare an inventory operating policy for the retail store.

(b) If the current policy is to order one month's supply at a time, what reduction in total costs can be achieved by using the inventory policy you propose?

**9** A beer distributor in a college town is concerned over the number of kegs of beer maintained in inventory. Although the beer is rarely in inventory long enough to turn stale and spoil, the money tied up in it is beginning to be of concern. The distributor would like to develop a better inventory policy and therefore asks one of the frequent student customers for help. How effective would the standard EOQ model be in this circumstance?

**10** Prepare a bill of materials for production of a ball point pen with the following parts:

(a) Top half cartridge
(b) Bottom half cartridge
(c) Plastic plunger
(d) Spring
(e) Ink cylinder
(f) Outside decorative ring
(g) Pocket fastener

**11** For the requirements listed in Table 7.14a and b, determine the order release schedule for finished goods (A) and a major subcomponent (B). It takes 2 B's for a finished A. The lead time for A is three weeks and B is two weeks.

### Table 7.14a A

|  | Week | | | | | | | | | | |
|---|---|---|---|---|---|---|---|---|---|---|---|
|  | 0 | 1 | 2 | 3 | 4 | 5 | 6 | 7 | 8 | 9 | 10 |
| Requirements |  | 10 | 6 |  | 8 | 6 |  | 12 |  |  | 15 |
| Inventory | 19 |  |  |  |  |  |  |  |  |  |  |
| Order release |  |  |  |  |  |  |  |  |  |  |  |

### Table 7.14b B

|  | Week | | | | | | | | | | |
|---|---|---|---|---|---|---|---|---|---|---|---|
|  | 0 | 1 | 2 | 3 | 4 | 5 | 6 | 7 | 8 | 9 | 10 |
| Requirements |  |  |  |  |  |  |  |  |  |  |  |
| Inventory | 24 |  |  |  |  |  |  |  |  |  |  |
| Order release |  |  |  |  |  |  |  |  |  |  |  |

**12** Perform the necessary computations to determine the order releases for the product data shown in Table 7.15a through e.

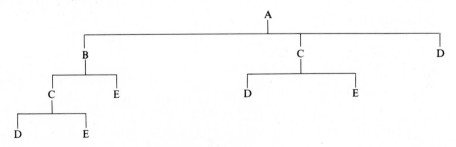

**Table 7.15a Part A**

| | Week* | | | | | | | |
|---|---|---|---|---|---|---|---|---|
| | 1 | 2 | 3 | 4 | 5 | 6 | 7 | 8 |
| Gross requirements | | | | | 100 | | | 150 |
| Scheduled receipts | | | | | | | | |
| On hand = 0 | | | | | | | | |
| Planned order release | | | | | | | | |

*Lead time = 2

**Table 7.15b Part B**

| | Week* | | | | | | | |
|---|---|---|---|---|---|---|---|---|
| Gross requirements | | | | | | | | |
| Scheduled receipts | | 130 | | | | 75 | | |
| On hand = 150 | | | | | | | | |
| Planned order release | | | | | | | | |

*Lead time = 1; usage = 1

**Table 7.15c Part C**

| | Week* | | | | | | | |
|---|---|---|---|---|---|---|---|---|
| | 1 | 2 | 3 | 4 | 5 | 6 | 7 | 8 |
| Gross requirements, spare parts | 10 | 10 | 10 | 10 | 10 | 10 | 10 | 10 |
| Scheduled receipts | 250 | | | | | | | |
| On hand = 20 | | | | | | | | |
| Planned order release | | | | | | | | |

*Lead time = 2; usage = 2

### Table 7.15d Part D

| | Week* | | | | | | | |
|---|---|---|---|---|---|---|---|---|
| | 1 | 2 | 3 | 4 | 5 | 6 | 7 | 8 |
| Gross requirements | | | | | | | | |
| Scheduled receipts | | | 140 | | | | | |
| On hand = 700 | | | | | | | | |
| Planned order release | | | | | | | | |

*Lead time = 1; usage for A = 2; C = 3

### Table 7.15e Part E

| | Week* | | | | | | | |
|---|---|---|---|---|---|---|---|---|
| | 1 | 2 | 3 | 4 | 5 | 6 | 7 | 8 |
| Gross requirements | | | | | | | | |
| Scheduled receipts | | | | | | | | |
| On hand = 50 | | | | | | | | |
| Planned order release | | | | | | | | |

*Lead time = 1; usage for B = 3; C = 1

13 Inventories are often used as barometers of economic activity. Periods of high economic growth tend to simulate low inventory levels and vice versa. If inventories are managed rationally, why would they vary with economic activity? (That is, why isn't the same order criterion used in all cases?)

14 Describe the inventory policies that have been observed in America during gasoline shortages. Is this observed individual behavior typical of organizational behavior in similar circumstances? Give specific examples to illustrate your discussion.

15 Describe your personal supply decision making behavior. Would you feel comfortable in using a decision model in making household purchases?

16 What incentive does a supply manager have to use a decision model for inventory decisions?

17 A supply manager has been observed to comment: "I'm the best supply manager in the company. I never run out of stock." What measure of effectiveness is the supply manager using? Is this appropriate? How can a broader set of objectives be incorporated into the performance evaluation of a supply manager?

## CASELETS

1. AJACK Plastics is a producer of polymer pellets. It manufactures the pellets from scrap plastic, fiberglass, and other recyclable materials. Arthur Jackson, the owner of the business, has become primarily a scrap broker who seeks

out bargain prices for used materials and sends them to the processing facility. Jackson is so involved in the buying of scrap materials that he has lost track of the production and storage consequences of his decisions. The plant is overrun with scrap, and significant production time is spent in finding the proper materials for production runs. Jackson's offer to build a warehouse has been received coldly by the plant manager, since he realizes it would be quickly filled to capacity with scrap. You have been hired by the plant manager to do a study which can be used to convince Arthur Jackson to change his supply strategy. In this case, outline the following:

(a) The general approach your study would take

(b) The data you would need

(c) The type of information you would provide the plant management to use in convincing Arthur Jackson that changes are necessary

2. GMA, a producer of mine equipment, has faced a continuing problem of keeping necessary supplies on hand. A typical unit has over 20,000 parts, including routine parts such as nuts and bolts and unique parts such as fabricated metal and special electronics. On a typical day, GMA may have twenty units in the plant waiting for some part. The parts problem has led to high in-process inventory costs as well as missed delivery dates. The present inventory system is based upon a forecast of units to be sold. Unfortunately, the forecast is not very accurate for specific units and some parts are overstocked while others are not ordered at all.

The company has a small computer which it uses for routine business applications. While the company has heard of MRP systems, it has not shifted to this type of inventory control system because of the lack of computer support.

For this organization outline the following

(a) What additional information or studies would you need before designing an inventory system for GMA?

(b) How would you measure the cost savings of a new inventory control system?

## CASE 7.1: THE ALCOHOLIC BEVERAGE COMMISSION

### Introduction

The alcoholic beverage commission (ABC) was faced with an increasingly embarrassing problem. Complaints were becoming more and more common regarding the state's liquor stores. Residents were upset that the state stores were frequently out of their favorite beverages.

The alcoholic beverage commission was concerned about these complaints but was uncertain as to what should be done. By state law, the state's liquor stores were limited in the amount of money which could be tied up on items in inventory. Due to the effect of inflation on liquor prices over the past several years, this formerly comfortable limit of $5 million was becoming increasingly tight. Legislation to increase the limit had failed during the previous legislative session due to the combined lobbying of the antiliquor and anti-government-spending forces. Possibilities of winning approval for an increased limit in the near future appeared dim.

The director of the ABC, Don P. Redwine, was lamenting his problem to the commissioner of finance and administration (F&A) one evening. The finance commissioner indicated that his group had some management expertise in this area that it was willing to lend to other state agencies. Redwine subsequently contracted to have an F&A consultant take a look at the liquor inventory problem.

## The Basic Problem

Don Redwine met with the F&A consultant, Wylbur Sumpter, and described the problem, emphasizing the effect of the monetary limit that had been placed on the liquor inventory. Redwine indicated that only 1000 kinds of beverages were normally kept in inventory in the total state system. Individual liquor stores placed orders through the state warehouse for the brands they wished to stock. Approximately 175 liquor stores were in operation throughout the state.

The state warehouse placed orders through the individual distributors each month. The decision on how much to order was based, for the most part, on the past experience of the director of the warehouse. The ABC director approved the order after making a check to be sure that the monetary limit of $5 million in inventory had not been violated.

The lead times for the different orders placed by the warehouse varied from two weeks to nearly half a year depending on the distributor and the type of product. Specialized items normally had longer lead times. The orders from the individual liquor stores were submitted once a month and a lead time of one week was common when the state warehouse had the items in stock. The individual stores typically placed their orders one week after the state placed its order each month.

## Data Collection

Sumpter began observing the state warehouse. He noted the flow of materials and gathered preliminary data on demands, lead times, and order processing times. In conversations with the warehouse manager, he identified one problem. The ordering pattern tended to give the warehouse employees an uneven workload which often resulted in delays in shipments to the individual ABC stores.

After this brief analysis of the problem, Sumpter began to collect and analyze the past demands from the entire state operation. The first set of data collected was the history of the inventory levels in the state warehouse. The inventory pattern identified from the data collection effort reinforced Sumpter's observation that inventory movement and receipt occurred unevenly throughout the month. As a result, the $5 million limit was reached only once a month for a two- to three-day span.

Table 7.16 Inventory item groupings

| Group | Number of brands | Number of bottles | Percent of inventory | Percent of inventory value |
|-------|------------------|-------------------|----------------------|----------------------------|
| A     | 257              | 185,713           | 26                   | 83                         |
| B     | 368              | 264,283           | 37                   | 16                         |
| C     | 375              | 264,284           | 37                   | 1                          |
| Total | 1000             | 714,280           | 100                  | 100                        |

Sumpter next turned to an analysis of the individual products in inventory. The classic 80-20 rule applied in this case as shown in Table 7.16.

The majority of the brands in group C had had little or no demand during the past year. Since the predominant inventory value was in the first group, Sumpter made the decision to examine those items initially.

Of the group A items, 178 had been out of stock during the past year. For almost all of these items, the safety stock was very limited, and the probability of running out of stock was high. A limited analysis of the group B items showed similar safety stock trends; however, the probability of shortages of these items was less because of lower demands for them.

## Analysis of Improved Inventory Operation Methods

Sumpter decided to look for improvements in the operation of the existing inventory system instead of concentrating on identifying optimal inventory policies.

First he examined the ordering schedules currently employed. The large inventories of Table 7.16 seemed to be avoidable. If more uniform inventory levels could be achieved, he reasoned that additional items could be carried in inventory, thus permitting the extra safety stock which seemed necessary. He discussed this problem with Don Redwine and reviewed the reasons for the current ordering policy.

The primary reason for the current policy seemed to be tradition. Originally, infrequent orders had been the rule at the central warehouse, to take advantage of quantity discounts. In recent years, however, these discounts had been reduced. Consequently, this reason for monthly orders had lost much of its original rationale. Another factor which favored the current monthly order period was state purchasing practices. The necessity of placing an order on a state register for bids made a fixed order period desirable to reduce clerical costs, but this factor had also been reduced in importance since the state had adopted a once-a-year bidding policy. That is, suppliers bid for state contracts for the entire year.

After reviewing the desirability of a more frequent ordering policy, it was agreed that such a policy would be feasible. Sumpter then developed an ordering program for the individual stores and the central warehouse by dividing the stores into four groups with nearly equal sales volumes. At the same time, he investigated the effects of placing orders four times a month at the central warehouse.

The expected impact of these changes was then measured by using historical data on demands and lead times to simulate the effects of the new policy. The results of this analysis were encouraging; the new policy permitted an increase in inventory capacity of nearly $800,000 by smoothing out the peak inventory level.

The impact of dropping the low-demand items from stock was also investigated. Data on these items showed a potential reduction of approximately $50,000 in inventory, thus increasing the additional inventory storage of the A items to $850,000.

The total impact of these changes was then estimated. Assuming an average price of $7.00 per bottle, the increase in inventory safety stock of A brands was estimated to be approximately 121,000 bottles. Dividing this total among the 257 group A items gave an average safety stock increase of 470 bottles per brand. Analysis of the previous year's demand data revealed that the additional 470 units in safety stock for each brand would have prevented nearly 70 percent of the out-of-stock situations.

The next aspect of the system to be studied was the safety stock being maintained on the group B items. Previous data collection efforts showed that the safety stock for many of these items was more than sufficient. A reallocation of part of this inventory to the group A items provided enough additional inventory to reduce anticipated out-of-stock situations by another 7 percent. The impact of all contemplated changes was to reduce the total out-of-stock occurrences of group A by 77 percent of the previous year's total.

## Improvements in Order Quantity and Safety Stock Parameters

While this improvement was encouraging, it still left the state with a substantial supply problem. Assuming the continuation of inflationary trends, the improvements seemed to be only stopgap measures. The solution to the problem of shortages seemed to require either an increase in the monetary limit or improvements in the ordering policies of individual stores. Since the first solution seemed unlikely, Sumpter turned to solving the problem of how to improve the selection of order quantities and safety stocks at each warehouse.

An analysis of a local ABC store showed that many items were overstocked and that abnormally large orders by that store were frequent. The store manager, when asked about this, said that ordering decisions were based on anticipating future shortages. In response to previous inventory difficulties, the manager was stockpiling items in anticipation of future problems. A quick survey of other stores showed this to be a common procedure.

The local policy of overstocking was creating the inventory problems of the alcoholic beverage commission. Seeking methods to improve upon this situation, Sumpter studied simplified inventory systems which were applicable to large numbers of items. He found no model which would have been practical for controlling the inventory level at every local warehouse. Sumpter decided that an alternative approach might be to develop an inventory control training program for the local store managers. His intention was to develop an approach that would enhance the intuition of local managers. Don Redwine was in favor of this approach and gave his approval to the establishment of a series of training programs.

Sumpter developed an interactive computer simulation program with which a local store manager could practice. The manager would make inventory decisions, and the computer would generate demands and order receipts. Five typical products were selected for inclusion in the simulation. The exercise was designed to handle twenty participants at once. The computer program also generated decisions for the remaining stores in order that input from all of the 178 stores would be included in the model. These decisions were based upon the twenty managers' policies and were intended to represent typical responses for the remaining stores.

A reward system was established as part of the simulation. Participants were ranked according to the cost of inventory maintained and the number of out-of-stock situations they encountered. Both factors were then weighted equally and an overall ranking of the participants were printed by the computer.

After a brief pilot test of the simulation, seminars were established throughout the state. The seminars were well received, and the managers, in general, responded favorably to the competitive features of the game. One important aspect of the seminars was that they provided the director an opportunity to discuss the changes being made at the state level. Improvements in the central warehouse operation were taken into account in the model, and the new order policies were included in it.

The typical response of a participant was to be conservative at first. Most managers continued their real-life practice of overstocking. However, as they gained experience with the situation, they quickly adopted a more aggressive approach to their inventory control decisions. The average store managers were able to reduce their inventory to sales ratios by 23 percent from their typical ratios. As a result of improvements in the state warehouse operation, the frequency with which items went out of stock during simulations was reduced by nearly 80 percent of the real-life level.

## Implementation of the Study Results

Don Redwine, impressed by the results of the simulation, decided to implement the recommendations made by Sumpter. The recommendation of spreading out larger orders was readily accepted by the warehouse manager. The reduction of the group C inventory drew notes of concern from the local store managers who had some business in these brands. However, the objections were not strong enough to delay implementation.

The training program had, in effect, been implemented. To achieve the greatest benefit from these sessions, the director had a procedure added to the simulation program which took the actual current computerized inventory records and gave rankings of the various stores. Given these rankings, store managers with extremely low rankings were asked to explain their problems to the director. Those managers at the top of the ranking list were formally recognized. The director rejected the idea of rewarding top ranking stores with higher-order priorities since this tended to give them a permanent advantage. However, he did indicate that the rankings would be used in determining salaries under the state's new merit pay system.

While the improvement in inventory management at the local stores could not be attributed entirely to the training exercise, initial improvements were sufficient to lower the overall inventory requirements to about $4.5 million, which seemed to give the alcoholic beverage commission enough flexibility to meet its demand for several years to come. A substantial public relations effort was undertaken to inform the legislature of the improvements. It was hoped that this effort would lead to more favorable legislative support in the future.

## Discussion Guide

1 The first phase of the study dealt with a commonsense approach to reducing inventory levels. Why didn't Ron Redwine think of this solution?

2 Why wasn't the conventional EOQ approach taken in this case? Was the approach applicable?

3 Do you feel that the ranking used in the training exercise was a fair measure of a manager's performance in a real-life setting? Would this training have a lasting impact on the performance of the manager?

4 Were there any other improvements which you think should have been pursued?

5 In evaluating the store managers, stock-outs were evaluated equally with inventory as measures of effectiveness. Was this appropriate? What impact would a different weighting make on the results?

6 Was the decision to reduce the number of type C items a good one? What trade-offs are being made in such a decision?

# EIGHT

## SERVICE DECISIONS

## SYNOPSIS OF THE CHAPTER

The needs and requirements of people often do not consist of goods but of services. However, total needs of a patron of an organization may include both goods and services. For example, people who are suffering from low income may appear at a welfare office to receive monetary assistance, but the office is also faced with providing service in the form of trained personnel to help the welfare applicants. An automotive parts warehouse sells parts to customers, but it also must staff the parts counter with trained personnel who can locate the proper parts for the customers.

Almost every organization finds itself faced with responding to needs for service on the part of the people with whom the organization deals. Organizations which do little but provide services instead of goods are becoming more numerous.

Many other organizations find their service components becoming steadily more dominant, providing more services instead of more goods to customers and users. The variety of services demanded from organizations make it difficult to generalize service-related decision problems, but most such organizations have the basic problem of matching service capacity with demand, the major topic of this chapter.

In meeting demand for services the fundamental problem faced is that demand is not constant, and as a result, it requires a varying fraction of service capacity. This chapter explains the repercussions of variation in demand and presents approaches that a service facility can adopt in order to satisfy service demand.

## MAJOR CONCEPTS PRESENTED IN THIS CHAPTER

1. The service division of an organization constitutes a special category defined by its purpose of providing services instead of goods.
2. Providing service can require a number of capabilities on the part of an organization, including facilities, inventories, and some products. But, the main work of a service organization is to provide trained personnel as needed.
3. Many service systems can be described as queuing systems.
4. The natural modes of responding to demand in service systems may be ineffective.
5. Variation in demand prevents a service system from satisfying customers by providing service capacity based upon average demand.
6. Service strategies based upon anticipating demand can be effective.
7. In some cases it may be necessary for a service division to attempt to revise demand for services.

## EXPECTATIONS OF THE STUDENT

The students, after studying this chapter, should be able to do the following:

1. Determine whether an organization exists primarily to provide service
2. Determine the specific services the organization provides
3. Explain the effects of the variation of demand
4. Define the queuing elements in a service system
5. Calculate the descriptive measures of a simple queuing system
6. Explain the difference between reacting to demand and anticipating it
7. Explain what advantage a service company can gain by managing demand
8. Explain how appointments can be used to manage demand
9. Devise a schedule for a fixed staff which can better satisfy demand than can the same staff restricted to only reacting to demand

## SMEDLEY MOTORS

Bill Smedley operated the Craston outlet of Minotaur Motors. His business catered to metropolitan and suburban customers and consisted of four distinct parts: selling new cars, selling used cars, selling parts, and repairing cars. During recent years, his profit margins on car sales had dropped sharply, largely because fewer cars were being sold. At the same time, more people either were having their cars repaired or were repairing them themselves.

Both car repair and parts sales were up sharply, and both services made excellent profit margins. Smedley's brisk business in parts had, however, created a problem for him in that he had a difficult time keeping the parts counter staffed with enough parts personnel. His usual procedure was to use a number of employees for swing duty; they either worked on car repairs or at the parts desk, as needed.

In Smedley's mind, the most stringent constraint preventing him from being able to keep enough workers at the parts counter was the newly signed contract with the repairer's union. The workers had objected to being ordered back and forth from the repair floor to the parts desk, so they had forced Smedley to a "block time" rule which stipulated that each work day for each worker had to include a "major segment."

The major segment of a work day was a six-hour continuous period during which the worker could be either at the parts counter or in the repair area. Smedley felt that this work rule had led to his being unable to keep the right number of workers on the parts counter. He neither liked to see long lines of customers at the counter nor to see counter staff lounging about with nothing to do. The problem of counter staffing began to worry him inordinately.

Smedley was complaining about the problem on the golf course one day to a fellow member of Rotary. His colleague was in the retailing business and had just read an article in a trade journal about a new system for staffing sales counters. The article, written by a management consultant, offered several useful suggestions for staffing.

Smedley, in a move that was completely out of character for him, contacted the consultant for advice. When he heard the consultant's fee, Smedley almost dropped the phone. However, he quickly devised a money-saving ploy. The annual businessman's golf tournament was coming up within a month, and his special guest was to be a baseball hall-of-famer. He offered the consultant an all-expense-paid golf outing that included being in the foursome with the baseball celebrity for a 50 percent reduction in his consulting fee.

The consultant, Paul Jackson, was intrigued by the offer and accepted. He stipulated that his work for Smedley would require no more than two days, but he did agree to supply Smedley with five technical papers that he could read and thereby learn how to do his own problem solving.

From his preliminary discussion with Smedley, Jackson felt that he already knew which typical problems of service systems applied to Smedley Motors and thought through those typical problems before selecting the briefing papers to send Bill Smedley.

# CHARACTERISTICS OF SERVICE DIVISIONS

Organizations with service as their primary goal are becoming a growing fraction of existing concerns. Service organizations are those whose primary activity is serving people, either singly or in groups. However, it is also true that many companies, previously devoted primarily to providing goods, are finding it advantageous to develop increasingly active service divisions. It is therefore becoming difficult to make a distinction between a service business and a goods business with a strong service division.

It is not critical to make the distinction between a predominantly service organization and an organization with a strong service component for the purpose of studying service problems. The problems are of a fairly general type and look much the same in either a business or a government setting.

Some organizations with important service components include the following:

| | |
|---|---|
| Regional distributor for product | Library |
| Hospital | Electric utility |
| Restaurant | Police department |
| Tax office | Municipal bus service |
| Television repair shop | University |

An organization may engage in a variety of activities, but the service component of these activities is readily identifiable.

Almost every company which produces goods for retail or wholesale must maintain a distribution system, and the dominant purpose of this system is customer service. It makes little difference whether the distributor is a central warehouse for one company or for a number of independent stores. The distributor must provide a predictable set of services. As an example of such a warehouse, consider the case of a regional beer distributor.

The beer distributor stocks a variety of brands and containers of beer, tries to maintain adequate inventories of beers so that orders can be filled quickly, and must have a sufficient number of trucks and drivers on hand to distribute orders. The distributor must somehow be aware of customers' current needs. This awareness requires personal contact with customers or contact through a staff of salespersons. His services to customers consist of taking orders for beer, distributing the orders, and taking inventory.

A hospital must service three main categories of patients: emergency care, necessary care, and elective care. These could be further divided into inpatients and outpatients. The hospital must provide facilities, supplies, and personnel. Facilities include ambulances, rooms, beds, and special equipment. Supplies include bedding, drugs, food, and numerous other items. Personnel include orderlies, nurses, administrators, clerks, drivers, druggists, and doctors.

A restaurant provides supplies, personnel, and facilities. The food may be very special, but it can be considered as a variety of supplies.

A tax office primarily provides trained personnel to help people with their tax problems.

A television repair shop also provides trained personnel.

A library provides books, and librarians, and a quiet place to read.

An electric utility provides a somewhat different service in that it provides it to numerous locations simultaneously. A further peculiarity is that electricity must be supplied immediately upon demand or else customers will feel that there has been a lack of service.

A police department provides a complicated array of services, but most of them require trained personnel, and the basic job of the police department is to place personnel in the right place in a large area at the right time.

A municipal bus service is supposed to provide transportation between most arbitrarily chosen pairs of points within its service area. The problems to be solved include routing, timing, and personnel assignment.

A university tries to provide a large number of degree programs to many students. In effect, it is providing trained personnel at the right times in the right places. There are supplies, such as books, and ancillary services, such as counseling, provided, but providing teachers is the university's primary service.

The list investigated encompasses diverse organizations and involves a variety of distinct services. From this list the main decision categories encountered are:

Matching of resources to demand
Personnel assignment
Inventory control
Resource allocation
Routing and distribution
Providing facilities

Of these topics, inventory is discussed in Chap. 7; resource allocation and some aspects of personnel assignment appear in Chap. 6; routing and distribution are treated in Chap. 10; and facilities decisions are the focus of Chap. 11.

The present chapter deals with the problem of matching resources with demand. Two likely situations may exist for a service division: either it must respond to demand by managing its personnel and the other resources it must provide, or it must somehow control demand to prevent it from exceeding the capability of the organization's resources.

## TECHNICAL PAPERS FOR SMEDLEY MOTORS

Paul Jackson correctly ascertained that Smedley Motors had two main problems: (1) providing enough counter staff to serve the customers and (2) a demand that consisted of pronounced peaks and valleys. He believed that Smedley might be able to induce some of the customers to change their habits enough to level out demand. With these thoughts in mind Jackson sent Smedley five briefing papers.

### The Nature of Service Systems—Briefing Number 1

Service systems are among the most common systems found in organizations. All experience the effects of service systems each day from the highways they travel on to the restaurants they eat at to the recreational facilities they frequent. No matter what service is being provided, the overall configuration of the system is as shown in Fig. 8.1.

The two major components of any service system are the waiting line, or queue, and the service facility. The service facility may have a single server or

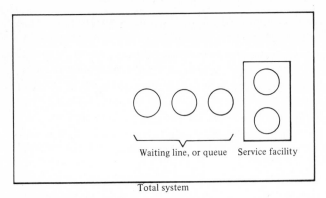

**Figure 8.1** The service station configuration.

many, or it may have several single-server stations. In the strictest sense, a multiple-service system consists of two or more servers but only one waiting line. An ice cream parlor that has its customers take a number as they enter and then services them in sequence is an example of a multiple-server system. A bank with a single, roped-off waiting line is another example. A supermarket on the other hand is a group of single-server queues, as is a typical set of toll booths on a turnpike. There are many ways that service systems may differ from one another.

The waiting line may differ from the configuration shown in Fig. 8.1 in that there may be no line at all but a dispersed array of customers as is commonly faced by an appliance repair business. In this case, the server travels to those waiting for service. Waiting lines may differ in other ways. The procedure for selecting the next customer to be served may employ a first-come–first-served, random, or priority rule, or it may use some other selection rule.

A line may be limited in the number of customers it can accommodate. Consider a facility which has a conveyor delivering items from a warehouse. There may be a limited storage area on the conveyor so that, once it is full, additional items cannot be discharged onto the conveyor, thus restricting its delivery rate.

The very nature of customer arrivals may influence the operation of a service system. The pattern of arrivals may be random and unstructured, or it may be totally scheduled. Random arrivals are fairly common in service systems that serve the general public, such as banks, gasoline stations, and retail stores. Batch arrivals are also common: mail deliveries come in batches as do passengers from transportation systems and arrivals of customers at entertainment events.

Scheduled arrivals are the rule at doctors' offices, clinics, and beauty shops. Although the arrivals are scheduled, variations in arrival times can make the providing of a consistent level of service difficult.

As Smedley reflected on the first paper sent to him by Jackson, he saw that his parts counter demonstrated many of the characteristics discussed. He saw that his operation was a series of single-server facilities, each with its own waiting line. Customers were served on a first-come–first-served basis in each line. Customer arrival patterns appeared to cause his problems. From 11 A.M. to 2 P.M. the counter area was filled with customers. There was a small, manageable early-morning business, and in the afternoon there was a similarly manageable clientele. Customers tended to arrive either singly or in batches typically consisting of two to six persons.

Smedley began to feel more comfortable about hiring Jackson. The paper he had read began to make sense and helped revise his view of the business he was in. He had never thought of his parts counter in these terms. He looked forward to reading the next paper.

## Some Misconceptions About Service Systems—Briefing Number 2

Managers of service systems often have significant misconceptions about the operation of their facilities. The true nature of many service systems is confusing and counterintuitive. The first problem that service managers must confront is the effect of the variation in arrival times and service times on the operation of the service system. If a server can process 80 units an hour and if the demand rate is 320 units per hour, it would seem obvious that four servers should be hired to handle the load. However, if neither the service time per customer nor the time between arrivals is constant, the decision to hire only four servers would be disastrous. Variations in service times and arrival patterns can make traditional staffing patterns invalid.

A second misconception that managers of service systems may have is that arrivals and services can be evened out over an entire day's operation. If 800 customers are expected in a day, a manager may provide service capacity for dealing with exactly 800 customers. The error in this approach is that services cannot be performed in advance of arrivals. Thus, excess service capacity during a period of low demand cannot be used to offset periods of high demand. This point is illustrated in Fig. 8.2. Capacity demand is lost and cannot be used to alleviate subsequent peak demands. Thus, using total capacity values as a guide to staffing without considering the variation in demand is inappropriate.

A third misconception of service system managers is that empty waiting lines are signals indicating the presence of excess capacity. A service facility manager

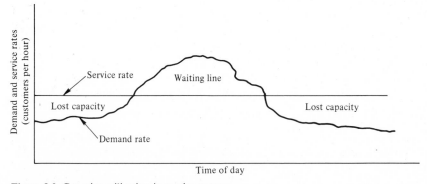

**Figure 8.2** Capacity utilization in service systems.

who sees a waiting line shrink and eventually disappear assumes that system capacity exceeds demand. This may not be the case. The system may be in perfect balance. Reducing service capacity when waiting lines are empty may be a poor operating strategy.

A fourth misconception affecting service system management is that measures of effectiveness can be based upon the rational criteria of clientele. In reality, a client of any service system reacts emotionally, no matter whether the client is a large company waiting for delivery of parts or an individual waiting in line at a bank. A fact of life is that people hate to wait. While waiting for service, their perceptions of service performance become distorted; service times seem much longer than they are. Basing service level decisions on rational measures while ignoring the emotional factors may produce service procedures that customers think of as inadequate.

The management of service systems requires matching capacity with demand as well as dealing with the psychological forces that accompany any waiting situation. A frequently told story illustrating this point concerns a set of elevators that were perceived to be very slow. After extensive studies of the elevators and their service, management concluded that the elevators were operating at a reasonable rate. However, the complaints continued until finally it was suggested that the psychological aspects of waiting needed to be addressed. Mirrors were placed on each floor as a diversion. The complaints about waiting conditions promptly evaporated; waiting time had been reduced successfully.

A final misconception in service system management is that service pricing and operational management are independent. An organization that lowers its price is hoping to attract additional business; the ensuing growth in business creates a sufficient increase in demand to necessitate an increase in capacity; costs subsequently rise, lowering the anticipated profit. The level of service provided may be a key to the pricing of the service, and the price may affect the required level of service.

---

As Smedley read this paper, he suddenly became aware that many of the problems he had encountered over the years could be attributed more to poor management than to a lack of capacity. Frequently, he would reassign a worker from counter duty to the repair area when counter lines became short. The result of his action in most cases was a quick increase in waiting lines. He had thought that the source of the problem was a sudden increase in demand, but the facility had probably been in balance when he had disturbed it by reducing capacity. He now understood what he was doing wrong. He turned to the next technical briefing with considerable enthusiasm.

## Queuing Models for Service System—Briefing Number 3

One class of formal models for the analysis of service systems is called queuing models. These models analyze a service system according to six general characteristics:

1. Arrival distribution—The model generally requires the specification of the arrival pattern along with the mean and standard deviation of the number of arrivals occurring during some unit of time.
2. Service distribution—The model generally requires the specification of the service pattern along with the mean and standard deviation of the service time.
3. Number of servers—Generally the models range from the single-server type to those for multiple servers (two or more).
4. Service discipline—The model requires identification of the order in which requests for service are processed. First-come–first-served (FCFS) is the most common discipline considered.
5. Limit on waiting line—In a few cases, there is a limit on the number of people that can line up for service. The common assumption of an infinite waiting line, however, is generally acceptable for most calculations.
6. Limit on demand population—In rare cases, there is a limit to the number of people who will ever use the system (e.g., a machine repairman may be responsible for only a fixed number of machines).

The simplest queuing model makes the following assumptions:

1. Arrival distribution—Poisson arrival rate—Essentially this assumption means that arrivals occur singly and in a random fashion.
2. Service distribution—Exponential—Essentially this assumption indicates that shorter service times are more likely.
3. Number of servers—single server.
4. Service discipline—FCFS.
5. Limit on waiting line—unlimited.
6. Limit on demand—unlimited.

From these basic assumptions, the arrival and service rates can be used to determine a number of characteristics of the service system. To demonstrate this model, consider everyone's favorite service system: the hospital clinic. Studies have shown that an orthopedic specialist can examine ten patients per hour. The clinic director would like to know how many patients to put on the orthopedist's schedule per hour. The answer seems obvious—Ten!

With the aid of queuing models, the impacts of various appointment schedules can be determined from the following derived relationships.

$\lambda$ = arrival rate (patients/hour)*

$\mu$ = service rate (patients/hour)

$\rho$ = utilization of system (i.e., fraction of time system is busy)

$$\rho = \frac{\text{arrival rate}}{\text{service rate}} = \frac{\lambda}{\mu}$$

*Please excuse the Greek letters, but they are the standard nomenclature of queuing models.

$P_o$ = proportion of time system is idle = $1 - \rho$

$L_s$ = average number of persons in system (waiting for service and being served)

$$L_s = \frac{\rho}{1 - \rho}$$

$L_q$ = average number of patients waiting

$$L_q = L_s - \rho$$

$W_s$ = average time in system including both waiting time and service time

$$W_s = \frac{L_s}{\lambda}$$

$W_q$ = average waiting time

$$W_q = \frac{L_q}{\lambda}$$

Consider a clinic appointment pattern that schedules six patients per hour. Thus,

$$\lambda = 6 \text{ patients/hour}$$

$$\mu = 10 \text{ patients/hour}$$

Given these rates, the characteristics of the service system will be as follows:

$$\rho = \frac{\lambda}{\mu} = 0.60$$

$$P_o = 1 - \rho = 0.40$$

$$L_s = \frac{\rho}{1 - \rho} = 1.5 \text{ patients}$$

$$L_q = L_s - \rho = 0.9 \text{ patients}$$

$$W_s = \frac{L_q}{\lambda} = 0.25 \text{ hours}$$

$$W_q = \frac{L_q}{\lambda} = 0.15 \text{ hours}$$

The clinic is only 60 percent utilized. From a patient's viewpoint, the operation is ideal. There are on the average only 0.9 patients in the orthopedist's waiting room, and each patient needs to wait only 0.15 hours on the average.

Clearly, the clinic director would never adopt such a slow operation. Trying eight appointments per hour:

$$\lambda = 8 \text{ patients/hour}$$

$$\mu = 10 \text{ patients/hour}$$

$$\rho = 0.80$$

$$P_o = 0.20$$

$$L_q = 3.2 \text{ patients}$$

$$W_s = 0.50 \text{ hours}$$

$$W_q = 0.40 \text{ hours}$$

The utilization has increased to 80 percent, but patients must now wait an average of 0.40 hours to see the orthopedist. There are more than three patients in the clinic on the average. Still the clinic director might wish to investigate other possibilities. Table 8.1 illustrates the system characteristics for various appointment schedules.

As shown in Table 8.1, the closer the appointment rate matches the service rate of the doctors, the longer the waiting time becomes. Why is this so? Whenever a decision is made to match arrival rates and service rates in a system, an assumption is made that no variation occurs in either pattern. The clinic assumes that a doctor processes a patient every six minutes and that a new arrival occurs every six minutes. Of course, this state of bliss never occurs. Doctors take longer on some patients than others and patients rarely adhere exactly to appointment times.

What actually occurs is a degree of variation in both arrivals and services. When such variation is present, the waiting line phenomena of Table 8.1 result. This "variation effect" must be carefully considered in making any service level decision.

The queuing model presented here is the simplest* of the many models that have been developed, but the variation effect illustrated above is reflected in all of the models from the simplest to the most complex.

Queuing models are ineffective in providing detailed analyses of many of existing service systems. Queuing models, in general, assume steady state conditions. That is, they present what would happen if the system conditions were to persist for a long period of time. In reality, system conditions change fre-

*For a discussion of multiple-server queues, see Technical Note 8.1.

**Table 8.1 System characteristics for different arrival rates**

| Appointments per hour | Utilization | Fraction idle time | Number in system | Number waiting | Time in system | Number waiting |
|---|---|---|---|---|---|---|
| 6 | 0.60 | 0.40 | 1.5 | 0.9 | 0.25 | 0.15 |
| 8 | 0.80 | 0.20 | 4.0 | 3.2 | 0.50 | 0.40 |
| 9 | 0.90 | 0.10 | 9.0 | 8.1 | 1.00 | 0.90 |
| 9.5 | 0.95 | 0.05 | 19.0 | 18.1 | 2.00 | 1.90 |
| 9.9 | 0.99 | 0.01 | 99.0 | 98.0 | 10.00 | 9.90 |
| 10 | Waiting line continues building and never stabilizes | | | | | |

quently as arrival patterns and other aspects of the system environment change. Thus steady state is rarely even approximated.

There are numerous technical difficulties in adapting queuing models to such phenomena as batch arrivals or services, unusual service rates, multiple-server queues, and numerous other realistic factors that make each service system unique. For this reason, conditional operating rules for managing service systems offer a more effective approach to managing service systems.

---

Smedley was somewhat disappointed after reading the third briefing paper. He had hoped that some simple procedure existed for straightening out his problems. While he did not understand the queuing formulas, the variation effect was a revelation to him. Having read the three briefing papers, Smedley was beginning to get a much clearer picture of how service systems perform. The fourth briefing paper, however, reversed the trend.

## Strategies in Service Systems—Briefing Number 4

**Operating Strategies—time varying demand** The most challenging service situations are those for which the arrival rate varies throughout the service period. Restaurants, banks, and movie theaters are a few of the many examples of this type of service facility. Traditional queuing models are inappropriate in such cases, since they assume a time-independent arrival distribution. An alternative method for analyzing such service systems is through the use of operating strategies.

An operating strategy is simply a set of rules that can be used in the management of the service system. All service systems are operated via some operating strategy no matter whether it is articulated. Traditionally, managers of service systems respond to long waiting lines by adding servers to the system. In one drugstore chain, the management has a written rule posted near the cashier that says: "When the line exceeds six people, ring bell for manager." Unwritten strategies have also been developed for the use of express lines, for waiting line management, and for specialized versus general service assignments for servers. Many service system managers operate according to such a reactive strategy. When long lines appear, extra service capacity is added. Another approach to scheduling capacity is to try to anticipate demand. The premise of an anticipatory scheduling system is that customer arrival rates can be predicted and service capacity should be assigned in anticipation instead of in reaction to arrivals. By scheduling capacity in anticipation of arrivals, long lines can be avoided.

Consider what happens in most service systems as capacity is added in reaction to arrivals: the results of such a procedure are shown in Table 8.2. During the morning off-peak period, the arrival rate is slightly less than the service rate and no line builds. At 11 A.M. a transition to peak demand occurs. The arrival rate increases to eighty people per hour, and a line of twenty people builds. The supervisor reacts by adding another server to the counter. The extra server is capable of handling the extra peak volume, but there is insufficient capacity to reduce the waiting line. At 1 P.M. the arrival rate drops to eighty per hour while

## Table 8.2 Results of assigning servers in reaction to arrivals*

| | |
|---|---|
| Morning off-peak:<br>(8 A.M.–11 A.M.) | Two servers on duty<br>Arrival rate = 50 per hour<br>Service rate = 60 per hour<br>No line builds |
| Transition period:<br>(11 A.M.–12:00 M.) | Two servers on duty<br>Arrival rate = 80 per hour<br>Service rate = 60 per hour<br>Line length at 12 M. = 20 people |
| Peak period:<br>(12:00 M.–1 P.M.) | Three servers on duty<br>Arrival rate = 90 per hour<br>Service rate = 90 per hour<br>Line length at 1 P.M. = 20 people |
| Transition period:<br>(1 P.M.–2 P.M) | Three servers on duty<br>Arrival rate = 80 per hour<br>Service rate = 90 per hour<br>Line length at 2 P.M. = 10 people |
| Afternoon off-peak:<br>(2 P.M.–3 P.M.) | Three servers on duty<br>Arrival rate = 50 per hour<br>Service rate = 60 per hour<br>Line length at 3 P.M. = 0 people |
| Afternoon off-peak:<br>(3 P.M.–4 P.M.) | Two servers on duty<br>Arrival rate = 50 per hour<br>Service rate = 60 per hour<br>Line length at 4 P.M. = 0 people |

*The variation effect has not been incorporated into this analysis for the sake of simplicity. To do so would make the results even more dramatic than are shown here.

the service capacity stays at ninety. By 2 P.M. the waiting line has dropped to ten people. Even during the afternoon off-peak period, the waiting line exists until 3 P.M. The average waiting line throughout the day has been six people.

Misconceptions about service scheduling include lack of understanding of the following principles:

1. Reacting to a long line by assigning an extra server may not reduce the waiting line. It may only keep the line from getting longer.
2. Removing servers when lines are short may result in the reoccurrence of the waiting line.

Anticipatory scheduling may alleviate many of the problems brought about by the reactive scheduling now practiced in many service facilities. Consider again the last example of arrival rates, but with service capacity assignments made according to a knowledge of past arrival patterns. The resulting patterns are shown in Table 8.3.

### Table 8.3 Results of assigning servers in anticipation of arrivals

| | |
|---|---|
| Morning off-peak:<br>(8 A.M.–11 A.M.) | Two servers on duty<br>Arrival rate = 50 per hour<br>Service rate = 60 per hour<br>No line results |
| Transition period:<br>(11 A.M.–12 M.) | Three servers on duty<br>Arrival rate = 80 per hour<br>Service rate = 90 per hour<br>Line length = 0 people |
| Peak period:<br>(12 M.–1 P.M.) | Three servers on duty<br>Arrival rate = 90 per hour<br>Service rate = 90 per hour<br>Line length = 0 people |
| Transition period:<br>(1 P.M.–2 P.M.) | Three servers on duty<br>Arrival rate = 80 per hour<br>Service rate = 90 per hour<br>Line length = 0 people |
| Afternoon off-peak:<br>(2 P.M.–4 P.M.) | Two servers on duty<br>Arrival rate = 50 per hour<br>Service rate = 60 per hour<br>Line length = 0 people |

In contrast to the reactive system, increased arrivals are expected and planned for during the 11 A.M. to 12 M. transition period. An extra server is added in anticipation of arrivals, and no waiting line forms. Since capacity during the peak hour matches the demand rate, and since no lines were allowed to form initially, the system continues to function smoothly. The average line length is zero, but no increase in the number of server-hours is required.

The example presented is an oversimplification of a service system's operation, but it demonstrates the principle of the anticipatory scheduling system. By anticipating customer arrivals and by scheduling servers to handle anticipated demand, waiting lines can be minimized. Since excess capacity is required to reduce a waiting line, service operation costs can be minimized by eliminating the formation of lines. This simple concept can be applied with a minimum of additional resources. The only requirements for implementing the system are adequate data, the derived anticipatory schedule, and the organizational commitment to making the system work.

The anticipatory scheduling system is an alternative to more common service capacity systems. It offers an operating strategy that anticipates waiting line problems instead of reacting to them. Three general strategies can be formulated for designing anticipatory service systems with time-varying demand:

1. Schedule service in anticipation of arrivals.
2. When there is a shortage of capacity to meet the total demand, postpone the shortage condition to a time as late as possible in the demand period.

3. Small waiting lines may represent a balanced system. Do not reduce capacity in such cases unless it is certain that capacity exceeds the arrival rate by a sufficient margin.

**Operating strategies—time-independent demand** An assembly operation is a class of service system with a demand rate which does not change over time. This operation consists of adding a component to a main assembly as it comes down an assembly line. Although the time between two consecutive arrivals of assemblies at the assembler varies according to some distribution, the overall rate remains constant throughout the day. Thus, the service strategy requires little more than a static determination of the proper capacity level. Although this problem can be complex, a solution, once identified, can likely be implemented without extensive supervision.

One issue of concern in designing an operating strategy for such a time-independent service system is whether to provide buffer storage for the service system. Consider the following example: An assembly line is adjusted to provide components to be assembled at the rate of 92 per hour; the assembler can attach the components at a rate of 100 per hour. At least 8 percent of the time the operator will be idle in such a system.

A design feature that can be used to reduce the idle time is to provide for the assembler a buffer stock of extra main assemblies which is sufficient to accommodate the expected idle time. Buffer stock may also be provided in anticipation of breakdowns or other stoppages of the line. Such a buffer strategy reduces idle time of the system but increases in-process inventory costs. However, the amount of in-process storage needed to accommodate the variation effect would be small if the flow capacities at various stages of the production line are nominally in balance.

Another decision required in time-independent service systems is what to do when the system becomes temporarily overloaded. In any arrival distribution there is some probability that a series of rapid arrivals will saturate the system's capacity. There is a tendency in such cases to react quickly by adding extra capacity to reduce the waiting line or to temporarily restrict additional arrivals. In most cases, such strategies are ineffective. If the arrival rate is truly time-independent, the system will clear itself naturally. Applying external adjustments to the system may be expensive or disruptive and are probably not needed.

To govern time-independent service systems, three additional strategies can be suggested:

1. Determine the appropriate operating level by use of data describing the arrival rate, service rate, and system characteristics. Service system models can be prepared by using queuing or simulation techniques.
2. The provision of buffer stock to limit service system idle time may be worthwhile in those cases where items can be stored at a reasonable cost.
3. Do not tamper with the system during temporary high-demand periods unless such intervention can be achieved at a reasonable cost and with minimum disruption of the other parts of the organization.

**Operating strategies—general systems** Another set of operating strategies can be proposed for general service systems without regard to whether they have time-varying or time-independent arrival rates. For service systems which permit multiple servers, the decision must be made whether to operate a single, pooled waiting line for all the service stations or one waiting line at each station.

Supermarkets typically have a waiting line behind each service station, whereas airport check-in facilities tend to have a single waiting line that feeds several servers at a ticket counter. The single waiting line is the more efficient facility due to its tendency to more steadily occupy all servers. However, there are factors that make multiple waiting lines more desirable.

A single waiting line requires a staging area for the collection of waiting customers. In systems where floor space is limited (e.g., in a supermarket), there may not be enough space for a single waiting line. Behavioral factors may also favor multiple waiting lines. For example, a customer may prefer doing business with a particular server. The single waiting line may also make the customer expect a longer wait than would multiple waiting lines. Many banks have resisted the introduction of single waiting lines because they believe that customers would expect a longer waiting time than they do with multiple lines.

Another operating decision to be made in general service systems is whether to designate one or more of the service stations as a special service facility (e.g., an express line in a supermarket). The establishment of a special service facility signals both physically and psychologically that one class of customers is to be given special consideration and, for this reason, may irritate some customers. However, the special-purpose station may prevent certain customers with special demands from creating long lines. For example, a bank may wish to remove its commercial customers from the normal teller windows. The special facility in some cases may simply add a constraint to a system that would have performed just as well without it. The special facility decision can only be made in terms of the overall criteria applied by management.

A third set of operational strategies deals with the scheduling of arrivals through the use of appointments (e.g., a doctor's office, an automobile garage). Regulating arrivals by appointment can alleviate the variation effect discussed earlier. On the other hand, appointment scheduling may increase system idleness. To keep idleness at a minimum, one operating strategy that may be used is to overload the system initially in order to maintain a backlog which will keep the system busy; a doctor's office may schedule an extra appointment at the beginning of the day in order to keep the system busy during those periods when appointment schedules are missed or when service is completed more quickly than expected. Appointment scheduling, if managed well, can be a very effective means of managing service systems. System idleness can be limited by providing a backlog of services to be performed.

Three additional operating strategies can now be added to the list:

1. A single waiting line can be an effective means of managing a service system if physical and psychological perceptions of customers are favorable.
2. Allocating some portion of service capacity to a special class of customers

acts as a constraint on the system. Careful attention should be given to such a decision to ensure that improving service to the special class of customers does not reduce system efficiency.

3. Appointment scheduling in service systems can be an effective tool for avoiding idleness in some cases.

Operating strategies offer convenient ways to avoid service system problems by better managing the existing capacity.

---

After reading the fourth briefing paper, Smedley felt saturated with service system philosophies and management principles. Although he had found the material to be interesting reading, the fourth paper had confused him, and he did not understand it very well. As a result, he had second thoughts about hiring a consultant, but he went on to the reading of the last briefing paper.

## Managing Demand—Briefing Number 5

Electric utilities are excellent examples of businesses which suffer from wide variability of demand and have devoted some thought to reducing the variability. Electricity demand in an urban community ordinarily has a pronounced afternoon and evening peak. There is a similar peak at about the time people arise for the day's work.

The ideal situation for an electric utility is to have a completely level demand all day, every day. This situation would permit the utility to keep a fixed amount of generating hardware running, and it could select the most efficient hardware to do most of the generating of electricity. In addition, maintenance planning would be greatly simplified, since the utility would always know just how many units it could have under repair at any time.

Due to the clear desirability of eliminating demand peaks, utilities have attempted to induce consumers to change their demand patterns so as to level the demand curve. Large industrial electricity consumers have been given preferential rates for electricity consumed during off-peak hours. Numerous industries have found the rebate sufficiently attractive to schedule some energy intensive operations during the night shift.

Electric utilities are probably the best example of businesses which have tried to manage demand instead of merely responding to it. Many smaller businesses regularly attempt to affect demand in the short run, but few have such a limited product line as an electric utility.

Department stores offer cut rates, sales, and other inducements to lure customers. Such moves are not permanent but are smaller-scale attempts to manage demand. Wholesalers often offer discounts on high-volume orders to encourage higher demand from customers.

Many businesses use a variety of promotions to increase demand, but few aim at reducing demand. Some organizations have a fixed demand for services that they would like to spread over a longer period, to reduce demand during peak periods. For example, a local taxing agency may offer a discount to taxpayers who pay early. Anyone who has waited in the last-minute tax lines understands why the tax office would like fewer people to delay.

Many service organizations would prefer to serve fixed demands rather than to adjust frequently to variable demand. There are a number of ways to do this.

Theaters presenting plays sell many tickets through travel agencies. The times of the presentations given to the agencies may be the less popular times. Thus, by selling only the tickets to performances at very popular times at the box office and the less popular tickets through travel agencies, a theater may be able to fill the seats at each performance.

Appointments are used in almost the same way in some businesses. From past experience a company may know that its officers have very well defined slack periods, so it may schedule all special appointments during only those periods.

A restaurant may find itself facing two or three daily surges of customers against a background of fairly slow business at other times. Several strategies are available. It can schedule a "happy hour" featuring low-priced alcohol at an off-peak time. It can offer an "early lunch" special to spread out its lunchtime peak. It can offer lower group rates for parties at off-peak times.

In most organizations the pattern is similar. Cost and price inducements lead the way. Special promotions, off-peak scheduling, and the adroit use of appointments are common devices for manipulating or leveling demand.

The nation's railroads were faced with inadequate demand for rolling stock and developed the "unit train" principle. A train of relatively constant length is assigned to an endless circuit between two points. For example, a unit train might pick up coal at a coal mine, transport the coal to the coast, and return to the mine to restart the cycle. The unit train is 100 percent utilized.

Managing demand is not possible in all settings and would not have a significant impact in others, but it is frequently possible and effective. Demand management represents a logical alternative to an organizational policy of merely reacting to fluctuations in service requirements.

---

After reading all five papers, Smedley was more than a little confused. He no longer thought he knew what to do. The last paper had suggested something different from what the others had advised. Smedley decided to phone Paul Jackson, even though the call was long distance.

Jackson, sensing Smedley's frustration over the phone, indicated that the operating strategy discussion was comprehensive and thus was more complicated than would be necessary for any specific organization. Smedley picked up the thread of Jackson's comment and suggested that his business volume only changed infrequently and he was not worried about that fact. However, Jackson insisted that he was committed to help Smedley and talked Smedley into keeping a record of the customer arrival rates at the repair area and at the parts counter for one week.

The results of the parts counter arrival survey were then summarized as shown in the column labeled "Average number of customers" in Table 8.4.

**Table 8.4 Arrival rate and capacity requirements**

| Time period | Average number of customers | Minimum capacity needed* (attendants) | Adjusted capacity requirements (attendants) |
|---|---|---|---|
| 10:30–11:00 | 56 | 3.50 | 4 |
| 11:00–11:30 | 125 | 7.81 | 9 |
| 11:30–12:00 | 180 | 11.25 | 12 |
| 12:00–12:30 | 362 | 22.62 | 25 |
| 12:30– 1:00 | 163 | 10.19 | 11 |
| 1:00– 1:30 | 75 | 4.69 | 5 |
| 1:30– 2:00 | 43 | 2.67 | 3 |

*Based on a service rate of 32 customers per hour.

Upon arriving at Smedley Motors, Jackson supplied the last two columns of Table 8.4 by summarizing the minimum capacity requirements and adjusting them. Adjustments were added for the "variation effect." A 10 percent allowance was provided for variation in arrival and service rates as well as for any other unusual circumstances. For the 10:30–11:00 time period, the adjusted requirements were found as follows:

Adjusted requirements $= 1.75 \times 1.10 = 1.92$ or 2 counter workers

Jackson obtained a copy of Smedley's existing counter schedule as shown in Table 8.5.

From the staff schedule, Jackson determined the actual capacity available during each half-hour for which arrival data had been collected (Table 8.4). The supply was then compared with capacity as shown in Table 8.6 and illustrated below:

10:30–11:00: Capacity supply

$= 16$ persons served per half hour $\times$ 3 servers available

$= 48$ customers able to be served

Demand $= 56$ customers

Capacity measure $=$ capacity supply $-$ demand $= 48 - 56 = -8$

**Table 8.5 Staff schedule**

| Shift schedule | Number of employees |
|---|---|
| 5:00–11:00 | 1 |
| 7:00– 1:00 | 1 |
| 9:00– 3:00 | 1 |
| 11:00– 5:00 | 6 |
| 12:00– 6:00 | 7 |

**Table 8.6 Staff availability compared with requirements**

| Time period | Staff availability | Existing capacity measure | Cumulative capacity measure |
|---|---|---|---|
| 10:30–11:00 | 3 | −8 | −8 |
| 11:00–11:30 | 8 | +3 | −5 |
| 11:30–12:00 | 8 | −52 | −57 |
| 12:00–12:30 | 15 | −122 | −179 |
| 12:30– 1:00 | 15 | +77 | −102 |
| 1:00– 1:30 | 14 | +149 | Surplus |
| 1:30–2:00 | 14 | +181 | Surplus |

The cumulative capacity measure column of Table 8.6 was the key to solving the waiting line problem. A negative measure indicated the formation of a waiting line, while a positive measure represented surplus capacity. The cumulative measure illustrated very dramatically the nature of the waiting line problem at Smedley Motors.

Jackson's next step was to look at the effect on the staff schedule of the general philosophy of anticipating waiting lines rather than reacting to them. More counter workers were required during the 11:00–5:00 shift in order to avoid the waiting line build-up from 11:30–12:00. He prepared an alternative schedule as shown in Table 8.7. The results of the new staff assignment were then determined as before in Table 8.8.

Jackson wrote a short report outlining his recommendations for staffing improvements. In the report, he discussed the difficulties inherent in Smedley's original schedule. Smedley had seemed to base his staff schedule on the arrival rate at the beginning of the hour rather than on capacity requirements for the entire hour. Thus, in the 11:00–11:30 period, Smedley saw surplus capacity which implied a lack of waiting line problems. However, the 11:30–12:00 demand exceeded capacity, and a waiting line began to build. Then the peak demand of the 12:00–1:00 time period began, and since the added capacity was not sufficient, the line continued to grow.

Jackson's staff schedule alleviated this problem to some extent by anticipat-

**Table 8.7 Alternative staff assignment**

| Shift schedule | Number of employees |
|---|---|
| 5:00–11:00 | 1 |
| 7:00– 1:00 | 0 |
| 9:00– 3:00 | 2 |
| 11:00– 5:00 | 13 |
| 12:00–6:00 | 0 |

**Table 8.8 New cumulative capacity measures**

| Time period | Staff availability | Proposed capacity measure | Cumulative capacity measure |
|---|---|---|---|
| 10:30–11:00 | 3 | −8 | −8 |
| 11:00–11:30 | 15 | +135 | Surplus |
| 11:30–12:00 | 15 | +60 | Surplus |
| 12:00–12:30 | 15 | −122 | −122 |
| 12:30– 1:00 | 15 | +77 | −45 |
| 1:00– 1:30 | 15 | +165 | Surplus |
| 1:30– 2:00 | 15 | +197 | Surplus |

ing the increase in arrivals during the 11:30–12:00 time period. As a result, no line would develop before the peak demand period began. Although a line did develop between 12:00–1:00, it was kept to the minimum level possible without increasing staff size.

Although the staffing schedule that Jackson suggested for the parts counter was a reasonable approach to that one aspect of Smedley's operations, Jackson knew from discussions with the owner that the union contract had also caused confusion on the repair floor.

"Do you have reliable records of your repair work for some time past?" he asked Smedley.

"Do birds fly? Listen, if there is anything a repairer knows, it's that you gotta keep all the records because some clowns will come back on you months later," said Smedley.

"Well, then, could you have someone summarize the last three months' worth of jobs into main categories? My idea is that we need to figure out how best to use the two-hour minor segment of time that our swing workers have available for the repair floor."

Smedley agreed, mildly surprised that Jackson had anticipated his next question. The accountant's assistant was put to the task of preparing the summary, which is shown in Table 8.9.

**Table 8.9 Three-month repair job averages**

| Repair category | Average number of jobs/month |
|---|---|
| Body work | 61 |
| Electrical repair | 43 |
| Tune-up | 267 |
| Oil-lube | 345 |
| Warranty maintenance | 137 |
| Send-outs | 97 |
| Transmissions | 45 |
| Motor work | 52 |
| Wheels, shafts, etc. | 203 |

Jackson had a few questions for Smedley about the data summary.

"I gather that 'send-outs' are jobs you send out for a specialized shop to do."

"Yeah. Radiators, gas tanks, some muffler work, armatures."

"Then those jobs don't occupy your shop workers very long?"

"No."

"What is warranty maintenance?"

"The warranty on new cars requires that the cars have a checklist of maintenance done at a dealer's shop, or else the warranty is null and void," said Smedley.

"What does this maintenance consist of?"

"Mostly tune-up and oil and lube type of stuff."

"Then, altogether, you really have an average of 749 tune-up and oil and lube jobs per month?" suggested Jackson. After Smedley saw how Jackson had added the numbers for the three categories, he nodded assent.

Jackson thought briefly and then asked, "Can we get a breakdown on those three categories by day of the month?"

Smedley put the accountant's assistant on this duty, and Jackson stopped in on his way to the golf tournament to see the figures, which appear in Table 8.10. He had a few questions.

"These twenty days are the twenty work days in the month?"

"Sure," replied Smedley.

"Why is there such a concentration of jobs during the first and last parts of the month?"

**Table 8.10 Daily averages of three categories**

| Day of month | Category | | |
| --- | --- | --- | --- |
| | Tune-up | Oil-lube | Warranty maintenance |
| 1 | 19 | 22 | 12 |
| 2 | 17 | 20 | 9 |
| 3 | 14 | 15 | 8 |
| 4 | 11 | 12 | 7 |
| 5 | 9 | 7 | 6 |
| 6 | 8 | 9 | 3 |
| 7 | 7 | 7 | 2 |
| 8 | 6 | 8 | 4 |
| 9 | 9 | 8 | 3 |
| 10 | 8 | 10 | 1 |
| 11 | 6 | 5 | 3 |
| 12 | 5 | 7 | 3 |
| 13 | 7 | 8 | 4 |
| 14 | 6 | 8 | 2 |
| 15 | 6 | 12 | 3 |
| 16 | 21 | 29 | 7 |
| 17 | 37 | 34 | 16 |
| 18 | 28 | 38 | 15 |
| 19 | 22 | 42 | 16 |
| 20 | 21 | 44 | 13 |

"Nobody knows for sure, but it seems that people only think about routine maintenance then."

Jackson thought a while and asked, "How long do a tune-up and oil and lube job take together?"

"Oh, maybe an hour-and-a-half or two hours," replied Smedley.

"And do these numbers mean that most tune-ups also have an oil and lube job?" asked Jackson.

"Well, sure," said a puzzled Smedley.

Jackson smiled and asked, "What do you think your regular customers would think about having a scheduled appointment for routine maintenance that you would guarantee them which would have them in and out in two hours and for which you would offer a 10 percent discount?"

"What? Why should I give a discount?" Smedley shouted.

Jackson laughed and said, "If you can schedule your routine jobs so as to level out the number of jobs per week and also fit them into the two hours available in the minor segment of your swing workers, you could get out, as I recall, thirteen routine jobs per day between 9:00 and 11:00. That makes 260 routine jobs out of 749 each month that you could take care of without pulling anyone off of major repairs."

Smedley snorted and said, "It can't be done. How could it be done?"

"Why not print up a flyer describing the idea and give it out to each of your customers when you do work for them. Over a few months, your schedule should begin to fill in, and I think you will find that the 9:00–11:00 period will be very popular." Then Jackson had to be off to the golf course.

Jackson was surprised to find that Smedley paid his consulting bill on time, and even more surprised when, three months later, he received a phone call from Smedley.

"Listen, Jackson, you're a genius," said Smedley.

"I know that, Bill, but what did I do this time?" asked Jackson.

"Well, I got to thinking about your appointment idea and decided to try it out. Doggone if the customers didn't go for it. Not only that, the swing workers liked knowing exactly what they were going to do every day. Before you knew it, the union steward came in and said that the other repairers were jealous. Well, I actually controlled my temper and said that I would see what I could do. So I put that kid Jewitt, you know, the assistant accountant, in charge of figuring out what to do. Well, Jewitt dug through the numbers on all the past jobs and figured out a kind of ideal repair schedule. So we started trying to schedule all kinds of jobs into the slots that were worked out. In no time, why it must have been less than two months, we were practically scheduled full up. We still can take a few jobs that show up without an appointment, but word seems to have gotten around, and doggone if the customers don't seem to like it. The union workers love it, too. They have as much as two whole weeks of jobs scheduled out most of the time, and for some reason, they like that."

"I'm really happy to hear that," said Jackson.

"Did you ever try that appointment thing somewhere else?" asked Smedley.

"Yeah, at an electronics repair center."

"Did it work there?"

"No."

# TECHNICAL NOTE 8.1 MULTIPLE-SERVER QUEUING MODEL

This model describes the simplest case in which more servers than one are used to deal with a queue. However, the model assumes that only one queue, not multiple queues, is being served. The assumptions are as follows:

1. Arrival distribution—Poisson
2. Service distribution—exponential for each server
3. Number of servers—$C > 1$
4. Service discipline—FCFS
5. Limit on waiting line—unlimited
6. Limit on demand—unlimited

The characteristics of the queuing system are determined according to well defined equations. The notations used in the equations are shown below:

$\lambda$ = average arrival rate

$\mu$ = average service rate per server

$\rho = \dfrac{\lambda}{\mu}$

$C$ = number of servers

$P_o$ = proportion of time system is empty

$$= \left\{ \left( \sum_{i=0}^{C-1} \frac{\rho^i}{i!} \right) + \frac{\rho^C}{C!\,(1 - \rho/C)} \right\}^{-1}$$

$L_s$ = average number of units (or persons) in system

$$= \left\{ \frac{\rho^{C+1}}{(C-1)!\,(C-\rho)^2} \right\} P_o + \rho$$

$L_q$ = average number of units in queue

$$= L_s - \rho$$

$W_s$ = expected time a unit (or person) must spend in system

$$= \frac{L_q}{\lambda} + \frac{1}{\mu}$$

$W_q$ = expected time a unit must spend in queue

$$= \frac{L_q}{\lambda}$$

The expected time a server requires to serve any unit that has gotten to the server is $1/\mu$; so the time relationship is

$$W_s = W_q + \frac{1}{\mu}$$

For instance, if a retail store has two servers and if the average customer arrival rate is 10 per hour, and if each server has an average service rate of 15 customers per hour during busy periods:

$$P_o = 0.50 \qquad W_q = 0.01 \text{ hour}$$

$$L_s = 0.76 \qquad W_s = 0.08 \text{ hour}$$

$$L_q = 0.09$$

In this case, the store has no customers at all half the time. The average number of customers is 0.76, but only an average of 0.09 customers are waiting in the queue. This means that most customers in the store are being served. In fact a customer should only expect to wait 36 seconds in the queue before a server will wait on him. Then it takes an average of 4 minutes for the customer to be served.

## QUESTIONS

**1** What is the variation effect? Explain, and describe a situation in which it occurs.

**2** Why might reducing service capacity when waiting lines are low be a poor strategy?

**3** "Service cannot be stored ahead." If this premise is true, how does the anticipatory scheduling system work?

**4** What are the objectives of a service facility trying to manipulate demand?

**5** Why is reacting to changes in demands for service a generally unsuccessful procedure?

**6** How was Smedley's staffing policy related to his parts customers' habits?

**7** Was Smedley able to solve his queuing problem at the parts counter by better scheduling?

**8** If a barber shop is a queuing system, what is its limit on queue length?

**9** If demand exceeds Smedley's parts service capacity between 12 M. and 2 P.M., is business "lost?" How?

**10** Why is making appointments an effective way to manage demand?

**11** How realistic are the simple assumptions of the queuing model in briefing number 3?

**12** What criteria must a service system satisfy before an anticipatory staffing system can be effective?

## EXERCISES

**1** Describe the service systems below in terms of the following criteria: number of servers, peak service time, single waiting line versus multiple waiting line, priority customers, special features. The service systems are as follows:

    (a) A typical supermarket check-out line

    (b) Check cashing at a bank drive-in window

    (c) The prescription window at a pharmacy

    (d) A ticket office at a movie theater

    (*e*) A concession stand at a football stadium

    (*f*) A doctor's office

    (*g*) An ice cream store that services customers according to a number picked up when they enter

**2** What is the purpose of assigning customers numbers when they enter a store? Is the system effective based upon your experience?

**3** Give examples of service systems in which arrivals occur in batches.

**4** Give examples of service systems in which services are performed in batches.

**5** Give examples of service facilities that have a limited waiting area.

**6** Give examples of service facilities that allow only a limited number of customers.

**7** Describe the difference between a multiple-server facility and a set of single-server facilities.

**8** From your experience, describe some instances where the variation effect was not given consideration in the management of the service facility.

**9** Describe some instances where you have observed misconceptions involving service system management.

**10** From your experience, give an example of a case where the service capacity utilization was affected by a change in the price of the product.

**11** A public library would like to determine the effectiveness of its checkout counter. Arrivals at the counter have been observed to follow a Poisson distribution with a mean arrival rate of 2 patrons per minute. Service time has been observed to be exponential with a rate of 2.2 patrons per minute. The library administrator would like to keep the average waiting time for service to less than two minutes. Is the current system meeting the desired level of performance?

**12** What would be the impact of adding an extra attendant at the checkout counter of the public library of Exercise 11?

**13** Two crews of city personnel have been assigned the task of replacing traffic lights and street lights as they fail. The number of requests which have been received in the pat are shown in Figure 8.3. It appears from the data that the arrival of requests is Poisson. Service data have also been collected as shown in Fig. 8.4. The service time appears to follow an exponential distribution.

    (*a*) From the data, determine the mean arrival rate and the mean service rate. Note that the mean service rate is the reciprocal of the mean service time.

    (*b*) Characterize the present system in terms of its performance measures.

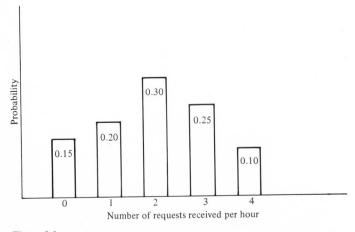

Number of requests received per hour

**Figure 8.3a**

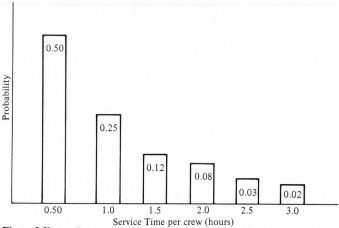

**Figure 8.3b**

**14** A department store's machine service center currently is run by a single maintenance worker. However, the store is considering putting an additional worker to work in the service center in order to reduce repair time and keep the store's machines operating a larger part of the time. Calculations from a queuing model yield the numbers in Table 8.11.

**Table 8.11**

| Number of service workers | Average time waiting for repairs | Total time until back in service | Average number of machines in shop |
|---|---|---|---|
| 1 | 1.6 days | 2.3 days | 6.9 |
| 2 | 0.1 days | 0.4 days | 0.9 |

If the extra maintenance worker will cost $12.50 per hour and if average machine downtime costs $38 per hour in lost profits, which alternative is better?

**15** The local department of motor vehicles serves walk-in customers who wish to renew their license plates. In the past, the office has been run by three clerks who could each individually process forty applications per hour. Each clerk works eight hours per day and takes a half hour for lunch. The customer demand rate is shown in Table 8.12. Identify a better operating strategy if all lunch

**Table 8.12**

| Time period | Customers | Number of clerks available |
|---|---|---|
| 8:00– 9:00 | 100 | 2 |
| 9:00–10:00 | 80 | 3 |
| 10:00–11:00 | 80 | 3 |
| 11:00–12:00 | 90 | 2.5* |
| 12:00– 1:00 | 140 | 2.5 |
| 1:00– 2:00 | 100 | 2.5 |
| 2:00– 3:00 | 80 | 3 |
| 3:00– 4:00 | 80 | 3 |
| 4:00– 5:00 | 70 | 1 |

*1 clerk is taking a half hour lunch break.

breaks must be given between 11:00 and 2:00. Assume that customers still in line at the end of the day are accommodated by overtime work.

16 How could the demand peaks be reduced in the example of Exercise 15?

17 What are some possible operating strategies that could be used to reduce gasoline waiting lines?

18 Is the fast checkout line at a supermarket an effective operating strategy? How could this strategy be evaluated?

19 Describe your personal behavior when confronted with a waiting line.

## CASELETS

1. The Precision Boat Company was faced with difficulties in handling items by use of lift trucks. The 1-million-ft² plant was served by fifty lift trucks from a central motor pool. Whenever a truck was needed in a manufacturing area, the operator would signal the need by turning on a flashing red light. The first truck seeing the light would serve that manufacturing area. The delay time in getting service had grown in recent years, so the company management science staff was assigned to see what could be done to decrease the delay time. After collecting data describing the demand for service and the service rate, the management science group used a queuing analysis to identify the optimal number of lift trucks needed. Much to their surprise, the model indicated that the company had five trucks too many. After checking all of the assumptions of the model, the management science group was convinced its model was correct. However, something was wrong!

   (a) For this situation describe the order in which items are serviced.
   (b) What is the likely discrepancy between the theoretical model and the true situation?
   (c) What can be done to improve the operation of the lift truck service system?

2. Saginaw State, a small liberal arts college, suffered from inadequate computer service. Demand had risen in the past five years from both the administrative and academic sides of the university. A study performed by the computer center staff had indicated that the existing and projected usage could be accommodated for at least two years. The problem was more one of inability to handle peak volume of demand. At the end of each month, the administrative data processing load was large, which reduced available computer capacity to handle the academic load. As the semester neared its end, the academic demand for computer time was unusually heavy. Both students and faculty had tended to postpone computer jobs, creating severe conflicts with heavier than normal administrative data processing.

   (a) Describe the service system problems at the Saginaw State computer center.
   (b) Provide suggestions for alleviating these problems.

# CASE 8.1: THE WATER RESOURCES DIVISION

## Introduction

The water resources division of the department of natural resources was in trouble. Delays in obtaining water use permits were often cited as reasons for lagging development in the state. The governor, originally an environmentalist, had recently changed focus. The governor had become concerned about attracting industry into the state and had given numerous talks criticizing the constraints placed on business by federal regulations.

During one talk to the Glaster Chamber of Commerce, a business executive confronted the governor, creating an embarrassing situation. The executive's firm had expansion plans underway, but it had been waiting two years for a water control permit from the *state*, not from the federal government. The governor turned to an aide and demanded that a report be prepared within a month, detailing the problems at the water resources division (WRD).

The governor's aide, Jack Benfield, called upon the services of the department of finance and administration to look into the problem at the WRD. Jim Prentice, an internal consultant, was given the job.

## Organization of the WRD

The water resources division, a division of the department of natural resources, was responsible for processing water use permits. Permits were processed through one of four departments: coal preparation, mine drainage, municipal, and industrial. The director of the permit section, Morris Dyer, was a longtime employee of the department.

Prentice met with Dyer to review the procedures used in processing a permit. He found that the same general process was followed regardless of the type of permit. Once an applicant requested a permit, an application form was numbered and sent to the applicant. When the application was completed, it was returned to WRD where it was checked for completeness. Most of the applications were initially incomplete and were returned to the applicant.

Completed applications were filed to await full review. The full review normally consisted of an office review and a field review. The field review procedures differed from section to section: in some cases, the field review was performed by

**Table 8.13 Permit processing statistics (1980)**

|  | Coal preparation | Mine drainage | Industrial | Municipal |
|---|---|---|---|---|
| Permit applications reviewed/month | 6 | 9.5 | 25 | 12 |
| Field reviews conducted/month | 5 | 3 | 4 | 1.5 |
| Permits returned to applicant/month | 2 | 4 | 8.5 | 0.5 |
| Average backlog of permits | 0 | 74 | 175 | 60 |

office personnel, and in other cases the review was done by field staff. In the municipal section, the field review was performed by the health department. The industrial section had the broadest range of permits to examine. In nearly all cases the office review could be completed in one day or less once the application was completed.

An analysis of permit processing activities for 1980 (Table 8.13) gives some idea of the workload of the various sections.

## Problems with the Existing System of Processing Permits

As Prentice delved into the situation at WRD he discovered a series of problems. The time to complete a review through the sections varied, but seemed to average three to six months. Delays were caused by many factors including the following:

1. The high rate of resubmissions
2. The time required to obtain a field review
3. The time to complete an office review

The high rate of resubmissions seemed to occur as a result of the applicants' inexperience in filling out the forms. In those cases where field staff were consulted in filling out the application, the incidence of incomplete applications seemed to diminish.

The delays caused by field reviews were attributed to several factors. First, there was considerable inconsistency in the treatment of reviews by the permit sections. In some cases, the field review was conducted prior to the office review and in other cases the reverse was true. The field review staff was in a separate administrative unit from the office staff, resulting in coordination problems. The review staff in some cases seemed to suspect that its reviews were ignored, and it gave lower priority to the field review aspect of the job. Workloads varied widely among field staffs, also.

The office review procedures were analyzed in depth. Several of the findings of the analysis included an apparent imbalance in staff among the four sections. In all sections, there was a significant amount of time-consuming work that was being done in addition to the reviews. The industrial section was the only one that spent as much as half its time on reviews in 1980 (Table 8.14).

**Table 8.14 User of time for reviews**

| Section | Professionals | Total time available per month, hours | Estimated time per month spent on reviews (1980), hours | Percent of time on reviews |
|---|---|---|---|---|
| Coal preparation | 3 | 480 | 32 | 7 |
| Mine drainage | 4 | 640 | 70 | 11 |
| Industrial | 4 | 640 | 300 | 47 |
| Municipal | 2 | 320 | 62 | 19 |

The limited time available for processing the waiting permits was poorly allocated. This problem seemed to be caused by inconsistencies in the way that permits were selected for processing in that there was not a procedure for assigning priorities. Finally, some of the delay was due to indecision on the part of the reviewer making the final determination on an application. If a decision was not reached quickly, the application went into "limbo" to be reviewed again at some later date.

Two general problems contributed to the permit delays in evidence at WRD: few performance objectives were used to evaluate the reviewers' activities; there were no goals established as to the number of reviews to be conducted monthly or the length of time it should take to complete a review. Thus, the reviewers were given no indication of the quality of their work.

The sections kept partial log sheets that showed some stages of processing for each permit and the date each stage was completed, but this log did not help in expediting applications, since it was difficult to compare the status of any two applications.

## Suggested Improvements in Permit Processing Procedures

After spending some time consolidating the information from his WRD observations, Prentice made a series of recommendations in a report to the director of the department of natural resources and sent a copy to the governor. The recommendations were grouped into four categories:

1. Information system improvements
2. Staffing improvements
3. Organizational improvements
4. Procedural improvements

### Information system improvements

1. *Establish performance goals*—Goals should be established for each review section, including the number of reviews to be processed each month and the length of time it takes to complete a review. At the end of each month, the section leader should be asked to report on the department's performance relative to the goals established.
2. *Establish planning and allocation sessions*—At the beginning of each week, the professional staff in each section should meet to determine which applications should be reviewed that week. The section leader should make available a list of the applications waiting to be processed. The professional staff should decide on the set of applications that could most effectively be processed during the coming week. The section leader should be responsible for ensuring that the selected applications were those with the highest priorities and that the resultant assignments were consistent with the section's performance goals.

3. *Establish an information log*—As each application request is received at WRD, it should be recorded in a log book. The purpose of the log is to provide complete information necessary for allocating work efforts and to provide data for measuring the attainment of performance goals. A cover sheet should be attached to each application to give a better indication of the progress of each application.

4. *Establish an advance planning system*—As requests for applications are received, these should be tabulated and used to anticipate future workloads. A system needs to be established that can predict future submission dates for applications. If such a system were developed, each section could anticipate future workloads. These projections could then be used in making staffing allocations.

5. *Increase effective review time*—Earlier analysis has shown that the time spent on reviews is often less than 50 percent of the available time in a section. A study needs to be conducted to determine how the additional time is being utilized. The first step in such a study would be to list the activities that are performed in addition to review. A follow-up study might involve the compilation of time sheets for reviewers on typical days in order to see how much time is being spent on each activity.

6. *Establish an expeditor–general-purpose reviewer*—One of the existing professional staff members should be trained to handle permits from all sections. The function of this person would be to assist those sections needing extra help because of absences or unexpected heavy workloads. The general-purpose reviewer could also be used as an expeditor to handle special applications as the need arises.

7. *Balance staff assignments*—The existing staff should be reassigned in order to balance out staffing of sections with their workloads. Based on 1980 figures, a better balance might be achieved by reassigning personnel from the mine drainage section to the industrial section.

## Organizational improvements

8. *Change field staff-office staff relationship*—Both the field staff and office staff should be placed under one administrator. Such a proposal would provide for better coordination between the field and office staff.

## Procedural improvements

9. *Improve sequence of field and office reviews*—The procedure for conducting field reviews needs to be scheduled more consistently. The field review should in most cases precede the office review, since findings from the site may indicate the need for additional information. By conducting the field review first, an extra office review may be avoided. Advance notice of field reviews can also improve overall field staff utilization by allowing the scheduling of visits to several sites on one trip.

10. *Review Forms*—A thorough study of the application forms is needed to see whether appropriate information is being collected, to see whether some questions can be deleted, and to see whether the wording on the forms can be improved. A survey of previous applications needs to be conducted to see which items of information being requested are the most frequent causes of incomplete applications. The wording of these particular requests should be reviewed.

11. *Improve completeness of forms*—The causes of incomplete applications, once identified, should be explored. Perhaps the percentage of complete forms could be increased if additional instructions were provided on the most troublesome parts of the application. Additional methods of improving completeness might be to send with the application the name of the field reviewer who can be of help when a question arises during the completion of the application. Training seminars for regular applicants might be another method for improving the completeness of forms.

## Implementation

The director of the department of natural resources read Prentice's report with great interest. For some time, the director had suspected that many of the problems with WRD were due to indecision on the part of the reviewers. It seemed that every permit was being reviewed numerous times in an effort to postpone a final decision.

However, the director knew that Morris Dyer was not the right person to effect Prentice's recommendations. Following up on the recommended reorganization of the office and field staff, the director decided to combine both groups under one administrative head. Morris Dyer was placed in charge of the coal preparation section, and Jerry Robe was named permit director. It was made clear to Jerry Robe that the backlog in all sections was to be removed within eight months. The director also endorsed the recommendations made by Prentice and asked for monthly status reports on their implementation.

## Postscript

Robe met with Prentice to go over each recommendation. Robe, a young, energetic bureaucrat, was excited by the challenge. The first three recommendations were adopted immediately. Robe also instructed his staff that he expected all of them to spend at least 80 percent of their time on reviews. Extraneous activities were to be given very low priority.

After the end of the year, the backlog had been reduced in every department but the industrial section. The federal government had begun requiring a new permit (NPDES) program for industrial plants that added extra burdens to the industrial section. Robe felt that a larger staff, funded by federal grants, would alleviate the industrial backlog.

The governor was especially pleased the next year to be able to make a repeat visit to the Glaster Chamber of Commerce to report on the progress made.

## Discussion Guide

1 Describe the WRD service system in terms of its service characteristics.

2 Describe the service system problems at the WRD.

3 Many of the recommendations made by Prentice were rather obvious. Why do you believe the management of WRD had been so negligent in its management?

4 Although Prentice did not appear to use any formal model in his analysis, he did suggest a series of operating strategies. What general principles did Prentice seem to use in developing these operating strategies?

5 What additional recommendations would you make?

# NINE

## SCHEDULING DECISIONS

### SYNOPSIS OF THE CHAPTER

This chapter examines the contributions of decision models in the scheduling of operations. It illustrates that scheduling decisions are complex, involving many variables, both quantitative and qualitative. As the case example illustrates, scheduling decisions are frequently made by experienced individuals using only their own judgment and intuition. Three modeling approaches to scheduling decisions are mathematical models, heuristic models, and decision support system models. Mathematical models are limited in their ability to model situations and the range of considerations they can accommodate. Heuristic models are rule-of-thumb procedures that provide good but not necessarily optimal solutions. Decision support systems are attempts to combine the experienced judgment of a decision maker with the analysis of a computer model to provide a decision system that is superior to either judgment or computer model.

### MAJOR CONCEPTS PRESENTED IN THIS CHAPTER

1. Scheduling decisions are very complex in that they involve numerous quantitative variables as well as a range of qualitative considerations.
2. The development of effective scheduling models is desirable because they offer the following potentials:
   a. Reducing the time involved to make a decision
   b. Reducing the amount of time required to train a scheduler
   c. Adjusting to the increasing complexity of the scheduling task
   d. Removing organization politics from the decision

3. To be effective, scheduling models must be designed to overcome numerous problems, including the following:
   a. Organizational conflict
   b. Workload imbalance
   c. Poor information flow
   d. Poor communications
   e. Improper product mix
4. A good scheduling model must have the following characteristics:
   a. Is dynamic and adaptive to change
   b. Makes use of a scheduler's experience
   c. Operates rapidly and requires minimal data
   d. Is able to accommodate qualitative considerations
5. Mathematical scheduling models are limited in their applicability to real scheduling situations.
6. Heuristic models offer "good" solutions to scheduling problems but may not provide optimal solutions.
7. Decision support systems are a blend of heuristic model and experienced judgment that can be more effective than either judgment or model.

## EXPECTATIONS OF THE STUDENT

The student, after studying this chapter, should be able to do the following:

1. Describe the nature and environment of scheduling decisions in typical organizations.
2. Describe the factors that would contribute to the development of a scheduling model.
3. Outline the requirements for a scheduling model.
4. Determine the best sequence for a two-machine scheduling problem in order to minimize the total time to complete a given list of jobs.
5. Apply several heuristic procedures to the solution of scheduling problems.
6. Develop the general format and structure for a decision support system.

## KEYSER REFRACTORIES

The Keyser Refractories Company produced refractory materials for use in steel, glass, and other industries. The Churchill plant had recently been the focal point of a series of studies conducted by Jim Meck and Janet Smith. Upon visiting the plant for another purpose, the consultants became aware of the shortcomings of the scheduling system being employed.

The scheduler's objective was to get orders out on time. Orders arrived via a teletype and were given to the assistant plant manager, Jake Monnell. Monnell had a magnetic board on which he kept track of orders. This schedule board was divided into weekly segments, and coded cards describing each order were placed on the board. At one time, he had tried to keep track of each order through each stage of production, but the task had become too involved. Monnell had only a limited amount of time to develop a schedule.

The corporate marketing department had a history of applying constant pressure on the plant to speed up the production of certain orders. As marketing began to exert more and more control over the plant, Monnell had become frustrated at the futility of trying to keep up with the changing orders. Every time Smith and Meck visited the plant, Jake Monnell was standing in front of the board muttering to himself and spewing clouds of blue smoke from his pipe.

Since the consultants had had previous experience in the plant, they were somewhat familiar with the existing management environment. The plant manager, Homer Marshall, had been present at several project meetings that had included Meck and Smith at the corporate offices in Potstown. At these meetings, Marshall had exhibited a timid demeanor before the corporate officials. While he would state his position on production matters, he would not confront corporate mangement with the problems caused by the frequent order changes made by the corporate marketing department.

Back home in Arkansas, Marshall became a very forceful administrator. He saw to it that Jake Monnell responded to all requests from corporate headquarters. In turn, Monnell was the one concerned with inserting marketing's constant barrage of disruptive demands into the schedule.

Henry Payson, the production supervisor for Keyser Refractories, had the unenviable task of responding to the frequent changes in the production schedule. He was constantly short of his production targets because inefficient mixes of products had to be scheduled. When he heard a rumor that a scheduling system might be developed, he looked upon the prospect as a vehicle of hope in a hopeless world, a means for producing better schedules, a way to increase production.

As Homer Marshall, Jake Monnell, and Henry Payson met with the consultants, two dominant criteria for developing an improved scheduling system emerged:

1. The system must give management some control in establishing job priorities, because along with a better schedule, management needed enough control over the schedule to comply with organizational factors beyond its control.
2. The system must be able to respond quickly to new conditions. As marketing and production staff called for schedule information, personnel at Churchill needed a quick response from the model in order to know whether to make commitments. In fact, the Churchill people hoped to be able to use this system to react to frequent changes in orders.

The scheduling problems at Keyser Refractories were similar to those that Meck and Smith had observed at many existing production facilities.

## GENERAL CONCEPTS IN SCHEDULING

Scheduling is a nightmare for many organizations. Consider, for example, a small plant manufacturing glass bottles. Its production scheduler must coordinate twenty to thirty orders per day. Two weeks prior to production, the scheduler must procure molds for each order from another plant and hire trucks to transport the finished material to its destination. On the day of production, the scheduler must be sure that no runs conflict and cause production bottlenecks. Space at both the loading dock and the warehouse is extremely limited; so the bottles must be scheduled to go directly from the packaging department to a truck. Coordinating this process requires minute-by-minute supervision. The scheduler was trained for this job over a four-year period and must make hundreds of decisions daily. Each decision could affect the company's ability to fulfill its contractual commitments.

Proper scheduling is such a vital element in many an organization's operation that its control may be a manager's most important function. There are several types of scheduling decisions required in organizations.

Project planning is the largest scale of operations requiring managerial scheduling. A mining company may lay out a ten-year development plan for a new underground mine. A shipyard may have to develop reasonable guesses for the timings of major steps in building a new type of ship. A federal agency may have to prepare sequential plans for covering new areas of responsibility. In general, project planning can involve virtually any kind of analytical tool, but a very common one is the PERT technique described in Chap. 4.

At a slightly less complex level, a manager may have to prepare the systematic procedures for maintaining smooth flows of operations in a production facility. If the plant is to do approximately the same sequence of work over and over, scheduling is essentially a process of assigning people and material in such a way as to balance the flows. For example, an aircraft plant which does nothing but make one type of aircraft over and over can be scheduled very tightly: every activity can be assigned a reliable standard time for its completion, and few unexpected problems will perturb the schedule.

The most common situation that must be scheduled is the following:

An unknown number of jobs must be completed.
Each job needs a distinct sequence of steps to complete it.
Each step on each type of job requires a fairly predictable amount of time.
The resources and labor which go into each step of each job is relatively consistent.

There are a number of possible variations to this outline, but it characterizes most operational scheduling environments.

There are uncertainties and unpredictable events associated with each batch of jobs to be scheduled, but, if jobs fit the description above, scheduling may be adequately accomplished by a mathematical procedure.

# THE ROLE OF MODELS IN SCHEDULING

Many organizations rely upon individuals who are specially trained to make scheduling decisions intuitively. A scheduler may be trained as an apprentice for many years to make decisions based on experience that control the operation of an organization.

The question arises as to why an organization with a well-trained scheduler would even consider using a decision model for scheduling. Several reasons can be suggested.

1. The time involved—A scheduler working from experience may take more time than is available to make a decision. Time becomes more critical as production processes become more highly automated, thus limiting the opportunities to adjust schedules.
2. The training required—Schedulers are valuable to an organization. If they leave it suddenly, they may be difficult to replace.
3. The complexity of the task—As processes become more complicated, the ability of even the best scheduler is taxed in trying to coordinate all phases of production. The organization may continue to give an outward appearance of smooth performance, but upon closer scrutiny it may be seen to be paying high costs for overtime, machine setups, and other inefficiencies that result from the scheduler's inability to keep pace with the complexity of the scheduling task.
4. Removal of organizational politics—Schedulers can gain considerable organizational authority in their jobs. In order to avoid misuses of power, an organization may find it necessary to use a model as an objective scheduling device.

The effects of bad scheduling can be hard to detect. From the vantage point of the highest managerial levels, scheduling decisions may appear to be rather mundane. As long as a company maintains reasonable customer satisfaction, the quality of scheduling will not be visible at those higher levels of management. Costs of poor scheduling are hard to identify and therefore unlikely to be evident to upper management. Thus, upper management is unlikely to become inspired to institute new scheduling procedures under ordinary conditions.

The impetus to use a scheduling decision model is likely to come from lower level management, such as the manager of an individual production facility. This manager may initiate the development of a scheduling model for a variety of reasons and, in doing so, may encounter a number of problems. First is the cost justification; it is hard to pin down the costs of poor scheduling. Consequently, rates of return for scheduling decisions are difficult to obtain. In addition, scheduling systems are so complex that a modeling effort may appear to be impossible. Finally, a scheduling model must overcome organizational inertia, since it may represent the first use of a computer on a real-time basis in the production function.

A further limitation is that few usable scheduling models are available. Most of the scheduling research done to date is not relevant to the situations faced by a scheduler. Real-world conditions that potentially limit the efficacy of a scheduling model are numerous, but most impediments seem to fall into one of the following categories:

1. Organizational conflicts—Scheduling is usually done by the production control department of an organization. Because of its function, the scheduling department must act as an intermediary between the marketing side of the organization and the production side. Marketing must respond to customer demands and sell whichever products or services the customers want. On the other hand, production supervisors prefer to produce high-volume, easy-to-produce products which increase productivity. Resolving disputes over the conflicting goals of production and marketing is a major problem in most scheduling departments.

2. Workload imbalance—Ideally a schedule should maintain a constant workload in all manufacturing departments. This goal is almost impossible to achieve, and an efficient workload during one hour may produce bottlenecks the next hour. Few schedulers are able to balance a schedule intuitively for more than a brief period. As a result there is likely to be either a glut of in-process storage or a number of idle workers.

3. Poor information flow—A scheduler must have information on manufacturing requirements, future needs, inventory levels, workforce, and machine capacities. In many organizations, this information has become computerized and is regularly available. Unfortunately, inventory records are not extremely accurate, future needs are often modified, capacities change, and management decides to alter its near-term production requirements. Even a short visit with a scheduler will likely be interrupted by numerous telephone calls changing information. As the information changes, so does the schedule.

4. Poor communications—Closely associated with information problems are those of communications. As schedules are changed, it is necessary to communicate the alternatives to everyone involved. Again, the scheduler must spend time on the phone communicating; at the same time, new changes await attention.

5. Improper product mix—Higher management may complicate scheduling by directing that a series of products requiring the same production facilities be manufactured. Rather than requiring products which would distribute production over the various production facilities, management may require a set of products all demanding time on a limited portion of the manufacturing facility.

A practical scheduling model must satisfy the following criteria:

1. It should be dynamic and adaptive to change.
2. It should make the greatest use of a scheduler's experience and intuition.

3. It should operate rapidly with minimal data input requirements.
4. It should not be restricted to the quantitative elements relevant to the decision.

As the consultants reviewed their notes on the problems faced by Keyser Refractories, they also researched the state of the art of scheduling techniques, looking for ways to solve the Keyser problem. Unfortunately, the state of the art was not very helpful, because existing theoretical methods seemed to have little to do with real-world scheduling problems.

Previous research on scheduling can be grouped into three general classifications:

1. Mathematical models, which give an "optimal" solution to a scheduling problem under a given set of conditions.
2. Heuristic approaches, which apply rules of thumb to the determination of a good but not necessarily optimal schedule.
3. Decision support systems, which take a tentative schedule from a scheduler, predict the consequences of the scheduler's intuitive decision, and iteratively repeat the same process until an acceptable solution is found.

## MATHEMATICAL MODELS IN SCHEDULING

Mathematical models have had limited effectiveness as scheduling tools, largely because the problems to be solved are quite complicated. However, even a cursory investigation of the principles underlying these models provides insight into scheduling.

For example, a mathematical solution to a problem can be constructed only when the problem is well defined. In the case of scheduling, one must be able to answer the question, What is your objective?

Mathematical scheduling algorithms generally address one of the following objectives:

Minimize the total processing time.
Minimize the number of late jobs.
Minimize setup time.
Minimize the sum of completion times.
Minimize the weighted completion times.
Minimize idle time.
Minimize total lateness of jobs.
Minimize maximum lateness of jobs.

This is not an exhaustive list of objectives, but it does indicate some of the criteria which can be applied in deriving a "good" schedule. However, it may be difficult to find people in an organization who will agree upon the choice of objective. If the sum of completion times for a set of jobs is minimized, then a really big job may be given the same value as a small job. If times are weighted

**Table 9.1. Example
processing times, in hours**

| Job | Machine A | Machine B |
|-----|-----------|-----------|
| 1 | 13 | 8 |
| 2 | 2 | 3 |
| 3 | 7 | 9 |
| 4 | 8 | 4 |
| 5 | 1 | 6 |
| 6 | 5 | 10 |

by job sizes and the weighted completion times are minimized, then large jobs may be given more importance than they are due.

However, consider a very simple scheduling problem with a very simple objective to demonstrate how well an algorithm can work in the ideal case. This algorithm is due to S. M. Johnson (1954), and it applies to jobs which must each be processed first on one machine (A) and then on a second machine (B). The algorithm consists of four steps:

1. Make up a table of the processing time on each machine for each job to be scheduled.
2. Find the smallest processing time in the table for either machine. In case of a tie, select either time arbitrarily.
3. If the smallest time is for machine A, schedule the corresponding job at the earliest remaining time on machine A. If the smallest time is for machine B, schedule the job as late as possible on machine B.
4. Delete the assigned job from the table and return to step 2.

Consider the example shown in Table 9.1.

The smallest processing time is one hour on job 5. Therefore, the first job chosen is 5. It is scheduled first on machine A. Job 2 is scheduled next on A since its processing time is the smallest once job 5 is deleted from the table. Job 4 is scheduled next because it has the smallest remaining time, and since the time of three hours occurs on machine B, job 4 is scheduled last. This process continues until the schedule is completed as shown in Table 9.2.

The two-machine schedule is optimal in that it minimizes the total time re-

**Table 9.2 The scheduled order of jobs**

| Job | Machine A | | Machine B | |
|-----|-----------|-----------|-----------|-----------|
| | Start time | Stop time | Start time | Stop time |
| 5 | 0 | 1 | 1 | 7 |
| 2 | 1 | 3 | 7 | 10 |
| 6 | 3 | 8 | 10 | 20 |
| 3 | 8 | 15 | 20 | 29 |
| 1 | 15 | 28 | 29 | 37 |
| 4 | 28 | 36 | 37 | 41 |

quired to complete the entire list of jobs. It also, incidentally, minimizes the total slack time.

As long as the times given for processing the jobs on the two machines are accurate, this schedule is the best available. Similar techniques can be applied to certain three-machine jobs, and other procedures exist in some more complicated cases, but as mathematical models begin to approach real-life complexity, they tend to become so complicated that they are either very expensive to use or very difficult to solve.

## HEURISTIC APPROACHES TO SCHEDULING

Heuristic approaches are much more adaptable than mathematical methods to solving scheduling problems. They are rules of thumb which can provide "quick and dirty" scheduling decisions. Consider the scheduling of the jobs with processing data as shown in Table 9.3.

Suppose that the date is now 9/4 and the scheduler wishes to determine which job to schedule next: A, B, C, D, or E. A common rule is "first-come–first-served," which dictates that the first job to enter the system is scheduled first. In this case, since job A entered on 9/1, it would be scheduled first. Jobs B, C, D, and E would then follow A in the schedule.

Another heuristic rule is the shortest-operation-time (SOT) rule which says: Schedule the job next that takes the least amount of time. Since the processing time for C is less than that of the other jobs, it would be scheduled first according to the SOT rule. The remaining schedule would then be jobs A, E, D, and B.

Researchers have developed numerous other heuristic scheduling rules. Panwalkar and Iskander (1977) have summarized over 100 such published rules. From their research, several general conclusions can be drawn as to the effectiveness of heuristic rules.

1. The first-come–first-served (FCFS) rule is ineffective and seems to have little redeeming virtue as a scheduled procedure.
2. The shortest-operation-time rule is effective as a simple rule in a variety of circumstances. Its major disadvantage is the extreme delay faced by jobs whose operation time is significantly longer than other jobs.
3. Heuristic rules can be applied in dynamic conditions; new jobs entering the systems are easily accommodated. For simpler heuristics, the calculations are

**Table 9.3. Example scheduling data**

| Job | Processing time, days | Time entered system | Due date |
|-----|------|------|------|
| A | 2 | 9/1 | 9/6 |
| B | 6 | 9/2 | 9/8 |
| C | 1 | 9/2 | 9/7 |
| D | 5 | 9/3 | 9/12 |
| E | 4 | 9/4 | 9/15 |

minimal and calculation times insignificant. The resulting schedules are adequate for simpler situations.

While heuristic approaches may be more readily adaptable than mathematical models, they too are limited according to two criteria: (1) They do not employ the experience and intuition of the scheduler effectively; (2) They do not include the qualitative aspects of scheduling, since most heuristics are based on quantitative priority rankings. An attempt to resolve these two problems leads to the next approach.

The underlying philosophy of the approach is that experienced judgment combined with computer support can provide better decisions than either experienced judgment alone or a model employing no judgmental input.

## DECISION SUPPORT SYSTEM APPROACH TO SCHEDULING

The decision support system (DSS) approach to scheduling incorporates experience into the modeling process as outlined in Fig. 9.1. The process begins with

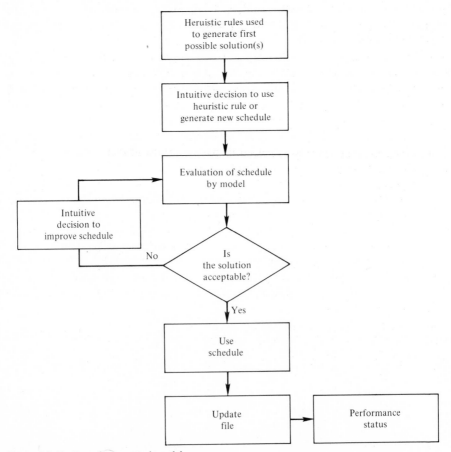

**Figure 9.1** Outline of conceptual model.

the generation of an initial solution. For simpler scheduling situations, a good beginning may be provided by heuristic rules that generate solutions more quickly than could have been generated from experience alone. The scheduler is then asked to improve on the starting solution. At this point, the decision maker's experience and intuition are applied to the problem. In this way, the procedure can include many important subjective elements in scheduling decisions.

Once a schedule has been determined, the model evaluates that schedule. The evaluation tool may be a rather straightforward calculation procedure which determines no more than the machine loadings for each processing stage. The role of the model is to evaluate the scheduler's decision. Typically, the output from this phase of the model will include estimates of job completion times for each job in the schedule, as well as measures of machine utilizations.

The scheduler reviews the output from the model and judges whether improvements can be made. The model is used over and over (iteratively). When satisfied with the current schedule, the scheduler stops the iterations and uses that schedule. The necessary decisions will be based upon a mix of subjective and quantitative criteria more complex than can be included in a purely mathematical model.

## THE KEYSER MODEL

The consultants decided to take the decision support approach to Keyser's scheduling and proceeded to develop a description of the product flow adaptable to this approach. The production process was organized into three stages shown in Fig. 9.2.

Raw materials enter the grinding stage first; a product may require raw materials which have been ground on any combination of the three grinders. The product flow cannot proceed to the next step without the completion of each grinding operation. Once all the raw materials are ground, the ground materials are weighed out (batched) and mixed. However, a product may have to wait prior to a step if the preceding product has not completed processing that step.

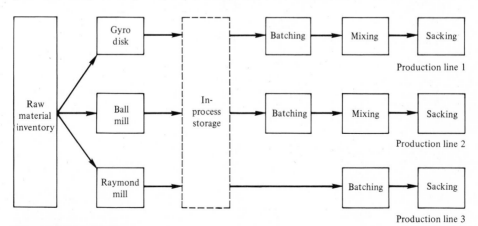

**Figure 9.2** Materials flow.

**Table 9.4 Order information**

CURRENT PRODUCT LIST

| PRODUCT NUMBER | PRODUCT NAME | AMOUNTS |
|---|---|---|
| 27 | SUPER STUFF 26 | 89.00 |
| 78 | GRAINY 1024 | 67.00 |
| 45 | HEAVY DUTY GUNK 13 | 550.00 |
| 34 | STICKY 37 | 800.00 |
| 21 | GUNNER MIX 69 | 340.00 |
| 70 | TACKY 25 | 150.00 |

Thus, checks must be made on the availability of the raw materials and on the progress of the prior product's batching before a product can be declared ready to begin its own batching step.

After preparing the flow description, the consultants developed a hypothetical example to illustrate the schedule produced. Six products were selected with order sizes as shown in Table 9.4.

The processing times and the production line for each product had been previously recorded for all products and were stored in the computer memory. All the scheduler had to do was to sit at the computer terminal and engage in a conversation with the computer.

The scheduling model begins by asking the scheduler to provide information on the products to be made and the tonnage required of each product. A conversation between the interactive scheduling program and the scheduler is shown below for the six products of Table 9.4. The question marks are prompts by the computer which are followed by the responses of the scheduler.

```
WOULD YOU LIKE TO UPDATE PRODUCT INFORMATION FILE?
?NO
WOULD YOU LIKE TO USE THE PRODUCT LIST ON FILE?
?NO
DO YOU WISH TO CREATE A NEW LIST OF PRODUCTS TO SCHEDULE?
?YES

PROCEDURE TO CREATE A NEW SCHEDULE

ENTER THE ID NUMBER OF THE PRODUCTS TO BE INCLUDED IN A NEW
    SCHEDULE AND THE TONS OF EACH TO BE PRODUCED
ENTER AN ID NUMBER OF ZERO TO INDICATE WHEN THE LIST IS COMPLETE

PRODUCT NUMBER
?27
AMOUNT (TONS) OF PRODUCT     SUPER STUFF 26
?89
PRODUCT NUMBER
?78
AMOUNT (TONS) OF PRODUCT     GRAINY 1024
?67
```

PRODUCT NUMBER
?45
AMOUNT (TONS) OF PRODUCT    HEAVY DUTY GUNK 13
?550
PRODUCT NUMBER
?34
AMOUNT (TONS) OF PRODUCT    STICKY 37
?800
PRODUCT NUMBER
?21
AMOUNT (TONS) OF PRODUCT    GUNNER MIX 69
?340
PRODUCT NUMBER
?70
AMOUNT (TONS) OF PRODUCT    TACKY 25
?150
PRODUCT NUMBER
?0

Once the data file is complete, the next step is to begin the iterative scheduling process.

WOULD YOU LIKE MODEL TO CREATE NEW INITIAL SCHEDULE?
?YES

The results of the initial schedule follow.

| PROD. NO. | PRODUCT NAME | GYRO DISK | BALL MILL | RAYMOND MILL | | BATCH/ MIXING | DOWN-TIME | SACKING |
|-----|-----|-----|-----|-----|-----|-----|-----|-----|
| 45 | HEAVY DUTY GUNK 13 | .00 | .00 | .00 | | .00 | 1.00 | 85.15* |
| | | .00 | .00 | .00 | LINE 1 | 84.15 | | 195.15† |
| 21 | GUNNER MIX 69 | .00 | .00 | .00 | | 195.15 | .50 | 212.65 |
| | | 10.20 | 11.22 | .00 | LINE 1 | 212.15 | | 239.85 |
| 78 | GRAINY 1024 | 10.20 | .00 | .00 | | 23.60 | .25 | 29.41 |
| | | 23.60 | .00 | .00 | LINE 2 | 29.16 | | 37.65 |
| 70 | TACKY 25 | 23.60 | .00 | .00 | | 61.10 | .25 | 73.80 |
| | | 61.10 | .00 | .00 | LINE 2 | 73.55 | | 92.45 |
| 27 | SUPER STUFF 26 | 61.10 | 11.22 | .00 | | 239.85 | .50 | 262.85 |
| | | 75.05 | 33.72 | .00 | LINE 1 | 262.35 | | 298.85 |
| 34 | STICKY 37 | .00 | 33.72 | .00 | | 298.85 | 1.00 | 339.85 |
| | | .00 | 60.12 | .00 | LINE 1 | 338.85 | | 403.85 |
| | | | | | | | | |
| TOTAL PROCESSING TIME | | 75.05 | 60.12 | .00 | LINE 1 | 403.85 | | |
| | | | | | LINE 2 | 45.40 | | |
| | | | | | LINE 3 | .00 | | |

| | |
|-----|-----|
| TOTAL DOWNTIME | 3.50 |

| | | | |
|-----|-----|-----|-----|
| TOTAL IDLE TIME | LINE 1-.00 | LINE 2-23.60 | LINE 3-.00 |
| FRACTION IDLE TIME | .00 | .26 | .00 |

*Beginning time of the operation
†Ending time of the operation

The schedule shown requires only a small amount of practice to be easily read. Product 45 requires no grinding time on any of the three grinders. Thus, each grinder shows a beginning and ending time of .00 for product 45. This product is batched, mixed, and sacked on production line 1, and it requires 84.15 hours to batch and mix the 550 tons of product 45. There is one hour of downtime required for cleanup after product 45 is mixed, and sacking starts immediately after downtime and takes 110 hours, ending at 195.15 hours.

Product 21 requires grinding of part of its materials on both the gyro disk and the ball mill. It, too, is processed on line number 1 and is completed at 239.85 hours.

The scheduler views the schedule above which was derived as the result of a heuristic decision rule, and decides whether improvements could be made. In this case, the scheduler decided that 403.85 hours could not be spared and therefore concentrated on only four of the products, revising the schedule accordingly.

WOULD YOU LIKE TO CREATE ANOTHER SCHEDULE????
?YES
ENTER THE PRODUCT ID NUMBERS IN THE SEQUENCE THEY ARE
    TO APPEAR IN THE SCHEDULE
ENTER A ZERO TO INDICATE WHEN YOUR SCHEDULE IS COMPLETE
PRODUCT -
?34
PRODUCT -
?70
PRODUCT -
?78
PRODUCT -
?45
PRODUCT -
?0

| PROD. NO. | | | | | | | BATCH/ MIXING | DOWN-TIME | SACKING |
|---|---|---|---|---|---|---|---|---|---|
| 34 | STICKY 37 | .00 | .00 | .00 | | | 26.40 | 1.00 | 67.40 |
| | | .00 | 26.40 | .00 | | LINE 1 | 66.40 | | 131.40 |
| 70 | TACKY 25 | .00 | .00 | .00 | | | 37.50 | .25 | 50.20 |
| | | 37.50 | .00 | .00 | | LINE 2 | 49.95 | | 68.85 |
| 78 | GRAINY 1024 | 37.50 | .00 | .00 | | | 68.85 | .25 | 74.66 |
| | | 50.90 | .00 | .00 | | LINE 2 | 74.41 | | 82.90 |
| 45 | HEAVY DUTY GUNK 13 | .00 | .00 | .00 | | | 131.40 | 1.00 | 216.55 |
| | | .00 | .00 | .00 | | LINE 1 | 215.55 | | 326.55 |
| | | | | | | | | | |
| TOTAL PROCESSING TIME | | 50.90 | 26.40 | .00 | | LINE 1 | 300.15 | | |
| | | | | | | LINE 2 | 45.40 | | |
| | | | | | | LINE 3 | .00 | | |

TOTAL DOWNTIME                                            2.50

TOTAL IDLE TIME       Line 1-.00       LINE 2-.00       LINE 3-.00
FRACTION IDLE TIME           .00             .00            .00

WOULD YOU LIKE TO CREATE ANOTHER SCHEDULE????
?NO

WOULD YOU LIKE TO SAVE THE PRODUCT LIST FOR FURTHER USE?
?NO

The new schedule better fit time limitations, requiring only 326 hours. The scheduler decided that the sequence was acceptable and terminated the interactive session. If the scheduler had so desired, additional iterations could have been performed with the model.

This scheduling procedure is based upon the decision calculus format developed by Little (1970). The goal of such a model is the updating of a manager's intuition. It does not attempt to derive an optimum solution. In fact, it implicitly recognizes that a quantitatively determined optimum solution cannot even be identified. However, such a procedure does satisfy the five criteria for a good scheduling model outlined earlier. These criteria were as follows:

1. It should be dynamic and adaptive to change.
2. It should make the greatest use of the scheduler's experience and intuition.
3. It should operate rapidly.
4. It should not be restricted to the quantitative elements relevant to the decision.
5. It should satisfy the company's scheduling standards.

Once the programming of the model was completed, the consultants visited the plant to help with its implementation. As they arrived at the plant, the plant manager informed them they were to attend a meeting with his entire staff. The manager's tone of voice was ominous.

The consultants could tell, as the staff filed into the room, that the meeting was going to be a rough one. As the discussion began, it was clear that the Keyser staff members were upset because they felt a model was being developed that would be restrictive and would ignore what they considered to be key issues. As the consultants explained the interactive nature of the model, their concern seemed to decrease, but only slightly.

It was clear that the staff did not fully understand the interactive nature of the system. In the past the staff members were accustomed to keying information into a terminal and receiving printouts several days later in the mail; so they expected the new scheduling model to operate in a similar fashion.

When Cheri Tweed demonstrated the system, the concern of the staff dissolved quickly. The staff was impressed by the instantaneous response of the system and finally began to understand the interactive nature of the system. Various members of the staff developed a hypothetical schedule and spent nearly an hour debating and revising it at the computer terminal.

Later, when the consultants met with the corporate sponsor of the scheduling work, they learned some revealing things about the modeling effort. "You know, you guys really sold that model. Once the Churchill people got on the terminal, the project was sold. Of course, Cheri was a help. She really captivated them."

# TECHNICAL NOTE 9.1 *N*-JOB, *M*-MACHINE SCHEDULING

A heuristic procedure for scheduling $N$ jobs on $M$ machines has been developed by Gupta (1971). Consider the job processing times of Table 9.5.

The steps in the procedures are as follows:

1. For each job, compare the processing time on the first machine $A$ with the processing time on the last machine $Z$.

$$\text{If } A \geqslant Z \quad \text{set} \quad K = 1$$

$$\text{If } A < Z \quad \text{set} \quad K = -1$$

$$\text{If } A = Z \quad \text{set} \quad K = 0$$

2. For each job, calculate the sum of processing times on each pair of successive machines. Select the sum that is the smallest (SUM).
3. Calculate $K/\text{SUM}$ for each job.
4. Sequence the jobs in the order of smallest to largest $K/\text{SUM}$ values.

For the example data, the calculations would be as follows:

### Job 1

$$\text{Since } 2 < 3, \quad K = -1$$

The successive sums are

$$2 + 6 = 8$$

$$6 + 5 = 11$$

$$5 + 3 = 8$$

Since the smallest sum is 8, SUM = 8

The $K/\text{SUM}$ value is then $-1/8$.
The $K/\text{SUM}$ values for each of the jobs are shown in Table 9.6.
The job sequence would be 1, 4, 3, 2, 5.

**Table 9.5**

|      | Machine |       |       |       |
| ---- | ------- | ----- | ----- | ----- |
| Job  | $M_1$   | $M_2$ | $M_3$ | $M_4$ |
| 1    | 2       | 6     | 5     | 3     |
| 2    | 4       | 2     | 7     | 1     |
| 3    | 8       | 3     | 6     | 4     |
| 4    | 5       | 2     | 1     | 5     |
| 5    | 6       | 1     | 3     | 4     |

**Table 9.6**

| Job | $K$/SUM |
|-----|---------|
| 1 | $-1/8$ |
| 2 | $1/6$ |
| 3 | $1/9$ |
| 4 | $0/3$ |
| 5 | $1/4$ |

## REFERENCES

Gupta, J. N. D.: "A Functional Heuristic Algorithm for the Flowshop Scheduling Problem," *Operational Research*, vol. 22, no. 1, March 1971, pp. 39–48.

Johnson, S. M.: "Optimal Two and Three Stage Production Schedules With Set-Up Times Included," *Naval Research Logistics Quarterly*, vol. 1, 1954, pp. 61–68.

Little, John D. C.: "Models and Managers: The Concept of a Decision Calculus," *Management Science*, vol. 16, no. 8, 1970, pp. B466–B485.

Panwalker, S. S., and Wafik Iskander: "A Survey of Scheduling Rules," *Operations Research*, vol. 25, no. 1, 1977, pp. 45–61.

## QUESTIONS

**1** What was the nature of the scheduling problems at the Churchill plant of Keyser Refractories?

**2** How was scheduling being performed at the plant?

**3** What contributions could a scheduling model make at the Churchill plant?

**4** How do the scheduling decisions presented in this chapter differ from the scheduling decisions that were modeled by PERT/CPM procedures?

**5** Why would an organization consider using a scheduling model?

**6** What are the typical problems encountered in developing and using scheduling models for decision making?

**7** What are the criteria for scheduling models? (Describe in your own words.)

**8** Why are mathematical models limited in their use in scheduling decision making?

**9** How do heuristic approaches differ from mathematical models in scheduling?

**10** What is the philosophy of the decision support system?

**11** How can the decision support system approach perform better than either intuitive or mathematical approaches?.

**12** How do the three approaches to scheduling rate with respect to the evaluation criteria?

## EXERCISES

**1** What are some valid measures of effectiveness for the scheduling function within an industrial firm that manufactures to order? To inventory?

**2** A company has established a rate of return of 30 percent for investments in computer-related projects. How would you measure the ROI for an interactive scheduling system?

**3** Describe the apprehensions that the following individuals would have with respect to the use of a scheduling system.

(*a*) Vice president of marketing

(*b*) Vice president of production

(*c*) Plant manager

(*d*) Customer

**4** Processing time for six jobs is shown in Table 9.7.
(*a*) Determine the processing sequence to minimize the total time to complete the jobs on both machines.
(*b*) Develop the job schedule for the sequence identified in (*a*).
(*c*) Explain why the Johnson procedure works.

## Table 9.7

| Job | $M_1$ | $M_2$ |
|-----|-------|-------|
| 1 | 2 | 6 |
| 2 | 3 | 1 |
| 3 | 4 | 7 |
| 4 | 1 | 8 |
| 5 | 5 | 9 |
| 6 | 8 | 3 |

**5** For the data in Table 9.8, do the following
(*a*) Determine the best processing sequence to minimize the total time to complete the jobs.
(*b*) Determine the idle time on both machines.
(*c*) How much better is this sequence than one that processes jobs in numerical order?

## Table 9.8

| Job | $M_1$ | $M_2$ |
|-----|-------|-------|
| 1 | 3 | 8 |
| 2 | 6 | 4 |
| 3 | 2 | 7 |
| 4 | 3 | 6 |
| 5 | 4 | 1 |
| 6 | 5 | 2 |
| 7 | 6 | 3 |

**6** A machine shop has decided to shift from its existing FCFS scheduling philosophy to another scheduling rule. Historical data was gathered for a two-week period of time as shown in Table 9.9.

## Table 9.9

| | Job | | | | | | | | | | | |
|---|---|---|---|---|---|---|---|---|---|---|---|---|
| | A | B | C | D | E | F | G | H | I | J | K | L |
| Arrival time | 1 | 1 | 2 | 3 | 5 | 7 | 9 | 9 | 11 | 11 | 12 | 14 |
| Processing time, days | 2 | 1 | 4 | 5 | 3 | 1 | 4 | 2 | 1 | 2 | 5 | 7 |
| Due date | 6 | 5 | 7 | 13 | 14 | 11 | 18 | 20 | 24 | 23 | 29 | 32 |
| Priority | H | M | M | L | L | M | M | M | H | M | M | L |
| H = high | | | | | | | | | | | | |
| M = medium | | | | | | | | | | | | |
| L = low | | | | | | | | | | | | |

The machine shop is initially empty and free at 12/1 to begin processing any of the jobs. For the heuristic rules listed below, determine the following:

(a) The average time the job was in the system
(b) The total number of late jobs
(c) The average lateness per job
(d) The number of high-priority jobs that are late

The following heuristic rules are to be investigated:

The first-come–first-served rule
The due date rule
The shortest-operation-time rule
A rule of your own development

Compute the performance of the heuristic rules and specify which is best.

7 A company has five machines through which each job must proceed as shown in Table 9.10.
(a) Using Gupta's procedure, determine the processing sequence.
(b) Prepare a schedule showing the start and finish times of each job on each machine.
(c) Determine the idle time on each machine.

## Table 9.10

| Job | $M_1$ | $M_2$ | $M_3$ | $M_4$ | $M_5$ |
|-----|-------|-------|-------|-------|-------|
| 1 | 1 | 2 | 3 | 1 | 6 |
| 2 | 4 | 6 | 7 | 2 | 2 |
| 3 | 5 | 3 | 8 | 4 | 5 |
| 4 | 2 | 2 | 7 | 9 | 1 |
| 5 | 6 | 4 | 3 | 6 | 8 |
| 6 | 3 | 3 | 2 | 5 | 2 |

8 What heuristic rules are commonly used to schedule the following operations:
(a) Homework assignments
(b) Computer jobs
(c) Emergency cases at a hospital
(d) Snow removal

9 How can a decision support system be used for training?

10 Evaluate the decision support system developed for Keyser Refractories according to the schedule criteria mentioned in the text.

11 A decision support system is to be prepared for scheduling students for classes. A student would have access to the system through a computer terminal. The system should ask students to enter courses to be taken and then provide them with a schedule. The system should also allow students to change the computer-generated schedule.
(a) Provide a typical computer-user dialogue to operate the decision support system.
(b) Give an example of how the output might look.

12 What obstacles would you normally expect to encounter in selling an organization on the use of a decision support system for scheduling?

13 How can the costs of poor scheduling be measured?

14 Describe the organizational characteristics that would be important for the successful implementation of a scheduling system.

15 Interview a scheduler to find out the following:
(a) The system he or she uses in scheduling
(b) Measures of effectiveness
(c) Training requirements

## CASELETS

1. The marketing group of General Products has been given the task of bringing eight new products to the market place. Each product may or may not require any of seven steps as shown in Table 9.11.

   The director of the marketing group has suggested that the products be worked on in numerical order. One of the group has suggested that some effort be given to determining the best sequence. The director is lukewarm to the idea and wants some evidence that the scheduling effort will pay off. Outline the following:

   (*a*) How the scheduling effort can be evaluated
   (*b*) How the product sequence can be found

2. Academy Packaging Company purchases cardboard from outside suppliers and transforms it into cardboard boxes to the specifications requested by its customers. The basic manufacturing flow is a two-step process of printing and and joining as illustrated below.

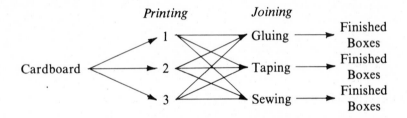

Orders typically call for small runs, since the company has a poor competitive position and cannot attract the more profitable higher-volume customers. An order is first sent to a printing operation where it is processed on one of three printers depending upon its size. During the printing phase the press must be initially set up. The setup time can be long depending upon the color, size,

**Table 9.11**

| Job | $S_1$ | $S_2$ | $S_3$ | $S_4$ | $S_5$ | $S_6$ | $S_7$ |
|-----|-------|-------|-------|-------|-------|-------|-------|
| | | | Steps required, time in weeks | | | | |
| 1 | 2 | ... | ... | ... | 5 | 3 | ... |
| 2 | ... | 3 | 4 | ... | 6 | ... | 4 |
| 3 | 6 | 2 | ... | 4 | 3 | 2 | ... |
| 4 | ... | 3 | 7 | ... | 4 | ... | 8 |
| 5 | ... | ... | 6 | ... | 5 | ... | ... |
| 6 | 8 | 2 | ... | 3 | 4 | ... | ... |
| 7 | 2 | 6 | ... | ... | 3 | ... | 4 |
| 8 | ... | 2 | ... | 3 | 4 | 6 | ... |

and joining method used in the previous job run. Setup times are typically longer than the actual run time.

Once the cardboard is printed, the next step is joining. Joining can be done by gluing, taping, or sewing. The setup time on machines that do gluing, taping, and sewing is short, and the run times are generally short.

A bottleneck exists at the printing operation. Management control of production is loose. Schedules are determined by the materials handler. Only rough and out-of-date estimates are available for the total processing time on each machine.

Nearly 100 orders are backlogged for production, and the plant is losing orders. As a result of this situation, the plant manager is under severe pressure to improve the production flow at the plant.

As a management consultant hired by the plant manager, outline the steps you would take to improve the scheduling procedures employed by the plant.

## CASE 9.1: CLARKSBURG SHIRT COMPANY

Clarksburg Shirt Company was a small contract garment manufacturer. Its major business was the production of shirts and blouses for major clothing lines. As competition from foreign imports grew, Clarksburg had problems in holding enough business to keep its work force employed. George David, the owner of the company, was sufficiently concerned about this problem to call the local university for advice.

Andrew Wolfe, a professor at the university, met with David and Luigi Petrucci, the plant manager, to discuss Clarksburg's problems. To improve sales, Clarksburg had three options as perceived by Wolfe:

1. Reduce contract prices.
2. Improve product quality.
3. Improve service.

David discounted the first two options. The prices being charged were already at the absolute minimum level. Product quality was high enough already. In reality Clarksburg Shirt was thought of as one of the best quality producers in the industry. In fact, David often wondered if the Clarksburg quality wasn't too good for the market being served.

Service improvements seemed to offer some opportunities for increasing sales. On several occasions, David has been told by clients that Clarksburg had the reputation of a producer that could not meet schedules.

Typically, a client would call Luigi Petrucci to discuss a potential order and get a commitment on a delivery date. If delivery dates and manufacturing concerns were resolved, the client would talk with David to negotiate a price.

Petrucci, although not college trained, was a master of the plant in all respects. He had the entire works in his head. With the aid of a summary sheet he kept, he had a fairly good running tally of the loading of the facility. He tried to

**Exhibit 9.1**

## For the Week of 4 Mar 1977 (1st Week)

| Lot | Style | Label | Fronts — Center side Top center | French front | Rev. w/lining | B.P. side Btn. stay | Rev. w/lining | Top center | Cuffs Sq. | Rd. | Fr. | 1 | 2 | None | Pkt 1 | 2 | Flap | Doz. |
|---|---|---|---|---|---|---|---|---|---|---|---|---|---|---|---|---|---|---|
| 5007B | 41000 | A. Richard | X | | | X | | | X | | | | X | | | X | X | 31 |
| 5007 | 41003 | A. Richard | X | | | X | | | X | | | | X | | | X | X | 15 |
| 736 | 5580 | M. Sharpe | | X | | X | | | | X | | X | | X | | | | | 136 |
| SO188 | 417417 | Damon | X | | | X | | | SS | | | | | | X | | | | 136 |
| 757 | SSSS | M. Sharpe | | X | | X | | | | X | | X | | | X | | | | 28 |
| 756 | SSS4 | M. Sharpe | | X | | X | | | | X | | X | | | X | | | | 23 |
| 50158 | 417625 | Damon | | | X | | X | | Bevel | | | | X | X | | | | | 137 |
| 758 | 6207 | M. Sharpe | | X | | X | | | SS | | | | | | X | | | | 68 |
| 759 | 6206 | M. Sharpe | | X | | X | | | SS | | | | | | X | | | | 42 |

| | | | | | | | | | | | | | |
|---|---|---|---|---|---|---|---|---|---|---|---|---|---|
| 24601 | 468 | J. House | X | | | X | X | | X | X | X | | | 205 |
| 2762 | 104 | K. Anderson | X | | X | | | X | X | X | X | X | | 35 |
| 752 | 6228 | M. Sharpe | | X | X | | SS | | X | | X | | X | 44 |
| 753 | 6230 | M. Sharpe | | X | X | | SS | | X | | X | | X | 10 |
| 50187 | 417415 | Damon | X | | X | | Bevel | | X | | X | X | X | 193 |
| 501879 | 417445 | Damon | X | | X | | Bevel | | X | | X | X | X | 28 |
| 501679 | 417684 | Damon | | X | | X | Bevel | | X | X | | X | X | 21 |
| 50177 | 417415 | Damon | X | | X | | Bevel | | X | | X | X | X | 83 |
| 50181 | 417714 | Damon | | X | | X | Bevel | | X | X | | X | X | 75 |
| 50176 | 417713 | Damon | | X | | X | SS | | X | X | | X | X | 45 |
| 754 | 6234 | M. Sharpe | X | | X | | SS | | X | | X | | X | 102 |
| 7549 | 6234 | M. Sharpe | X | | X | | SS | | X | | X | | X | 52 |

Total = 1531
Damon = 728

**Exhibit 9.1 (Continued)**

## For the Week of 11 Mar 1977  (2d Week)

| Lot | Style | Label | —Fronts— Center side Top center | French front | Rev. w/lining | B.P. side Btn. stay | Rev. w/lining | Top center | —Cuffs— Sq. | Rd. | Fr. | 1 | 2 | None | —Pkt— 1 | 2 | Flap | Doz. |
|---|---|---|---|---|---|---|---|---|---|---|---|---|---|---|---|---|---|---|
| 50182 | 417655 | Damon | | | X | | X | | Bevel | | | | X | X | X | | | 49 |
| 50166 | 417626 | Damon | | | X | | X | | Bevel | | | | X | X | | | | 146 |
| 50172 | 417634 | Damon | | | X | | X | | Bevel | | | | X | X | | | | 75 |
| 50171 | 417677 | Damon | | | X | | X | | SS | | | | | X | | | | 40 |
| 21895 | 1462 | J. House | | | X | | X | | X | | | | X | X | | | | 244 |
| 21894 | 1461 | J. House | X | | | | X | | SS | | | | | X | | | | 70 |
| 1504 | 225PT-11 | Pissilio | X | | | X | | | | X | | X | | | X | | X | 11 |
| 50173 | 417538 | Damon | | | X | | X | | Bevel | | | | X | X | | | | 161 |
| 50163 | 417716 | Damon | | | X | | X | | Bevel | | | | X | X | | | | 26 |
| 100 | ASST | Pissilio | X | | | X | | | | X | | X | | | X | | X | 22 |

| | | | | | | | | | | | | | |
|---|---|---|---|---|---|---|---|---|---|---|---|---|---|
| 1008 | ASST | Pissilio | X | X | X | X | X | | | X | | X | 142 |
| 1505 | ASST | Pissilio | X | X | | SS | | | | X | | X | 64 |
| 2637 | 42330 | A. Klein | | | X | | X | | | | X | X | 41 |
| 50191 | 417699 | Damon | | | | SS | | | X | | | | 91 |
| 50174 | 417709 | Damon | | X | | SS | | | X | | | | 41 |
| 21896 | 1468 | J. House | Pullover | | | X | | X | X | | | | 51 |
| 7254 | 5426 | E. Picone | X | X | | SS | | | | X | | X | 66 |
| 7257 | 5425 | E. Picone | X | X | | SS | | | | X | | X | 68 |
| 50154 | 417800 | Damon | Not cut | | | | | | | | | | 8 |
| 2646 | 4200 | A. Klein | Not cut | | | | | | | | | | 35 |
| 2653 | 4204 | A. Klein | Cut | | | | | | | | | | 40 |
| 2657 | 47645 | A. Klein | Not cut | | | | | | | | | | 35 |
| 2648 | 42868 | A. Klein | Not cut | | | | | | | | | | 40 |

Total = 1424
Damon = 629

**Exhibit 9.1 (Continued)**

For the Week of 18 Mar 1977  (3d Week)

| Lot | Style | Label | Fronts — Center side Top center | French front | Rev. w/lining | B.P. side Btn. stay | Rev. w/lining | Top center | Cuffs Sq. | Rd. | Fr. | 1 | 2 | None | Pkt 1 | 2 | Flap | Doz. |
|---|---|---|---|---|---|---|---|---|---|---|---|---|---|---|---|---|---|---|
| 50175 | 417708 | Damon | | | X | | X | | Bevel | | | | X | X | | | | 71 |
| 50189 | 417638 | Damon | | | X | | X | | Bevel | | | | X | X | | | | 72 |
| 50190 | 417719 | Damon | X | | | X | | | SS | | | | | X | | | | 81 |
| 24128 | 2060 | J. House | X | | | | X | | X | | | | X | | X | | | 98 |
| 50196 | 417694 | Damon | | | X | | X | | Bevel | | | | X | X | | | | 101 |
| 50197 | 417723 | Damon | X | | | X | | | SS | | | | | X | | | | 133 |
| 10747 | 5298 | C. Klein | X | | | | X | | | X | | | X | X | | | | 4 |
| 10747C | 5298 | C. Klein | X | | | | X | | | X | | | X | X | | | | 19 |
| 24138 | 1462 | J. House | X | | | | X | | X | | | | X | X | | | | 97 |
| 50192 | 417716 | Damon | | | X | | X | | Bevel | | | | X | X | | | | 64 |
| 50193 | 417717 | Damon | | | X | | X | | SS | | | | | X | | | | 49 |
| 50194 | 417676 | Damon | Cut | | | | | | | | | | | | | | | 119 |
| 50195 | 417678 | Damon | Cut | | | | | | | | | | | | | | | 148 |
| 50189A | 417638 | Damon | Cut | | | | | | | | | | | | | | | 32 |
| 24137 | 1461 | J. House | Not cut | | | | | | | | | | | | | | | 26 |
| 21849 | 1168 | J. House | Not cut | | | | | | | | | | | | | | | 29 |

Total = 1165
Damon =  872

**Exhibit 9.1 (Continued)**

## For the week of 25 Mar 1977 (4th Week)

| Lot | Style | Label | —Fronts— Center side Top center | French front | Rev. w/lining | Btn. stay | B.P. side Rev. w/lining | Top center | —Cuffs— Sq. | Rd. | Fr. | 1 | 2 | —Pkt— None | 1 | 2 | Flap | Doz. |
|---|---|---|---|---|---|---|---|---|---|---|---|---|---|---|---|---|---|---|
| 50198 | 417724 | Damon | Cut | | | | | | | | | | | | | | | 28 |
| 50189 | 417415 | Damon | Not cut | | | | | | | | | | | | | | | 10 |
| 50200 | 417417 | Damon | Not cut | | | | | | | | | | | | | | | 8 |
| 7354 | 5425 | E. Picone | Not cut | | | | | | | | | | | | | | | 10 |
| 7346 | 5426 | E. Picone | Not cut | | | | | | | | | | | | | | | 8 |
| 7345 | 5426 | E. Picone | Not cut | | | | | | | | | | | | | | | 8 |
| 24643 | 2161 | J. House | Not cut | | | | | | | | | | | | | | | 13 |
| 24648 | 1462 | J. House | Not cut | | | | | | | | | | | | | | | 2 |
| 2683 | 4233B | A. Klein | Not cut | | | | | | | | | | | | | | | 2 |
| 2679 | 4256B | A. Klein | Not cut | | | | | | | | | | | | | | | 2 |
| 996 | 6563 | Finity | Not cut | | | | | | | | | | | | | | | 5 |
| 50202 | 417415 | Damon | Not cut | | | | | | | | | | | | | | | 15 |
| 50203 | 417415 | Damon | Not cut | | | | | | | | | | | | | | | 9 |
| 50204 | 417417 | Damon | Not cut | | | | | | | | | | | | | | | 17 |

Total = 1435
Damon = 902

319

**Exhibit 9.1** (Continued)

## For the Week of 1 April 1977 (5th Week)

| Lot | Style | Label | —Fronts— Center side | | | B.P. side | | | —Cuffs— | | | | | | —Pkt— | | | Doz. |
| | | | Top center | French front | Rev. w/lining | Btn. stay | Rev. w/lining | Top center | Sq. | Rd. | Fr. | 1 | 2 | None | 1 | 2 | Flap | |
|---|---|---|---|---|---|---|---|---|---|---|---|---|---|---|---|---|---|---|
| 50201 | 417628 | Damon | Not cut | | | | | | | | | | | | | | | 5 |
| | ASST. | Resilio | Not cut | | | | | | | | | | | | | | | 9 |

Total = 148
Damon = 90

his earnings in additional facilities, but most of his money went for gold purchases. When the depression struck, Spiegel was ready to act.

Using his gold reserves, Spiegel bought out bakeries throughout the northeastern United States. He saw to it that the Sunnyside name became well known in each area by making bread donations to the local soup kitchens. Sunnyside Bakeries succeeded in its efforts, and after the depression Sunnyside was virtually without competition.

The business continued to grow under the direction of Spiegel's sons. Although market share declined in some areas, Sunnyside was still the leading competitor in each of its market areas.

In 1980, Spiegel's grandson John, the president of the firm, saw a major opportunity for growth: Dixie Bakeries, a large producer in the south, had encountered financial difficulties. John Spiegel was therefore able to use his company's strong financial position to purchase Dixie. The combined strength of the two companies gave Sunnyside the facilities to become the leading producer of bakery products in the nation.

The major problems caused by the merger were due to the haphazard nature of the combined bakery facilities, sales districts, and distribution routes. Spiegel decided that these problems had forced him into a complete reexamination of the distribution system at Sunnyside, so he called Ralph Young, director of distribution, to his office, explained his concerns, and instructed Young to develop a totally new distribution system for Sunnyside. Young began his assignment immediately.

## DISTRIBUTION SYSTEMS

Distribution is the process of getting goods and services to consumers. Retail goods sold in large quantities require extensive distribution. Consider, for example, a tube of toothpaste. The tube is assembled at a factory. The distribution problem to be solved is how to be sure that the system exists for consistently placing tubes of toothpaste on retail shelves.

There must be one or more bulk shipping points or warehouses. The locations of these warehouses must be chosen. If there are multiple warehouse locations, then they must be either built, bought, rented, or leased. Alternatively, the toothpaste company may ship all of its product to another company which specializes in wholesale distribution.

Regardless of the choice of distribution network, the company will have to ship some toothpaste itself. If it controls the complete distribution network, it may employ a variety of types of transportation. Railroads, trucks, and ships are the most likely bulk carriers. The company may own its carriers, rent or lease them, or it may rely upon commercial carriers. In any event, it must choose a mix of modes of transportation.

If a company controls its own extensive distribution network, it has an additional set of related decisions to make. It must decide upon the boundaries of distribution regions to be served by specific carriers and warehouses. It must determine routes between customers and distribution points. It must ascertain the amounts to be shipped from point to point in its distribution network.

In summary, a distribution manager is concerned with a number of related decisions:

1. Transportation systems selection—What mix of transportation systems should be used in moving the product?
2. Lease, rent, or buy decisions—Should the organization lease, rent, or buy the transportation equipment and storage facilities it will need?
3. Distribution network decisions—What type of distribution network should be used (e.g., warehouse, direct customer shipment, retail outlets, etc.)
4. Route decisions—What route should the product take from the manufacturer to the various distribution points?
5. Distribution quantity decisions—How much should be shipped from each manufacturing facility or shipping point to each order site?
6. Boundary assignment decisions—What area should be serviced by each distribution point?

Although a number of additional decisions are required by the distribution manager, those listed above are the major points of concern in setting up a distribution network.

In a practical setting, it is often difficult to place a given distribution-related problem into any one category. A problem may be more general and contain only a few aspects that have to do with distribution. Also, distribution problems may be inextricably intertwined.

Transportation system selection may be primarily determined by financial conditions, making operational considerations secondary. Locale may severely limit transportation options. On the other hand, there could be so many available alternatives that only a mathematical model, using a technique such as linear programming, can sort them out.

Lease, rent, or buy decisions may be similarly complicated since a large number of possibilities are likely to present themselves. However, these decisions may be complicated by transportation considerations to the extent that both categories of decision must be weighed together.

Decisions with regard to warehousing and shipping points are in large part determined by transportation and purchase decisions. However, the choice of the type of distribution network may precede all other decisions, making this choice relatively independent.

Transportation, purchase, and network decisions can be part of the policy or strategic decisions of a company. If this is the case, these decisions are quite difficult to model and may be able to be determined only by complicated debate and negotiation within the organization. In many cases these categories of decision appear not to be made at all but to acquire solutions gradually over time.

Given that the first three categories of decisions have been made, dividing areas into service regions, assigning routes, and optimizing shipment quantities can be described as operational decisions. These are the types of distribution decisions that can more readily be solved with the assistance of models.

After reflecting on the charge given to him by Spiegel, Young decided that the approaches to the first three decision areas at Sunnyside were fixed. Truck transportation was the only practical means of delivery of baked goods. Young's own staff had prepared studies showing that Sunnyside should purchase its trucks rather than lease or rent them. The network pattern of manufacturer-to-retailer had been found to be the most economical; the short shelf life of bakery products made warehouse systems impractical. As a result, Sunnyside operated a large number of small bakeries that produced a complete line of products and did not use warehouses at all.

Young did see a number of ways he might improve on the route, distribution quantity, and boundary assignment decisions. In fact, he and his staff had begun a study during the previous year which would have realigned the boundaries for each salesperson's territory. As a result of pressure from the sales force, however, the study had been abandoned.

Young said to himself, "I'm going to strike while the iron is hot this time and finally get the sales districts set up on a rational basis."

## THE SALES DISTRICT DECISION

Each sales representative at Sunnyside Bakeries was responsible for calling on retail outlets in his or her sales district to take orders for bakery shipments. Sales representatives visited steady customers once a week and lower-volume customers every other week. Those retail outlets that did no business with Sunnyside were visited often, but irregularly, to be given sales pitches. The existing sales district boundaries resulted in workloads that were uneven. A salesperson in a district requiring many regular weekly and biweekly calls was penalized by not having the opportunity to seek new business, since sales commissions were weighted to encourage the development of new business.

Each sales district consisted of a series of sales areas (see Fig. 10.1). For each sales area, Sunnyside maintained a computerized summary of the number of retail outlets in each category:

$N_1$ = number of retail stores to visit weekly

$N_2$ = number of retail stores to visit biweekly

$N_3$ = number of retail stores to visit as time permits

As the company had grown, so had the number of sales districts. When a new district was added, the existing sales staff acted like a mother hen protecting her chicks. No one wanted to give up favorite areas. Sales representatives tried to dump parts of their sales areas with heavy workloads and minimal opportunities for new business into the new sales districts. The result of this process was a collection of sales districts that gerrymandered haphazardly across the map.

Young decided to establish a quantitative decision model that would assign

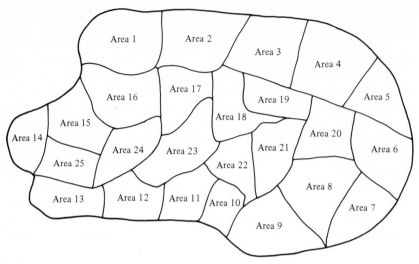

**Figure 10.1** Sales areas in sales district 1.

sales areas to sales districts in a way that would smooth the workloads. To develop the model he needed two things:

1. A measure of evenness to be used in comparing sales districts
2. A procedure for assigning sales areas to sales districts

The workload measure that Young decided to use was

$$W = \frac{T - N_1 t_1 - N_2 t_2 - T_L}{N_3}$$

where  $W$ = time available for visiting retail outlets in category three
$N_1, N_2, N_3$ = numbers of retail outlets in each category
$T$ = total time available per month
$t_1, t_2$ = time required per month to visit retail outlets in categories one and two
$T_L$ = estimate of lost contact time per month due to transit time between retail outlets

The overall workload variation in assignment was measured by

$$V = \frac{\underset{i}{\text{Max }} W_i - \underset{i}{\text{Min }} W_i}{\overline{W}}$$

where  $V$ = evenness measure for a sales area assignment
$W_i$ = workload measure for $i$th sales district
$\overline{W}$ = average workload measure for all sales districts

This measure was considered to show fair assignments when $V$ was small. Although the development of an evenness measure was a fairly easy task, the assignment process was more difficult. Young asked one of his technical staff, Laurence Butler, to explore the available systems for making assignments.

Butler reported back that all he could find were some mathematical models that were expensive to use and uncertain in their applicability to a problem of this type. Butler explained that the assignment process involved making a number of either/or choices: either the sales area was assigned to a district or it wasn't. The computer procedures for solving these problems were time-consuming and did not guarantee that a solution could be found. Butler was also concerned that qualitative factors could not be accommodated by such models. What Butler proposed was quite different.

Butler outlined a model that would be used as a decision support system. The model would be interactive in nature and would ask the user to make assignments of sales areas to sales districts. The model would then automatically determine the code number of each retail outlet that was to be assigned to each district. The workload measure would then be calculated for each district and an overall even-

**EXHIBIT 10.1 Sample computer dialogue**

FOR EACH SALES DISTRICT, INDICATE THE SALES AREAS TO BE INCLUDED.
A STATUS CHECK WILL BE PROVIDED AT THE END OF EACH ASSIGNMENT PHASE.

SALES DISTRICT

? 1
SALES AREAS
? 1, 3, 4, 5, 8, 10, 21

WORKLOAD STATUS

| SALES AREA | N1 | N2 | N3 | |
|------------|-----|-----|-----|---|
| 1          | 21  | 12  | 14  | |
| 3          | 12  | 15  | 12  | |
| 4          | 15  | 28  | 15  | |
| 5          | 18  | 20  | 16  | |
| 8          | 20  | 13  | 37  | |
| 10         | 18  | 12  | 21  | |
| 21         | 10  | 8   | 4   | |
|            | 114 | 108 | 119 | |

WORKLOAD MEASURE = .16 HOURS PER CATEGORY 3 STORES PER MONTH
TOTAL TIME TO VISIT ALL CATEGORY 3 STORES = 6.4 MONTHS
NUMBER OF STORES VISITED PER MONTH = 19

ness measure calculated. The total area of the sales district would be used to estimate the lost time. Young approved of the concept and said, "Get after it."

The model was developed as outlined, and Butler arranged a demonstration for Young in the computer terminal room. A map of the sales territory, divided into sales areas, was on the wall next to the computer terminal. Butler sat Young at the machine and after Butler gave him a few instructions, Young analyzed a set set of area assignments in sales district 1 (see Exhibit 10.1). The interactive program installed by Butler was easy for Young to use. He simply had to respond with district and area numbers when the computer prompted him with question marks.

Young had assigned areas 1, 3, 4, 5, 8, 10, and 21 to sales district 1. The result of the assignment was an estimated time of .16 hours per month to visit each category 3 store. Since the standard visit to a category 3 store required one hour, one sales representative would require more than six months to visit all these stores. Only nineteen category 3 stores could be visited by the district salesperson per month.

The model next provided the user with an opportunity to add or delete sales areas from the sales district assignment as shown in Exhibit 10.2. This new assignment was somewhat more favorable to the district salesperson, since it allowed more time for developing new business.

**EXHIBIT 10.2  Revision of initial assignment**

```
DELETE
?  8
   ADD
?  12

              WORKLOAD STATUS

SALES
AREA        N1       N2       N3
```

| SALES AREA | N1 | N2 | N3 |
|---|---|---|---|
| 1 | 21 | 12 | 14 |
| 3 | 12 | 15 | 12 |
| 4 | 15 | 28 | 15 |
| 5 | 18 | 20 | 16 |
| 10 | 18 | 12 | 21 |
| 12 | 12 | 20 | 12 |
| 21 | 10 | 8 | 4 |
| | 106 | 115 | 94 |

WORKLOAD MEASURE = .23 HOURS PER CATEGORY 3 STORE PER MONTH
TOTAL TIME TO VISIT ALL CATEGORY 3 STORES = 4.4 MONTHS
NUMBER OF STORES VISITED PER MONTH = 21

**EXHIBIT 10.3 First round summary**

| SALES DISTRICT SUMMARY | | |
|---|---|---|
| SALES DISTRICT | WORKLOAD MEASURE | |
| 1 | .23 | |
| 2 | .18 | |
| 3 | .26 | MAX |
| 4 | .25 | |
| 5 | .12 | MIN |
| · | | |
| · | | |
| · | | |
| 43 | | |
| | AVG .22 | |
| TOTAL WORKLOAD VARIATION = .64 | | |

Once an assignment was completed for a sales district, the model asked the user to allocate sales areas to the next district. The sequence of steps in this process was the same as before. Once all the sales district assignments were complete, the workload measures and the overall workload variation measure were calculated and presented as shown in Exhibit 10.3.

This initial evenness measure indicated that the range between workload measures from the maximum loaded sales district to the minimum loaded district was significant. By looking at the workload measures for each district, Young could guess how to reassign sales areas. With each change in assignment, the workload variation declined as shown in Fig. 10.2.

After seven iterations, the workload variation had declined substantially. The final four iterations consisted primarily of fine tuning to satisfy qualitative criteria. Once the assignments were satisfactorily completed, Young prepared a

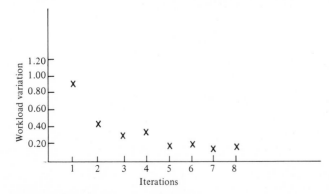

**Figure 10.2** Workload variation reduction.

report for Spiegel which outlined the procedure for area assignment and described its results.

Spiegel was delighted with the report but realized that it would excite considerable controversy in the sales staff. To overcome anticipated opposition, Spiegel proposed a small bonus for each sales representative assigned a new sales area. For salespersons with a significant proportion of reassigned areas, the total bonus would be a substantial fraction of their monthly salaries and commissions. Due to this inducement, few changes in Young's assignment plan were demanded by sales representatives.

## THE SHIPPING DECISION

The new manufacturing facilities added as part of the Dixie acquisition forced Sunnyside to totally rethink its shipment policies. In the past, a given manufacturing facility had been designated as a supplier for a set of sales areas. These assignments had been made haphazardly, and Young knew that cost savings could result from improved shipment decisions. Because Butler was still working on sales district assignments, Young asked another of his analysts, Mary Kruger, to help him on the shipping decision.

As defined by Young, the shipping decision was simple: "How much should we ship from each manufacturing plant to each sales area?" Kruger recognized this as the classical transportation problem she had studied in college.

Approaching the shipping problem as a transportation problem requires formulating the shipping problem in a matrix format as shown in Fig. 10.3. Each manufacturing plant labels a row in the matrix, while each sales area labels a

| Manufacturing plant | 1 | 2 | 3 | $\cdots$ | $n$ | Plant capacity |
|---|---|---|---|---|---|---|
| A | $C_{A1*}$ | $C_{A2}$ | $C_{A3}$ | $\cdots$ | | |
| B | $C_{B1}$ | $C_{B2}$ | $C_{B3}$ | $\cdots$ | | |
| C | $C_{C1}$ | $C_{C2}$ | $C_{B3}$ | $\cdots$ | | |
| . | . | . | . | | | |
| . | . | . | . | | | |
| . | . | . | . | | | |
| M | | | | | | |
| Sales area requirement | | | | | | |

*Cost of shipping from plant A to sales area 1.

**Figure 10.3** The transportation matrix format.

column. In each cell of the matrix, the cost of shipping from the manufacturing plant to the sales area is recorded.

The goal of the transportation procedure is to determine the amount that should be shipped from each plant to each sales area in order to minimize total cost. The procedure itself was straightforward, but Kruger had trouble deciding exactly how to describe the items being shipped.

In the classical transportation model, only one kind of item is considered. Sunnyside had dozens of different items, ranging from bread to donuts, to be shipped in a single truckload. A further complication was that plant capacity was measured in pounds of product, while sales area requirements were ordered as the number of units of each item.

Kruger decided to express the allocation problem in terms of the common unit of pounds of product to be shipped from each plant to each sales area. Area requirements were converted into pounds for the allocation effort. To demonstrate the allocation procedure, Kruger set up a small problem to show her programmers.

The matrix shown in Fig. 10.4 contains the complete description of the sample transportation problem. It shows that plants A, B, and C, respectively, can produce 10,000, 12,000, and 16,000 pounds of bakery goods over the planning period. The sales areas are 1, 2, 3, and 4, which respectively require 14,000, 10,000, 8000, and 6000 pounds of goods over the same period. Costs are given on an average basis. However, bread is the dominant item shipped; so, the cost of shipping goods from A to 1 of $2.10 per 1000 pounds is likely to be the cost of shipping bread.

Kruger first described how an initial solution could be obtained from the allocation problem. She used an approach, called the *northwest corner rule*, which allocates as much as possible to the most northwestern corner (row A and column 1 in this case). In the sample problem, Kruger showed how 10 units should be assigned in the A-1 cell. To have exceeded this amount would have exceeded the capacity of plant A. Since no remaining allocations can be made in the A row, the most northwestern corner cell becomes B-1. Since only 4 units remain to be allocated to the first sales area, an allocation of 4 units is made in cell B-1. The

|  | 1 | 2 | 3 | 4 | Plant capacity X 1000 lb |
|---|---|---|---|---|---|
| A | 2.1 | 3.4 | 2.8 | 2.5 | 10 |
| B | 1.8 | 2.2 | 2.9 | 2.2 | 12 |
| C | 2.6 | 1.7 | 1.8 | 1.9 | 16 |
| Sales area requirement, X 1000 lb | 14 | 10 | 8 | 6 | |

**Figure 10.4** Sample transportation problem (costs in $/1000 lb).

| | 1 | 2 | 3 | 4 | Plant capacity, X 1000 lb |
|---|---|---|---|---|---|
| A | 10 ⌐2.1 | ⌐3.4 | ⌐2.8 | ⌐2.5 | 10 |
| B | 4 ⌐1.8 | ⌐2.2 | ⌐2.9 | ⌐2.2 | 12 |
| C | ⌐2.6 | 2 ⌐1.7 | 8 ⌐1.8 | 6 ⌐1.9 | 16 |
| Sales area requirement, X 1000 lb | 14 | 10 | 8 | 6 | |

**Figure 10.5** Northwest corner allocation.

most northwestern corner cell remaining is B-2. In this case, 8 units can be allocated. The procedure continues, ending with the allocation pattern of Fig. 10.5.

Next, Kruger explained how to decide whether a different allocation would have been preferable. To illustrate this step, Kruger showed what would happen if a unit were allocated to cell A-2 (see Fig. 10.6).

If 1 unit were added to cell A-2, then 1 unit would have to be subtracted from cell A-1 to match the plant capacity. Similarly if 1 unit were subtracted from cell A-1 then 1 unit would have to be added to B-1. This in turn requires that a unit be subtracted from cell B-2 to meet demands in areas 1 and 2 exactly. The impact of this switching would be a total change of

$$\$(+\ 3.4\ -\ 2.1\ +\ 1.8\ -\ 2.2)\ =\ +\ \$0.90/\text{unit}$$

Since the total cost would be increased, there would be no reason to allocate any shipment to the A-2 cell. The same process continues until each cell is evaluated. The evaluation for the B-4 cell is shown in Fig. 10.7.

In this case, the cost effect will be

$$\$(+\ 2.2\ -\ 2.2\ +\ 1.7\ -\ 1.9)\ =\ -\ \$0.20/\text{unit}$$

With a cost decline of \$0.20/1000 pounds, it would indeed be wise to transfer shipment to cell B-4. Since every shipment allocated to B-4 saves .2 units, the

| | 1 | 2 | 3 | 4 | Plant capacity X 1000 lb |
|---|---|---|---|---|---|
| A | 10 − ⌐2.1 | + ⌐3.4 | ⌐2.8 | ⌐2.5 | 10 |
| B | 4 + ⌐1.8 | 8 − ⌐2.2 | ⌐2.9 | ⌐2.2 | 12 |
| C | ⌐2.6 | 2 ⌐1.7 | 8 ⌐1.8 | 6 ⌐1.9 | 16 |
| Sales area requirement, X 1000 lb | 14 | 10 | 8 | 6 | |

**Figure 10.6** Check on northwest corner solution.

|  | | 1 | 2 | 3 | 4 | Plant capacity, × 1000 lb |
|---|---|---|---|---|---|---|
| A | 10 | 2.1 | 3.4 | 2.8 | 2.5 | 10 |
| B | 4 | 1.8 | 8 – 2.2 | 2.9 | 2.2 | 12 |
| C |  | 2.6 | 2 + 1.7 | 8 — 1.8 | 8 – 1.9 | 16 |
| Sales area requirement, × 1000 lb | | 14 | 10 | 8 | 6 | |

**Figure 10.7** Evaluation of cell B-4.

question that remains is, how much can be allocated to B-4? Fig. 10.7 can be used to answer this question. Any addition to B-4 will bring about reduced shipments from B to 2 and from C to 4. With a current allocation of 8 units to B-2 and 6 units to C-4, the most that can be transferred to B-4 is 6 units. The new allocation pattern is shown in Fig. 10.8.

Kruger explained that the evaluation process would continue until all the cell evaluations were positive, indicating that any reallocation would increase costs. At that point, the process would stop, having found the optimal shipping pattern. In Sunnyside's case, although 126 manufacturing plants and 629 sales areas needed to be considered, Kruger claimed that the evaluation could be done very quickly because it could be done by an existing computer program.

The transportation model was subsequently formulated and run on Sunnyside's computer. One of the advantages the model provided was that it could also assess the value of selected manufacturing facilities. Several facilities of dubious worth were given zero production capacities in the model to see whether closing them had a significant impact on total shipping costs. Management studied the results of the analyses and made a decision to close three bakeries.

Some adjustments of the model data were required to more accurately include truck capacity limitations, but after fine tuning, the cost reduction procedures indicated by the model were implemented.

|  | 1 | 2 | 3 | 4 | Plant capacity × 1000 lb |
|---|---|---|---|---|---|
| 10 | 2.1 | 3.4 | 2.8 | 2.5 | 10 |
| 4 | 1.8 | 2 2.2 | 2.9 | 6 2.2 | 12 |
|  | 2.6 | 8 1.7 | 8 1.8 | 1.9 | 16 |
| Sales area requirement, × 1000 lb | 14 | 10 | 8 | 6 | |

**Figure 10.8** Revised allocation pattern.

## THE ROUTE DECISION

In addition to accepting the changes in the distribution system, the corporate staff at Sunnyside became enthused about reevaluating other procedures. In one of the staff meetings devoted to outlining the changes, a respected Sunnyside employee suggested that they also study the routing of their delivery trucks.

Route decisions up to that point had been made by the truck drivers themselves. As a result, decisions tended to be influenced by such factors as the location of the best spot for lunch and that of the driver's home. However, as energy costs rapidly increased, the need for a more efficient method of routing deliveries became steadily more apparent, and Young asked Butler to study the routing problem.

Butler discovered that the company employed 458 drivers, each with a unique daily route. To realign each of these routes without the aid of a computer would have been impossible. The procedure that Butler proposed to use was "the traveling salesman model." This procedure reduces the routing decision to an analysis of a data base such as that of Table 10.1, which contains sample data Butler used to demonstrate his thoughts to Young. Distances between various locations— a truck garage at a bakery and five stores—are shown in Table 10.1.

The trucks begin each day at the garage and must visit each store before returning to the garage. The question is, which route should the truck take?

Intuitively, it appears that the truck should go from the garage to store B since this distance is the shortest. From store B the next closest store is A, so the route is established, garage-B-A. From A, the closest store is D. Each store is subsequently added to the route based upon its closeness to the previous store in route. The overall route is

$$\text{Garage-B-A-D-E-C-garage}$$

The total miles are

$$14 + 8 + 13 + 9 + 30 + 25 = 99 \text{ miles}$$

In demonstrating this procedure, Butler explained that, although it appears attractive at first, eventually "choosing the shortest route next" results in making poor selections. When the truck finishes at store E, its only remaining choice is

**Table 10.1  Travel matrix, distance in miles**

|         | Garage | Store | | | | |
|---------|--------|-----|-----|-----|-----|-----|
|         |        | A   | B   | C   | D   | E   |
| Garage  | x      | 20  | 14  | 25  | 15  | 32  |
| Store A | 20     | x   | 8   | 21  | 13  | 14  |
| Store B | 14     | 8   | x   | 16  | 13  | 15  |
| Store C | 25     | 21  | 16  | x   | 20  | 30  |
| Store D | 15     | 13  | 13  | 20  | x   | 9   |
| Store E | 32     | 14  | 15  | 30  | 9   | x   |

C at a distance of 30 miles; from C to the garage is another 25 miles, both long distances.

Butler showed that the mileage from one point to another was not the only criterion. The total travel distance should be considered at each step. For example, although the distance from the garage to store C does not appear to make C the best first stop, the other ways of including store C on the route may involve greater total distances. One aid to analyzing the route trade-offs is to subtract from each column the minimum value in that column as shown in Table 10.2.

The route is now selected by choosing the unvisited location with the lowest reduced distance in the row of the present location.

The route selected using the reduced travel distance matrix is

$$\text{Garage-C-E-D-A-B-garage}$$

The total travel distance in this case is

$$15 + 10 + 9 + 13 + 8 + 12 = 67$$

However, a tie exists in making the choices, and the other choice in breaking the tie produces

$$\text{Garage-C-E-D-B-A-garage}$$

The total travel distance for this alternative is

$$15 + 10 + 9 + 13 + 8 + 10 = 65$$

Butler classified the route selections that he had illustrated as merely *heuristic procedures*. That is, they were simple-to-use techniques that did not guarantee optimal results but gave "good" solutions. Optimal solutions in such cases would require the use of mathematical procedures such as branch-and-bound methods or network techniques. Butler explained that the available computer software was reliable for route decisions with no more than 25–30 stores. For larger problems, the amount of computer time required to obtain an optimal solution was frequently not worth the improvement it provided over simple heuristic procedures. Young felt that even the heuristic approach could produce worthwhile cost savings.

**Table 10.2 Travel matrix with reduced distances, in miles**

|          |        | Store |   |   |   |   |
|----------|--------|-------|---|---|---|---|
|          | Garage | A | B | C | D | E |
| Garage   | x      | 12 | 6 | 0  | 6  | 23 |
| Store A  | 0      | x  | 0 | 6  | 4  | 5  |
| Store B  | 2      | 0  | x | 1  | 4  | 6  |
| Store C  | 15     | 13 | 8 | x  | 11 | 1  |
| Store D  | 5      | 5  | 5 | 5  | x  | 0  |
| Store E  | 22     | 6  | 7 | 15 | 0  | x  |

Butler and Young began discussing the implementation of a route determination program and discovered that their biggest hurdle would be the collection of the travel distance data. It was simply not feasible to physically measure the time or distance between all store combinations. They decided to use maps to obtain rough estimates of travel distances. Although the maps were not exact, they gave distances that closely matched those that were checked by actually driving the routes.

Once the new routes were determined, they were presented to the drivers. Threats of strikes and resignations ensued. Management held firm, and, eventually, the new routes were implemented. But on several routes, improvements in travel time and gasoline consumption did not occur as expected. The truck drivers on these routes were followed, and it soon became apparent that the drivers had ignored their route instructions. A general check of procedures seemed advisable.

Using expected gasoline consumption and mileage estimates, an audit was conducted of the performance of the driver of each route. Those drivers that had peculiar performance characteristics were followed. Seven drivers were found to be ignoring the route sequences given them. The uncooperative drivers were called in to talk to their region managers who promised to put critical letters into their personnel files unless the drivers began to follow their assigned routes. Over time most discrepancies in routes were corrected.

## NETWORK MODELS IN DISTRIBUTION DECISIONS

Many distribution decisions like the route decision above can be thought of as having the structure of networks. A network is an interconnected series of collection points and transportation links as shown in Fig. 10.9. A manufacturing plant has a number of alternative routes by which to ship its product to a warehouse. A network model treats each of the links in the transportation network as a decision point. A specific procedure is then developed to determine the optimal route from the origin to the warehouse via a sequence of decision points.

Network models exist for such decisions as determining the following:

1. The minimum path from origin to destination
2. The maximum flow from the origin to some destination

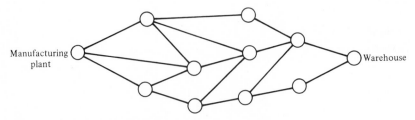

**Figure 10.9** Representative network.

3. The network path which connects all points in the network in order to optimize some criterion
4. The optimal route reaching each point in a network (i.e., the traveling salesman problem).

Although network models have existed for many years, their usefulness and their acceptance by management has been limited. Several reasons can be suggested for this fact:

1. Many network models are computationally time-consuming. Realistic distribution problems are typically immense in size, and even the most advanced computer routines have difficulty in solving such problems.
2. Distribution decisions have subjective features that existing network models cannot accommodate. The desirability of a certain path sequence may not be related to cost, time, or any other quantitative measure.
3. Distribution decisions may be multiobjective in character. Existing network models involve single objectives.
4. Data requirements such as intercity mileages, flow capacities, or times may be difficult to satisfy.

Geoffrion (1976) has reported on a distribution study at Hunt-Wesson as the type of decision effort that has been conducted with existing modeling technology, and there is reason to believe that network techniques will become more useful in practical decision making in the future. Computers are becoming more powerful; computer programs are becoming more accessible to users; and researchers are constantly researching new ways to reduce computational difficulties.

Heuristic or intuitive techniques can still be used to produce "good" solutions until the time that the more powerful computational tools become sufficiently reliable and inexpensive to replace them.

## REFERENCE

Geoffrion, Arthur M.: "Better Distribution Planning With Computer Models," *Harvard Business Review*, July–August 1976, pp. 92–99.

## QUESTIONS

1 What were the various distribution problems encountered at Sunnyside Bakeries?
2 If the distribution problems remained unsolved, what would be the likely consequences for Sunnyside?
3 How can the effectiveness of the following distribution decisions be measured?
    (a) Boundary decisions
    (b) Shipping decisions
    (c) Route decisions
    (d) Transportation system selection

4 What are the different types of distribution decisions faced by some organization that you have observed? Give an example of each.

5 What are the distribution problems of the following organizations? Describe them.
  (a) Movie distributor
  (b) A newspaper publisher
  (c) An electrical utility

6 Why did Sunnyside not consider shipping its product by rail or plane?

7 What kinds of equipment and facilities would be involved in make, lease, rent, or buy decisions at Sunnyside?

8 Why did Sunnyside not institute centralized warehouses as part of its distribution system?

9 Why was Sunnyside opposed to allowing the truck drivers to select their own routes?

10 Sunnyside might have avoided redistricting altogether by simply giving bonuses to disadvantaged sales representatives. What was the company's incentive for revising sales districts?

11 Why did Sunnyside use an optimizing algorithm to determine shipment quantities instead of a heuristic approach or an interactive program?

12 How would the solution to a transportation problem indicate that a shipping point should be eliminated from the distribution network?

13 What are the likely implementation problems encountered as a result of using a model to reallocate boundaries?

14 Why is it difficult to use an "optimizing" model in boundary assignments?

15 Why is it easier to use an optimizing model for shipping decisions than it is for boundary assignments?

16 How do you personally make route decisions?

17 How are distribution decisions related to those of supply decisions and facilities decisions?

18 Are distribution decisions best described as planning decisions or as operating decisions?

19 What are typical distribution decisions made by governments?

# EXERCISES

1 Describe the types of distribution decisions that have to be made by an oil company.

2 Describe the types of distribution decisions that have to be made by a hospital.

3 National problems with water supply have been described as a distribution problem. What is meant by this?

4 Describe some industries that have higher than normal distribution costs. What makes their costs high?

5 A company with a large number of manufacturing facilities throughout the country must decide upon a management organization plan for its distribution department. Should it be a centralized, or a decentralized, organization? Why?

6 Describe the general characteristics of an organization which would have no need for any type of distribution system.

7 A state would like to redistrict its statewide precincts to comply with one-person–one-vote doctrine. For a state with five congressional districts do the following:
  (a) Develop an evenness measure to compare different precinct assignments.
  (b) Develop an outline of computer dialogue and output formats that could be used in making such a decision.

8 A university department has decided to realign its student advising assignments. Alphabetical assignments are to be made to each of five advisers. The percentage of students with last names beginning with each letter has been found to be as shown in Table 10.3.

## Table 10.3

| Student last name | Percent of students | Student last name | Percent of students |
|---|---|---|---|
| A | 4 | N | 4 |
| B | 5 | O | 4 |
| C | 4 | P | 4 |
| D | 8 | Q | 1 |
| E | 5 | R | 2 |
| F | 3 | S | 11 |
| G | 4 | T | 5 |
| H | 4 | U | 2 |
| I | 2 | V | 2 |
| J | 3 | W | 6 |
| K | 3 | X | 1 |
| L | 4 | Y | 1 |
| M | 7 | Z | 1 |

(*a*) Determine an adviser assignment that equalizes the advising load between all the faculty. Assignments to each adviser must be in continuous-alphabetical order.

(*b*) Prepare a description of the procedure you used.

**9** For the transportation data shown in Table 10.4, determine the optimal shipping pattern.

## Table 10.4

| Plant | Warehouse | | | Plant capacity, unit |
|---|---|---|---|---|
| | 1 | 2 | 3 | |
| A | 6 | 2 | 4 | 10 |
| B | 3 | 5 | 7 | 25 |
| C | 2 | 6 | 1 | 25 |
| D | 4 | 2 | 4 | 25 |
| Warehouse capacity, tons | 50 | 15 | 20 | |

**10** Suggest an initial allocation procedure which gives a better solution to the transportation model than the northwest corner rule.

# CASELETS

1. Continental Conservationists, a group of 60s radicals, grouped together to form a company specializing in alternative energy forms. With special permits from the U.S. Forest Service, Continental gained permission to collect fallen timber from the forests for use as fuel wood. The idea seemed to be not only

civic-minded, but profitable. As originally planned, the only costs were for chain saws, trucks, and a few administrative expenses. Labor was generally volunteer. As the operation came into being, however, an unexpected cost was incurred. The problem of getting the wood to the consumer had not been considered. Since the typical consumer did not have a truck, Continental had to deliver wood itself. Since Continental was constantly gathering its wood from different forest sites in the state, decisions had been made on how to supply each customer with wood.

    (a) Describe the distribution problems facing Continental.

    (b) What would you suggest Continental do to solve its distribution problems?

2. The Fergus County school system was faced with a series of complaints from parents about the delivery of their children to schools. Bus routes in existence would frequently deliver some children to school up to an hour-and-a-half early and would not pick up some children until one hour after school was over. The school system had a fixed number of buses to cover the routes, with some buses collecting students for several schools. Other buses would make more than one entire set of deliveries (collect students and deliver them). Complicating the problem was the fact that each of the schools began at different times.

    (a) Outline how this distribution problem could be solved.

    (b) What measure of effectiveness would be appropriate in this case?

## CASE 10.1: THE GRAPTON SANITATION DEPARTMENT

### Introduction

The City of Grapton was confronted with deficits of nearly $30,000 per year during the prior two years' operation of the city's sanitation department. The finance committee of the city council had proposed a 30 percent increase in sanitation fees to recoup the financial losses. Many of the community's older citizens campaigned against the proposal, which led the city council to reject the finance committee ordinance on its second reading.

    Mayor Davis Seneca was left to devise new options for putting the sanitation department back on a sound financial basis. He asked the sanitation department director, Chris Bond, to cooperate with mayoral aide Kelly Barnes, who had been assigned by the mayor to solve this problem. Barnes was asked to study the sanitation department's operations and report back to the mayor.

### Initial Investigations

The sanitation department's dominant activity was collecting domestic garbage. Records listed the time that each truck arrived at a disposal site and the amount of waste discharged. Billing records contained the number of families along each route, and the number of dwellings. The present routes, the truck assignments, and the number of workers on each truck were also available. Routes were assigned so that one truck served each of the city's seven wards. The union contract spelled out a minimum crew size per truck (three plus a driver) and prohibited more than one route realignment per year.

Barnes spent two days riding sanitation trucks in order to observe the collection operations firsthand. Although the workers were initially distant, they began to use the opportunity to air their gripes and make suggestions on how service could be improved. They also liked the notice that arose from an article in the *Grapton Times*, "Female Observer Rides with Garbage Trucks." Barnes recorded rough measurements of the times required to do different operations.

After gathering the initial data and insights into the problem, Barnes began her analysis of the distribution of workload between the seven trucks. Since each ward had about the same population, the sanitation department had felt that routes determined by ward boundaries would be in balance. Table 10.5 shows the average times at which each truck finished its assignment per day of the week. As shown in the table, there was considerable variation in completion times from route to route.

Truck 2, the busiest, completed its collections nearly an hour-and-a-half after truck 7. The total idle time for the trucks was also found to be approximately seven hours per week.

Barnes had learned that labor costs were the largest component of garbage collection costs and guessed that substantial savings could be obtained by reassigning routes. In order to test alternative routes, however, Barnes needed an appropriate workload measure. She decided to sample some of the routes, and develop a way of predicting the amount of waste generated. At the same time, Barnes was looking for a way to compare alternative cost reduction ideas.

After two weeks, Barnes met with the mayor and Chris Bond. She began by describing her activities to date and then showed her findings on current completion times. While the mayor seemed surprised by the imbalance, Chris Bond indicated little dismay at the findings.

**Table 10.5 Average completion times**

| Truck | Monday | Tuesday | Wednesday | Thursday | Friday | Weekly average per truck |
|---|---|---|---|---|---|---|
| 1 | 1:29 | 1:43 | 2:01 | 1:15 | 1:32 | 1:36 |
| 2 | 2:52 | 3:10 | 3:20 | 2:57 | 2:45 | 3:01 |
| 3 | 2:01 | 1:46 | 2:22 | 2:07 | 2:16 | 2:06 |
| 4 | 1:26 | 1:43 | 2:06 | 2:04 | 2:12 | 1:54 |
| 5 | 2:21 | 2:33 | 2:42 | 2:16 | 2:32 | 2:29 |
| 6 | 1:45 | 2:16 | 2:07 | 2:08 | 2:10 | 2:05 |
| 7 | 1:32 | 1:42 | 1:07 | 1:21 | 1:44 | 1:29 |
| Daily average | 1:55 | 2:08 | 2:15 | 2:01 | 2:10 | |
| Idle time | 1:35 | 1:22 | 1:15 | 1:29 | 1:20 | |

"I'm not surprised; it takes me so long to figure out a route that I'm generally stuck with it. I know I could improve the assignments, but I just don't have time."

"I understand your problem, Chris," said the mayor. "How much money could be saved if Kelly can develop a better procedure for route assignments?"

"Just let me say that if Kelly could find a quicker way for assigning routes, it would be a great help to me. I might be able to reduce the overall route times by 10 percent. That would give us even more idle time, and we might be able to reassign some of our men to special collections that now require overtime. We really need two or more trucks each week for a full day for these jobs. I would also like to know if we could perhaps eliminate extra helpers on some of our routes. I know we're going to face some union pressure to keep them on, but I think normal attrition will permit us to reduce our workforce without layoffs."

Barnes presented an equation she had developed for determining the total time to cover a route and illustrated how the different alternatives could be tested. She proposed to build a model that would permit a quicker response to needs, and she outlined her data requirements. She received both the approval and the budget she needed.

Barnes decided that her model should take a route assignment generated by the sanitation department director and calculate the total time required by the assignment. Then the director could use his wealth of experience in making route assignments to produce a "good" but not necessarily an "optimal" assignment. Barnes further decided that the model should be operated in the interactive mode on a computer terminal. She collected data and built the model.

Barnes scheduled a meeting with Chris Bond to explain her procedure, which included dialogue with a computer at a computer terminal. While Bond was unfamiliar with model development, he was able to understand Barnes' model, but was hesitant about using the time-sharing terminal.

To test Bond's understanding of the model, Barnes first worked with him to generate a preliminary route assignment which would contain significant idle time. As city blocks were assigned to a route, they were marked on a master sheet, and the route was recorded. This initial assignment was done for the Monday-truck 1 route and gave an estimated completion time of 3:02 P.M. This initial assignment procedure took approximately twenty-five minutes, including extensive questions and delays, as Bond had gained understanding of the process, but he could readily see how to reduce the route's idle time.

Subsequent assignments were made for truck 1 for the remaining days of the week. The Friday assignment took only ten minutes as Bond became more proficient at the process. As they continued, Bond began to learn how substantial time savings could be achieved by extending routes across ward boundaries. The model seemed to meet Bond's needs and expectations, and he readily accepted the process as a means for investigating cost reduction programs.

## Application of the Model

Bond's first serious effort at route alignment eliminated the need for one truck one day a week, but he felt that even greater reductions could be made if he were to reapply the same process; so he developed a new set of route assignments which deviated from conventional ward boundaries. This new alignment of routes allowed for the completion of the total collection without the use of three trucks for one day of the week.

One of Bond's major headaches was special collections. Past experience had shown that these three trucks would be capable of handling all of the special collections during the week. Bond was elated by the new schedule—it could save money. The savings on special collections were estimated to be $6 per hour. Over the past years, there had been an average of 1256 hours per year of special collections. Since the volume of special collections did not seem to be increasing, Bond estimated the savings to be

$$\text{Annual savings} = \$6/\text{hour} \times 1256 \text{ hours/year} = \$7536/\text{year}$$

Bond next asked Barnes to alter the formulas for calculating the collection time to reflect the decrease of one helper per route. Bond proceeded to realign the routes to reflect the new workforce level and produced a tight time schedule for each truck to finish by a 3:30 P.M. quitting time. The savings from the reduction of seven helpers was calculated to be

$$\text{Annual savings} = 7 \text{ helpers} \times \$7600/\text{helper} = \$53,200$$

However, overtime was expected to result from this plan, and the expected costs of the annual increase in overtime had to be subtracted. Estimated annual overtime costs under this plan were $5200; so the total estimated savings would be

$$\$53,200 - \$5200 = \$48,000$$

Bond felt that the reduction of helpers could be accomplished by natural attrition rather than by firings. Route assignments were again made under the new assumption that residential pickups were to be made only at curbside. The result of this process was the elimination of one truck. The estimated savings from this plan were primarily due to workforce reductions and were as follows:

| | |
|---|---|
| One driver (supervisor) | $ 8,500 |
| Three helpers @ $7600 | $22,800 |
| Fuel, maintenance of truck | $ 5,000 |
| Miscellaneous expenses | $ 2,000 |
| Total savings | $38,300 |

The alternative of replacing the existing twice-a-week collections with once-a-week collections was the next cost reduction program investigated. It was assumed that the number of cans per trip to be collected would double under this plan. This program reduced the number of trucks needed to four. The estimated savings were estimated to be as follows:

| | |
|---|---|
| Three drivers (supervisor) | $ 25,500 |
| Nine helpers @ $7600 | $ 68,400 |
| Fuel, maintenance of trucks | $ 15,000 |
| Miscellaneous expenses | $ 6,000 |
| Salvage (two trucks) | $ 10,000 |
| Total savings | $124,900 |

## Table 10.6 Evaluation of different alternatives

| Alternative | Savings/year |
|---|---|
| Better alignment of routes | $ 7,536 |
| Reduce helpers on each truck | $ 48,000 |
| Curbside collection | $ 38,300 |
| Once-a-week collection | $124,900 |

While this alternative contained the most attractive cost savings, it was considered the most difficult to implement politically. Similar suggestions had been made in surrounding communities and had been soundly rejected by their citizens.

Barnes prepared a report for the mayor on each option and the possible consequences of that option as shown in Table 10.6. The report was given to the mayor who took the results to David Fowler, the local sanitation workers' union leader.

## Meeting between the Mayor and the Sanitation Workers' Union Leader

David Fowler, an astute judge of public sentiment, realized that his union would be on shaky ground if it staged an attack on the recommendations without making proposals for reducing the department's budget. Grapton's citizens had shown an increasing discontent with the growing costs of municipal government.

Since each of the proposals required increased workloads for individual workers, Fowler felt that he could gain union support if he would obtain incentive pay for the increased tonnage collected. He proposed that each worker receive an incentive for each ton collected above the current average of 8 tons per day. The mayor agreed to the concept in principle, and Fowler then agreed not to oppose the first three recommendations, but he said the adoption of the fourth alternative would lead to a long and bitter strike.

## Analysis of Incentive Proposals

The mayor briefed Barnes on the union's proposals and asked her to reevaluate the cost savings, which she did as shown below:

### Alternative no. 2

Increased tonnage =

$$9.5 \text{ tons/day per truck} - 8.0 \text{ tons/day per truck incentive} = 1.5 \text{ tons/day}$$

Incentive costs =

$$1.5 \text{ tons/day} \times 200 \text{ days/year} \times 3 \text{ workers/truck} \times 7 \text{ trucks} \times C_I(\$/\text{ton}) = 6300 C_I$$

where $C_I$ = incentive payment for extra tons collected ($/ton) per worker

*Alternative no. 3*

Increased tonnage = 9.0 tons/day − 8.0 tons/day = 1.0 tons/day

Incentive costs = 1.0 tons/day × 200 days/year ×

$$\times \; 4 \text{ workers/truck} \times 4 \text{ trucks} \times C_I \text{ (tons/day)} = 3200 C_I$$

Barnes determined that if $0.50/ton were accepted as the incentive rate this would reduce the original anticipated savings to:

Reduce helper savings = $48,000 − $4200 = $43,800

Curbside collection savings = $38,300 − $3600 = $34,700

The mayor was pleased with the results and decided to offer the union the $0.50/ton rate in the hopes that this would foster a spirit of goodwill and improve the overall chances of the acceptance of one of the cost reduction plans.

## City Council Action

The mayor briefed the council on the study and then gave a synopsis of the alternative cost reduction plans. As he expected, the council focused its attention on the second and third alternatives. Eventually a vote of 10–4 by the city council passed an ordinance to provide for curbside collections.

With the passage of the ordinance, the mayor made a few concluding remarks thanking the council for its support on this matter. "I think we've accomplished something significant tonight. We have restored fiscal stability to one of our city's vital departments. In doing this, we have avoided increasing the financial burden of government on our citizens. At the same time, we have asked our citizens to help us directly in keeping our costs under control by placing garbage cans at curbside. The encouraging response to this proposal gives me a great deal of confidence in keeping our city on the track of fiscal responsibility."

## Discussion Guide

1 Do you feel that the basic approach of this case was correct? Would an optimum-seeking approach have been better?

2 Do you think the model was properly validated? Explain your reasons.

3 Do you think the union leader could have obtained a better settlement?

4 The proposals presented to Fowler generally pointed toward reducing his union local's membership. Why did he not complain?

5 Why did the city not consider giving a garbage collection contract to a private firm, as many cities have done?

# ELEVEN

## FACILITY DECISIONS

### SYNOPSIS OF THE CHAPTER

Facility decisions must be made by all kinds of organizations, public and private. At the operational level, decisions consist primarily of how best to do specific tasks such as selecting a site, designing a building, determining the best use for an area or for equipment, and revising or replacing expensive equipment.

This chapter presents four such decisions. The first requires the choice of a new facility's location. The second consists of laying out a new building. The third requires optimizing the use of existing equipment, and the fourth is the determination of a preferred replacement policy.

The reader should note that a variety of techniques are used to make the decisions in the chapter. As in most of the chapters in this book, decisions range from being greatly assisted by formal models to being only slightly assisted.

Some of the models are task-specific. The line optimization procedure uses theoretical knowledge about output to design an experiment. The plant layout analysis makes use of a computer model applied only to layout problems.

At the other extreme, the plant location model in this chapter was made by application of commonsense criteria followed by an intuitive assessment. The replacement model in this chapter requires very little formal modeling but does employ simple economic reasoning.

### MAJOR CONCEPTS PRESENTED IN THIS CHAPTER

1. Major organizational decisions tend to determine some facility policies as part of a larger strategy.
2. At the operational level, decisions include:
   a. Where should we locate?
   b. Where should we place our different units within the facility?

c. What process flow should we adopt?

d. How should our work stations be designed?

e. At what speed should our production units operate?

f. When should we replace particular pieces of equipment?

3. The location of a new facility must be chosen by weighing the impacts of a variety of factors at different candidate locations. These factors include the following:

   a. Labor force

   b. Transportation

   c. Raw materials

   d. Climate

   e. Pollution

   f. Energy

   g. Capital and operating costs

4. Whether a floor plan or a plant layout is prepared by hand or with computer assistance, it will require that the importance of relationships between parts be provided by knowledgeable individuals.

5. A plant layout can be done much more quickly with the aid of a computer algorithm.

6. The experimental design for a line optimization project requires that the designer have a theoretical knowledge of the line's operating characteristics.

7. Questions of when to replace or repair equipment are often solved by evaluating the expected operating and capital costs of alternatives.

## EXPECTATIONS OF THE STUDENT

The student, after studying this chapter, should be able to do the following:

1. Identify the most important criteria according to which locations for new facilities should be evaluated

2. Identify the portion of organizational decisions which are primarily concerned with facilities

3. Work through a plant layout procedure by hand by assigning closeness measures to plant departments and calculating total closeness ratings

4. Design a machine rate optimization experiment by using a theoretical output curve and the golden section search equation

5. Choose the optimal replacement life for equipment by calculating expected operating and capital costs

## MANCHESTER CANDIES

Cedric Richardson, vice president in charge of international operations of Manchester Candies, had been given the responsibility of installing a new candy manufacturing facility in the United States. A British-based company, Manchester

Candies had seen its wafer style of candy become popular with diet-conscious Americans, and, over the years, many of its products had been licensed for production by American candy companies.

Manchester was deciding whether to produce some of its own brands in America; so a pilot plant was to be built for the manufacture of selected candies. Test marketing in Ohio had shown "Little Wafe" and "Duke's Ducat," two popular British brands, to have potential American market appeal. The pilot plant would therefore concentrate on these two brands.

Richardson first studied the direct requirements of the products. Little Wafe was a wafer-type candy bar that was relatively difficult to manufacture. The primary ingredients were corn starch, flour, sugar, and a chocolate layer. Duke's Ducat, on the other hand, was relatively simple, consisting of a chocolate disk filled with rum-flavored caramel.

Most of the required raw materials were generally available in the United States, except for the chocolate, which was to be made from cocoa beans, milk, and other ingredients according to Manchester's special process.

Richardson had hired the U.S. management engineering firm of Steinway and Associates to help make recommendations as to plant location and other facility decisions. Benedict Taylor was the primary consultant assigned to the project.

Taylor met Richardson initially in London for a briefing on the project. Richardson, a meticulous individual, demanded a thorough analysis of each facility decision, including the location of the facility, its layout, and the detailed operations of the two production lines.

Although Taylor was impressed with Richardson's apparently rational approach to decision making, matters of style seemed overly important to Richardson. Time and again, Richardson emphasized that he wanted the entire project handled with class. He wanted to avoid public quarrels over the location decision. In the 1970s Volkswagon had become a party to a public dispute between two American states that were battling to attract a new VW plant; Richardson above all wished to avoid such disputes.

Richardson was also concerned with the qualitative aspects of the plant decisions. He wanted a facility that would give the impression of elegance. He felt that the name "Manchester Candies" should always summon a positive connotation. Accordingly, he wished to avoid embarrassing conflicts with either labor unions or environmental protection groups.

Taylor was perplexed by Richardson's concern for style. Most of Steinway's studies of facility issues were based upon purely economic factors. Steinway was, in fact, accustomed to initiating political disputes in order to gain special favors for clients with respect to taxes, land acquisition, and utility rates. Richardson clearly did not want Steinway to handle Manchester's project with the methods it commonly employed.

As he started the location study, Taylor was also thinking through the range of facility decisions which Steinway could propose to the candy makers in the hope that Manchester would consider other projects in addition to that of the existing consulting contract.

# WHAT ARE FACILITY DECISIONS?

Facility decisions vary in scope from the total corporate strategy for capacity expansion to the location of an entire physical plant to the replacement of a particular piece of equipment. Organizations at one time or other are faced with decisions such as the following:

Should we expand?
If we expand, by how much should we expand?
Should we increase capacity in a sequence of steps?
Should we increase the capacity of existing facilities or build new ones?

Decisions such as these may be strongly affected by the strategic plans of the organizations. Capital budgeting and financial planning may dominate considerations, instead of the need for facilities. But at the operational level of choosing the characteristics of facilities and seeing to it that they operate properly, there are a number of facility decisions that must be made in most organizations. These decisions are as follows:

1. Where should we locate?
2. Where should we place our different units within the facility?
3. What process flow should we adopt?
4. How should our work stations be designed?
5. At what speed should our production units operate?
6. When should we replace particular pieces of equipment?

Such facility decisions deal with the location, organization, utilization, and replacement of an organization's physical plant. Operational facility decisions may significantly affect production decisions, and, in many cases, some such decisions may be considered to double as production decisions.

Models for facility decisions may be very specialized, as is the case in layout planning. In other decisions involving such areas as process flow and operating speeds, a specialized model may be required or a general model such as linear programming may be applicable. It is the job of the decision analyst to adapt a wide variety of available models to the particular facility decisions being made, and it is the job of the decision maker to use model analyses in an effective fashion.

# THE LOCATION DECISION

As Taylor reflected on Richardson's directive, he tried to picture the location decision in general terms. With many previous clients, Taylor had found that the decision to build a new plant was made hastily. All too often, an organization would install extra capacity instead of improving the use of its existing capacity; but since Manchester had no existing capacity in the U.S., Taylor felt that a capacity utilization study would not be germane.

Multiplant strategies were another dimension to the location decisions that often concerned Taylor. Frequently, an organization would make a decision to build additional capacity without giving any thought to the impact of the new facility on its other facilities. Again, the Manchester study seemed to exclude multiplant interaction problems, since the new plant would be the only one in the United States.

The one aspect of the location complicating the decision was that of regional warehouses. Richardson had indicated that no more than four regional warehouses could be built in addition to a main warehouse at the plant itself. Thus, the plant location decision could not be made without choosing warehouse locations simultaneously.

Taylor's preferred approach to choosing plant locations was to start by outlining the factors he had found by experience to be important. Corresponding to each factor, he would then prepare a statement of desired attributes. The major location factors that Taylor felt to be most important were the following:

1. Labor force
2. Transportation
3. Raw materials
4. Climate
5. Community
6. Pollution
7. Energy
8. Government
9. Capital and operating costs

For each of these factors, Taylor listed the attributes desired by Manchester Candies:

1. Labor force—No history of labor confrontation; workers willing to do routine jobs
2. Transportation—Good highway network; rail and barge connections unnecessary
3. Raw materials—Ready access to dairy farms, sufficient water supply, proximity to harbor for unloading cocoa beans
4. Climate—Unimportant except for impact on raw material deliveries
5. Community—Small community preferred where the plant would become a major contributor to the local economy
6. Pollution—Unpolluted source of water desired; lack of local concern over pollution produced by plant
7. Energy—Stable supply of natural gas
8. Government—Sympathetic to business
9. Capital and operating costs—Important, but not the major consideration

Starting from these brief characterizations, Taylor searched his files for possible locations. Feeling that raw materials were the most restrictive factor,

Taylor first tried east coast locations. He then searched through other areas, trying to find regions that fit the largest number of high-priority characteristics.

The search produced three regions for further analysis. In each of these regions, Taylor identified a likely industrial site. Since a warehouse network would have to be established in conjunction with any plant location chosen, Taylor's next step was to identify the best warehouse configuration for each region.

After the warehouse locations were identified, Taylor had one of his employees determine the costs for each site. A table was then prepared showing the ability of each site to satisfy Manchester's needs.

Taylor debated with himself over whether to develop a mathematical model or a ranking system for comparing the sites. On previous jobs, clients had requested that such quantitative aids be provided. The ranking schemes generally assigned numerical scores to each site's ability to satisfy each criterion. Weights reflecting relative importance were then developed for each criterion so that a weighted score could be prepared for each site. Mathematical models he had used included a plant location integer programming model.

Taylor had found from experience that clients who came from a technical background generally preferred the ranking system of comparison. These decision makers were uncomfortable with qualitative considerations and liked to have their decisions reduced to numbers. Richardson on the other hand seemed comfortable with both quantitative and qualitative evaluations. With this fact in mind, Taylor merely prepared a comparison table for each of the alternatives (Table 11.1) without numerical interpretations.

At Taylor's presentation of the table in London, Richardson was pleased with the site comparisons. As Taylor began to elaborate on each of the characteristics, it became clear to him that Richardson knew what he wanted. In contrasting site 1 and site 2, site 2 was better on only two points than site 1: gas availability and capital cost. In neither case was site 2's advantage significant. Therefore, Richardson eliminated site 2 from further consideration.

In a similar comparison, site 1 seemed better than site 3. Before making the final decision, Richardson decided to go to America and visit both sites. The local civic and business leaders at each site put on an impressive show for Richardson, and he felt that either site would make an excellent choice. The towns were Nitral, South Carolina, and Pocahontas, West Virginia.

In order to break the tie between locations, Richardson planned a week in each area, Pocahontas first. As was his custom, Richardson took a 5-mile morning hike. Richardson stepped out in his dilapidated hiking clothes and found the hilly terrain to be fascinating. On his hike in the area, Richardson was deep in the woods when he tripped over a wild grapevine and fell 20 feet into a ravine. Badly bruised, Richardson limped to an old farmhouse nearby to seek help.

The Steed family, without hesitation, took Richardson into their home, cleansed his bruises, and fed him a substantial breakfast. Then they took him into town in their 1949 Ford. As they let him off at his motel, Mrs. Steed handed Richardson a sack of fresh biscuits and a pint of elderberry jelly. Richardson skipped the trip to Nitral and returned to England. He wrote a report recommending that Pocahontas be selected.

## Table 11.1 Site characteristics

| Characteristic | Site 1<br>Pocahontas, W.Va. | Site 2<br>Hampson, Ky. | Site 3<br>Nitral, S.C. |
|---|---|---|---|
| 1. Labor force | Unskilled; female; may be limited supply | Semiskilled; labor activity strong; sufficient supply | Semiskilled; limited labor activity; short supply |
| 2. Transportation | Limited at present; major highway expansion expected within 2 years | Good north-south routes; limited east-west routes | Limited access; no existing development plans |
| 3. Raw materials | Dairy and water supplies plentiful; 350 miles from seaport | Dairy supply limited at present but could develop; water pollution problems; 450 miles from seaport | Dairy supply available but future growth limited; 200 miles from seaport |
| 4. Climate | Average temperature—52°F; temperature range—0–90°F; 32 inches of rain/year | Average temperature—57°F; temperature range—10–100°F; 24 inches of rain/year | Average temperature—63°F; temperature range—30–100°F; 20 inches of rain/year |
| 5. Community | Rural area; poor schools; limited amenities | Rural area; poor schools; limited amenities | Rural area; poor schools; limited amenities |
| 6. Pollution | Clean environment; no problems | Polluted streams; plant would cause limited damage | Clean environment; no pollution problems |
| 7. Energy | Limited gas lines but could be built | Gas available | Gas available |
| 8. Government | Very favorable; tax advantages | More inclined to heavy industry; limited tax advantages | Very favorable; tax advantage; free rent for 5 years |
| 9. Capital cost | $20.2 million | $19.9 million | $20.6 million |
| 10. Annual costs | $5.2 million | $6.2 million | $5.8 million |

## FACILITY LAYOUT DECISIONS

Manchester Candies made an announcement that the construction was to begin in six months. Richardson was pleased that the company had accepted his word, and he was pleased with Benedict Taylor's work. Richardson asked Steinway to do the layout of the new plant and specified that Taylor be Steinway's operative on the job.

In the past, Taylor had successfully used three computerized layout procedures: ALDEP (automated layout design program), CORELAP (computerized relationship layout planning), and CRAFT (computerized relative allocation of facilities technique). ALDEP and CORELAP were used when an entirely new layout was desired, while CRAFT was best applied to improving an existing layout. Taylor chose to use the CORELAP software for the Manchester job, since the problem was to lay out a new plant.

The facility was conceptually broken down into nineteen departments which represented the manufacturing and service function of the facility. To better understand plant requirements, Taylor reviewed the processing steps in the planned facility and toured similar manufacturing facilities in England. The chocolate process consisted of the series of operations: cleaning and roasting of cocoa beans, grinding of the beans, mixing of the ingredients. Cake manufacture and the congé operation were other operating steps after which the cakes were coated with chocolate. Once the bars were made, they were wrapped, packed, and shipped.

Production offices, engineering offices, administrative offices, quality control areas, a cafeteria, and rest rooms were also on the list of facilities to be included in the plans, as were warehouse space and intermediate storage space. Estimates of the space requirements for all of the departments are shown in Table 11.2.

Each of the plant layout programs uses a measure of effectiveness in the layout process. In the case of CORELAP, an activity relationship chart must be prepared for each pair of departments to fix the degree of closeness between them. These relationships are described by numerical indices as shown in Table 11.3.

In order to obtain the best values for each relationship at the Pocahontas plant, Taylor interviewed each of the production managers at the British facilities. Where conflicts arose, Taylor tried to resolve the conflicts according to his own best professional judgment. The result of Taylor's interviews was Table 11.4.

For department 11 (cake production), the only departments that were considered important in closeness were departments 16 (mixing) and 17 (grinding). Grinding preceded cake production in the manufacturing sequence and mixing followed it. By assigning higher closeness values to the mixing and grinding departments, Taylor intended that they would be located near the cake production.

CORELAP's first calculation step in the assignment process is the computation of the total closeness rating (TCR) for each department. The TCR value is simply the sum of each of a department's rating values. For department 11 the

## Table 11.2 Department space requirements

| Department number | Department | Space requirement, ft² | Department number | Department | Space requirement, ft² |
|---|---|---|---|---|---|
| 11 | Cake production | 7,300 | 21 | Cafeteria | 1,400 |
| 12 | Congés | 23,000 | 22 | Washroom and rest rooms | 2,700 |
| 13 | Little Wafe production | 8,000 | 23 | Production offices | 1,500 |
| | | | 24 | Engineering offices | 2,100 |
| 14 | Duke's Ducat | 8,900 | 25 | Administration offices | 4,700 |
| 15 | Wafer construction | 2,500 | 26 | Quality control lab | 1,000 |
| 16 | Mixing | 2,500 | 27 | Little Wafe pack and ship | 9,000 |
| 17 | Grinding | 8,000 | 28 | Duke's Ducat pack and ship | 9,000 |
| 18 | Warehouse | 12,100 | | | |
| 19 | Storeroom | 700 | 29 | Clean and roast | 12,000 |
| 20 | Immediate storage | 1,400 | | | |

**Table 11.3 Relationship codes
and numerical values**

| Relationship of one department's closeness to another | Numerical value |
| --- | --- |
| Preassigned | 7 |
| Absolutely necessary | 6 |
| Especially important | 5 |
| Important | 4 |
| Ordinary closeness | 3 |
| Unimportant | 2 |
| Undesirable | 1 |

TCR is 40. The relationship chart is then reordered with the highest TCR-rated department listed in the first column (Table 11.5).

For each department, the total area to be laid out must be broken into unit blocks before space can be assigned. In this case, Taylor decided to base his layout on 12- by 12-ft unit squares.

For example, in department 14, the total area of 8900 square feet is divided into sixty-one blocks (8900/ 12 × 12). These sixty-one blocks can be formed into a rectangle of seven blocks by eight blocks plus additional blocks to make up the remainder of 8900 total square feet.

Department 14 has the highest TCR; so it starts the layout as shown in Fig. 11.1. The department with the highest closeness rating with department 14 is then added to the layout (in this case, department 28). If there is a tie, the closest department with the highest TCR is added next. The exact method of placing the next department onto the layout can be found in the CORELAP user's manual. The result of adding department 28 to the layout is shown in Fig. 11.2.

Once departments 14 and 28 have been added to the layout, the next department must be selected. There are four departments that have closeness ratings of 4 with department 14 (20, 21, 22, 23), and one department (22) with a closeness rating of 4 with department 28. Since department 20 has the highest TCR it is added next to the layout (Fig. 11.3).

This process continues until the final department has been added to the layout as shown in Fig. 11.4.

Looking at the completed layout, Taylor thought to himself, "Ye gad." The layout was totally unacceptable. A general truism was illustrated: Relationships that seem so obvious to the intuitive mind must be explicitly designed into any model.

There was no apparent reason for the model to attach departments 19, 24, and 25 to the right side of the building. The intuitive mind would have used up the space inside the left end first. Irregular shapes of departments are not acceptable in practice, but the model used was not designed to dwell on the shape of the building.

**Table 11.4 Activity relationship chart**

| | 11 | 12 | 13 | 14 | 15 | 16 | 17 | 18 | 19 | 20 | 21 | 22 | 23 | 24 | 25 | 26 | 27 | 28 | 39 |
|----|----|----|----|----|----|----|----|----|----|----|----|----|----|----|----|----|----|----|----|
| 11 | 0 | 2 | 2 | 2 | 2 | 4 | 4 | 2 | 2 | 2 | 2 | 2 | 2 | 2 | 2 | 2 | 2 | 2 | 2 |
| 12 | 2 | 0 | 2 | 2 | 2 | 5 | 2 | 2 | 2 | 4 | 2 | 2 | 2 | 2 | 2 | 4 | 2 | 2 | 1 |
| 13 | 2 | 2 | 0 | 2 | 5 | 2 | 2 | 2 | 2 | 4 | 2 | 4 | 2 | 2 | 2 | 3 | 5 | 2 | 2 |
| 14 | 2 | 2 | 2 | 0 | 2 | 2 | 2 | 2 | 2 | 4 | 4 | 4 | 4 | 2 | 2 | 3 | 2 | 5 | 2 |
| 15 | 2 | 2 | 5 | 2 | 0 | 2 | 2 | 2 | 2 | 5 | 2 | 4 | 4 | 2 | 2 | 3 | 3 | 2 | 2 |
| 16 | 4 | 5 | 2 | 2 | 2 | 0 | 2 | 2 | 2 | 2 | 2 | 2 | 2 | 2 | 2 | 2 | 2 | 5 | 5 |
| 17 | 4 | 2 | 2 | 2 | 2 | 2 | 0 | 2 | 2 | 2 | 2 | 2 | 2 | 2 | 2 | 2 | 2 | 2 | 5 |
| 18 | 2 | 2 | 2 | 2 | 2 | 2 | 2 | 0 | 2 | 2 | 2 | 2 | 2 | 2 | 2 | 4 | 2 | 2 | 2 |
| 19 | 2 | 2 | 2 | 2 | 2 | 2 | 2 | 2 | 0 | 2 | 3 | 2 | 2 | 2 | 2 | 2 | 2 | 2 | 2 |
| 20 | 2 | 4 | 4 | 4 | 5 | 2 | 2 | 2 | 2 | 0 | 2 | 2 | 2 | 2 | 2 | 2 | 2 | 2 | 2 |
| 21 | 2 | 2 | 2 | 4 | 2 | 2 | 2 | 3 | 2 | 2 | 0 | 2 | 2 | 2 | 2 | 2 | 2 | 4 | 2 |
| 22 | 2 | 2 | 4 | 4 | 2 | 2 | 2 | 2 | 2 | 2 | 2 | 0 | 2 | 2 | 2 | 2 | 4 | 2 | 2 |
| 23 | 2 | 2 | 2 | 4 | 2 | 2 | 2 | 2 | 2 | 2 | 2 | 2 | 0 | 2 | 2 | 2 | 2 | 2 | 2 |
| 24 | 2 | 2 | 2 | 2 | 4 | 2 | 2 | 2 | 2 | 2 | 2 | 2 | 2 | 0 | 2 | 2 | 2 | 2 | 2 |
| 25 | 2 | 2 | 2 | 2 | 2 | 2 | 2 | 2 | 2 | 2 | 2 | 2 | 2 | 2 | 0 | 2 | 2 | 2 | 2 |
| 26 | 2 | 4 | 3 | 3 | 2 | 2 | 2 | 4 | 2 | 2 | 2 | 2 | 2 | 2 | 2 | 0 | 2 | 2 | 2 |
| 27 | 2 | 2 | 5 | 2 | 3 | 2 | 2 | 2 | 2 | 2 | 2 | 4 | 2 | 2 | 2 | 2 | 0 | 2 | 2 |
| 28 | 2 | 2 | 2 | 5 | 2 | 2 | 2 | 2 | 2 | 2 | 2 | 4 | 2 | 2 | 2 | 2 | 2 | 0 | 2 |
| 29 | 2 | 1 | 2 | 2 | 2 | 2 | 5 | 2 | 2 | 2 | 2 | 2 | 2 | 2 | 2 | 2 | 2 | 2 | 0 |

**Table 11.5 Reordered relationship chart**

| | 14 | 13 | 15 | 20 | 22 | 26 | 12 | 18 | 27 | 28 | 17 | 16 | 11 | 23 | 21 | 29 | 25 | 24 | 19 |
|----|----|----|----|----|----|----|----|----|----|----|----|----|----|----|----|----|----|----|----|
| 11 | 2 | 2 | 2 | 2 | 2 | 2 | 2 | 2 | 2 | 2 | 4 | 4 | 0 | 2 | 2 | 2 | 2 | 2 | 2 |
| 12 | 2 | 2 | 2 | 4 | 2 | 4 | 0 | 2 | 2 | 2 | 2 | 5 | 2 | 2 | 2 | 1 | 2 | 2 | 2 |
| 13 | 2 | 0 | 5 | 4 | 4 | 3 | 2 | 2 | 5 | 2 | 2 | 2 | 2 | 2 | 2 | 2 | 2 | 2 | 2 |
| 14 | 0 | 2 | 2 | 4 | 4 | 3 | 2 | 2 | 2 | 2 | 2 | 2 | 2 | 4 | 4 | 2 | 2 | 2 | 2 |
| 15 | 2 | 5 | 0 | 5 | 2 | 3 | 2 | 2 | 2 | 5 | 2 | 2 | 2 | 4 | 2 | 2 | 2 | 2 | 2 |
| 16 | 2 | 2 | 2 | 2 | 2 | 2 | 5 | 2 | 2 | 2 | 2 | 0 | 4 | 2 | 2 | 2 | 2 | 2 | 2 |
| 17 | 2 | 2 | 2 | 2 | 2 | 2 | 2 | 2 | 2 | 2 | 0 | 2 | 4 | 2 | 2 | 2 | 2 | 2 | 2 |
| 18 | 2 | 2 | 2 | 2 | 2 | 2 | 2 | 0 | 2 | 2 | 2 | 2 | 2 | 2 | 2 | 5 | 2 | 2 | 2 |
| 19 | 2 | 2 | 2 | 2 | 2 | 4 | 2 | 2 | 2 | 2 | 2 | 2 | 2 | 2 | 3 | 5 | 2 | 2 | 0 |
| 20 | 4 | 4 | 5 | 0 | 2 | 2 | 4 | 3 | 2 | 2 | 2 | 2 | 2 | 2 | 2 | 2 | 2 | 2 | 2 |
| 21 | 4 | 2 | 2 | 2 | 2 | 2 | 2 | 2 | 4 | 4 | 2 | 2 | 2 | 2 | 0 | 2 | 2 | 2 | 2 |
| 22 | 4 | 4 | 4 | 2 | 0 | 2 | 2 | 2 | 2 | 2 | 2 | 2 | 2 | 2 | 2 | 2 | 2 | 2 | 2 |
| 23 | 4 | 2 | 2 | 2 | 2 | 2 | 2 | 2 | 2 | 2 | 2 | 2 | 2 | 0 | 2 | 2 | 2 | 2 | 2 |
| 24 | 2 | 2 | 2 | 2 | 2 | 2 | 2 | 2 | 2 | 2 | 2 | 2 | 2 | 2 | 2 | 2 | 2 | 0 | 2 |
| 25 | 2 | 2 | 2 | 2 | 2 | 2 | 2 | 2 | 2 | 2 | 2 | 2 | 2 | 2 | 0 | 2 | 0 | 2 | 2 |
| 26 | 3 | 3 | 3 | 2 | 4 | 0 | 4 | 4 | 2 | 2 | 2 | 2 | 2 | 2 | 2 | 2 | 2 | 2 | 2 |
| 27 | 2 | 5 | 2 | 2 | 4 | 2 | 2 | 2 | 0 | 0 | 2 | 2 | 2 | 2 | 2 | 2 | 2 | 2 | 2 |
| 28 | 5 | 2 | 2 | 2 | 4 | 2 | 2 | 2 | 2 | 0 | 2 | 2 | 2 | 2 | 2 | 2 | 2 | 2 | 2 |
| 29 | 2 | 2 | 2 | 2 | 2 | 2 | 1 | 2 | 2 | 2 | 5 | 2 | 2 | 2 | 2 | 0 | 2 | 2 | 2 |

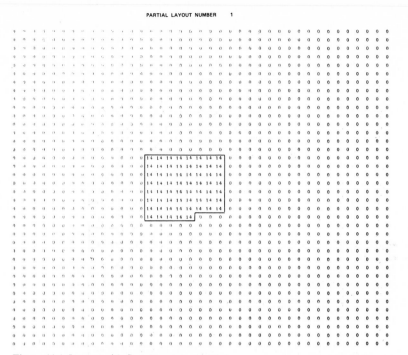

**Figure 11.1** Layout with first department added.

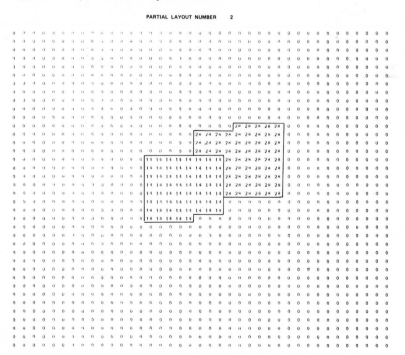

**Figure 11.2** Layout with second department added.

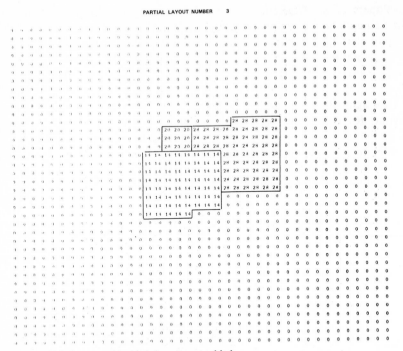

**Figure 11.3** Layout with third department added.

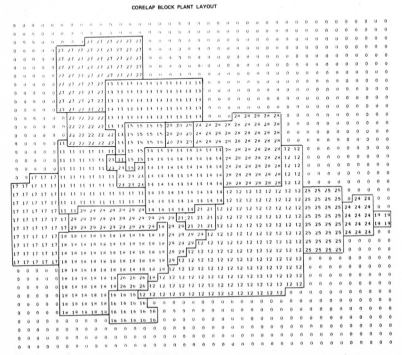

**Figure 11.4** Layout with all departments.

The developers of the CORELAP system, realizing that significant human input would be necessary to make the model successful, had designed an interactive version of CORELAP that allowed the user to fix certain facilities in given locations. Taylor accessed the interactive version of CORELAP and began to change the original layout to make it acceptable. After twenty-two iterations between Taylor and the machine, the layout of Fig. 11.5 evolved.

Taylor flew again to England and met with Richards in Manchester to review the layout. Richardson saw the layout as a substantial improvement over the company's two-story plant in Manchester. Taylor was very proud of his use of the computer to generate the layout, but Richardson seemed dubious of the computer's value. "You Yanks seem to want to use the computer on everything. I bloody well can't see where a computer did anything but confirm the obvious."

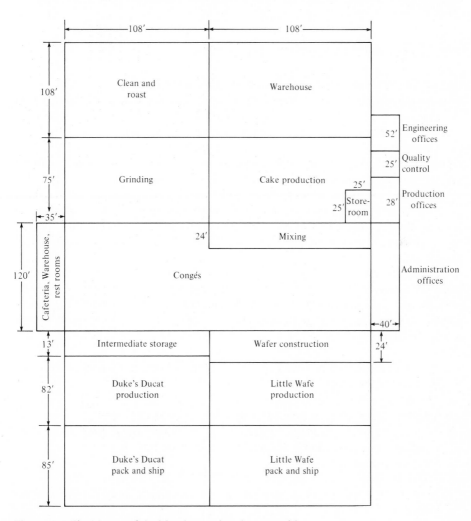

**Figure 11.5** Final layout of the Manchester plant (not to scale).

Taylor responded that the computer was actually just a scratch pad. With Taylor's guidance, it could generate many layout alternatives in a short period of time. In effect, the computer served as a fast computational device directed by the intuitive abilities of the decision maker.

Taylor and Richardson shared dinner the evening prior to Taylor's departure for America. Richardson, as it turned out, had an ulterior motive for the meeting. He surprised Taylor by unexpectedly offering him the plant manager's job at the American facility. As an added inducement, Richardson informally indicated that Taylor could quickly become vice president of American operations if the venture proved successful. Taylor, a consultant all his working life, was tempted by a chance to settle down in one place. Although he asked for time to think over the decision, he was already sure that he would take the job, and shortly after he did accept.

## THE LINE OPTIMIZATION DECISION

One of Taylor's first actions as plant manager was to hire his old college friend, Chick Hutchins, as his chief engineer. Hutchins had spent most of his career in the chemical industry, where many of the production problems were similar to those at the Pocahontas plant (the name chosen for the American facility).

One of Hutchins's first jobs was to decide on the proper line speed for the automatic cup-filling step in making the Duke's Ducat product. This was a problem similar to one Hutchins had worked on before at Amalgamated Chemicals.

His basic approach to the problem was to use an experimental optimization procedure. In this approach, he would conduct experiments on the process by running the cup-filling line at different speeds. By carefully controlling the line speed settings, a very good line speed could be identified with a minimum of experimentation.

Before the line optimization experiment could begin, however, a measure of good performance was needed. Hutchins asked the plant accountant to suggest a performance measure for the line. The accountant suggested profit as the most appropriate measure, and indicated further that profit was influenced by the following factors:

1. Production capacity relative to the theoretical maximum number of products the line can produce
2. The selling price of the product
3. The amount of scrap produced in making the product
4. The quality of the product, or the lack of it, which might result in product rejection once the product has left the production line
5. Labor requirements
6. Material costs
7. Maintenance costs, including wear on the machinery, preventative maintenance, etc.

8. Downtime on the production line because of machine breakdowns, clogging of products, etc.
9. Equipment capitalization
10. Changeover costs
11. Overhead

Hutchins was dismayed by this information. To estimate each component in the profit equation would take an extensive amount of time and effort. In fact, Hutchins doubted whether some of these factors could even be measured for a single product line. After giving this problem some thought, Hutchins decided to try to isolate those factors which would likely be affected by changes in the line speed.

He ascertained that the only factors which would be influenced by line speed changes were: (1) production capacity, (3) the scrap rate, (4) the eventual product quality, (7) maintenance costs, and (8) machine downtime. Hutchins felt that his experiments with line speed changes would be modest enough to prevent the need for significant changes in staffing of the line.

Product quality and maintenance seemed likely to be affected by line speed, but it was difficult to see how these factors could be measured. Hutchins did learn from the engineers that these factors would likely be affected only slightly as compared to the other factors.

The three remaining factors, production capacity, scrap rate, and downtime, were each related to production quantity according to the relationship

$$P_f = P_o - PL_{dt} - PL_s$$

where $P_f$ = final production (units/shift)—actual amount of good product produced each shift

$P_o$ = line speed setting (units/shift)—theoretical maximum production per shift

$PL_{dt}$ = production loss due to downtime (units/shift)—measured as downtime multiplied by the original line speed setting

$PL_s$ = production loss due to scrap (units/shift)—measured as amount of scrap produced per shift.

Given this relationship, it became clear that line speed adjustments could be evaluated on the basis of final productivity of the line without an evaluation of the total profit equation. This fact was advantageous, since productivity figures were normally kept for each line. Consequently, no new data needed to be collected.

The basic approach Hutchins suggested for optimizing the line was to conduct a set of sequential experiments. The relationship between line speed and production was thought to be as shown in Fig. 11.6. Line speed was measured in pumps per minute (ppm), and the theoretical relation between production of cups of acceptable quality and line speed suggested a simple way to design the optimizing experiments.

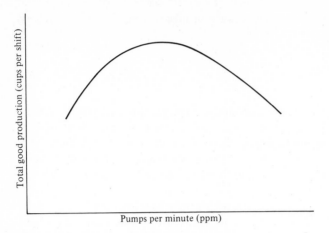

**Figure 11.6** Conceptual relationship between line speed and production.

As an example of this procedure, Fig. 11.7 illustrates the information that two line speed observations gave about the optimum line speed. As the figure shows, the line speed of 151 ppm gave higher output than that of 159 ppm. Because of the peaked shape of the production curve, line speeds from 159 to the line maximum of 172 ppm were excluded from the experiment, since the production curve should continue to drop above 159 ppm. Therefore, the optimum line speed was expected to be in the interval below 159 ppm. A third experiment at a speed of 146 ppm is illustrated in Fig. 11.8.

The interval below 146 ppm was excluded from the analysis, since production would not increase below 146 ppm. Thus, the optimum line speed was narrowed to the 146 to 159 ppm interval.

Subsequent experiments would have limited the interval further until an

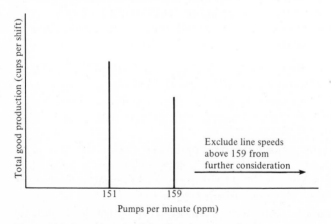

**Figure 11.7** Sample result of two line-speed experiments.

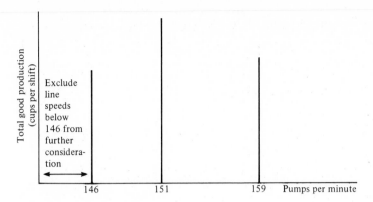

**Figure 11.8** Sample results after three experiments.

approximate optimum line speed was found. Developing the experimentation procedure, Hutchins codified these specific implementation details:

1. The experiments should be conducted for a specific number of shifts in order to prevent random variation in production from unduly influencing the optimizaton procedure. The number of shifts needed for the experiment should be determined by the theoretical criteria placed on results.
2. If any experiment results in disruptive and unacceptable production, the experiment should be terminated at once. The mean production for this experiment would be set at an arbitrarily low value which would be the worst production value for any of the experiments and would subsequently narrow the search for the optimum line speed.
3. The reduction in the search interval width should be rapid as a result of using this procedure. The reduction is in accordance with the relation

$$R = (0.6180)^{N-1}$$

where $R$ = percent reduction of original search interval
$N$ = number of experiments

The choice of experiments is important to reducing the number of trials required to locate an optimum procedure. Several methods are available for choosing the experiments. The method selected by Hutchins for the line speed experiment is known by the name *golden section search*. In this method, the placement of experiments is identified from the relationship

$$d = 0.3820L$$

where $d$ = distance from end of interval at which experiment should be conducted
$L$ = width of interval which contains optimum line speed

The line speed control box allowed speed adjustments over the interval from 138 to 172 ppm. Thus, the value of $L$ was 34, (i.e., 172 to 138). Therefore, the placement of the first experiment would be calculated as

$$d = 0.3820L$$

$$d = 0.3820(34)$$

$$d = 13 \text{ units}$$

This means that the first two experiments should be conducted approximately 13 ppm from each end of the interval. This would place the experiments at 151 ppm and at 159 ppm. Results of early experiments and the corresponding intervals appear in Fig. 11.9.

As a result of the first two experiments, the optimum line speed was limited to the interval 138 to 159 ppm. The value of $L$ was then 21 ppm, and the new value of $d$ was

$$d = 3820L$$

$$d = 0.3820(21)$$

$$d = 8$$

An experiment was then placed at 8 ppm from the ends of the 138 to 159 ppm interval. Since there was already an experiment at 151 ppm, the only new experiment needed was at $138 + 8 = 146$ ppm.

As the experimental interval is reduced, only one new experiment is needed for each trial. Experiments were placed sequentially at 151, 156, and 154 ppm, according to the placement formula.

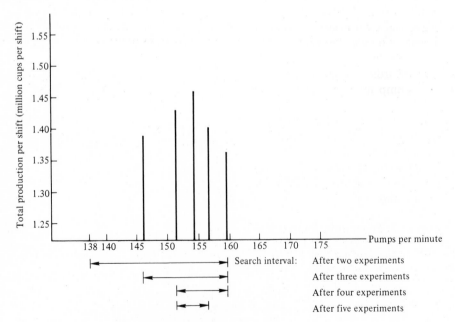

**Figure 11.9** Experimental optimization results.

Upon completion of the experiments, Hutchins was ready to recommend a line speed of 154 ppm. He explained the experiments and then made his formal recommendation to Taylor, who was impressed with the results and promptly implemented the line speed. Hutchins later found an efficient speed for the second production line, and due to his efforts, profits blossomed.

## THE PUMP REPLACEMENT DECISION

The Pocahontas plant operated at an unexpectedly high level during its first year of operation. As a result of the line speed work done by Chick Hutchins, the productivity of the two candy lines was 10 percent higher than that of comparable lines in England. One cost item, however, was out of line with costs encountered in England: the cost of pump replacement was much higher than it should have been.

Taylor had originally shrugged off the difference in replacement cost as being due to the British habit of never throwing anything away. After studying relevant data, though, he began to suspect that the replacement decisions themselves might be faulty. Taylor asked Hutchins to look into the question and report back.

Hutchins's first action was to look up the maintenance records for the pumps. The maintenance shop kept a set of records which described the work it performed, primarily for the purpose of billing the production departments. The form used is shown in Exhibit 11.1. It contained data that Hutchins felt were the key to the pump replacement issue.

Since an item tag number identified each piece of equipment in inventory, it was possible for Hutchins to identify the pumps listed on the sheets. At the completion of each maintenance job, a tag or sticker was attached to maintained equipment showing the time of the last action taken. Each pump had a stroke counter, and this count was also recorded on the service tag.

The records for six months of maintenance gave Hutchins enough data to estimate pump maintenance costs. He summarized the costs as shown in Table 11.6.

This statistical summary identified the costs of pump maintenance over time. For example, it cost an average of $95.90 for maintaining the pump during the service period between 0.6 to 0.8 million pumps. According to company policy, all pumps were replaced after 1.6 million strokes.

Hutchins decided to use the data to study the relative capital costs of replacement and maintenance. For this study, he assumed that a new pump had

**Exhibit 11.1 Pocahontas maintenance record**

| Date | Item tag number | Time since last service | Maintenance action | Maintenance charge |
|------|-----------------|-------------------------|--------------------|--------------------|
| 6/23 | C263A | 5/1 | Bearing replacement | $52.50 |
| 6/23 | A432T | 6/2 | Pump clogging | $10.20 |
| 6/24 | B264H | 5/7 | Loss of pressure | $80.20 |

## Table 11.6 Pump maintenance cost summary

| Stroke count at service, million strokes | Average maintenance costs, $ |
|---|---|
| 0.0–0.2 | 80.60 |
| 0.2–0.4 | 92.70 |
| 0.4–0.6 | 91.80 |
| 0.6–0.8 | 95.90 |
| 0.8–1.0 | 112.90 |
| 1.0–1.2 | 150.60 |
| 1.2–1.4 | 180.90 |
| 1.4–1.6 | 210.30 |

a retail price of $240 and no resale value. Hutchins's summary is shown in Table 11.7. In this table Hutchins assumed a standard lifetime for a pump of 1 million strokes.

The analysis in the first row of Table 11.7 shows that the average capital cost per million strokes, if pumps were replaced after 0.2 million strokes, would be $1200 (i.e., $240/0.2). The maintenance costs during this period were expected to total $80.60 or $403 per million strokes. The average total costs would be $1603 per million strokes.

For a strategy of replacement after 0.4 million strokes, the capital costs would decline to $600 per million strokes. The average maintenance costs would increase to $433.30 per million strokes, but the average costs in this case would drop to $1033.30 per million strokes.

By studying the last column in the table, Hutchins discovered that the lowest average cost would be achieved at a replacement strategy of 1.0 million strokes. Contrary to what Taylor had thought, the pumps should have been replaced more often than had been company policy, and he recommended to Taylor that the implied policy be adopted. Taylor accepted the rcommendation, and the plant's pump replacement costs fell to about the British level.

## Table 11.7 Replacement cost summary

| Replace after, in million strokes | Average capital cost, $/million strokes | Cumulative maintenance cost, $ | Average maintenance cost, $/million strokes | Average total cost, $/million strokes |
|---|---|---|---|---|
| 0.2 | 1200 | 80.60 | 403.00 | 1603.00 |
| 0.4 | 600 | 173.30 | 433.30 | 1033.30 |
| 0.6 | 400 | 265.10 | 441.80 | 841.80 |
| 0.8 | 300 | 361.00 | 451.30 | 751.30 |
| 1.0 | 240 | 473.90 | 473.90 | 713.90 |
| 1.2 | 200 | 624.50 | 520.40 | 720.40 |
| 1.4 | 171 | 805.40 | 575.30 | 746.30 |
| 1.6 | 150 | 1015.70 | 634.80 | 784.80 |

# FACILITY MODELS IN RETROSPECT

The facilities decisions addressed at the Pocahontas plant are representative of facilities decisions facing many organizations. Models for assisting in these decisions may take the form of a quantitative analysis or of a logical framework for structuring a qualitative decision. The plant layout decision, for example, employed a decision model which was little more than a structured approach to the problem.

In the plant layout problem, the model served to assist intuition in the decision process. The decision to place a particular department in a particular location was one that could have been made by either the model or the decision maker; the model facilitated the process by giving the decision maker a quick evaluation of alternatives.

The plant location decision began with quantitative criteria, but the difficulty of assigning specific numerical goals to the criteria led to their being expressed qualitatively. The decision was still too complex and was decided by Cedric Richardson intuitively. At the other extreme, the cost model for the pump replacement problem was a more quantitative assessment of alternatives.

In all cases, managerial judgment can supersede model solutions, and some models require a mix of qualitative and quantitative criteria. For instance, in the line optimization problem, qualitative criteria had to be imposed on experiments in order to prevent the continuation of destructive operations.

The one common thread in all of these problem solution techniques is structure. Each solution process used a well-structured, organized approach to defining an acceptable solution.

# REFERENCES

Armour, G. C., and E. S. Buffa: "A Heuristic Algorithm and Simulation Approach to Relative Location of Facilities," *Management Science*, vol. 9, no. 1, 1963, pp. 294–309.

Lee, R. C., and J. M. Moore: "CORELAP—Computerized Relationship Layout Planning," *Journal of Industrial Engineering*, vol. 18, no. 3, 1967, pp. 195–200.

Seehof, J. M., and W. O. Evans, "Automated Layout Design Program," *Journal of Industrial Engineering*, vol. 18, no. 12, 1967, pp. 690-695.

Sepponen, R.: "Corelap 8 User's Manual," Department of Industrial Engineering, Northeastern University, Boston, 1969.

Wilde, D. J., *Optimum Seeking Methods*, Prentice-Hall, Englewood Cliffs, N.J., 1964, pp. 32–52.

# QUESTIONS

1 Why did Richardson not insist upon a quantitative method of comparing the Pocahontas, Hampson, and Nitral sites?

2 What major strategy or policy decisions at Manchester led to the decision to build a U.S. plant?

3 What would the Pocahontas plant's layout be if the relationship code between departments 14 and 20 were 1 instead of 4?

4 What considerations lead to the choices of relationship codes between departments? For example, why should packaging and shipping have a high closeness code in most companies?

5 How did Hutchins know the theoretical shape of the production line production curve? Do you agree with that curve?

6 Can you suggest a faster search procedure in the line optimization experiment than the golden section search? If so, explain this procedure.

7 The calculations in Table 11.7 are only accurate if future costs can be expected to be the same as historical costs. What effect would including the effect of inflation have on these calculations, and how would that change the replacement decision?

8 How much more per pump would Hutchins have expected the company to spend if its policy were to replace pumps after 1.6 million strokes instead of after 1.0 million strokes? How much more is the cost per million strokes?

9 If the demand for the Manchester Candies from the Pocahontas plant were to suddenly double, what changes would be likely to occur in the plant's operations? What facility decisions would the corporate office in England be forced to consider?

10 Processes produce data as well as products. How can the data be used to improve the productivity of the process?

11 The American steel industry has been accused of not replacing plants and equipment in a cost-effective manner. Why were replacement models not used in this case?

# EXERCISES

1 What are some of the facility decisions that have been made recently in your community? What were the factors influencing the decision?

2 Evaluate location decisions that have been made with regard to the local school system.

3 Interview representatives from a local company to determine the factors that led to their plant location decision.

4 What are the locational advantages and disadvantages of your local community?

5 You are given the task of locating a shoe manufacturing facility in your state. Evaluate different location alternatives, and indicate where you would locate the facility.

6 Devise numerical values for each characteristic of Table 11.1. Then devise a quantitative method of using the values to compare the merits of the three sites. Is this method preferred over that used in the Manchester Candies case?

7 Examine the layout of the kitchen facilities in your home. Provide a revised layout and explain the logic of it.

8 Prepare an activity relationship chart for your college campus. Consider the following activities:
   (a) College of business
   (b) College of arts and sciences
   (c) College of engineering
   (d) College of education
   (e) Library
   (f) Football stadium
   (g) Dormitories
   (h) Parking facilities
   (i) Cafeteria facilities
   (j) Intramural sports facilities
   (k) Basketball arena
   (l) Administration offices

9 Prepare a totally new layout of a facility by using an automated computer program (if available). Evaluate the existing layout in contrast to yours. What are the likely reasons for inefficiencies in the existing layout?

10 Prepare a relationship chart and layout of your study area.

11 Develop a general step-by-step procedure for conducting a layout study.

12 Visit a local plant and examine the existing layout.

13 Identify the important criteria in making layout decisions.

14 Evaluate the layout of a local retail store from the following prospectives:
   (*a*) Store manager
   (*b*) Customer

15 What are the advantages of an experimental optimization approach over a trial-and-error approach? Disadvantages?

16 Suppose the yield *y* of a process has the general equation

$$y = -4X^2 + 16X + 2$$

Use the golden section search to approximate the optimum value of *X* over the interal of $X = 0$ to $X = 10$.

17 Discuss the criteria used by you or your family in deciding whether to replace a family car.

18 Motors used in the manufacture of a product are replaced when they fail. From maintenance records, data have been collected on failure patterns as shown in Table 11.8. The motors cost $825. Is the current maintenance policy appropriate?

## Table 11.8

| Hours of operation | Maintenance and lost production cost, $ |
|---|---|
| 10,000 | 82.60 |
| 20,000 | 93.80 |
| 30,000 | 102.50 |
| 40,000 | 241.30 |
| 50,000 | 396.20 |
| 60,000 | 578.90 |

19 What factors other than economics enter into a replacement decision?

20 A replacement policy is to be developed for a component of any assembly-line machine. What are the costs that should be considered in developing this replacment policy?

21 Could a computer program design a plant layout without any human intervention? Why?

22 What criteria should a young married couple with small children use to choose the location of their new home? What criteria will probably dominate the decision?

# CASELETS

1. The College of Engineering at Walker State University consisted of six departments of engineering. Each department had roughly one floor of space for offices and classrooms. Laboratory space was divided among the departments on the ground and basement floors.

   Over the years, the enrollments and research loads of the various departments grew and the building filled to capacity. However, since some departments grew faster than others, there was an imbalance in the needs of each department. Consequently, space utilization in the departments varied significantly.

The new dean of the College of Engineering decided to establish a better procedure for space allocation. This was sure to be a controversial issue since the departments were very protective of their space.

(*a*) Outline the approach that you might take in reallocating space in the college.

(*b*) How would you ensure an even utilization of space on a long-term basis?

2. A fast food chain has decided to locate a new outlet in a town of approximately 50,000 people. As with most cities of its size, business began to shift out of the central business district in the 1970s. One major shopping mall, located 3 miles outside of the city, was the main shopping area. Several highways also had developed significant business growth with numerous fast food restaurants, discount stores, and supermarkets.

From past studies, the fast food chain had identified traffic volume as the most significant factor in determining a location's success. The second most important factor was the population under 16 years of age that was within a ten-minute drive of the store.

(*a*) Outline how you would make the location decision.

(*b*) What data would be needed and how would you collect them?

(*c*) How would the different locations be evaluated?

## CASE 11.1: THE WILLIAMSTOWN FIRE STATION

Williamstown was in the process of building a new fire station, and the vacated building was to be used for office space for other city departments. The departments to be allocated space in the old building were the police, safety, civil service, and purchasing departments. In addition, the fire chief insisted that the fire department be allowed to maintain some office space in the building.

Each of the department heads made a plea to the mayor, Thomas Costain, to provide his department with extra space. Once the requests were received, the mayor could see that significant compromises would have to be made: the building contained only 8635 square feet of space, and the department heads had collectively requested 10,750 square feet.

### Department Heads' Meeting

Faced with this conflict, the mayor called a department heads' meeting to allow each of the departments to present its case and submit to questioning from the other departments.

James Weston, the chief of police, led off the discussion with the observation: "We must provide for better juvenile counseling. Right now, the juveniles that the court has assigned to us must come down to the station. They are being counseled in an area close to the prison. Needless to say, they can't help but feel that they are still in custody in such an environment. We want them to stop thinking of themselves as prisoners and develop a more positive attitude."

Bill Jones, the head of the purchasing department, interrupted at this point. "Surely, Jim you aren't saying that you are going to use the entire 700 square feet you requested to do nothing but counseling."

"Bill, if you would let me finish, you could answer your own question. We also need an evidence room. The supreme court is tying our hands again. If we don't keep complete security on all evidence, they can throw a case out of court. As you know, just this past week, we had the entire front end of a car in as evidence. If we don't have better control of evidence, we're going to have criminals infesting our streets."

"You sound convincing Jim, but what amount of space will you need for counseling and protection of evidence?" asked Adam Swenson, the civil service director.

"Well, we figure that we'll need at least 5000 square feet. The remaining 2000 square feet in our request is for a second squad room with showers and lockers for our officers. You know, we only have one facility now, and that's on the west end of town. When officers are in the east end, they end up being forced to make a lot of unnecessary trips back and forth. The rest of the space will be used for record storage, meetings, and general-purpose needs."

"Jim," the mayor interrupted, "Consider two alternatives—no space or your minimum. What are your absolute minimum needs?"

"Well, the way I figure it, we have to have at least 5000 square feet if we are to do the job a police department in this size of a city should do," said the chief in response to the implied threat.

"Thanks, Jim," said the mayor. "Bill, what does the purchasing department need?"

"As you know, the state auditor has just issued a directive that we keep records on purchases for the past five years. We only keep records for two years now, and we'll need the 1000 square feet we requested for records storage."

"Wait a minute," said the safety director, Beryl Watson. "I thought that the city had just purchased a microfilm system. Won't that reduce your space needs?"

"Well, I suppose so, but we still must keep paper records of the current year's purchases."

"Assuming that the original records are kept for only one year, what space will you need for those records and the microfilmed copies?" asked the mayor.

After a hurried calculation, Bill replied, "I guess we could get by on 500 square feet."

"Thanks, Bill. Adam, what does the civil service department need with the 800 square feet you requested?"

"Well, Mayor, we would like to set up an office on this side of town. As you know, our present office is in a highly congested area and we really don't have the space to accommodate all the business we have to handle. Besides, we would like to have our own testing area instead of having to use the rooms in the post office all the time."

"Adam, I've helped you give those tests to fire department job applicants, and I don't see anything wrong with using the post office," interrupted Nick Pearson, the fire department chief.

"Well, I guess we could get by without the space, but we did have other uses in mind for the room when tests aren't being given. We could do without if we had to. We need at least 300 square feet, however, for a second office."

"Thanks, Adam. Beryl, the safety department is next," said the mayor.

"Mayor, we requested 250 square feet to use for our school safety program. We need the space to store equipment and to have an area to put on safety programs for clubs and civic groups. You know, a lot of people will be using this building and it would be nice if we could have a permanent safety display area."

"Beryl, I believe in safety and it would sure make our job easier," stated Chief Weston, "but why can't the schools provide you the space you need?"

"Well, they could, Jim, but we just feel that we could be more effective by being located here."

"We saved our present occupants for the last," said the mayor. "Nick, I thought you wanted out of here."

"We do, mayor, but it's important for us to keep two of our emergency ambulance units here. We can keep the travel time to emergencies at a minimum that way. It will take 1000 square feet for them, and we requested an additional 700 square feet for auxiliary storage. I guess that since the rest of you are making concessions, we could get by on 1000 square feet if we had to."

"Let's see," said the mayor, "I've summarized our discussion up to now on this sheet of paper. Let me put it up here on the blackboard." (The figures are shown in Table 11.9.)

"It looks like we can accommodate each of your minimum needs, if that's all right with everyone."

"I'll make a motion to that effect," prompted Jim Weston.

"I second," replied Nick Pearson.

"It may be OK for your guys, but it looks like the safety department may not get anything," Beryl Watson shouted rather loudly.

"I don't particularly like the low minimum either, Beryl, but we have to set priorities on a thing like this," stated Adam Swenson. "I call for the question."

"All those in favor?" asked the mayor. "Those opposed? The vote is 4 to 1 that we accept the minimum requirements as presented. Now, we have to decide

**Table 11.9**

| Department | Desired space | Minimum requirements |
|---|---|---|
| Police | 7,000 | 5,000 |
| Purchasing | 1,000 | 500 |
| Civil service | 800 | 300 |
| Safety | 250 | 0 |
| Fire | 1,700 | 1,000 |
| Total | 10,750 | 6,800 |

how to allocate the space which remains after we take out the minimum requirements. Any suggestions?"

"Why don't we do it on the basis of our percentage of the total city budget?" suggested Jim Weston. "That way, we'll maintain the status quo."

"That makes no sense, Jim," stated Nick Pearson. "We always make decisions like that. Why don't we try to make this one a decision that is based upon some rationality? Although the actual space to be allocated is not that much, why don't we make an example of this. Mayor, didn't you just hire a new administrative intern? Maybe we could ask her if some of her college training couldn't help us. What do the rest of you think?"

"I don't like the idea of some college student deciding a matter like this," objected Beryl Watson.

"I didn't say that she would decide the issue," responded Nick. "All I said was that she may have some ideas on how we could solve this problem."

"Well, I'll go along with the idea only if it doesn't commit us to following her recommendations without a further meeting," interjected Jim Weston. "Too many times these hot-shot students make recommendations that would disrupt our whole organization. Look what happened over in Westman. That study of their police force has got everyone in an uproar."

"I assure you that we won't go behind your backs on this," the mayor emphasized. "It's just a trial run. Without any strong objections from the rest of you, I'm going to proceed as Nick suggested."

## Model Development and Results

Subsequent to the department heads' meeting, the mayor met with Janet Romano, the administrative intern. The mayor briefed Romano on the department heads' meeting and asked her to suggest a procedure for dealing with the problem. The mayor continued by saying he had to have an answer within two weeks. She asked for time to give the problem some thought before she made any suggestions as to how to proceed. The mayor added that they had only limited financial resources to solve the problem.

The next day, Romano returned to the mayor's office to give him her suggestions for solving the space allocation problem.

She began, "Mayor, the problem of deciding which departments should receive the space seems to me to be a resource allocation problem; that is, you are trying to allocate the available space to achieve a desired objective. The technique known as linear programming should be able to solve this problem."

After receiving the approval of the mayor, Romano met with the department heads to collect data for the model. These meetings revealed that there was no single estimate for the cost per square foot of alteration; it varied according to the use intended for the space. The cost per square foot of space eventually used was an average of the costs for different uses. While this procedure would not give an exact answer, it would permit obtaining a rapid solution. Romano set up her model for processing through the computer.

Assuming the priorities of departmental needs provided by the city advisory

**Table 11.10**

| Department | Total space allocation, ft$^2$ | Desired space, ft$^2$ | Alteration cost |
|---|---|---|---|
| Police | 5,000.0 | 7,000 | $100,000 |
| Fire | 1,094.4 | 1,700 | 8,850 |
| Safety | 250.0 | 250 | 1,750 |
| Civil service | 800.0 | 800 | 6,400 |
| Purchasing | 1,000.0 | 1,000 | 8,000 |
| Total | 8,144.4 | 10,750 | $125,000 |

committee and using a budget of $125,000, the computer model produced the allocations shown in Table 11.10.

It was apparent that not enough money was available to transform the entire space into new facilities. Of the 8635 square feet available, budgeted funds were sufficient to alter only 8144.4 square feet of space. Romano scheduled a meeting with the mayor, who was disturbed by the results, but not surprised.

"I was afraid this would happen," he said. "The city council approved only $125,000 this year and construction costs have really gone up. I know of nothing else to do but to return to the council and request additional funds. How much more money do we need?"

"I don't know right now," replied Romano, "but I can play with the model to find out."

Romano returned to work and revised the model, increasing the budget in increments until there were sufficient funds to remodel the entire 8635 square feet of floor space. This analysis showed that an additional $4415 was necessary for a total expenditure of $129,415. This new solution gave the allocations shown in Table 11.11.

With these results in hand, Romano returned to the mayor's office. After a discussion of the results, the mayor decided to call a meeting of his department heads to discuss the results with them. The mayor indicated to Romano that he hoped to use these results as guidelines but that small changes would likely be required for architectural reasons. He also invited the city architect to the meeting.

**Table 11.11**

| Department | Total space allocation, ft$^2$ | Desired space, ft$^2$ | Alteration cost |
|---|---|---|---|
| Police | 5,000 | 7,000 | $100,000 |
| Fire | 1,585 | 1,700 | 13,265 |
| Safety | 250 | 250 | 1,750 |
| Civil service | 800 | 800 | 6,400 |
| Purchasing | 1,000 | 1,000 | 8,000 |
| Total | 8,635 | 10,750 | $129,415 |

## Department Heads' Meeting

At the beginning of the meeting, the mayor outlined what had transpired since the last meeting. He then distributed a copy of Romano's results to each department head and sat for a moment awaiting comments.

Jim Weston, chief of police, muttered to himself, "I knew this would happen, mayor. Why is my department being penalized so much?"

"Jim, it just cost too much to make the changes you requested. If we had allocated the police department more space then we would have to take more than twice the space from other departments."

"Yes, Mayor, I understand that, but shouldn't our requests be given a higher priority?"

"We discussed that point with the revenue sharing committee, and, in fact, they did consider your request to be of greater priority. But the costs of your alterations were so great that it affected our total allocations."

"Jim, you still have the greatest amount of floor space and consume the greatest portion of the budget," Nick Pearson added.

"What about the safety department?" asked Beryl Watson. "We didn't get anything initially, and now you're saying that we can only have half of our request."

"It's just a matter of priorities," replied the mayor. "Our advisory committee did not feel that your requests should have higher priorities than other departments. Politicians are always talking about the importance of citizen input to public decisions. I'm confident that the allocation solution plan we have reflects the desires of our citizens and provides us with an efficient utilization of our resources."

After some additional discussion of the plan, the mayor asked the city architect, Charles Simms, to comment on the likelihood of his being able to develop architectural designs from the solution.

"Well, Mayor, I have a few suggestions to make. First, I notice that several departments have requested space for general meeting rooms. Why don't you provide one general-purpose room for meetings? We can take allocations from each department to develop this room if you like."

"I notice from the general agreement around the table that a room of that type would be desirable," replied the mayor.

"As for the remaining space," continued the architect, "I think you realize that this is an old building and we may not be able to design rooms to meet the square foot allotments exactly, but we should be fairly close."

"Janet, what do you think?" the mayor asked Janet Romano, his administrative intern.

"Since our data was based upon estimates to begin with," she replied, "I think it would be appropriate to make whatever minor adjustments are required."

"Fine," replied the mayor. "I detect that the consensus among the group is to adopt the plan Janet has proposed. Janet, I would like to thank you for showing us how to solve a problem of this type. During the rest of the summer I'm sure that we'll be calling on you again to help us."

## Discussion Guide

1 Was an approach based upon square foot allocations appropriate? Should a procedure have been used which would have allocated space on an all-or-nothing basis? That is, should the department have received an entire unit of space for one particular function instead of a square foot amount which may have been only half a room?

2 How else could the city have approached this decision problem? What approach do you think would be best?

3 If you had been on the advisory committee, how confident would you have been in your ability to establish numerical priorities for ranking the different department requests?

4 Could the final results have been obtained without resorting to an LP model?

5 What was the value of the model in this case?
   (a) To analyze a complex series of decisions?
   (b) To provide the appearance of objectivity?

## FOUR

## SUMMARY

# INTRODUCTION TO PART FOUR
# SUMMARY

In the earlier three parts of the text, decision areas were separated, as much as possible, into distinct categories. This part seeks to summarize the major points of the earlier parts, including the various warnings as to the limitations of models and how to deal with some of the difficulties inherent in real-life modeling.

This chapter presents an instance of modeling and decision making involving a confluence of problem categories. Since this instance is typical of real-life modeling situations, it is presented to demonstrate how difficult it is in practice to separate decisions into the pedagogical categories of the prior chapters.

The pressure of time constraints on the modeler is shown to be a major factor in choice of modeling technique. Other limitations on the modeling and decision process are described, including internal organizational conflicts which may prevent resolution of difficulties.

Some aspects of the case presented end successfully, some unsuccessfully. A complicated decision situation often has such mixed results. On balance, the overall modeling project would be judged a success, but the seeds of its eventual undermining are also in evidence.

It is hoped that this chapter will tie together the concepts of the rest of the book and leave the reader with an appropriate appreciation for the complexity of using models and making decisions in real life.

# TWELVE

## MODELS IN
## REAL LIFE

## SYNOPSIS OF THE CHAPTER

Real-life decision situations do not lend themselves to simple descriptions in many cases. This chapter emphasizes some of the complications attendant to decision making and modeling. Because the goal of the preceding chapters was to elucidate specific problem areas, the complications have not been stresssed. However, real-life problems are often difficult to identify, problems tend to cross managerial categories, mixtures of solution techniques may be required, and time pressure or other constraints may interfere with the modeler's ability to model and with the decision maker's leeway in making decisions. This chapter addresses these issues.

## MAJOR CONCEPTS PRESENTED IN THIS CHAPTER

1. The first step in solving a problem is identifying the problem.
2. The decision expected as a result of modeling a problem tempers the definition of the problem.
3. Time pressure may significantly alter the approach to a decision and may restrict the number of alternatives considered.
4. If an analytical study's recommendations are to have a chance of being implemented, the factual basis of the recommendations must be correct.
5. Hypotheses used to construct modeled alternatives must be specified carefully in reports on model analyses.
6. The final decision may require information about related factors that the modeler did not consider.

7. The decision maker's skill, confidence, and personal style may affect how successfully a decision is implemented.
8. Not all problems can be solved in real-life situations.
9. Many problems have causes and symptoms which cross the domains of several organization disciplines.
10. Models rarely make decisions, but provide information to the decision maker.
11. A modeler must select the aspects of the problem which must be modeled and what kind of model to use.
12. There is a variety of roles that model, modeler, and decision maker may play.
13. Solutions to problems may present more problems, which may in turn interfere with the implementation of those solutions.
14. Dealing with people must be the dominant consideration in making and implementing decisions effectively.

## EXPECTATIONS OF THE STUDENT

The student, after studying this chapter, should be able to do the following:

1. Identify cross-disciplinary complications that may be anticipated in specific cases
2. Recognize factors which may obscure the nature of a problem
3. Realize the need for decision making initiative on the part of the modeler
4. Look for the kinds of roles that modeler, model, and decision maker play in specific situations
5. Anticipate aspects of a decision which must be emphasized to enhance its implementation
6. Specify the people considerations which must be built into a decision to improve its chances of success

## GALBIS INTERNATIONAL

Galbis International's Mix Plant in Minnesota was apparently making products at its maximum pace. Conventional wisdom within the company held that the GalbMinn Mix Plant was capacity bound. The company president, Bill Ragdale, was not convinced that capacity was the plant's limitation. He believed that poor management might be the real constraint.

Ragdale had decided that the capacity restrictions on three product lines at GalbMinn had to be eliminated. Either the management in the Minnesota plant would have to be improved, or, if the plant really was capacity bound, one or more new production lines would have to be installed at the nearby Iowa plant. Ragdale's choices were determined; he simply needed more facts. He called in his best internal consultant, John Smith.

"John, you've been with our management sciences division now for, what, two years?"

"Yes, sir."

"What do you know about GalbMinn?"

"Only what I've heard. Everyone says that it's the most complicated plant we've got."

"Why?" asked Ragdale.

Smith hesitated, then said, "As best as I can make out, the plant makes a number of special construction products, and practically all of them use the same raw materials and preparation steps. If one mixer is down, three or four complete production lines are down. Also, the plant has apparently grown over time so that production flows zigzag all over the floor."

"I want you to go out there. Find out all you can about the Supel, Algel, and Domet lines. I'm thinking about putting in new lines to make those products at GalbIo. We have the raw materials there, and we may have extra preparation capacity there."

Smith had studied the Iowa plant thoroughly. "Yes sir," he said. "The way that plant runs, it has considerable extra capacity on the prep side. I don't know whether it will fit in with those product lines you named. I'm not that familiar with them."

"Well, find out all you need to know and give me a full report," said Ragdale.

"Uh, how long do I have?"

"I need the information before I have to make the first cut on the budget," said Ragdale. He flipped through his desk calendar. "That's three weeks."

"Three weeks?" asked Smith plaintively.

"Yup. You'd better get moving," said Ragdale.

Smith made arrangements quickly and flew to Minnesota the next morning. On the plane, he tried to map his strategy.

"I could just determine that the Minnesota plant is up against capacity and leave it at that," he thought. "I think Ragdale has already decided to put in new lines at Iowa, anyway. Well, I'll see what I find out. One thing is for sure. I'll never be able to put together any kind of large computer model in three weeks. It will take me a week to write the report!"

## REAL-LIFE PROBLEM SOLVING

The early stages of a problem solving activity consist of identifying the problem. The GalbMinn decision seemed deceptively simple in its infancy: Should the corporation shift production capacity from one plant to another? It would seem that a simple "yes" or "no" would have sufficed.

However, the decision was not that simple. If the Minnesota plant was not capacity bound, then improved management might have resulted in an adequate increase in production. One fact that Smith did not have at hand was how much capacity was required. Was a small increase or a large one required? If new lines at the Iowa plant were installed, how much would they cost? Would additional product sales be enough to pay for the expansion?

At the time Smith arrived at the Minnesota plant, none of these questions had occurred to him. It should not be surprising that this is so. He had little information to help him form opinions, and he was unfamiliar with the plant to be studied.

Ragdale also knew little about the plant. He had toured it, but he had had little contact with operational data from it. He knew that Supel-13 had a large market nationwide, and he believed that Galbis could increase its market share of that product sharply. He was not sure about Algel or Domet products, but he had heard that GalbMinn's capacity to produce those products was constrained. He could have approved appropriations for any capacity additions he wanted, but a corporate rule held that an investment had to average a 35 percent return, and he would not violate that rule.

The small amount of accurate information that Ragdale had in hand is not uncommon in a decision making environment. Decisions regularly must be made on short notice and before a deadline. Often, the implications of the decision are poorly understood at the time it is discovered that it must be made. It is rarely possible to make leisurely decisions.

Studying the operations at GalbMinn could have shown a variety of possibilities for resolving the capacity problem. These possibilities included the following:

1. Temporizing, i.e., waiting for better information or for pending market shifts
2. Shutting down some product lines at GalbMinn and adjusting to the reduced output
3. Shifting some GalbMinn production to new lines at GalbIo
4. Shaking up the GalbMinn management
5. Changing the Minnesota plant's product mix
6. Changing the Minnesota plant's scheduling procedures
7. Building an entire new plant to replace the old one
8. Installing new capacity at GalbMinn
9. Installing new capacity at GalbIo and maintaining existing production at GalbMinn

Some of these alternatives would have required corporationwide policy decisions before they could have been adopted. Any moves drastically affecting the company's product mix or its capital investments would have been felt in Galbis offices all over the world.

The problem that John Smith flew to investigate had the potential to be simple, and it had the potential to be complicated.

## GALBIS INTERNATIONAL'S MINNESOTA PLANT

Located on as flat a piece of earth as could be found anywhere was GalbMinn. The plant had over 2000 employees and operated three shifts five days a week. Weekends were devoted to maintenance and cleanups, which were extensive. Smith was greeted warmly by the plant manager, Paul Storey, and the assistant plant manager, Mike Ackerman. They know that Smith had come with carte blanche from président Ragdale.

The two men promptly arranged a meeting including Smith, themselves, and the three product line managers. They explained how they did things and what their problems were. Within an hour, Smith asked to tour the plant. Joe Black, the Supel manager, was his guide on a complete look at the facility. The tour took most of the day, but at a brief wrap-up with Storey, Smith asked for a long list of data and a thorough briefing session with the five managers the next morning.

In his motel room, Smith sketched a diagram of the plant and studied it until he became too tired to concentrate. His late-night efforts paid off the next morning as he found himself alert and well organized. He fired out rapid requests for data, checked his notes with all five men, asked questions of each product line manager, and queried Storey and Ackerman about their special concerns.

That afternoon, as Smith headed for the airport, he carried a briefcase loaded with notes, drawings, and photocopies of numerous layouts, schematics, and data sheets. He was already beginning to see how to proceed.

Back at corporate headquarters Smith sought out the corporate production manager, Ham Rice. He reviewed his preliminary findings, discussed the concerns of the plant personnel, and tested several of his ideas on Rice. He was delighted to discover that Rice had, and would give him, several additional pieces of information that he needed.

Smith next talked to Richard Walsh, the corporate marketing director. By the end of that discussion, Smith knew enough to begin his data analysis.

The hypothesis he had formed was that the sloppy way that GalbMinn was laid out made it impossible to add the equipment required to increase its capacity. However, he believed that there were a few things that could be done to improve production efficiency by a significant amount. It further appeared that a single new product line at GalbIo might be justified.

To test his hypothesis, he decided he would write a computer program in FORTRAN which could calculate machine utilizations, total revenues, and total profits for any given mix of products during a simulation of one week's operation at GalbMinn. However, the list of all products made at the plant was too numerous to include in the model, so he decided to model only those few products that had the largest volumes of sales. It turned out that only thirteen products accounted for 75 percent of the total tonnage.

The three lines at GalbMinn were dry, wet, and solid lines. The dry line was ordinarily called the Supel line, the wet line was called the Algel line, and the solid line was called the Domet line. According to Bill Ragdale, the most important alternative that Smith felt he should consider was installing one or more new lines at GalbIo, and products from the wet and dry lines were the most reasonable ones to move from GalbMinn. Accordingly, he merely summarized the solid products in all of his analyses, effectively reducing the number of items he had to consider to eight.

The solid line averaged about 205 tons per week in output. The tonnage of the dominant items from the other two lines is summarized in Table 12.1.

Although all three lines shared many of the same raw materials and prep-

**Table 12.1 Supel and Algel weekly output**

| Supel line | Weekly output, tons | Algel line | Weekly output, tons |
|---|---|---|---|
| Supel–13 | 61 | Algelbond | 53 |
| Supel–3 | 45 | Algelso | 67 |
| Supel–6 | 13 | | |
| Supel–27 | 27 | | |
| Supel–C | 218 | | |
| Supel–M | 21 | | |
| Total | 385 | Total | 120 |

aration steps, Smith did not feel that he had time to model the sharing of resources. He wrote a short memo to Ragdale explaining GalbMinn's materials management problems and suggested an algorithm which might alleviate this difficulty at GalbMinn. He then excluded the solid line from all further consideration and wrote the production simulation program to deal only with the eight wet and dry products he had chosen.

## RESULTS OF THE GALBMINN MODEL

Smith's model showed that the production times per ton that the Minnesota personnel had given him would only account for a small part of the available time on the Algel line. That line could have easily produced four times the product that it did. Smith attributed this low output to the inability of the plant to produce enough raw materials to keep all three lines busy.

The dry line was a different story. The six major products, made at their average weekly rates, would occupy almost all of the available time on the line. The Supel line's dominant production constraint was its ability to package products.

Smith decided to use his model to determine how much profit could be made on the two lines if they were each devoted to only one product. His computer analyses are summarized in Table 12.2.

Most of the products could not be sold in the quantities that a dedicated line could turn out. Information obtained from the corporate marketing manager in-

**Table 12.2 Weekly profits from lines dedicated to single products**

| Product | Line | Tons per week | Weekly profit, $ | Production constraint |
|---|---|---|---|---|
| Supel–13 | Dry | 450 | 400,500 | Packaging |
| Supel–3 | Dry | 450 | 1,390,500 | Packaging |
| Supel–6 | Dry | 450 | 2,794,500 | Packaging |
| Supel–27 | Dry | 450 | 715,500 | Packaging |
| Supel–C | Dry | 450 | 841,500 | Packaging |
| Supel–M | Dry | 450 | 931,500 | Packaging |
| Algelbond | Wet | 450 | 737,000 | Mixing |
| Algelso | Wet | 429 | 1,059,630 | Grinding |

dicated that Supel-3 could achieve a demand of 8000 tons per year, Supel-C might reach 15,000 tons per year, and Algelbond and Algelso could each be promoted to perhaps 6000 tons per year. By studying his price-cost lists along with the available market projections, the priorities for GalbMinn production seemed to Smith to be as follows:

1. Make 8000 tons/year of Supel-3 due to profit margin.
2. Make 15,000 tons/year of Supel-C due to volume.
3. Make 630 tons/year of Supel-6 due to margin.
4. Make Supel-13 due to potential volume.

Study of these strategies proved to Smith that Supel-13 should not be made at GalbMinn at all. There was adequate demand for the other products on the dry line that it could be fully utilized by filling demand for the higher–profit margin items. It appeared that the only way Supel-13 would be a good product to make would be if it could be turned out in large volume. This conclusion brought Smith back to Ragdale's apparent inclination to install new capacity for making some GalbMinn products at GalbIo.

While he had been at the Minnesota plant, Smith had discovered that several tons of raw materials were arriving at GalbMinn daily by rail from GalbIo. He also knew that the company-owned mines in Iowa produced all of the raw materials used in making Supel-13. Smith needed to know three more facts: how much the installation of a dedicated Supel-13 line at GalbIo would cost, how much materials preparation capacity the Iowa plant could spare for the new line, and how many tons of Supel-13 the company could realistically expect to be able to sell.

He found out that the likely market region for sales of Supel-13 from the Iowa plant included companies with a continuing demand for the product of about 120,000 tons per year. Marketing felt that a 15 percent market share would be a reasonable goal if the company were to decide to become competitive in the Supel-13 market. Profit per ton to Galbis from Supel-13 would be about $800 if the product were to be priced at a competitive level. A quick calculation showed

$$\text{Expected profit} = \$800 \times 0.15 \times 120{,}000 = \$14{,}400{,}000$$

Smith reasoned that the corporate rule stipulating that an investment had to return at least 35 percent gave him a way to estimate the maximum permissible cost of a new Supel-13 line at GalbIo:

$$\text{maximum cost} \times 0.35 = \$14{,}400{,}000$$

$$\text{maximum cost} = \$41{,}143{,}000$$

Smith's next step was to ask Ham Rice how much the single production line would cost at the Iowa plant. Rice promised to check with engineering and get back to him. The next day, Rice called Smith and told him that the cost estimate was $35 million.

With the last piece of the puzzle in place, John Smith wrote his report. He advocated dropping Supel-13 production at GalbMinn and recommended installing a Supel-13 line in Iowa, using that plant's excess materials preparation capacity, which he had calculated to be adequate for the purpose. He explained the degree of market penetration that the product would have to make into the western Great Lakes market area to justify the investment, and he described how the new line must be operated.

His report said, "Supel-13 is an easy-to-make product that is even made by mom-and-pop operations in their garages. The only way that Galbis can change ingrained buying habits is to be the cost leader in this market. To be the cost leader, it is not sufficient to use the natural advantage of owning all of our own raw materials. We must also reduce the production cost per ton to a minimum by dedicating the production line exclusively to Supel-13. If the line is diverted to making other products part of the time, this will only hurt the competitive position of Supel-13, which we currently list at $1720 a ton but sell for $1500 or less."

## THE DECISION

The final decision on whether to install the Supel line in Iowa was Bill Ragdale's. The corporation had the money; the question was whether the move would be right. He had to consider a number of related issues:

1. Could the existing carriers transport the additional 18,000 tons per year of Supel-13 that the Iowa plant would produce, and could the carriers move the tonnage fast enough to make Galbis competitive?
2. Could marketing change its selling habits and those of its salespeople sufficiently to obtain a 15 percent share of the regional market for Supel-13?
3. Was restricting the new line to the production of only one item a good idea? And if it were a good idea, how could it be enforced.
4. If Supel-13 were pulled out of GalbMinn, should the transition be abrupt or gradual?
5. Were Smith's data and analyses correct?
6. Should the company simply continue with business as usual and avoid all activities containing an element of risk?

Ragdale decided that, if the company were never going to take any risks, its competitors would eventually drive it out of business. Also, one of Ragdale's biggest pleasures in life was taking corporate risks. Thus, if Smith's report held up under scrutiny, Ragdale would install the new line at GalbIo. He sent a copy of the report to the following:

Helmut Diacopolous, GalbIo plant manager
Paul Storey, GalbMinn plant manager
Ham Rice, corporate production manager
Bill Petersen, corporate information systems manager
Harmon Cage, corporate marketing manager

He also sent each man a copy of Smith's memo which had described GalbMinn's scheduling difficulties and offered a solution. The recipients were given ten days to read, absorb, and check the two documents before they were to meet with Ragdale and give their recommendations. None of the five was given any clues as to Ragdale's inclination or concerns.

The meeting itself was short, lasting less than thirty minutes. Although no one wanted to express overtly negative views about anything Ragdale had decided to do, he skillfully overcame such concerns and quickly managed to enlist everyone in a fully professional discussion of Smith's report and memo.

Storey explained that his main problem at GalbMinn was providing enough raw materials to keep all three lines running at the same pace as orders were received. He enlarged somewhat upon Smith's description of this problem, and he declared that the computerized procedure for materials scheduling advocated by Smith would relieve this bottleneck significantly.

Bill Peterson clearly disliked having his department's work dictated to him by John Smith, but under close questioning by Ragdale he said that he could and would have the scheduling system installed at GalbMinn within two weeks.

Ham Rice agreed with everything Smith had written. He was pleased with the direction of the discussion because it appeared to him that production would be made considerably smoother at GalbMinn as a result of the meeting.

Harmon Cage was the unhappiest manager present. He was a former salesperson, and his views were largely those of a salesperson. He disliked having to tell his salespeople that they were to push Supel-13 to the degree implied by Smith's report. However, when Ragdale asked whether marketing could sell the 18,000 tons per year target of Supel-13, pride got the best of him and he swore that it could be done.

Helmut Diacopolous was asked the question about which Ragdale was most concerned. "If we put in this new line at your plant, will you reserve it exclusively for Supel-13? I don't intend to put it in if it's going to be tied up with Supel-6 when it's supposed to be ready to run Supel-13," said Ragdale.

Diacopolous was ambivalent about the addition to his responsibilities, but he felt that if he handled it well it could lead to his advancement. He agreed to keep all other products off the Supel-13 production line.

Ragdale double-checked on one more point. He verified with Diacopolous that GalbIo had adequate excess materials preparation capacity to feed the new line. With that, Ragdale was satisfied. The meeting ended, and the new line was approved. During the meeting Ragdale had decided that there was no logically compelling reason to produce small amounts of Supel-13 at GalbMinn, and he sent an executive order eliminating that product from the plant that very day.

## DEFINING THE PROBLEM

The Galbis International case demonstrates that managerial decision making can be quite involved. The decisions themselves are rarely clearcut at the time the first question arises. The first step in the decision process is likely to consist of determining the nature of the problem. Often, this single step constitutes a solution because the statement of a problem may well imply its solution. For example, if a student studying managerial decision making finds that the problem is not knowing enough of the text material, the solution is, clearly, to study the textbook.

Not all problems can be easily described, and few have readily apparent solutions. Not all problems have pleasant solutions, and some problems have no solutions at all. Thus, the first phase of the decision process consists of isolating a problem which is capable of being addressed.

An individual called upon to solve some difficulty may be told, "We have a problem. Fix it." (Or the same thing with more and longer words.) Someone assigned a task may be given an incorrect description of that task. Misdirection and misunderstandings are common during the beginning stages of a decision making process.

It is rarely the case that a problem can be isolated as pertaining to only a restricted phase of an organization's activities. Just as a fuse repeatedly burning out implies a larger failing of an electrical system, a small impediment to an organization's efficiency may reflect a pervasive lack of purpose. Consider the following examples.

A federal agency finds itself unable to monitor all of the activities for which it is responsible. Reason: Congress has assigned the agency more than it can do.

A production facility is falling steadily further behind in making deliveries. Reason: Corporate policy restricts the plant from maintaining adequate inventories.

The productivity at a plant is falling every year. Reason: The corporation will not invest capital to replace out-of-date equipment because it is diverting funds toward the acquisition of other, unrelated companies.

Electric power plants find themselves unable to burn cheap, American coal and instead burn expensive, imported oil. Reason: Incompatibility between federal energy and environmental policies.

Although a textbook may select those situations for presentation which present clearly delineated problems, real life is unlikely to be so cooperative. Operational problems are usually impossible to isolate from the environment of organizational planning and policy decisions.

For instance, the capacity problems at Galbis International's Minnesota plant were largely a result of a corporate policy of making a very long list of products. Instead of focusing on a limited array of products which could be turned out efficiently at each plant, every company plant was allowed to increase its product list to any length. As new products were added or as new capacity was needed, machines and storage units were installed anywhere there was space. The corporation never focused upon a definite portion of the possible sales market and thus could not intelligently limit itself to a restricted product list.

The de facto expansion policy was to "tack on" equipment at existing plants. No facility was ever designed to do just one well-defined task, and if such a facility had been installed, it would have been quickly corrupted by additional tasks. This lack of direction in corporate policy was the root cause of most difficulties throughout the company. It is not at all certain that the GalbIo Supel-13 line will remain dedicated to that one product for long.

At no time has the Galbis management realized that its fundamental problem is its approach to policy and planning decisions. This problem remains invisible.

## INTERDISCIPLINARY COMPLICATIONS

Just as it may be difficult to properly identify the problem to be addressed, it may also be difficult to isolate a problem into a single discipline. It is convenient in a textbook to cite situations which permit a specific solution technique, but many real-life impediments to success straddle two or more organizational disciplines.

At GalbMinn, John Smith discovered that there was a large backlog of unfilled orders. The causes were complex and intertwined. The component causes were as follows:

Corporate policy determined how orders were recorded in the order entry system.
The order release required that only complete orders be shipped.
Most orders included requests for some dry products, some wet products, and some solid products.
Wet products have a very brief shelf life, solid products last almost forever, and dry products can be stored for six months.
Orders were always filled by completing the wet part of the order last.
Wet products had the lowest priority among all products made at GalbMinn.
All parts of an order except the wet part might be complete for months, waiting for the wet part.
Salespeople were unaware that the composite orders they wrote were causing long delays in filling orders.

Only one aspect of Smith's report on the GalbMinn operations alleviated the backlog of orders. The new materials scheduling algorithm installed by the management information personnel speeded up production, thus helping fill orders faster.

However, Smith also wrote a separate memo describing the order entry system's limitations and proposing a few ways to correct them. He suggested that salespeople be instructed to file separate orders for each of the wet, dry, and solid categories, that the order entry system be changed, that the order release system be changed, and that production priorities be continuously juggled to reduce the order backlog.

None of Smith's suggestions was adopted. Corporate headquarters opposed changing order entry and order release, the management information department rejected the idea of reprogramming the order entry files, marketing refused to change the instructions it gave its salespeople, and the GalbMinn management insisted that its priorities were inflexible.

The order backlog is a real problem which can be described simply, but it is complicated by the fact that it crosses several corporate domains. It is caused by a mixture of operational, planning, and policy limitations. This problem would not fit well under the topical heading of any chapter in this book. It is not a simply defined problem.

## SPECIALIZED INFORMATION

Throughout this book, discussions requiring specialized areas of expertise have been avoided. However, it must be pointed out that real-life decision making cannot be accomplished without the assistance of experts in various disciplines.

Accountants, computer programmers, statisticians, physical scientists, economists, financial experts, market analysts, industrial psychologists, sociologists, and other diverse experts must help in providing the technical information necessary to understand and make decisions. Vendors who sell goods and services to the organization represent another valuable source of information.

Anyone desirous of better understanding decision making within specialized disciplines should study those topics specifically. The scope of this book naturally precludes them.

## MODELS—THEIR SCOPE AND ROLE

Rarely is a model the final arbiter of a decision. There are manufacturing processes which, of necessity, are largely controlled by computer algorithms, but the decisions required of the computer in these cases are mechanical. Models are the dominant determinant of a decision in many cases, but the decision must be of a simply stated operational nature for this to be true.

A model usually provides information to the decision maker, and this information may be crucial or only mildly interesting. The value of the model in the decision process is dependent upon the decision, the decision maker, and the decision making environment. The role of a model in making a decision is strongly determined by its importance, the time available, its complexity, and the interaction between the model and the modeler.

## TIME LIMITS AND COMPLEXITY

John Smith faced a stringent time constraint on his study of GalbMinn. This is the usual situation for a modeler. The decision maker must quickly determine what to do and passes this urgency on to decision support personnel.

The longer a modeler has to develop a model, the more complexity can be installed in it. However, complexity is not necessarily of value. A Pareto principle could be stated as follows:

Eighty percent of the value of a model is derived from twenty percent of its possible complexity.

Models provide only poor approximations of reality, and overemphasis on details may be merely busywork.

Smith would have been faced with the usual modeler's difficulty with or without a time constraint. Lack of time eliminated some of his options. In any event, he would have had to decide what type of model to devise, what it should do, and what he should attempt to model.

Does a model seek to imitate everything about a decision making situation? This would seem to be an impossible goal. For example, consider modeling a city. Could every person in that city be individually modeled and contained in the model? Certainly not. A modeler must select the features to be modeled much as an artist selects what features of a landscape to include in a painting.

If only a portion of a situation is to be modeled, which portion should it be? Since a decision maker must surely consider only a portion of a decision making environment, perhaps it would be best to try to imitate the decision maker's decision process. However, this solution to the selection of model details imposes upon the model the role of trying to reproduce the decision maker's conclusions. This may be the proper role of a model. Smith decided to try to model the production lines at GalbMinn, and he only modeled two of the lines. He further limited his model to producing only eight items. The modeler must decide whether the model is to be deterministic or stochastic, i.e., whether the modeled details are to be viewed as certain or uncertain. Although everything in the universe appears to be stochastic (uncertain), deterministic models are often effective. In other cases, only stochastic models will suffice. Smith's time constraints caused him to select a deterministic approach to modeling production. He used average values for production times and simple values for the revenues and costs he needed in the model. His intention was to obtain average production time and expected profits that would result from specific outputs of products.

Assuming that all of the issues above have been decided, the modeler must decide whether the model will be an optimizing model or a descriptive one. An optimizing model tells how to obtain the "best" results. A descriptive model simply shows what given conditions would cause to happen. There are instances when one type of model is more appropriate than the other, largely due to the decision making environment itself.

Many decision makers are irritated by so-called optimal results. However, other decision makers are irritated by the seemingly wishy-washy nature of descriptive results. The decision maker's style may be the determinant of the modeler's choice of model.

Smith's FORTRAN model of GalbMinn was descriptive; it only reported the consequences of running a specific product mix. In his report, Smith was careful to explain how his model worked and what product mixes he had studied. His clarity of presentation was such that no one accused him of being wishy-washy.

The modeler must choose what objective or objectives the model must address. Ideally, the decision maker will provide sufficient direction to make this choice easier, but the modeler must at least determine which objectives will receive the greatest scrutiny.

Although Smith paid attention to a number of GalbMinn problems, the thrust of his primary report was how to increase profits; he implicitly adopted the enhancement of profits as the objective of his modeling effort. This objective was in fact the correct one in Ragdale's view, and he found Smith's work to be very helpful.

The more important a decision to the organization, the more complex the modeling process. A purely operational decision can be solved by use of a well-defined model. An organizationwide policy question may involve so many diverse objectives that it is almost impossible to model it in a simple manner. A sequence of special-purpose models may be required. For example, cost, labor, forecasting, and resource allocation models may all have to be employed to plan organizational expansion.

The more difficult a problem is to model, the less likely a model is to be relied upon by a decision maker. In simpler cases, it may be relied upon strongly. The exact role of a model relative to the decision maker is difficult to prescribe in general.

## ROLES OF MODEL, MODELER, AND DECISION MAKER

There is a range of roles that a model can play in the decision process. To a large degree this role of the model is determined by the extent to which the decision maker's experience and intuition enter into the final conclusion. Although the explicit mode of interaction between a decision maker and a model may not be articulated, possible mixtures of roles are shown in Table 12.3.

Both the modeler and the decision maker must be aware of the distribution of analysis between model and manager. John Smith designed a model which was intended to generate solutions from the problem statement. Bill Ragdale intuitively evaluated Smith's report, checked the data, and cast Smith's solutions in an implementable form.

One might insist that John Smith employed his own experience and intuition to a considerable degree in deciding what problem to address, what to model, what data to acquire, what type of model to prepare, and how to write the type of report Ragdale would find useful.

**Table 12.3 Integration of intuition and experience with decision models**

| Approach | Role of model | Role of intuition and experience |
|---|---|---|
| 1 | Generate solutions from problem statement. | Evaluate solution, make necessary problem formulation changes. |
| 2 | Train decision maker to improve intuition. | Generate solutions. |
| 3 | Generate initial solution. | Improve upon initial solution. |
| 4 | Develop solution procedure after observing intuition. | Provide basis for modeling. |
| 5 | Provide computational aids to evaluate intuition. | Generate solutions. |

It is true that Smith was the decision maker in his role of developing a detailed analysis of the GalbMinn problem. The roles of modeler and manager are similar in that each has his or her own part to play in the modeling-decision process and each must use all the objective and subjective tools at his or her disposal.

## IMPLEMENTATION OF DECISIONS

Implementation of decisions is a difficult process. The basic reason for this fact seems to be that people resist change, and decisions usually dictate change. However, it must be noted that there is little known about how to implement decisions effectively. This is a topic which would seem to be in need of scientific study.

One roadblock to successful implementation of a proposed solution to a problem is that the solution may not specify how it is to be enacted. Anyone who has had a sick automobile can empathize with the difficulty of implementing the solution "overhaul the transmission." Few drivers have any idea how to repair transmissions, but as a solution to the car's ailment, "overhaul the transmission" is a clear directive.

John Smith indicated that Galbis should install a new production line. Yet, the process of installing a $40 million set of equipment is scarcely trivial. The implementation of Smith's suggestion presented someone with a considerable array of new problems.

One way to avoid presenting solutions to problems which in turn create new problems might be to insist that no solution is to be considered complete until it is planned all the way through implementation. Management would then be required to provide anyone assigned to problem solving with access to the various professionals necessary to flesh out the details of an implementation procedure.

Sometimes, all that is required to make techniques for resolving a difficulty effective is readable documentation—clear instructions for how to do what the decision maker has proposed. Often, readable documentation is omitted from the written accounts of new procedures. Computer users, in particular, wage a constant battle in trying to obtain understandable instructions for using computer programs.

It might be that implementation of goals could best be enhanced by skillful management. The decision maker who enlists aid in making a decision must become aware of the characteristics of the decision which require further analysis or documentation. Perhaps the prevalent expectation in the past has been that a quantitative analyst could be entrusted with the entire solving process. Whatever the cause for unacceptable implementation of decisions, this particular problem requires constant attention on the part of management.

## DEALING WITH PEOPLE

In all organizations, people are the most important working units. Quantitative techniques for making or assisting decisions tend to ignore the unpredictable nature of people.

Long ago, it was widely believed in some industries that management consisted only of setting piecework rates for workers. The workers theoretically would manufacture units at a rapid rate so as to make a high wage. Once a factory's output became fairly high, management would cut the piecework rate, theoretically forcing the workers to work faster in order to make the same wages.

This viewpoint held the seeds of its own demise. The workers quickly ascertained the pointless nature of working faster and contrived to establish de facto work speeds which were not permitted to increase. People and their attitudes cannot be excluded from the considerations in decision making.

Not only must the attitudes of workers be considered, so must the attitudes of all levels of management. Quantitative analytical tools can be very effective in exposing solutions to problems and the proper management options to adopt, but inept or antagonistic applications of such tools can be counterproductive.

Sometimes, organizational politics must be factored into a decision. The feelings or habits of certain individuals must be explicitly considered. In almost all cases, the common needs and attitudes of people need to be implicitly included in decision making deliberations. Rare it is that a purely mechanistic decision can be effective.

## SUMMARY

This book has attempted to present a number of decision categories in which decision models have been used effectively. The use of models has been presented as a cooperative activity between the decision maker, the model, and the modeler.

Some disadvantages of models have been demonstrated along with their advantages. It has been emphasized that the vast array of qualitative factors be considered as part of the modeling and decision processes, although it is not possible to provide formulas for using qualitative information.

The standard constraints of interpersonal dealings have been included in the discussions as integral parts of the decision process. Politics, emotion, likes and dislikes, incentives, goals, and the needs of people have all entered into the cases outlined throughout the book.

Students may not study any of the technical fields which deal with support data needed in making many decisions, but it is hoped that, having read this book, the student will move on to the role of decision maker with a better understanding of how to solicit information from those fields.

## QUESTIONS

1 What decision did Bill Ragdale originally contemplate making?

2 What decision did John Smith actually model?

3 What additional concerns did Smith express about the GalbMinn operation?

4 In addition to his main report, Smith submitted memos suggesting improvements in two procedures at GalbMinn. What were these procedures?

5 One of the procedures mentioned in Question 4 received attention; the other did not. What are the reasons for these responses to Smith's suggestions? Explain your answer.

6 There are several good reasons why the marketing manager did not want to instruct his salespeople to promote sales of Supel-13. What are three of these reasons?

7 How does restricting a production line to making one product lower production costs?

8 Why did Galbis not consider the entire United States as the market region for sales of Iowa Supel-13?

9 Is a ROI of 35 percent an uncommonly large requirement for justifying an investment?

10 How did Smith calculate the profit margin per product? Suggest a procedure for such a calculation. What data would you need?

# EXERCISES

1 Management is an art and not a science. Any efforts to quantify this art are bound to fail. Do you agree with this statement? Support your answer with specific illustrations.

2 There is not enough time to "rationalize" decisions. You have got to use your intuition to the best of your abilities. Do you agree with this statement? Support your answer with specific illustrations.

3 Numbers are only one part of the overall decision. Therefore, decision models are not very useful. Do you agree with this statement? Support your answers with specific illustrations.

4 Decision models require an understanding of so much math that few managers are going to use them. Do you agree with this statement? Support your answer with specific illustrations.

5 Organizational politics are involved in any major decision. As a result, only less important decisions can be modeled successfully. Do you agree with this statement? Support your answer with specific illustrations.

6 From your personal experience, what were some decisions that were made that could have been improved by use of a decision model?

7 Are decision models more likely to be successful on the job or in personal decisions?

8 How have your impressions about decision models changed as you have read this book?

9 At this time, what additional training do you feel you need in the area of decision models?

10 Do you believe that the study of decision models has helped your personal decision making? In what respect?

# INDEX

# INDEX